MW00615763

A RAGE TO CONQUER

ALSO BY MICHAEL WALSH

A RAGE TO CONQUER

TWELVE BATTLES THAT CHANGED
THE COURSE OF WESTERN HISTORY

MICHAEL WALSH

ST. MARTIN'S
PRESS
NEW YORK

First published in the United States by St. Martin's Press,
an imprint of St. Martin's Publishing Group

www.stmartins.com

The Library of Congress Cataloging-in-Publication Data is available upon request.

ISBN 978-1-250-28136-4 (hardcover)
ISBN 978-1-250-28137-1 (ebook)

Our books may be purchased in bulk for promotional, educational, or business use.
Please contact your local bookseller or the Macmillan Corporate and Premium Sales
Department at 1-800-221-7945, extension 5442, or by email at
MacmillanSpecialMarkets@macmillan.com.

First Edition: 2025

10 9 8 7 6 5 4 3 2 1

For Lance Morrow

REVEILLE

We must recognize that war is common, strife is justice, and all things happen according to strife and necessity.

—HERACLITUS OF EPHESUS (C. 500 B.C.)

μῆνιν ἄειδε, θεά, Πηληϊάδεω Ἀχιλῆος / The wrath of Peleus' son, the direful spring
  Of all the Grecian woes, O Goddess, sing!

—HOMER, THE *ILIAD*

Auferre, trucidare, rapere, falsis nominibus imperium, atque, ubi solitudinem faciunt, pacem appellant.
  To ravage, to slaughter, to usurp under false titles, they call empire, and where they make a desert, they call it peace.

—TACITUS, *AGRICOLA*, CHAPTER 30 (98 A.D.)

Mark where his carnage and his conquests cease!
He makes a solitude, and calls it—peace.

—BYRON, *BRIDE OF ABYDOS*, CANTO XX (1813)

Like or find fault; do as your pleasures are: Now good or bad, 'tis but the chance of war.

—SHAKESPEARE, *TROILUS AND CRESSIDA* (1602)

It's all God's will: you can die in your sleep, and God can spare you in battle.

—LEO TOLSTOY, *WAR AND PEACE* (1867)

De l'audace, encore de l'audace, toujours de l'audace!

—GEORGE S. PATTON, JR., BY WAY OF DANTON AND
FREDERICK THE GREAT

Everything in war is very simple, but the simplest thing is difficult.

—CARL VON CLAUSEWITZ, *ON WAR* (1832)

CONTENTS

TO FIGHT FOR

The more ignorant men are, the more convinced are they that their little parish and their little chapel is an apex to which civilization and philosophy have painfully struggled up the pyramid of time from a desert of savagery. Savagery, they think, became barbarism; barbarism became ancient civilization; ancient civilization became Pauline Christianity; Pauline Christianity became Roman Catholicism; Roman Catholicism became the Dark Ages; and the Dark Ages were finally enlightened by the Protestant instincts of the English race. The whole process is summed up as Progress with a capital P.

—GEORGE BERNARD SHAW, NOTES TO *CAESAR AND CLEOPATRA* (1899)

WAR HAS BEEN AN ESSENTIAL PART OF THE HUMAN CONDITION AS long as there has been a human condition; there is nothing inhuman about it. It is the principal agent of societal change, waged by men on behalf of, and in pursuit of, their gods, women, and the sheer joy of combat, and in so doing to impose their will upon other men through extreme violence. Destructive though it is and must necessarily be, war is a primary engine of both scientific and cultural progress, driving both external technology and the inner exploration of the soul through the arts. Its terrible wrath and beauty compels us to ask ourselves what it means to be human, superhuman, subhuman, inhuman, antihuman. It is essential, elemental, masculine. It is an important facet of every culture, from the highest civilization to the lowliest primitivism. For better or worse, our world is unthinkable without it. Then again, our chimp ancestors could have told us that.

In the long view, no problem is ever fully solved, no border settled, no solution final, no religious faith universally embraced as supreme. Such is the eternally recurrent nature of human contentiousness; in this regard at least, Nietzsche was right. But it is absurd to say, as contemporary political correctness has it, that war, or at least violence, never solves anything; in fact, it provides at least a temporary, and often quite long-lasting, solution to most of the world's most intractable conflicts. The battlefield is not the place for negotiation. It is the place for extreme, dispositive violence. It is not abnormal; as we shall see, it is *merely* a mechanism by which *policy* is conducted *with* means other than jaw-boning. Few major conflicts end without a winner, and certainly none of the epochal battles considered herein: great martial, cultural, and civilizational turning points, after which the world was never the same.

Change is, as Heraclitus continues to remind us, the only permanence. Nonetheless, war brings at least a temporary stasis. It rearranges the pieces on the chessboard, offering each second or third generation (because that is usually the distance separating conflicts) a chance to have a throw of the dice, to test itself in the eternal human contest of wits, strength, and will. The Trojan War (a poetic interpretation of *something* that happened in antiquity) announced the millennia-old conflict of East vs. West—a war we are still fighting today, with the front lines more or less at the Bosphorus, as they were in Homer's time. Wars are not ended at the bargaining table; all the great confrontations of history have ended violently. It is only when wars temporarily have been halted via "negotiated settlements" that they inevitably continue. "Negotiation" rarely settles anything; rather, it is the face-saving after-effect of either victory or defeat. If you're negotiating, you're losing.

A look at the long list of warlike peoples and bellicose great powers that no longer exist—from the Parthians to the Prussians—is proof enough of the theorem. Peace is not the absence of war but the temporary aftereffect of its conclusion. War may be hell, but it brings peace. Like every great commander before him, the American Civil War general William Tecumseh Sherman articulated this principle when he wrote during the hostilities to the Confederate commander John Bell Hood:

> You cannot qualify war in harsher terms than I will. War is cruelty, and you cannot refine it; and those who brought war into our country deserve all the curses and maledictions a people can pour out. I know I had no hand in making this war, and I know I will make more sacrifices to-day than any of you to secure peace.

Since the end of the Second World War, this is a lesson entirely forgotten by the political leadership of the United States, a defect that is likely to have unhappy consequences for the nation as it approaches its 250th birthday.

A successful war is one that accomplishes its objective. That might be territorial gain, plunder, the definitive elimination of a deadly rival, or simply a matter of physical and cultural survival. One of the first wars in Roman history was fought over women. According to Livy, the early Romans, faced with a dearth of females and thus having no prospect of survival beyond the living generations, fought a war with their Sabine neighbors, a war conceived in treachery that resulted in the abduction of the most desirable and fertile Sabine women but which ensured the survival of the young city. When some years later the Sabine men mounted a military campaign to liberate them, the kidnapped Sabine women, rather than rebelling against their new husbands, interposed themselves between their new masters and the Sabine men who had come to rescue them:

> Then the Sabine women, whose wrong had given rise to the war, with loosened hair and torn garments, their woman's timidity lost in a sense of their misfortune, dared to go amongst the flying missiles, and rushing in from the side, to part the hostile forces and disarm them of their anger, beseeching their fathers on this side, on that their husbands, that fathers-in-law and sons-in-law

should not stain themselves with impious bloodshed, nor pollute with parricide the suppliants' children, grandsons to one party and sons to the other.

"If you regret," they continued, "the relationship that unites you, if you regret the marriage-tie, turn your anger against us; we are the cause of war, the cause of wounds, and even death to both our husbands and our parents. It will be better for us to perish than to live, lacking either of you, as widows or as orphans." It was a touching plea, not only to the rank and file, but to their leaders as well. A stillness fell on them, and a sudden hush. Then the leaders came forward to make a truce, and not only did they agree on peace, but they made one people out of the two. They shared the sovereignty, but all authority was transferred to Rome.

The men had made the war; the women—the objects of the conflict, now allied with the stronger of the two parties—had forced a peace, to the Romans' benefit and at the cost of the Sabines' independence.

The present volume, a companion to *Last Stands* (2020), continues that book's central thesis that war is of necessity and biology a masculine preserve. A world without belligerent men might be a world without war—but there has never been a successful society ruled directly by women. Western attitudes regarding the proper relationship of men and women extend back to, and originate with, the earliest voices of our literature —the Bible, Hesiod, and Homer—and those attitudes are inextricably tied up with warfare and the battlefield: the quintessentially male, unsafe space, whose danger must be embraced rather than be denied, regretted, or ameliorated. Any culture that is forced to rely on women in combat is destined to lose, and lose badly.

It is to be emphasized that this is an interpretative cultural and military history: the principal battles are viewed in the context—sometimes a very long context—in which they occurred. A reader expecting a dry enumeration of unit movements will be disappointed; one open to seeing (mostly) well-known battles in the broader cultural milieu that gave rise to them may find himself enlightened.

One thing the reader will not find is the anachronism that has come to be called "presentism." In simple terms, this is defined as judging the actions of the past by the standards of the present, a dangerous error on several counts. First, history is a one-way street: we are able to examine the lives and actions of people in the past, but they could not possibly conceive of our existence except in the broadest possible terms. Second, it presupposes that modern—and ever-changing—social and cultural standards are always to be preferred to the manifest benightedness of the past. This is an outgrowth of the cultural Marxist notion of the "arc of history," which itself derives from the classically Marxist postulation of the "iron laws of history." In turn, the origin of these "laws" are an outgrowth of (1) the late eighteenth and nineteenth century's passion for taxonomy and (2) a bastardized Christian notion of a teleological universe, parodied so memorably by Voltaire in the character of Dr. Pangloss in *Candide*, who believed that we are living in the best of all possible words. Throw in the benign autosuggestion of the French psychologist Émile Coué (1857–1926), who enjoined his patients to say and believe: *ous les jours à tous points de vue je vais de mieux en mieux* (every day in every way, I am getting better and better), and you have the modern, supercilious view of the march of history.

Third, and most important for our purposes here, it prevents and occludes historical understanding and accuracy in the service of contemporary ideologies of every stripe. Today, for example, we look upon the institution of human slavery with horror, often associating it exclusively with the African slave trade in the New World. And yet the most cursory reading of history—and not just Western history, either—demonstrates that slavery is as old as mankind itself. The ancient Hebrews did it, the Greeks did it, the Romans did it, the Turks did it, and it is still ongoing today in some countries of the world, mostly but not exclusively Islamic. Toppling statues and chipping names off buildings, however, does nothing to rectify what we currently perceive as a moral wrong. All we, the living, can do is *not do it*. And thus it is with all instances of "presentism." In order for us to live our lives by our moral precepts, we must allow the people of the past to have lived their lives their way as well.

Accordingly, we shall examine a tangled skein[1] of conflicts from the beginnings of Western history to the present, battles and campaigns each of which at their conclusion left our world a very different place: changed, changed utterly as Yeats says in "Easter, 1916." Not all victories have happy endings. Each generation must be ready to fight for its freedom—if freedom any longer matters. And it will only matter as long as there are real men willing to fight.

Since the Trojan War, the earliest[2] war in Western history and the cornerstone of Western literature as well, the men of the West have been studying and practicing the art of war. The phrase itself is culturally significant, for while it may derive from the Chinese military philosopher Sun Tzu's treatise, 孫子兵法, known to us in translation as *The Art of War*,[3] the notion that war is an "art" is quintessentially Western. It absolves its participants from the mistranslation of the Mosaic biblical commandment, "thou shalt not kill," because while faith in any of the Abrahamic religions proscribes murder it does not preclude righteous killing. Indeed, in both Christianity and Islam, it is wholeheartedly endorsed via the apologias of the Augustinian "just war" and the Koran's advocacy of jihad. The ancient Hebrews were as warlike as anybody else, according to their holy book waging genocidal war on the Canaanites in order to claim the land that, according to their scriptures, was promised

---

1. The original title of Sherlock Holmes's literary debut in 1887, changed to *A Study in Scarlet* before publication. "There's the scarlet thread of murder running through the colourless skein of life, and our duty is to unravel it, and isolate it, and expose every inch of it," observed Doyle.

2. Variously dated by scholars to the late thirteenth or early twelfth century B.C.; Homer's poem dates from the eighth century B.C. That a war actually happened there is no longer in doubt.

3. A regrettable model: "To fight and conquer in all our battles is not supreme excellence; supreme excellence consists in breaking the enemy's resistance without fighting." A Greek or Roman would consider such a notion the height of dishonor. It is illustrative that the Chinese have never won a war against a Western power but exceed all other nations in the destructiveness of their civil wars.

them by their god, although there is little or no historical evidence that such a conflict ever happened.

Still, war is foundational to every society, in every epoch. Pacifistic, nonviolent cultures rarely survive first contact with an outside enemy. However much it offends current Western sensibilities, war will never vanish, never be abolished,[4] and never lose its attraction for young and virile men.

With it often comes a definitive conclusion, arriving suddenly, even overnight. Most of the battles contained herein conform to that observation. In 331 B.C. Alexander the Great could hardly have anticipated that he would change the course of Western history during his final confrontation with the "Great King" Darius III at the Battle of Gaugamela. When Caesar accepted the surrender of Vercingetorix at Alesia in 52 B.C., he could not have known he had just fathered one of the principal nation-states of Europe, the "handmaiden" of a Church that had not yet announced itself, but would build itself upon the ashes of Rome. As Constantine watched his rival Maxentius drowning in the Tiber after a brief clash of arms at the Milvian Bridge outside Rome in October of 312, did he have a vision of the triumph of a new, Christian *pontifex maximus* (once one of Caesar's titles) sitting not only upon the throne of Empire but upon that of St. Peter and ruling over the largest faith on earth? Unlikely. But they all knew something had happened.

The Germans call these moments in time *Wendepunkte,* turning points, when the polite but malignant fiction of the "arc of history" suddenly ricochets off some unknown object or force and heads in a completely different direction. Indeed Clio, the Muse of History, is herself a born dramatist, staging at the Catalaunian Plains in 451 one of the great clashes between East and West as the dying gift of Rome, the great mother of the West, expiring in the childbirth of Europe, protecting her progeny with her last breath.

Clio, however, takes no sides and has no stake in the outcome. There are no "iron laws" of history, and man's attempt to project human emotions onto impersonal events in an effort to foretell the future is always

---

4. See the Kellogg-Briand Pact of 1928, which outlawed war.

doomed to failure. Civilizations rise and fall, and some in fact never even rise. None lasts. There is a futility to fidelity to god and country, a bitter irony, as every soldier knows. Soon to confront death himself in Flanders's fields, Wilfrid Owen (1893–1918) articulated the sentiment of a generation—likely, of every generation—in his poem, "Dulce et Decorum est":

> *If you could hear, at every jolt, the blood*
> *Come gargling from the froth-corrupted lungs,*
> *Obscene as cancer, bitter as the cud*
> *Of vile, incurable sores on innocent tongues,—*
> *My friend, you would not tell with such high zest*
> *To children ardent for some desperate glory,*
> *The old Lie:* Dulce et decorum est
> Pro patria mori.

But is that really a lie? In the fourth act of Shakespeare's *Hamlet*, the Danish prince encounters an advance guard from the Norwegian army of Fortinbras, marching through Denmark on their way to battle "the Polack" over a worthless scrap of land. Frozen by inaction, Hamlet admires their willingness to fight and die over nothing: "What is a man if his chief good and market of his time be but to sleep and feed? A beast, no more," he soliloquizes.

> *Witness this army of such mass and charge,*
> *Led by a delicate and tender prince,*
> *Whose spirit with divine ambition puffed*
> *Makes mouths at the invisible event,*
> *Exposing what is mortal and unsure*
> *To all that fortune, death, and danger dare,*
> *Even for an eggshell. Rightly to be great*
> *Is not to stir without great argument,*
> *But greatly to find quarrel in a straw*
> *When honor's at the stake. How stand I, then,*
> *That have a father killed, a mother stained,*
> *Excitements of my reason and my blood,*

And let all sleep, while to my shame I see
The imminent death of twenty thousand men
That for a fantasy and trick of fame
Go to their graves like beds, fight for a plot
Whereon the numbers cannot try the cause,
Which is not tomb enough and continent
To hide the slain?

Hamlet thus curses himself for his inaction, his cowardice; the fight might be meaningless, but what does it matter? The fight is *everything*—even for an eggshell.

And so, for all their horror, wars are fought, and will continue to be fought, as long as men of hot blood are there to fight them. All that is required are men who have studied and internalized the timeless principles of warfare as embodied by their fellow warriors from Achilles to Patton, and understand how to put them to best use. As it happens, these have been best articulated by a German veteran of the Napoleonic Wars whose most famous aperçu has been consistently mistranslated and thus misunderstood, leading to all sorts of subsequent mischief: Carl von Clausewitz. It is to him we now turn to conduct our tour of the great battlefields of Western history, for it was there that we were born.

One

CLAUSEWITZ ON WAR

War is no pastime; it is no mere joy in daring and winning, no place for irresponsible enthusiasts. It is a serious means to a serious end, and all its colorful resemblance to a game of chance, all the vicissitudes of passion, courage, imagination, and enthusiasm it includes are merely its special characteristics. . . . War, therefore, is an act of policy. Were it a complete, untrammeled, absolute manifestation of violence (as the pure concept would require), war would of its own independent will usurp the place of policy the moment policy had brought it into being.

—CLAUSEWITZ, *ON WAR*, CHAPTER 1

IN 1832, MARIE VON BRÜHL, THE RECENTLY WIDOWED WIFE OF THE Prussian general Carl[1] von Clausewitz, published her late husband's near-encyclopedic, practically Aurelian thoughts on his lifelong profession in a work that we know today as *Vom Kriege* (*On War*). She did

---

1. The spelling of his Christian name with a "C" rather than the German "K" emphasized his links to the classical tradition. See also Carl Philipp Emanuel Bach and Carl Maria von Weber for other examples.

so with characteristic but customary feminine trepidation in her introduction to her husband's unfinished masterpiece, cut short by his death from cholera in 1831 at the age of fifty-one:

> It goes without saying that I have no intention whatever of regarding myself as the true editor of a work that is far beyond my intellectual horizon. . . . Those who knew of our happy marriage and knew that we shared everything, not only joy and pain but also every occupation, every concern of daily life, will realize that a task of this kind could not occupy my beloved husband without at the same time becoming thoroughly familiar to me.

Marie was far too modest. Without her loving attendance to the manuscript—many manuscripts, really, recording her husband's *pensées* on war over decades of practical experience both in the field encountering Napoleon at the disaster of Jena/Auerstedt and later near Waterloo, and reforming the Prussian military system from the relative safety of Berlin—we would not have this martial version of Aquinas's *Summa Theologica* in anything like its current form.

It is impossible to overestimate Clausewitz's perspicacity and influence, or his continuing relevance. Although his work has been widely misunderstood[2]—in part thanks to a crucial mistranslation of his most famous aphorism, which has colored much that has been written about him since, hinging on the English words "by" and "with"—it has only grown in influence since publication, however tepidly it was at first received. Wrote one reviewer in the *Preussische Militair-Literatur Zeitung* shortly after publication in 1832:

---

2. Not the least by Adolf Hitler, who in his final testament of April 29, 1945, wrote: "*Dass ich ihnen allen meinen aus tiefsten Herzen kommenden Dank ausspreche, is ebenso selbstverständlich wie mein Wunsch, dass sie deshalb den Kampf unter keinen Umständen aufgeben mögen, sondern, ganz gleich wo immer, ihn gegen die Feinde des Vaterlandes weiterführen, getreu den Bekenntnissen eines grossen Clausewitz.*" (That I give them all my thanks from the bottom of my heart is as self-evident as my wish that, as always, under no circumstances should they give up the fight against the enemies of the Fatherland, faithful to the creed of the great Clausewitz.) He shot himself the next day.

The streams whose crystal floods pour over nuggets of pure gold, do not flow in any flat and accessible river bed but in a narrow rocky valley surrounded by gigantic Ideas, and over its entrance the mighty Spirit stands guard like a cherub with his sword, turning back all who expect to be admitted at the usual price for a play of ideas.

The sophisticated reader will at once sense the resonances, beginning with the end of Milton's *Paradise Lost* ("The brandished sword of God before them blazed/ Fierce as a comet") and continuing through to German romanticism: we are in the realm of the demonic spirit Samiel from Carl Maria von Weber's opera *Der Freischütz* (first performed in 1821) and only eleven years before Richard Wagner's *The Flying Dutchman*. The quintessential romantic landscape painter Caspar David Friedrich (1774–1840) was an exact contemporary of Clausewitz. Floods, gold, rivers, rocky valleys, and, above all, man's relationship with nature are the essential elements of German romanticism, and it is within that context that we must consider Clausewitz. Neither art nor war exists in an intellectual or spiritual vacuum.[3]

A veteran of the Napoleonic Wars, Clausewitz had seen his nation's military capability destroyed at the twin battles of Jena/Auerstedt in 1806 and was himself taken captive by the French. Fortunately for him, he fell into the operational cracks of the ongoing change in France from the noblesse oblige of the ancien régime to rigorous revolutionary egalitarianism; while only vaguely aristocratic by birth, he was an adjutant to Prince August Ferdinand of Prussia, which won him special treatment in captivity. Many Prussians, especially the older ones, had decided after their shellacking at the hands of Napoleon that the future lay with France. They had seen their kingdom soundly, embarrassingly

---

3. One significant precedent was *De re militari* (Concerning Things Military) by the fourth-century Roman historian Vegetius. Written somewhere between 383 and 435, the book's real influence came a thousand years later, when it was published in Utrecht in 1473. As *On War* would four centuries afterward, it became a bible of various European militaries, and remained so into the nineteenth century.

beaten by the highly trained and motivated Grande Armée and shorn of half its territory by the Treaties of Tilsit in 1807. Outmaneuvered by Napoleon at the height of his powers, the command-heavy Prussians under Friedrich Wilhelm III were unable to counter the Corsican's tactical mobility, his mastery of the entire battlefield, the training and dedication of his troops, and his own inspirational leadership in the field. But mostly, they had to confront his innovative approach to warfare, which time and again allowed him to surprise and defeat numerically larger forces.

As a lightly monitored prisoner in France for little more than six months[4] after the disaster at Jena, Clausewitz was unimpressed with the country. Far from its being a new kind of nation, he thought France a country in moral and spiritual decline, culturally decadent, its glories already in the past (no matter their brief recrudescence under Napoleon). He saw France as vulgar Rome to nascent Germany's vigorous neo-Hellenism, as exemplified by Goethe. As he pondered what had gone wrong with the military force bequeathed to Prussia by Frederick the Great, which now lay in ruins, he began articulating a theory of warfare that would serve Prussia and Germany better in the future. This is what he decided:

- War is nothing but a duel on a larger scale.
- War is thus an act of force to compel our enemy to do our will.
- War is never an isolated act.
- In war, the result is never final.
- Only the element of chance is needed to make war a gamble, and that element is never absent. No other human activity is so continuously or universally bound up with chance.
- In the whole range of human activities, war most closely resembles a game of cards.
- War is no pastime; it is no mere joy in daring and winning, no place for irresponsible enthusiasts.

---

4. His imprisonment was not onerous, lasting from December 30, 1806, to July 9, 1807.

- War, therefore, is an act of policy.
- War is merely the continuation of policy **with** other means. [*Der Krieg ist eine bloße Fortsetzung der Politik **mit** anderen Mitteln.*]

Here we have the essence of the first chapter of book 1, "On the Nature of War,"[5] and everything that comes thereafter in the hundreds of pages that follow flows from these salient observations. I have provided the German original for the final point because it is crucial to our understanding of what is Clausewitz's most famous observation. Or, rather, our misunderstanding of it, owing to both a mistranslation of the German word for "with" and the double meaning of the word *die Politik* in Clausewitz's native language. Thus, "War is merely the continuation of **policy with** other means" is now commonly rendered "War is merely the continuation of **politics by** other means," when the author clearly is characterizing war as political *policy* **with** the additional element of violence to make it more persuasive. He continues:

*So sehen wir also, daß der Krieg nicht bloß ein politischer Akt, sondern ein wahres politisches Instrument ist, eine Fortsetzung des politischen Verkehrs, ein Durchführen desselben **mit** anderen Mitteln.*

We see, therefore, that war is not merely an act of policy/a political act but a genuine political instrument, a continuation of political intercourse/dealings/interaction, carried on with other means.

It's critical to understand this small but important distinction because it changes the entire way we view Clausewitz's philosophy. If war really is a "continuation of politics by other means," this implies that diplomacy has failed and thus has effectively ceased. This interpretation appeals to those who believe that "war never settles anything" and that, in an inexplicably oft-quoted phrase (there is nothing particularly clever

---

5. In a note written around 1830, Clausewitz wrote: "The first chapter of Book One alone I regard as finished. It will at least serve the whole by indicating the direction I meant to follow everywhere."

about it) attributed to Churchill—although the words were apparently uttered by Harold Macmillan[6]—"Jaw-jaw is better than war-war."

It also implies that war is a morally lesser form of "politics" in the sense we now employ the word: partisan but nonviolent wrestling for greasy-pole advantage in the competition for the taxpayers' money and the opportunity to boss them around. In the Clausewitzian sense, however, it more often means state *policy*, which is a compendium of goals and desires to be achieved on behalf of the state by any means necessary: the ultimate form of persuasion.

> Consequently, it would be an obvious fallacy to imagine war between civilized peoples as resulting merely from a rational act on the part of their governments and to conceive of war as gradually ridding itself of passion, so that in the end one would never really need to use the physical impact of the fighting forces—comparative figures of their strength would be enough. That would be a kind of war by algebra. Theorists were already beginning to think along such lines when the recent wars taught them a lesson. The thesis, then, must be repeated: war is an act of force, *and there is no logical limit to the application of that force.* [Emphasis mine.]

Thus, warfare is a perfectly acceptable element of state policy, a tool of the trade, not a last resort. "War by algebra" may seem attractive, the spectacle of two mathematically inclined gorillas beating their chests until one becomes intimidated and retires—but that isn't the way it works in reality. Drawing up Tales o' the Tape looks persuasive in print, but once in the ring a fighter's punching power and defensive skills can offset height, reach, and weight, as long as he has the heart and the stomach and the tactical command to do what's necessary to win.

And while Clausewitz describes the concept of *absolute war*—war to the end—as the logical end-state of belligerence, he never argues that all wars should be fought to annihilation: "No one starts a war—or rather, no one in his senses ought to do so—without first being clear in

---

6. According to Churchill's official biographer, Martin Gilbert, what Churchill actually said was, "Meeting jaw to jaw is better than war."

his mind what he intends to achieve by that war and how he intends to conduct it. The former is its political purpose; the latter its operational objective." What he did not endorse, however, is the more modern concept of a "proportional" war or a "strategy of limited aim"—concepts that have brought the United States to grief in every war it has fought from Korea on, and with not a single military or diplomatic victory to show for it.

Clausewitz lived and wrote as the nation-states of Europe were beginning to assemble into their more or less contemporary forms, which coincided directly with German nationalism and the idea that peoples united by language, history, and culture ought to live in a state of their own.[7] After Napoleon was put back in his box on the far-off island of Saint Helena, France was returned to something resembling its pre-Revolutionary shape. Although the Holy Roman Empire had been dissolved in 1806, and its French-imposed successor, the Confederation of the Rhine, had replaced it as an assemblage of the various German states and principalities, the Prussians under Bismarck created the modern German nation under Kaiser Wilhelm I in 1871.

The wars that had raged across Europe were not only among the most savage in continental history but the most militarily sophisticated up to that time. Napoleonic innovations in strategy and tactics forced every other fighting force in Europe to adapt or be annihilated; many of them, such as the Prussian army, had to be destroyed before being reconstituted. But though Napoleon himself was at last safely locked away—he died in 1821, just six years after the Battle of Waterloo—the lessons he had taught did not go unheeded.

The Little Corporal[8] forced Europe to rethink its approach to warfare.

---

7. Europeans at this time were also fighting for nationalism elsewhere; Byron died at Missolonghi in Greece in 1824 fighting for Greek independence from the occupying Turks. As the contemporary European Union shows, however, this theory, essential to the formation of the modern nation-state, is under serious challenge from the globalists, who admit of no distinction between and among peoples, and seek to remove the nation from the equation, leaving only the state.

8. The nickname was affectionate, dating from Napoleon's early career as an artilleryman, when he would sometimes lie on the ground to sight his guns. To the end, his men adored him.

Rather than move a single lumbering mass of men, horses, artillery, and supplies to the battlefield, Napoleon created the idea of multiple individual corps, self-contained, highly mobile small armies that lived off the land instead of being tethered to long, vulnerable supply trains, could either fight independently under some of his best commanders or, after spectacular forced marches, converge at just the right moment to apply maximum force at the point of greatest impact. This flexibility and maneuverability time and again allowed him to defeat numerically superior allied forces, attacking their component parts individually and crushing each in turn. He employed lighter field guns, twelve-pounders,[9] than did his opponents, enabling him to move them around like chess pieces on the battlefield and assemble optimal firepower where and when it was needed most. "I tried to converge all our forces on the point I wanted to attack," he once said. "I massed them there."

One characteristic great military minds share is the ability to foresee the shape of the battle while it is in motion: not where the enemy is at the moment but where he will be minutes from now: we might term this *kinetic generalship*. In three decisive battles against the Persians— the Granicus, Issus, and Gaugamela—Alexander overcame the superior forces of the Achaemenid emperor Darius III by knowing the exact moment to lead his Companions in a ferocious cavalry charge signaled by a gap in the Persian center that Alexander's tactics had themselves provoked. This devastating right hook delivered the Macedonian Greek horsemen directly into the heart of Darius's order of battle, creating havoc in the camp and forcing the king in two successive encounters to flee the field, and thus lose his wife, his children, his fortune, and eventually his empire and his life.

Alexander and Caesar[10] were Napoleon's great twin influences, and he resembled them both in many ways, combining elements of surprise, discipline, endurance, audacity, and clarity of objective. For all three generals, total victory was the only exit strategy. Alexander never lost a battle, Caesar never lost a campaign. Napoleon burned across

---

9. During the American Civil War these guns were called "Napoleons."

10. In exile, Napoleon composed a study of Caesar's tactics, *Précis des Guerres de César*, which was eventually published in 1836.

the European skies like a comet, practically undefeated, until fatally weakened by his pyrrhic victory at Borodino and the ensuing disaster of the retreat from Moscow in 1812, then crushed at the Battle of the Nations at Leipzig the following year. The last stand at Waterloo in 1815 was thus, seen in this light, the last glow of the Roman candle that had been the emperor before whom all Europe had trembled.[11]

The Napoleonic era coincided with the first full flush of Romanticism across Europe. One needs only glance at Jacques-Louis David's famous portrait *Napoleon Crossing the Alps* (c. 1801–5) to see it in motion. There is the First Consul,[12] in full military uniform, cape billowing, seated on a rearing, wild-eyed, white charger with the mountains looming behind, his right arm extended to indicate "forward," but his face looking directly at the viewer: a man in command of himself, his troops, and Nature herself, and very much conscious of it. It was an idealized portrait of warfare in all its militaristic and political glory, the fulfilment not just of masculinity but of man.

Omitted of course were the hideous wounds, the suffering, the eviscerations of warfare. On the battlefield, disease and death were everywhere; if the bullets or cannonballs didn't get you, a bug or a bleed-out surely would. No stranger to such misery, and adumbrating Sherman, Clausewitz—who had seen and encountered the Black Swan that was Napoleon Bonaparte in the flesh—looked at it this way:

> Kind hearted people might think that there was some ingenious way to disarm or defeat an enemy without too much bloodshed and might imagine this is the true goal of the art of war. Pleasant as it sounds, this is a fallacy that must be exposed: war is such a dangerous business that the mistakes which come from kindness are the very worst. The maximum use of force is in no

---

11. "*E avanti a lui tremava tutta Roma,*" says the heroine at the end of Act Two of Puccini's *Tosca* (1900) after she murders Scarpia. The opera is set during the Napoleonic Wars.

12. The title Napoleon gave himself after seizing power in 1799 from the Directory in the wake of the French Revolution; the echoes of ancient Rome are clear, as they were with his later title, Emperor of the French (1804–1814/15). In May of 1804 he also crowned himself Emperor of Italy.

way incompatible with the simultaneous use of the intellect. . . . This is how the matter must be seen. It would be futile—even wrong—to try and shut one's eyes to what war really is from sheer distress at its brutality.

If this seems on some level a left-handed apologia, it is. An acceptance of pain and suffering, and of the brevity of life, was part of human understanding, right up to the middle of the twentieth century. No one, from the Greeks and Romans on, thought he would live forever, or even much past forty. The question was not whether you would die but *how* you would die, and whether it would be a good death, a noble death, a death that meant something, which added something to your life; a death that rounded it off with a capstone. Death was not just the end of life, it was its culmination— for men, at least. (For women, the functional equivalent was childbirth.)

Consider how the deaths of warriors are described in Homer's *Iliad*. Almost every wound is fatal, and the wounded man drops to the ground, scrabbling at the earth, "groaning, clutching the bloody dust," as blackness overcomes him and his soul departs his body for its journey to the underworld—the eternal shadows of an afterlife that strikes us as far more like hell, or perhaps Limbo, than the Christian heaven. There are hardly ever any last words for the heroes; Hector, stabbed through the throat by Achilles's spear, is a notable exception. Millennia later, ordered into battle, into the teeth of the guns, Napoleon's men did so not only bravely but enthusiastically, with praise for the emperor on their lips. That the French soldiers—and not only the French—did so willingly is unimaginable today. But they did.

There's a quote attributed to Napoleon (although no one can quite point to it, and leading scholars are disinclined to credit its authenticity): *On s'engage partout, et puis l'on voit* (Start the battle and see what happens). But there's a certain Clausewitzian spirit about it, and it has influenced later historical figures such as Lenin, who cited it in 1923 in "Our Revolution":

Napoleon, I think, wrote: *"On s'engage et puis . . . l'on voit."* Rendered freely this means: "First engage in a serious battle and then see what happens." Well, we did first engage in a serious battle in October 1917, and then saw such details of development (from the standpoint of world history they were certainly details) as the Brest peace, the New Economic Policy, and so forth. And now there can be no doubt that in the main we have been victorious.

Another who took it seriously was Sir Evelyn Baring, later the British consul-general in Egypt at the time of General Charles Gordon's heroic defense of Khartoum in 1884–85. As a lieutenant in the Royal Artillery, he made a study of Napoleon's tactics, published in 1870 through the Royal Military Academy's Staff College at Camberley:

Napoleon's motto was, "On s'engage partout, et puis l'on voit," which must not be taken to mean that he began a battle without any definite plan at all, but rather that his system of fighting was so elastic that it could bend itself to suit the altered circumstances of any particular case. In short, Napoleon was one of those men whom Goethe eloquently describes in his *Wahlverwandtschaften*[13] as bending circumstances to suit their will, whilst his adversaries, by often blindly refusing to admit the influence of special events, were, in point of fact, at the mercy of any accident which might arise.

Like Alexander and Caesar, Napoleon was *sui generis,* a one-off who combined genius, ruthlessness, and malevolence with a strange kind of egoistic innocence that never permitted him to doubt himself or his purpose. For Alexander, following in his father's footsteps to launch an attack on nascent Europe's existential rival, the Achaemenid Persian Empire, was self-evidently necessary—and history would have judged him harshly had he not. For Caesar, the conquest of Gaul, at the cost of perhaps a million Celtic lives, was not only good for Rome, it was also

---

13. Goethe's third novel, published in 1809. The title, which can also describe a chemical reaction, has been translated as *Elective Affinities,* but it might be better translated as *Related by Choice.* The plot concerns an aristocratic married couple who invite the man's friend and the wife's orphaned niece to live with them on their rural estate, with predictably explosive results.

good for the Gauls themselves. For Napoleon, the bringing of Gallic reason, a revised legal code, and the creation of the Confederation of the Rhine to replace the moribund Holy Roman Empire was only natural. After Charlemagne, Napoleon was the first Pan-European, the logical successor not only to Alexander and Caesar but also to Constantine the Great.

His sway over the European imagination was, for a time, absolute. No place, it seemed, was safe from his depredations; mothers across Europe would frighten their children with stories about him, and no crowned head slept easily while he was in the field. Although Napoleon was ridiculed by the British cartoonists as "Boney," a preening, malevolent midget, the English nevertheless felt compelled to eliminate the French navy as a threat, which they did under Nelson at the Battle of Trafalgar off the Spanish coast on October 21, 1805, thus ending Bonaparte's plans for an invasion of Great Britain and forcing his attention back to continental Europe. Regarded as a vulgar Italian Corsican parvenu by the European aristocracy (he didn't even speak French very well!) as well as a true son of the regicide Revolution, Napoleon united the nations of Europe in multiple coalitions against him, although his principal enemies were Britain and tsarist Russia.

Napoleon left no overall theory of war behind him, but one of his most celebrated generals, Antoine-Henri Jomini, did.[14] His prescriptive, diagrammatic, even geometric *Traité de grande tactique* (1805) and his *Précis de l'art de la guerre* (1838) became standard texts in the war colleges of the world, including at West Point before the Civil War, where many of the readings at the time were in French, the language of war.[15] Among his principal admonitions was to always maintain numerical superiority at each point of attack—especially the "decisive" point—while harassing the enemy's lines of communications and defending one's own.

Clausewitz, Jomini's contemporary and rival, advocated no system,

---

14. Jomini saw the Napoleonic wars from both sides, serving both with the Grande Armée and the Russian army at various times.

15. Ulysses S. Grant may have read them; he was at West Point from 1839 to 1843.

no *gradus ad Parnassum* to conquest. Like all great theoreticians, he was an original; descriptive schools of theory followed. Bach may have codified the twelve-note tempered scale, and in so doing created the framework for the edifice of modern tonal music, but he was operating on his own. The Prussian's famous contemporary Ludwig van Beethoven burst through the bonds of the classical sonata form in the *Eroica Symphony* (1805) because he had to, not because he wanted to. In battle, Alexander took men on horseback and turned them into the Companion cavalry. Caesar transformed the ordinary foot soldier, in his maniples, centuries, and legions, into a peerlessly flexible weapon of war. And Napoleon's influence upon Clausewitz cannot be underestimated—which is why *Vom Kriege* is still read and embraced today.

Nevertheless, *On War* is not the Schlieffen Plan in embryo.[16] Indeed, Clausewitz explicitly rejects the notion that there can be any such thing. Far from being the Prussian archetype of the by-the-book soldier,[17] Clausewitz is a romantic hero with a bent for the empirical. Even as he lays out his strictures for the proper understanding of the nature of war, Clausewitz is still far more in tune with Byron—who adored Napoleon—than his Prussian contemporaries:

> *For the Angel of Death spread his wings on the blast,*
> *And breathed in the face of the foe as he passed;*
> *And the eyes of the sleepers waxed deadly and chill,*
> *And their hearts but once heaved, and for ever grew still!*
> —BYRON, "THE DESTRUCTION OF SENNACHERIB" (1815)

For Clausewitz, the shock of Napoleon was, in the late art critic Robert Hughes's famous formulation, the shock of the new. For a decade, Europe fumbled for a response, for no one had seen anything like it. As Shakespeare said of Caesar in his eponymous play, "Why, man, he doth bestride the narrow world like a Colossus."

---

16. Although *Vom Kriege* was certainly a major influence—along with Homer and the Bible—on Helmuth von Moltke (1800–1891), who became Prussian chief of staff in 1857.

17. Indeed, Clausewitz took Montesquieu for his literary model.

Is this, then, the Great Man theory of history? Certainly, compared with Marxism, it is. Marxism prescribes, Teutonically, rules, iron laws, which govern the affairs of men, which has given rise to a quintessentially modern liberal notion that history has a kind of moral sentience. This sentiment was made famous by Martin Luther King, Jr., referencing the abolitionist Theodore Parker, in a 1958 article in *The Gospel Messenger*: "The arc of the moral universe is long, but it bends toward justice." It was Los Angeles rabbi Jacob Kohn of Sinai Temple who, in a New Year's message, replaced the words "moral universe" with "history," and this is the form in which the passage is most quoted today. More Shakespearean, more Caesarean, Clausewitz subscribes to Brutus's maxim that:

> *There is a tide in the affairs of men.*
> *Which, taken at the flood, leads on to fortune;*
> *Omitted, all the voyage of their life*
> *Is bound in shallows and in miseries.*
> *On such a full sea are we now afloat,*
> *And we must take the current when it serves,*
> *Or lose our ventures.*

The "current" of which Shakespeare speaks, Clausewitz calls "friction" (*Friktion*). Friction is everything that can and will go wrong, which in war is everything. Facing Napoleon at Austerlitz,[18] the Austrians and the Russians were certain they had planned for every eventuality with a "scientific" approach to warfare. In one of his most dazzling victories, Napoleon ran rings around them via a combination of subterfuge, lightning troop movements, and ruthless efficiency; even the weather worked in his favor—fog or mist, as it happened. As Prince Andrey, one of the main characters in *War and Peace*, ruefully comes to realize in the battle's aftermath: "In war the most deeply considered plans (as he had seen at Austerlitz) mean nothing, and that everything depends on

---

18. Considered in depth in chapter 8.

the way unexpected movements of the enemy, which cannot possibly be foreseen, are met."

> What kind of theory and science can there be when conditions and circumstances are indeterminate and can never be defined, and the active strengths of the warring parties are even more indefinable? No one can, no one ever could, know what the positions of our army and the enemy will be at this time tomorrow, and no one can know the relative strengths of the various detachments. . . . What kind of science can there be when, as in all practical matters, nothing can be defined, and everything depends on an incalculable range of conditions which come together significantly at a moment that no one can know in advance?

Tolstoy's sprawling novel is an ode to the power of friction, in both his characters' personal and professional lives, in the face of "science."

The mid-nineteenth century was, after all, the apotheosis of taxonomy. Darwin, aboard the *Beagle,* formulated his theory of evolution based on painstaking observation; he published the results in *On the Origin of Species* (1859) and *The Descent of Man* (1871), turning the scientific world upside down. In music, Richard Wagner developed his notion of the "all-encompassing work of art" (*Gesamtkunstwerk*), at first theoretically in his treatises on the subject, such as *Opera and Drama* (1851) and then put to the test in the first of his "Ring" cycle music dramas, *Das Rheingold* (1869). Karl Marx published *Das Kapital* in 1867. Even a work of fiction such as Melville's *Moby-Dick* (1851) includes extracts and an etymology, and features an exhaustive exploration of whaling practices while relating the tale of Ahab's search for the White Whale.

Indeed, the nineteenth century may be regarded as the apotheosis of Europeanism as well, an age of exploration and discovery, both in the sciences and in the arts, a prolonged intellectual and emotional struggle to come to grips with the essential questions of civilized existence: Who are we? Where did we come from? What does the rest of the world look like? Where are we going? How do we relate to our environment? How do we plumb our souls? Science explored the externals, mapping the world beyond, while artists pushed deeply into minds and hearts. Our modern system of specialized study and credentialism—all trees, no forest—would be utterly alien to these people who saw the world as a unity toward which all disciplines strove. Wagner, no less than Darwin, no less than Marx.[19]

Yet everywhere there was conflict. Wars and rumors of wars. Wars of conquest and revenge. Pitched battles in the heart of Europe and on the peripheries of the world as the Europeans saw things: in the Americas, in the Far East, in Africa. The seamless workings of the Great Watchmaker, first described in William Paley's *Natural Theology: or, Evidences of the Existence and Attributes of the Deity* (1802) and which set out the concept of "intelligent design" and the teleological argument in favor of God, suddenly seemed hard to defend in the face of so much apparent chaos. Surely a great and loving God could not have meant to include the slaughter of thousands, millions, in His perfectly designed universe?

Friktion is Clausewitz's singular contribution to the philosophy of war, made in the context of the upheavals of the first half of the nineteenth century. He had seen friction in action at Jena, and he had watched as the Prussian "scientific" way of war had so quickly and easily succumbed to the onslaught of creative, controlled Napoleonic chaos. From this, Clausewitz developed his idea of the "trinity":

> War is more than a true chameleon that slightly adapts its characteristics to the given case. As a total phenomenon its dominant tendencies always make war a paradoxical trinity—composed of primordial violence, hatred, and enmity, which are to be regarded as a blind natural force; of the play of chance and probability within which the creative spirit is free to roam; and of its element of subordination, as an instrument of policy, which makes it subject to reason alone.

Each leg of the stool represented an aspect of society: the people, roused to war; the military and its commanders, ready to fight it on their behalf; and the government, which would direct the course of

---

19. All three are the subjects of Jacques Barzun's seminal study, *Darwin, Marx, Wagner: Critique of a Heritage* (1941).

action according to policy. "The passions that are to be kindled in war must already be inherent in the people; the scope which the play of courage and talent will enjoy in the realm of probability and chance depends on the particular character of the commander and the army; but the political aims are the business of government alone."

We note that Clausewitz makes explicit allowances for the "creative spirit . . . the play of courage and talent." This makes war almost sound like a performance—which of course it is, although deadly serious. But it is also fully in keeping with the author's romantic (however analytical) inclinations regarding war. A career soldier who—although being a protégé of both Scharnhorst[20] and Gneisenau[21]—never felt his talents were fully recognized by his political superiors and who eventually left the Prussian service to work with the Russians during Napoleon's Russian campaign, returning to the Prussian service after Waterloo.

Clausewitz famously—and perhaps surprisingly given his admiration for Napoleon—gave the advantage to the defense in his book, even though the emperor was almost always on the attack. But the defense often has the advantages of fortifications or at least fighting on home turf, while the attackers traditionally must have three-to-one superiority in manpower to mount a successful assault. Clausewitz, however, understood that no plan survives first contact with the enemy. That the enemy gets a vote. That, as former heavyweight champion Mike Tyson would later put it: "Everybody has plans until they get hit for the first time." After that, plans, no matter how carefully wrought, largely go out the window, and Friction and Fortuna now play the lead roles.

What is this *Friktion* of which Clausewitz speaks, and to which he devotes so many pages of *Vom Kriege*? This element, let us call it "uncertainty," is the key to understanding his theory of war, and it leads inexorably, but perhaps surprisingly, to the main thesis of this book, which is that human history in fact turns on *Friktion* and (to continue our

---

20. Gerhard Johann David von Scharnhorst (1755–1813), the father of the Prussian army.

21. August, Count Neidhardt von Gneisenau (1760–1831), Clausewitz's friend and mentor; he died in the same cholera epidemic as did Clausewitz. Germany later named battleships after both Scharnhorst and Gneisenau.

German theme) *Wendepunkte*—"turning points"—that forever alter its course.

Anything can change the course of a battle, and thus of a war, and thus of history. An improperly conceived battle plan. A failure of nerve. Outmoded technology. A bridge poorly defended, or blown too soon. The drowning of an emperor. Hunger, want, thirst, cold. A fresh infusion of troops. Forces concealed from the enemy. The weather. Surprise, and a lack of will or capacity or courage with which to react to it. A savvy leader understands this:

> If one has never personally experienced war, one cannot understand in what the difficulties constantly mentioned really consist, nor why a commander should need any brilliance and exceptional ability. Everything looks simple; the knowledge required does not look remarkable, the strategic options are so obvious that by comparison the simplest problem of higher mathematics has an impressive scientific dignity.

In other words, friction. "Friction is the only concept that more or less corresponds to the factors that distinguish real war from war on paper," writes Clausewitz. Comparing a war machine to a real machine, he notes, "This tremendous friction, which cannot, as in mechanics, be reduced to a few points, is everywhere in contact with chance, and brings about effects that cannot be measured, just because they are largely due to chance." And so we are back to chance, and to Napoleon's perhaps apocryphal—but quintessentially Clausewitzian—observation.

For this is, in Clausewitz's experience and in the experience of every combat soldier who ever fought before or since, the essential nature of war. Clausewitz—*le plus Allemand des Allemands*[22]—never actually uses the famous phrase "the fog of war" in his treatise, although he comes close. "War is the realm of uncertainty; three quarters of the factors on which action in war is based are wrapped in a fog of greater or lesser uncertainty," he writes in book 1, chapter 3, "On Military Genius." Later:

---

22. "The most German of Germans." Hubert Camon, *Clausewitz* (Paris, 1911).

"In the dreadful presence of suffering and danger, emotion can easily overwhelm intellectual conviction, and in this psychological fog it is so hard to form clear and complete insights that changes of view become more understandable and excusable." In other words, *Nebel* (fog) is *Friktion*. And *friction* is generally the decider between victory and defeat.

In this light, Clausewitz addresses a quintessentially romantic concept: the nature of genius in war. In "On Military Genius," he notes, "We are aware that this word is used in many senses, differing both in degree and in kind. We also know that some of these meanings make it difficult to establish the essence of genius. But since we claim no special expertise in philosophy or grammar, we may be allowed to use the word in its ordinary meaning, in which 'genius' refers to a very highly developed mental aptitude for a particular occupation." He then proceeds to define "genius" in a way that would do the early Romantics proud: "Genius consists in a harmonious combination of elements, in which one or the other ability may predominate, but none may be in conflict with the rest." It was Clausewitz's belief that military genius could only appear in countries with "the higher degree of civilization"—an assertion disproven by history, as it happens—but his frame of reference was Alexander, Caesar, and Napoleon.

In *War and Peace*, Tolstoy has no use for theories of martial inspiration, mocking "the remarkable and lofty faculty that goes by the name of genius, which is so lovingly ascribed to Napoleon." He offers this observation on the nature of *friction* and military genius via one of his principal characters:

Prince Andrey stood back amazed at what they were all saying. Ideas which he had long held and often thought about during his military service—that there was no such thing as a science of warfare, and never could be, and therefore there could be no such thing as "military genius"—struck him now as entirely true and self-evident. "What kind of theory and science can there be when conditions and circumstances are indeterminate and can never be defined, and the active strengths of the warring parties are even more indefinable? No one can, no one ever could, know what the positions of our army and the enemy will be at this time tomorrow, and no one can know the relative strengths of the various detachments. . . . What kind of science can there be when, as in all practical matters, nothing can be defined, and everything depends on an incalculable range of conditions which come together significantly at a moment that no one can know in advance?"

Another element of warfare that resonated with the Romantics was its resemblance, in many of its salient aspects, to sex. Deeply physical, deeply emotional, inflamer of passions, destroyer of judgment, a process of (however briefly) self-annihilation, rife with intimate bodily fluids, *la petit mort* as opposed to *la grande mort,* but no less seductive. Sex was always an animating principle in war, beginning with the *Iliad* and Achilles's compelled forfeiture of the beautiful slave girl, Briseis. The sinister, syphilitic roué, Pandarus (whence comes our verb "to pander"), makes this quite explicit in the ribald song he sings to Helen and Paris in Shakespeare's profoundly cynical play, *Troilus and Cressida*:

O love's bow Shoots buck and doe:/ The shaft confounds, Not that it wounds,/ But tickles still the sore./ These lovers cry Oh! oh! they die!/ Yet that which seems the wound to kill, Doth turn oh! oh! to ha! ha! he!/ So dying, love lives still.

As the poet Percy Bysshe Shelley (1792–1822) writes in *Queen Mab:* "How wonderful is Death,/ Death, and his brother Sleep!/ One, pale as yonder waning moon/ With lips of lurid blue;/ The other, rosy as the morn/ When throned on ocean's wave/ It blushes o'er the world;/ Yet both so passing wonderful!" Dead at twenty-nine, Shelley certainly found out quickly enough.

Poets who actually experienced war echoed the comparison; however obliquely, it was frequently on their minds. "We are the Dead. Short days ago/ We lived, felt dawn, saw sunset glow,/ Loved and were loved,/ and now we lie/ In Flanders fields," wrote John McCrae (1872–1918). The Anglo-Jewish poet Isaac Rosenberg (1890–1918), son of Lithuanian immigrants, killed in the closing days of the war, perhaps said it best in "Returning, We Hear the Larks":

Death could drop from the dark
As easily as song—
But song only dropped,
Like a blind man's dreams on the sand
By dangerous tides;
Like a girl's dark hair, for she dreams no ruin lies there,
Or her kisses where a serpent hides.

Generally speaking, women do not expect to die violently at the hands of other women; for males, the possibility is never very far from one's mind: in street confrontations, bar fights, armed robberies, riots, and of course in war itself. A confrontation with death was something to be expected if not actually sought, if only to exorcise the ghosts of fear and cowardice that haunt all young men. During the American Civil War, the anticipation of one's first experience of combat was called "going to see the elephant," a fabulous beast not hitherto encountered by American farm boys. In *War and Peace*, Tolstoy expressed the concept like this:

Who is there? There, beyond this field, and the tree, and the roof lit by the sun? No one knows, and you would like to know; and you're afraid to cross that line, and would like to cross it; and you know that sooner or later you will have to cross it and find out what is there on the other side of the line, as you will inevitably find out what is there on the other side of death. And you're strong, healthy, cheerful, and excited, and surrounded by people just as strong and excitedly animated. So, if he does not think it, every man feels who finds himself within sight of an enemy, and this feeling gives a particular brilliance and joyful sharpness of impression to everything that happens in those moments.

Tolstoy here is describing the emotions of the Russians as they prepare for their first encounter with the French and the great—and thus far, offstage—elephant named Napoleon. The passions are engaged, the senses heightened, but fear is not much of a factor. Curiosity, and the understanding that God and Fortuna determine the outcome of battle, far outweigh it. "What are we facing tomorrow?" Prince Andrey, the voice of paralyzing reason, asks before the battle of Borodino. "A hundred million chances which will be decided on the instant by whether we run or they run, whether this man or that man is killed."

A word about something not often considered by armchair generals but that once was an intrinsic part of warfare, and that is the traditional "offer of battle," which has to do with more than simple considerations of weather and terrain. War is often compared to chess (or chess to war), but there is also something of the mating dance about it. In Greek and Roman times, competing sides first sought out the most advantageous terrain for the size and nature of their armies. Not just the high ground, or a flat plain upon which to let loose scythed chariots, or the passive defensive fortifications afforded by a handy river or mountain range. Rather it had to do with the psychological preparedness of the opposing forces, and their commander's judgment about the ideal time to engage. It was a form of martial seduction.

In the ancient world, there was a fighting season, which generally ran from late spring to mid- to late autumn. Until the advent of mechanized transportation, weather was generally dispositive in the northern hemisphere, which was why Hannibal's surprise attack upon Rome from the north in 218 B.C., over and through the snow-covered passes of the Alps, came as such a shock. Similarly, after a month of dithering, Napoleon knew he was in a race against time once he decided to retreat from a burned-out Moscow on October 19, 1812. It was a fatal delay, which allowed General Winter to chew up his forces. Between the lack of sustenance owing to the Russians' scorched-earth policy and the weather, the Grand Armée evaporated; of the 612,000 men under arms who entered Russia, only about 112,000 returned to the western frontier. The emperor himself, like a modern Darius III, fled back to Paris before his troops in order to get ahead of the catastrophic news and try to salvage his doomed empire.[23]

---

23. According to the *Encyclopedia Britannica*, "Among the casualties, 100,000 are thought to have been killed in action, 200,000 to have died from other causes, 50,000 to have been left sick in hospitals, 50,000 to have deserted, and 100,000 to have been taken as prisoners of war. The French themselves lost 70,000 in action and 120,000 wounded, as against the non-French contingents' 30,000 and 60,000. Russian casualties have been estimated at 200,000 killed, 50,000 dispersed or deserting, and 150,000 wounded."

Accordingly, we read in Caesar's *Commentaries*, for example, that "battle was offered," and sometimes declined until both generals felt they had the strategic advantage. The smallest things—a swamp here, a hillock there, the troops' state of readiness, or lack of sleep—loomed large. At Gaugamela, Alexander kept the Persians guessing as to when he would attack (they suspected a highly unusual night assault), and so Darius kept his men at the ready all night; Alexander, by contrast, slept in late and awoke, refreshed and ready to fight; he knew he had victory in the bag. At Waterloo, Napoleon delayed the start of his attack on Wellington until nearly noon, waiting for the field to dry from the heavy rains of the night before, but the delay gave Marshal Gebhard Leberecht von Blücher's Prussian troops an extra few hours to join up with the Anglo-Dutch army and thus win the day. Even as late as both the First and Second World Wars, as motors replaced horses and airplanes replaced balloons, weather conditions played an important role. Planes couldn't fly in bad weather, nor could airborne spotters see the enemy. Spring mud and winter snows continued to hamper the effectiveness of combat forces. The much-bruited "arc of history," then, should perhaps be better viewed not as a crescent or arc but an eternal circle: the worm Ouroboros, the sacred serpent of ancient Egypt and Greece forever devouring its tail.

And yet men fight, with pride and even eagerness. In *War and Peace*, on the eve of the decisive Battle of Austerlitz, callow Nikolai Rostov unexpectedly comes face-to-face with the Russian tsar, Alexander I. The effect on him is electric:

> Rostov was not far from the trumpeters, and with his keen sight had recognized the Tsar and watched his approach. . . . Stopping in front of the Pávlograds, the Tsar said something in French to the Austrian Emperor and smiled.
>
> Seeing that smile, Rostov involuntarily smiled himself and felt a still stronger flow of love for his sovereign. He longed to show that love in some way and knowing that this was impossible was ready to cry.
>
> "Oh God, what would happen to me if the Emperor spoke to me?" thought Rostov. "I should die of happiness!"

To die for, instead of merely to fight and kill for. This is the secret of motivation, discipline, and military success, although it is rarely if ever stated as such. Alexander knew it, as did Caesar, Constantine, Aetius, Bohemond, Napoleon, and Patton. Let the men see you, whether charging furiously at the head of the Companions, confidently swathed in the red cloak of Caesar, or strutting with the swagger stick[24] and the ivory-handled *pistoles* of Patton. As in love, so as in war: passion is one of the prime motivators, and when a commander can get his troops to focus that ardor on his own person, victory is often the result.

And yet, *friction*. Little in war is predictable; the key is to stay focused as the fight develops. "Lose a man," said Napoleon, "but never a moment." In this respect, warfare is not a chess game in which defeat, once apparent, is also inevitable. The turning points of history are only clear in retrospect. Like a well-written screenplay, history is a continuous narrative, with each scene and sequence flowing inexorably (but not predestined) into the next. Sometimes things happen *in spite of* what came, or did not come, before and not *because* of it. History is the dispassionate record of human activity, and it is through the eyes and the frame of humanity that we must view it.

What does remain constant, though, is the quality and nearly unique abilities of its best wartime commanders, men who could focus their decision-making processes in real time and, in some sense, actually slow down time itself as they watched the battle unfold, often over tremendous distances. Planning of course is an important aspect of it— knowing the terrain, choosing the battlefield, mastering the logistics, having the right subordinate commanders to execute major tactical decisions (and even make them), and personally possessing just the right combination of bravado and sagacity to inspire the troops to follow. *Pace* Tolstoy, time and again we see that men with a real genius for war seize the moment. And when that moment coincides with a pivotal point in the annals of humanity, the result is a new world.

In the battles and conflicts described herein, few participants knew

---

24. A symbol of authority that dates back to the centurion's staff of the Roman legions.

at the time they were involved in epochal events, save perhaps the victorious commanders whose iron will and battlefield acumen had in part
forced the issue. And yet even they could not suspect how long-lasting
an effect their moments of glory would have.

Turning-point battles are not always recognized as such at the time.
Alexander's triumph over the Achaemenids was won at Gaugamela, yet
he still needed to chase Darius all the way to Bactria, in central Asia,
before he encountered the Great King's corpse—and even then he kept
pushing on, to India. A brief battle at the Milvian Bridge north of Rome
seemed at first to end the Second Tetrarchy and to partially settle the
question of who was to be ruler of the Romans of the western empire;
but there were still battles to be fought against Licinius before the Empire was united under a single ruler once more.

Not even Constantine the Great suspected at the time that the death
of Maxentius, weighted down by his armor and drowning in the Tiber,
would lead ineluctably to the founding of a new imperial capital called
Constantinople on the site of ancient Byzantium at the Strait of Bosphorus, where Europe meets Asia. Nor would he have thought that the
eventual installation of Christianity, once a minor Jewish heresy until
Saul of Tarsus—Saint Paul—transformed it into a faith, would ultimately became the state religion of the Empire and gradually assume
Rome's former spiritual and temporal authority, including the office of
pontifex maximus,[25] today still held by the Pope.[26]

Where we go from here, no one knows. All we do know is that it
will continue until the end of the West. New societies, new cultures,
are struggling to be born, with no guarantee of improvement. The West
faces a crossroads in a Clausewitzian fog, past which it cannot see, no
matter how hard we peer. Our roadmap ends with us, and it is up to us
either to force new trails or expire by the wayside. All we can do—all
we must do—is study the past, understand how we got here, connect its
lessons into coherent, essential narratives, tally the forces in play, and

---

25. The Latin root of the word *pons* means "bridge," while *fex* derives from the verb "to
make." Thus the *pontifex maximus* was the chief bridge builder between the human world
and that of the divine. Hardly a negligible office.

26. It passed to him in 381 A.D., when the emperor Gratian declined it.

harness or suppress them as best we can, aware that as we do so we are making history just as surely as our forebears did. And know that we will not live to know the ultimate outcome.

Let us start, then, at the beginning: in the late Bronze Age. Mycenaean Greeks, their ships pulled up on the littoral, their camps pitched on the beach, stare across a wide plain at the topless towers of Ilium on the west coast of Anatolia. With the gods of both sides watching from above, West is about to collide with East—and with this epic clash does our history properly begin.

TWO

ACHILLES AT ILIUM

In Troy, there lies the scene. From isles of Greece
The princes orgulous, their high blood chafed,
Have to the port of Athens sent their ships,
Fraught with the ministers and instruments
Of cruel war: sixty and nine, that wore
Their crownets regal, from the Athenian bay
Put forth toward Phrygia; and their vow is made
To ransack Troy, within whose strong immures
The ravish'd Helen, Menelaus' queen,
With wanton Paris sleeps; and that's the quarrel.

—SHAKESPEARE, *TROILUS AND CRESSIDA*

LEAVE IT TO THE BARD TO SO PITHILY SUM UP THE DRAMA OF THE first great military conflict in Western history, the Trojan War, which was fought around 1200 B.C. near the end of the Mycenaean Late Bronze Age. Beginning with Homer, this elemental conflict has been the inspiration for artists, poets, storytellers, and military strategists and historians for three thousand years. After all, it has everything: Helen, the most beautiful woman in the world, with the frisson of questionable virtue; two royal brothers, the great king Agamemnon and the Spartan king Menelaus; the feckless coward Paris, whose abduction of the very willing Helen[1] ignites the conflict; and two mighty heroes, Achilles for

---

1. Genealogically, Helen is a descendent of Zeus himself by Leda, whom he seduced in the

the Greeks and Hector, the cream of the Trojan warriors, who must battle to the death for honor, country, and glory. That's the quarrel.

For a long time, the war of which the Poet sings and with which classical iconography begins was thought to be fanciful. Homer lived during the ninth or eighth century B.C., after the Late Bronze Age Collapse, and around the time of the rediscovery of writing among the Greeks. He is by reputation the author of both the *Iliad,* which describes a relatively brief period near the end of that ten-year conflict, and the *Odyssey,* which relates the epic, decade-long journey home from Troy of the wily Greek chieftain Odysseus in the teeth of everything that gods and monsters could throw at him. It wasn't until 1870–71 that the site of Troy was finally located at Hisarlik in present-day Turkey, amid the excavations of the long-vanished city begun by Frank Calvert and Heinrich Schliemann. Today, scholars consider the layers known as Troy VI/VIIa to be the location of the city of which Homer sang.

Yet even without archaeology, we've somehow known for millennia that something happened in the eastern Mediterranean between the earliest Greeks and a people living in Anatolia near the Dardanelles. To assume that the ancient bards simply invented a national epic out of whole cloth, however embellished it might be, is to grab the sword by the blade instead of the hilt. That is the conceit of modernity; why posit a conspiracy so vast when the recognition that there is some truth in every legend answers the challenge of Occam's Razor without turning one into a superstitious peasant or a credulous rube?

Then who, historically, were the Trojans? Our best guess is that they were a people called Luwians, a branch of the Hittites, who were attacked by the Mycenaean Greeks somewhere around 1200 B.C. The Hittites, a people familiar to us from the Old Testament, were Indo-Europeans

---

form of a swan. The episode was a favorite of artists from Greco-Roman times through the Renaissance, in part because it allowed painters and sculptors to frankly depict a beautiful naked woman in the act of copulation, albeit with an animal. W. B. Yeats wrote a particularly expressive poem on the subject, "No Second Troy," after Maud Gonne finally rejected his various marriage proposals and married John MacBride, who was shot by the British after the Easter Rising of 1916. The poem was published in 1924.

who tangled frequently with the ancient Egyptians and fought one of the earliest battles of which we have knowledge, the Battle of Kadesh (1274 B.C.) against the pharaoh Ramesses II, which resulted in the first known peace treaty in history.

What's fascinating, however, is that the Trojan War comes near the end of both Mycenaean and Hittite history; shortly thereafter came what historians refer to as the Late Bronze Age Collapse, which essentially destroyed Mediterranean civilization in just half a century. We're not quite sure why, but the archaeological evidence from Troy indicates that the city had suffered extensive war damage. This was also a time of severe earthquakes, droughts, and famines, which led to political instability, the collapse of trade, and invasion by a new set of intruders known as the Sea Peoples. They appear to be a kind of Mediterranean forerunner of the Vikings, conducting lightning raids on the coastal settlements of Greece, Anatolia, and Egypt. In any case, cities fell, palaces crumbled, and even the written language of the Mycenaeans, known as Linear B, was abandoned; by the time classical Greek civilization arose some eight hundred years later, nobody could read it. Thus the Trojan War wasn't just the last stand of the Trojans but of the whole pre-ancient world the storied conflict has come to represent and embody.

Whatever the cause, the city known to the Greeks as Ilion finally fell into desuetude around 1180 B.C., although the ruins remained for centuries longer. They might have still been visible in Homer's day. We know from Arrian,[2] whose military biography *The Campaigns of Alexander* is one of our primary sources of information about the Macedonian conqueror, that one of the first things Alexander did upon crossing the Hellespont and setting out to crush the Achaemenid Persian Empire was to stop at Troy, the beginning of all things:

---

2. Lucius Flavius Arrianus Xenophon, known as Arrian (c. 86–160 A.D.) was a Greek historian and student of Stoic philosophy born in Nicomedia in the Roman province of Bithynia and a Roman citizen. He served as a provincial Roman official, a military commander, a consul of Rome, and the governor of Cappadocia. The book is also known as *Anabasis* and deliberately modeled in title and structure on Xenophon of Athens's great work of the same name from 370 B.C.

One account says that Hephaestion[3] laid a wreath on the tomb of Patroclus; another that Alexander laid one on the tomb of Achilles, calling him a lucky man, in that he had Homer to proclaim his deeds and preserve his memory. And well might Alexander envy Achilles this piece of good fortune; for in his own case there was no equivalent: his one failure, the single break, as it were, in the long chain of his successes, was that he had no worthy chronicler to tell the world of his exploits.

The *Iliad* is one of the most brutal and unblinkingly violent books ever written. Its vivid descriptions of combat with spear, arrow, and sword set the standard for acceptable levels of bloodshed in both art and entertainment. Those coming to the *Iliad* for the first time know that the operative word, the very first word of the poem, in fact, is *rage*—μῆνιν (*mēnin*), or *wrath*—the choleric rage of Achilles, the Greeks' greatest warrior, which manifests itself throughout the story—even though for a very long time, Achilles is an offstage character, fuming and sulking in his tent with Patroclus—until it releases itself in a spasm of slaughter that ends with the death of Hector. And then, in one of the most remarkable and surprising endings in Western literature, the great rage subsides, dissipates, and this most sanguinary of epics closes on a fleeting moment of reconciliation between Achilles and Priam, Hector's father, and the funeral of Hector. Even amidst all this death, there is still life, and love.

There is, however, not a word about the Trojan Horse, the sack of Troy, the slaughter of most of its inhabitants, the escape of Aeneas, and the fate of the Trojan women: Hecuba, Priam's queen; Andromache, Hector's grieving widow; Helen, the cause of all the trouble, returned to Menelaus; and Cassandra, taken as Agamemnon's slave and concubine.[4]

---

3. Hephaestion was Alexander's dearest companion, the Patroclus to his Achilles.

4. "In the few days covered by the *Iliad*'s narrative, no cities will be stormed and the war will not be brought to conclusion," writes Caroline Alexander in *The War That Killed Achilles* (2009), "But the rebellion that would have played in heaven will take place on earth."

Their fates Homer's and later poets' audiences already knew,[5] as they knew of the events leading up to the launch of the thousand ships, and Greek poets and playwrights mined the vein of these stories for centuries more, secure in the knowledge they didn't have to fill in the backstory.

The sanguinary tone is established in the poem's opening stanza, quoted here in the heroic rhyming couplets translation of Alexander Pope, issued in six volumes between 1715 and 1720. Pope's magisterial treatment not only made his career (he was in his twenties when he began the work) but restored Homer to pride of place in classical scholarship during the Augustan age, and set English poetry firmly on a course it followed until the Romantic era.[6]

> *Achilles' wrath, to Greece the direful spring*
> *Of woes unnumber'd, heavenly goddess, sing!*
> *That wrath which hurl'd to Pluto's gloomy reign*
> *The souls of mighty chiefs untimely slain;*
> *Whose limbs unburied on the naked shore,*
> *Devouring dogs and hungry vultures tore.*
> *Since great Achilles and Atrides strove,*
> *Such was the sovereign doom, and such the will of Jove!*

We know at once that we are in for war, not only hand-to-hand combat with primitive weapons but also its aftermath: dead bodies, stripped of their armor and left for the birds and the dogs to eat unless quickly whisked away. Rather than a pitched battle between great armies, the Trojan War is, in Homer's telling, largely a series of single combats. There are chariots, but no cavalry. Greeks and Trojans seek one another out, combatants square off, often exchanging brief biographies regarding their lineage and places of origin. During the fight, they immediately look for their opponent's weak spot, the chink in the bronze

---

5. See, for example, *The Trojan Women* by Euripides, first performed in 415 B.C., which begins just moments after the sack of Troy.

6. "It is a pretty poem, Mr. Pope," said Richard Bentley the British clergyman, classical scholar, and master of Trinity College, Cambridge, upon being asked his opinion of the translation, "but you must not call it Homer."

armor that allows the tip of the spear or the sword into the body. Often this is near the collarbone, at the base of the throat, the place where the lifeblood throbs and from which it is most easily spilled. Naturally, the poet lovingly records every gruesome moment, as in this passage from Book V celebrating the prowess of the ferocious Greek hero, Diomedes, who in this encounter slays the Trojan, Pandarus:[7]

> *He spoke, and rising hurl'd his forceful dart,*
> *Which, driven by Pallas, pierced a vital part;*
> *Full in his face it enter'd, and betwixt*
> *The nose and eye-ball the proud Lycian fix'd;*
> *Crash'd all his jaws, and cleft the tongue within,*
> *Till the bright point look'd out beneath the chin.*
> *Headlong he falls, his helmet knocks the ground:*
> *Earth groans beneath him, and his arms resound;*
> *The starting coursers tremble with affright;*
> *The soul indignant seeks the realms of night.*

Note the mention of Pallas Athena here. In Homer's world, the gods are very much active participants in the affairs of men. They are, in fact, the *friction* of which Clausewitz later wrote, the emblems of things beyond man's control or ken, ascribed to Até, the goddess of delusion, rashness, and folly, and also the qualities the word itself describes. Not only do the gods watch the action from Olympus or Mount Ida but they also often interpose themselves in it, deflecting an arrow or a blow, and sometimes even whisking their favorites off the field should danger threaten. They can even be themselves briefly wounded by mortals, as Ares, the god of war, is by Diomedes. Indeed, as the classical scholar Mary Lefkowitz argues in *Greek Gods, Human Lives: What We Can Learn from Myths* (2003), it is the gods who are Homer's real principal characters, not the humans who function as their playthings, occasional sexual partners, bastard offspring, and fleeting objects of affection, but

---

7. The "shining archer." Quite a different personage from Shakespeare's, but then so are all the other historical characters in *Troilus* as well.

for whom any feelings are necessarily evanescent. As she notes, "The most important ancient Greek religious text was the *Iliad*."

In the Hebrew Torah and the Christian Old Testament, God creates Eve to be a companion and helpmeet for Adam. Not so in the Greco-Roman theogonies. Instead, Woman is created as a *punishment* for Man—"a great calamity"—inflicted upon mankind for the sins of Prometheus, the Titan who stole and gave fire (science, technology, the means of self-improvement) to Man.

> And it stung high thundering Zeus deep to the spirit, and angered him in his heart, when he saw the far-beaconing flare of fire among mankind. At once he made an affliction for mankind to set against the fire. . . . When he had made the pretty bane to set against a blessing, he led her out where the other gods and men were, resplendent in the finery of the pale-eyed one whose father is stern. Both immortal gods and mortal men were seized with wonder then they saw that precipitous trap, more than mankind can manage. For from her is descended the female sex, a great affliction to mortals as they dwell with their husbands—no fit partners for accursed Poverty, but only for Plenty . . . a bane for mortal men has high-thundering Zeus created women, conspirators in causing difficulty. (Hesiod, *Theogony*, translation by M. L. West)

Even for men who chose not to wed, there was no escape from their curse. To die old and childless meant having to fend for yourself even as age took its toll, and upon your death your unworthy relatives, some of them quite distant, would split up your estate. "Then again, the man who does partake of marriage, and gets a good wife who is sound and sensible, spends his life with bad competing constantly against good; while the man who gets the awful kind lives with unrelenting pain in heart and spirit, and it is an ill without a cure. Thus there is no way of deceiving or evading the mind of Zeus, since not even Iapetos' son, sly Prometheus, escaped the weight of his wrath, and for all his cleverness a strong fetter holds him in check."

It gets worse. In Hesiod's other religious foundational text, *Works and Days*, this first woman is called Pandora, crafted in part by Athena and Aphrodite (two of the three goddesses involved in the Judgment of Paris, the wellspring of the Trojan War), who infused the new creature with "a bitch's mind," one who would arouse a "painful yearning and consuming obsession" in men. "In her breast the Go-between, the dog-killer [Hermes], fashioned lies and wily pretences and a knavish nature by deep-thundering Zeus' design; and he put in a voice, did the herald of the gods, and he named this woman Pandora, 'Allgift,' because all the dwellers on Olympus made her their gift—a calamity for men who live by bread."

The story of Pandora and her famous box is well known to us, although its origins and lesson have been forgotten. Like innumerable myths and fairy tales (see also the works of the brothers Grimm), it has been sanitized out of all recognition, cleaned up for polite and, latterly, "progressive" company, all of its horror and meaning bled from it until livid. Pandora, the poisoned gift, is presented to mankind complete with a stoppered amphora containing all the ills that mortal flesh is heir to:

> For formerly the tribes of men on earth lived remote from ills, without harsh toil and the grievous sicknesses that are deadly to men. But the woman unstopped the jar and let it all out, and brought grim cares upon mankind. Only Hope remained there inside in her secure dwelling, under the lip of the jar, and did not fly out, because the woman put the lid back in time by the providence of Zeus the cloud-gatherer who bears the aegis. But for the rest, countless troubles roam among men: full of ills is the earth, and full the sea. Sicknesses visit men by day, and others by night, uninvited, bringing ill to mortals, silently, because Zeus the resourceful deprived them of voice. Thus there is no way to evade the purpose of Zeus.

This sexual predicament—misogyny, some might call it—lies at the heart of the masculine rage of the *Iliad* and precipitates all of the action. The shades of Helen and Briseis, however, unavenged and unfulfilled, loom over the entire poem; they are the cause of all the death and destruction wrought on earth for the amusement of the gods. When, in Euripides's play *The Trojan Women* (415 B.C.) the wronged Menelaus and his wife, Helen, finally come face-to-face in the ruins of Troy, his first instinct is to drag her back to Greece and kill her:

> HELEN. King Menelaus, thy first deed might make a woman fear. Into my chamber brake thine armèd men, and lead me wrathfully. Methinks, almost, I know thou hatest me. Yet I would ask thee, what decree is gone forth for my life or death?
> MENELAUS (struggling with his emotion). There was not one that scrupled for thee. All, all with one will gave thee to me, whom thou hast wronged, to kill!
> HELEN. And is it granted that I speak, or no, in answer to them ere I die, to show I die most wronged and innocent?
> MENELAUS. I seek to kill thee, woman; not to hear thee speak!
>
> (translation by Gilbert Murray)

She talks her way out of it, of course, and legend has it that they remain married until the end of their days.[8]

In book 3 of the *Iliad*, composed hundreds of years before Euripides's play, the wronged Menelaus and the seducer, Paris, square off in single combat to decide the issue of Helen. It's a remarkably sensible alternative to the mass slaughter of heroes who have no particular love for the House of Atreus and couldn't care less about Helen, whom they regard as a slattern. Menelaus is far from the Achaeans' most potent warrior, and Paris is a lover, not a fighter, who would rather lounge in his palace bedroom with his purloined paramour than battle like his brother, Hector. Both men miss a death strike with their spears, but Menelaus grapples with Paris, breaking his sword over Paris's helmet. He then grabs the hapless Trojan by his helmet's horsehair crest and begins to drag him away, choking him with the strap. However, the goddess Aphrodite, who has a special fondness for Paris,[9] envelops him in mist

---

8. Helen is in some ways the forerunner of the Sabine women of Roman mythology: she goes with whichever conqueror can carry her away.

9. He did, after all, choose her as the most beautiful of the goddesses over both Hera and

and spirits him miraculously back to his bedroom, then fetches Helen to him for some more lovemaking.

Furious, Menelaus demands to be acknowledged the victor in the duel and, in the heavens, Zeus agrees. But Hera, the goddess of marital fidelity—despite, or perhaps because of, her brother/husband Zeus's constant infidelities—vehemently demurs: she hates Paris and the Trojans with a mad passion and wishes to see the city razed. In the face of her wrath Zeus, of course, immediately folds, the truce is broken and the war continues.

The gods, thus, act as the frictive elements in this, the first of our Western wars. Over the poem's 15,693 lines, both major and minor divinities will take part, not only the principal gods and goddesses, but also important lesser gods including, notably, Hephaestus. The god of both blacksmiths and fire, he is the one who not only forges Achilles a new suit of armor[10] after he loses his when Patroclus is killed and stripped of it by Hector, but also intervenes on Achilles's behalf during his battle with the river god, Scamander. The gods also quarrel among themselves, as Zeus has to put down various rebellious lesser gods and struggle with his own indecision (he starts by favoring the Trojans but ends up favoring the Greeks) and his mixed feelings about justice and propriety.

Zeus's principal adversary, however, is his own wife, "cow-eyed" (a Homeric compliment in Pope's translation, large eyes in women being a prized sexual trait) Hera, "of the white arms." Hera was supposed to have been even more beautiful than the goddess of love, the sexy Aphrodite, but her position in the hierarchy made her essentially unapproachable. She is the original incarnation of the captious wife,[11] but still capable of deploying her sexual charms and wiles to bend Zeus to her will. When the Greeks appear to have the upper hand in book 14,

---

Athena; accordingly, the latter two consistently root for and assist the Greeks. The nude beauty contest (Paris of course insisted the goddesses be naked) is memorialized in countless works of art as *The Judgment of Paris,* most famously by Peter Paul Rubens in 1639.

10. At the behest of the nymph Thetis, Achilles's mother.

11. Her counterpart in German mythology is the hectoring Fricka, Wotan's wife, in Wagner's *Ring of the Nibelung.*

Hera (Juno in Latin) gets Aphrodite's assistance in dolling herself up, then heads over to Zeus's man cave atop Mount Ada and screws him senseless: *"At length, with love and sleep's soft power oppress'd/ The panting thunderer nods, and sinks to rest."*

With Zeus sleeping off *la petite mort,* Hera calls upon Poseidon to rally the Greeks, whose makeshift defensive wall has been breached, their trenches overrun, several of their leaders wounded, including Diomedes and Ulysses; beaten back to their ships, they are poised to break under Hector's furious assault. But this proves to be the high-water mark of the Trojan offensive. Once Achilles takes the field in book 19 following the death of Patroclus, the advantage is entirely on the Achaean side, and Achilles's defeat of Hector in book 22 represents the martial climax of the epic.

After such a build-up, the duel between the heroes comes as something of an anticlimax, and a morally repellant one at that. The Trojan army has retreated behind the city's fabled walls, and Hector finds himself trapped on the outside, accompanied only by his brother Deiphobus, with Achilles bearing down on him. He resolves to fight, but his nerve fails him; he runs, and Achilles is forced to chase him around the walls until at last the Trojan hero squares off to face the enraged Greek.

Hector offers Achilles a noble deal: that the victor shall not desecrate the loser's corpse. But Achilles, his fury now roused to fever pitch, will have none of it. *"Talk not of oaths (the dreadful chief replies,/ While anger flash'd from his disdainful eyes),/ Detested as thou art, and ought to be,/ Nor oath nor pact Achilles plights with thee."*

It's not a fair fight. Achilles throws his spear, but Hector ducks beneath its path; unseen by Hector, Athena retrieves the weapon and brings it back to Achilles. Now it's Hector's turn: his javelin hits Achilles square in his Hephaestus-forged shield and bounces off harmlessly. Hector calls to Deiphobus for another spear, but his brother has vanished—he was just an apparition—and Hector is in fact alone. Hector draws his sword and charges Achilles, only to realize that Achilles somehow has his spear back. In his last moments, Hector realizes that Athena has interceded on the Achaean side and resigns himself to his doom. *"'Tis true I perish, yet I perish great:/ Yet in a mighty deed I shall expire,/ Let future ages hear it, and admire!"*

Achilles plunges his spear into Hector's throat at the base of the neck. Hector sinks into the dust, with one last wish, that Achilles not leave his body to the dogs but return it to his parents, Priam and Hecuba, for proper burial. Achilles scornfully spurns the dying man, but Hector's last words are chilling:

Thy rage, implacable! too well I knew:/ The Furies that relentless breast have steeled,/ And cursed thee with a heart that cannot yield./ Yet think, a day will come, when Fate's decree/ And angry gods shall wreak this wrong on thee;/ Phœbus and Paris shall avenge my fate,/ And stretch thee here, before this Scæan gate.

But even a dying man's curse cannot still the Greek champion's rage: *"Then his fell soul a thought of vengeance bred;/ (Unworthy of himself, and of the dead)."* Achilles punctures the dead hero's ankles, laces them with thongs, ties Hector to his chariot, and drags his body around the city before the horrified eyes of Priam and Hecuba watching from the walls. The destruction of Troy, and the death, rape, or enslavement of its people—the spoils of war—is now a foregone conclusion.

In killing Hector, though, Achilles has sealed his own doom. As he debates taking the field against the Trojans to avenge Patroclus, he knows full well his mother's prophecy: he can return to Phthia and live a long but uneventful life back home, or go out in a blaze of glory at Troy. Throughout the first half of the poem, the first option seems more attractive, especially as he's been humiliated by Agamemnon with the loss of his slave girl, Briseis. But the death of Patroclus at Hector's hands decides it for him.

What else motivates this wrath, a rage so great that it practically cannot be contained? A deadly combination, sex and honor. It's often forgotten that while the *Iliad* begins *in medias res* and concludes before the Fall of Troy, its inciting incident has to do with a woman, two of them in fact, and neither named Helen. The first is the beautiful maid Chryseïs, captured previously by a Greek raiding party and given as a slave/concubine to Agamemnon. The other is Briseis, also beautiful, who was awarded to Achilles. As the poem opens, Chryses, the father of Chryseïs, arrives in the Greek camp to plead for the return of his daughter. *"Relieve a wretched parent's pain,"* he begs, *"And give Chryseïs to these arms again."*[12] When Agamemnon haughtily refuses, Chryses, in a prayer to Apollo, calls down a deadly plague, which immediately ravages the Greek camp.

The Greeks learn from a soothsayer that Agamemnon's obdurate selfishness is the cause of their misery. Under duress, Agamemnon returns the girl to her people but demands Briseis from Achilles as the price of his appeasement. Although Achilles peacefully surrenders the maiden to Agamemnon's tent, something snaps, triggering his fury. Achilles is not only shamed by the loss of Briseis (whom he has come to love), but he's blindingly resentful that such degradation should come at the hands of someone he regards as nowhere near his equal. Indeed, the only reason Achilles finally agrees to let Patroclus borrow his armor—to stand in for him as a pseudo-Achilles—is to goad the rest of the Greeks into demanding the return of Briseis and thus permit him and his Myrmidons to take the field again.

Further, Achilles never wanted to be there, on the Trojan shore, in the first place. The Trojans never harmed him: "What cause have I to war at thy decree?/ The distant Trojans never injured me." Instead the blame is to be placed squarely on the Atreides[13] brothers, pompous Agamemnon,[14] and the horned cuckold, Menelaus, as Achilles begins openly rooting for a Trojan victory to embarrass and disgrace Agamemnon.

So the sexual component of the *Iliad* cannot be overestimated. True, the woman who started it all, round-heeled Helen, appears only infrequently—as does Paris, for that matter. Neither of them evinces any shame, although Helen does understand that she is the cause of all this

---

12. The constructive genius of Homer is evident from the start: this is the same dramatic situation we encounter, far more poignantly, at the poem's close when old Priam uses practically the same words to implore Achilles to release Hector's body for burial.

13. Frank Herbert's choice of a family name for Paul Muad'Dib in his *Dune* series was a deliberate evocation of the accursed family.

14. Who will get his comeuppance at the hands of Orestes in Aeschylus's play of the same name, the first in the *Oresteia* trilogy that is the foundation of the Greek theater, first performed c. 458 B.C.

misery. The sexual pairings of Zeus and Hera, Paris and Helen, and Hector and Andromache are all quite different. Only the final duo is sympathetic; only they have young progeny at stake, in the form of the baby Astyanax, Hector's infant son to whom, we know from *The Trojan Women*, fate will be especially unkind.

The ancients, however, understood the similarity of the sounds of sex and the sounds of death: the cries, the moans, the gurgles, whether of passion or bloodletting. Semen and blood are closely related, essential elements of masculinity, as each thrust of spear or sword or loins reminds us. Zeus, immortal, is nevertheless conquered by death, at least temporarily, in his romantic encounter with Hera. The act of penetration and its consequences echo throughout the poem. For every body that lies dead on the plain, a woman will have to be impregnated, suffer the pangs and dangers of childbirth, and give birth to the next generation of heroes. They also fight, who carry on the bloodlines.

To modern Western sensibilities, this seems achingly primitive, a caricature of "toxic masculinity." But it's not. The ancient Greeks separated the sexes in almost every aspect of society. Men worked, and fought, in the fields. Women worked in the home. Men proved their worth in battle, or in the political arena; marriage and motherhood were the realms of the feminine. Women could not be citizens, nor could they own or inherit property. Above all, they were not to be trusted; their desirable bodies, their deceptive and potent sexuality, and their physical weakness that forced them to duplicity, were in the eyes of the Greeks things to be feared and controlled, for the sake of the family and of the *polis*. Women were to be seen and not heard, and never to be talked about in weighty conversations. "A modest silence is a woman's crown," wrote Sophocles, while Pericles was quoted by Thucydides as saying, "The greatest glory will accrue to the woman who is talked about least among men, whether for good or ill."

It goes without saying that women were never to be found armed on the battlefield, nor were they expected to be; if women were fighting on your behalf, you were losing. Their job was replenishment of cannon fodder. The Romans, successors to the Greeks as the dominant culture of the Mediterranean, understood this. They could rebound from the most crushing defeats by Hannibal—at Trebia, Lake Trasimene, and most notably at Cannae—thanks to the fecundity of their women and the virility of their men. Women, it was felt, do not desire or even tolerate constant, overt conflict, which is why they evolved forms of female combat that do not require them to pick up a sword, a shield, or a rifle. A glass of poison here, a stiletto there, or a willing lover, convinced to do murder . . .

On the other hand, Greek men, citizens, were free to take their pleasures as they found them, with mistresses, prostitutes, slaves, or boys. "Happy the lover who exercises in the gymnasium and then spends the rest of the day at home in bed with a beautiful boy," wrote Theognis of Megara, a sixth-century B.C. lyric poet. Indeed, same-sex physical acts between males were characteristic of Greek culture, especially pederasty—although a great distinction was made between the virile penetrator and the one submissively penetrated. The friendship between Achilles and Patroclus, as with that between the priapic Alexander and Hephaestion, possibly, probably included sex.[15] Boys were desirably buggered until their beards came in, after which they could be advanced into public life by means of their former lovers; a form of career advancement.[16]

Heterosexuality, however, was the predominate social value: the boasting about lineage that precedes many of the combats in the *Iliad* illustrates the store that was put in licit paternity. The paternal line was determinative of your initial place in life, but mothers were of emotional importance; Thetis, for example, plays a significant role in the

---

15. According to Plutarch, Alexander admitted of two vices: sleep and lust. His lust he could slake with various captured women and boys, the spoils of war available to every soldier of that time, or perhaps with his male companion, Hephaestion, although the ancient historians make no reference to such a relationship, instead referring to the general, who had been friends with Alexander from boyhood and was his most trusted companion, merely as *Philalexandros*. Projecting contemporary sexual attitudes onto men and women who lived and died twenty-five hundred years ago is a fool's errand; as we see even as recently as the last century, male relationships—especially in war—could be intense without ever becoming sexual.

16. Julius Caesar was haunted all his public life by rumors spread by his enemies that as a young ambassador to court he had been the catamite of Nicomedes IV, the king of Bithynia.

Iliad, whereas Achilles's father, Peleus, the king of Phthia, is only mentioned in passing. Yet one of Achilles's names—his surname, in fact—is Pelides, son of Peleus, and he's sometimes referred to by that name in the epic. And his sexual passion for Briseis, "his wife," is clear: it's her loss, after all, that triggers his rage, and when she is finally returned to him, Agamemnon makes it a point to assure Achilles that he never slept with her.

Helen of Troy—really, she's Helen of Sparta—is the most famous abductee in ancient history, but not the first. Indeed, the first recorded event in Western history, as limned by Herodotus—the "Father of History"—in the opening pages of his seminal work, *The Histories* (c. 430 B.C.), involves the abduction of a woman:

> And on the fifth or sixth day after they [the Phoenicians] had arrived, when their goods had been almost all sold, there came down to the sea a great company of women, and among them the daughter of the king; and her name, as the Hellenes also agree, was Io the daughter of Inachos. These standing near to the stern of the ship were buying of the wares such as pleased them most, when of a sudden the Phoenicians, passing the word from one to another, made a rush upon them; and the greater part of the women escaped by flight, but Io and certain others were carried off. So they put them on board their ship, and forthwith departed, sailing away to Egypt. In this manner the Persians report that Io came to Egypt, not agreeing therein with the Hellenes, and this they say was the first beginning of wrongs.

From Io, it was but a short step to the revenge-kidnapping by the Greeks of the Phoenician princess Europa (from whom the continent derives its name). This was followed by the abduction of Medea of Colchis, which eventually led to the Trojan prince Paris's abscondment with Helen, wife to Menelaus of Sparta—and thus to the Trojan War. Hesiod, it seems, may have been right.

Who was this Helen, who has so enchanted us for millennia? About the woman herself, we know very little. According to legend, she was the daughter of Zeus, the most beautiful woman in Greece, if not the world, and had once before been abducted by Theseus before being res-cued by her brothers, Castor and Pollux, known as the Dioscuri (sons of Zeus). All the heroes, including Odysseus, had wooed her, but she chose Menelaus, the king of Sparta, in part because her sister, Clytemnestra, was married to Agamemnon. After Paris was killed during the battle for Troy, she briefly married Deiphobus, Hector's brother, but betrayed him to the vengeful Menelaus during the sack of the city, and returned to live out her days with the Greek in Sparta, happily ever after.

Other versions of her story, retailed most notably in the play *Helen* by Euripides (following Herodotus's account written thirty years ear-lier), has it that Helen never made it to Troy with Paris but that she was replaced with a phantom Helen and in fact had been pining for Mene-laus all along from her refuge in Egypt. She is surprised to learn from returning Greeks after the Fall of Troy that she is public enemy number one, but after much confusion Menelaus is shipwrecked in Egypt, re-united with the real Helen, and they return together to Sparta.

It's not the historical, or quasi-historical, Helen that fascinates us, however, but her various incarnations in mythology, poetry, the plastic arts, and drama. Like some of the other major characters in the *Iliad*, she has transcended quasi-history to exist as an icon of female beauty, passion, and even treachery. She's a hot potato whom nobody but Paris really wants but no one can figure out what to do with; she brings down the walls of Troy for a reason almost none of the combatants (especially Achilles) can fathom.

As Troilus observes of the problem Helen presents in Shakespeare's "problem play," *Troilus and Cressida*:

> *Why keep we her? the Grecians keep our aunt:*
> *Is she worth keeping? why, she is a pearl,*
> *Whose price hath launch'd above a thousand ships,*
> *And turn'd crown'd kings to merchants.*
> *If you'll avouch 'twas wisdom Paris went—*
> *As you must needs, for you all cried "Go, go,"—*
> *If you'll confess he brought home noble prize—*
> *As you must needs, for you all clapp'd your hands*
> *And cried "Inestimable!"—why do you now*

The issue of your proper wisdoms rate,
And do a deed that fortune never did,
Beggar the estimation which you prized
Richer than sea and land? O, theft most base,
That we have stol'n what we do fear to keep!

Sitting around a council of war, Hector, Paris, Troilus (another of Hector's many brothers), and Priam debate the wisdom of returning Helen to the Greeks, but none of them can think of a reason that's quite compelling enough, while Paris naturally opposes any such course of action. It is left to mad Cassandra to give the Trojans the advice they need to hear, but of course will not follow: *"Cry, cry! Troy burns, or else let Helen go."*

Shakespeare's Helen is something of a nullity, oblivious to the Hesiodean chaos she's caused, the unholy number of men who have died for her. Instead, she flirts and exchanges ribald jokes with Pandarus, portrayed in the play not as the treacherous archer of the *Iliad* but a lecherous and disease-ridden procurer whose amatory machinations bring Troilus and Cressida to grief, and who bequeaths the audience his suppurating vilenesses in the bitter valedictory that closes the play.

Many of the men on both sides regard Helen as little more than a drab, especially the nasty Greek slave, Thersites, who between offering various creative synonyms for venereal disease sums up the situation by observing, "After this, the vengeance on the whole camp! or rather, the bone-ache! for that, methinks, is the curse dependent on those that war for a placket . . . all the argument is a cuckold and a whore." Shakespeare's audiences readily understood the bawd: "bone-ache" was slang for syphilis, while a "placket" technically refers to the slit in a woman's petticoats nearest the pudendum; in vulgar terms it simply means "cunt." Shakespeare's spectacularly crude sexual idioms are so freely indulged in order to make a larger point: that when it comes to subterfuge, deception, combat, and bodily fluids, sword thrusts and pelvic thrusts are not dissimilar, and, however pleasurable, are indulged in by us humans each at our own peril. Yet so great is the power and attraction, how can we not? Playthings of the gods—and goddesses—indeed.

There are few if any heroes in Shakespeare's dyspeptic retelling of

Homer. Achilles has Hector murdered by his thugs. Cressida is a bimbo who, when returned to the Greeks, immediately tumbles for Diomedes. Nestor is a windy bore. Only Ulysses emerges with any dignity. Such was the view from the early seventeenth century, from one of its greatest minds.

Even in this most masculine of primal conflicts, the two female protagonists of the *Iliad*—Athena and Helen—are always present, even when they are not on stage. Paris's lust for Helen precipitates the larger conflict; he is the actor, she the object. (The various alternate endings the Greeks gave her, not to mention Shakespeare's stilettoed portrayal, indicate what a cipher she in fact is.) But without her, there is no story. Helen is the embodiment of a Western view of Woman: that she is self-sufficient. She just *is,* and the men (who are always *becoming*) discover their destinies through her, whether she cares or not. By contrast, the more masculine goddess Athena takes an active role throughout, casting the decisive vote in favor of Achilles when she intervenes in his showdown with Hector. And yet it is Helen whose name has echoed more seductively down the ages, the eternal object of desire.

They, however, are not the only important women in the *Iliad*. There is also Briseis, whose forfeiture to Agamemnon at the outset sets Achilles along his fatal path. Briseis has seen her father and husband slaughtered by Achilles when the Greeks took her city of Lyrnessus, but she has since fallen in love with him as his captive. Achilles also considers her his wife; his anger at Agamemnon when he is forced to give her to the king is therefore compounded by his love for her and the shame of his effective emasculation at the hands of a man he despises. It is a poor hero, after all, who cannot maintain control of his woman—who under Greek custom and law was his property.

In her final appearance in the poem, Briseis makes their relationship explicit. Weeping over the body of Patroclus, she declaims: *"Achilles' care you promised I should prove,/ The first, the dearest partner of his love;/ That rites divine should ratify the band,/ And make me empress in his native land."* She is one of the most sympathetic characters in the *Iliad*, a spoil of war who would have become the queen of the Myrmidons in Phthia had Achilles lived. But by reentering the fray upon the death of his closest friend, Achilles must now fulfill the prophecy and trade the prospect of life and happiness in this world for the surety of everlasting glory.

Through the magic of etymology, Briseis has also found a fitting afterlife. Starting around the time of the medieval romance, the *Roman de Troie*,[17] her name morphs first into Briseida and then, via Boccaccio in *Il Filostrato*, to Criseyde—possibly via a conflation with Chryseïs—in Chaucer's epic, *Troilus and Criseyde* (c. 1380), and ultimately to Shakespeare's Cressida.

The tragic hero of the poem, of course, is Hector, the crown prince, who must pay for the sins of his brother with his life. His defeat by Achilles (and Athena, with her thumb on the scale) spells the doom of Troy and most of the males within it—including his baby son, Astyanax, who will be ripped from his mother Andromache's arms and hurled from one of Troy's high walls. Hector very nearly, almost singlehandedly, carries the day during the poem's middle section, and the Greeks fear him more than any other Trojan warrior. But once Hector kills Patroclus, mistaking him for Achilles, Fortune turns inexorably against Troy. We can forgive him his one, human moment of panic, when he initially flees from his encounter with the invincible Achilles outside the Trojan walls before turning to face his fate like a man.

After the fall of the city, the women were violated and then given as spoils: Queen Hecuba is raped by Ajax the Lesser and given to Odysseus; Andromache must become the consort of Neoptolemus, son of Odysseus; and Helen is returned to Menelaus. Finally, the seer Cassandra (also molested by Ajax minor) is handed over to Agamemnon and returns with him to Argos, where she is killed, while he meets the grisly fate she has foreseen at the hands of his wife Clytemnestra and her lover, Aegisthus—chopped to pieces, defenseless, in his bath.

The battle for Troy is a pivotal point in Western history, adumbrating what will be a Manichean conflict between West and East—the two sides alternating between muscular cultural confidence and perfumed decadence—that continues to this day. The West's origin story, it continues to resonate down through history, straight through to the Arab

---

17. Written by the French poet Benoît de Sainte-Maure in the middle of the twelfth century, which helped reignite interest in classical antiquity.

Muslim attacks on New York City and the Pentagon in 2001, which announced its latest phase. Like it or not, it is *the* Forever War.

Its first, Homeric, incarnation was begun in rage and yet ends not in violence but in some sort of forgiveness and mercy. Priam, guided by Hermes, his wagon laden with gifts, secretly enters the Grecian camp and visits Achilles in his famous tent. He has come to beg for the body of his son that he might give him the proper burial the dying Hector had begged for but which the callous Achilles had denied him. "The king his entry made:/ And, prostrate now before Achilles laid,/ Sudden (a venerable sight!) appears;/ Embraced his knees, and bathed his hands in tears;/ Those direful hands his kisses press'd, embrued/ Even with the best, the dearest of his blood!"

At last, Achilles's rage subsides; the mighty fire cools. Priam, invoking the memory of Achilles's own father, has touched a chord deep within that savage breast. "Alas, what weight of anguish hast thou known,/ Unhappy prince! thus guardless and alone/ To pass through foes, and thus undaunted face/ The man whose fury has destroy'd thy race!/ Heaven sure has arm'd thee with a heart of steel,/ A strength proportion'd to the woes you feel." Achilles relents: Priam will have Hector's body, and a truce shall obtain for eleven days—and on the twelfth the war shall resume. We catch one last glimpse of Briseis as Achilles bids farewell to Priam and the old man departs:

> Then gave his hand at parting, to prevent
> The old man's fears, and turn'd within the tent;
> Where fair Briseïs, bright in blooming charms,
> Expects her hero with desiring arms.

It's a lovely, unexpected conclusion, the work of a master storyteller. The epic opens and closes with a father begging for the return of his child, with Achilles back in the arms of Briseis, and with a continuing standoff between the Achaeans and the Trojans. Plants and callbacks, reversals of fortune, the intervention of Fortune herself, or *friction* in the form of the gods—it is the foundation of Western dramatic art, including all subsequent epic poetry, plays, novels, and the cinema; in his

Poetics, Aristotle went to school on Homer, codifying the principles of storytelling for every subsequent generation.

As with any successful franchise, there have been sequels galore. Among the most notable is the French composer Hector (!) Berlioz's five-act grand opera, *Les Troyens,* based on Virgil's *Aeneid* (itself the original sequel) with a libretto by the composer. It's written in two sections—the first set among the besieged Trojans and including the fatal arrival of the Trojan Horse, the second concerning the fugitive Trojans at Carthage and the tragic love affair between Dido, the Carthaginian queen, and the noble Aeneas, one of the survivors of the sack of Troy, whose destiny it is to found the city of Rome. Due to its sheer size and scope, as well as some ill will between Berlioz and the director of the Paris Opera, the first performance at the Théâtre Lyrique in 1863 included only the second half, and it was in that form— *The Trojans at Carthage*—that the work was performed (infrequently) for many years.

It was not until 1890, more than two decades after the composer's death in 1869, that the work was heard largely in the form Berlioz intended, although there still were cuts and elisions. Today the opera is generally given complete, as befits its masterpiece status. The martial Greek acts, 1 and 2, are austere, chilly. The ghost of Hector appears to Aeneas and tells him to prepare to flee the doomed city for Italy. Its heroine, Cassandra (a mezzo-soprano), tries to warn the Trojans of the dangers of the Horse—left by the Greeks as an "offering" to Athena and brought inside by the Trojans so as not to offend the goddess—but to no avail; as the Greeks storm the city, she and other women of Troy kill themselves while Aeneas flees, Cassandra's last words, *"Italie,"* ringing in his ears. His destiny is now clear.

The acts set in Carthage, by contrast, are warm and lush. The Trojans have landed, temporarily, at the Phoenician city on the North African coast, and come to the aid of its queen, Dido, also a mezzo. The score includes the oft-excerpted "Royal Hunt and Storm" orchestral music, but even this does not prepare us for the astonishing beauty of the celebrated love duet, *"Nuit d'ivresse et d'extase"* (Night of rapture and boundless ecstasy), a lyrical flowering practically unique in the composer's oeuvre, instilling these figures from the remote past with the breath of life in a way that only music can.

As we know—from Virgil, from Henry Purcell,[18] and from Berlioz—it will end badly. No matter how much he loves Dido, Aeneas, son of Aphrodite, must press on to Latium and there found a city even greater than Troy: the Eternal City, Rome. As the love duet concludes in rapture, Hermes magically appears and, striking Aeneas's cast-off shield, thrice intones "*Italie!*" Forsaken, Dido watches the Trojan ships sail away and, cursing Aeneas, kills herself, with visions of Hannibal's revenge on Rome dancing in her head. Her brief evocation of the great duet's principal theme just before her suicide adds the final touch of pathos to the tragic tale.

Les Troyens is not just the "exotic and irrational entertainment" of Dr. Johnson's famous jibe about opera but a work that transforms the men and women of mythic prehistory into fully realized human beings. This is art's special power. Across a span of more than three thousand years, Achilles, Odysseus, Hector, Cassandra, and the others live on. Achilles got his wish: cultural immortality for one brief, radiant moment of existence in which he embodies the tragic human condition of Western man. The Trojans may have lost the war but, in their one shining moment, like Achilles, they also gained immortality by dying young. Meanwhile the Greeks endured, creating a civilization that lasted for not hundreds but thousands of years, bequeathing their legacy to posterity and setting Western civilization on a course from which, for better or worse, it has only recently begun to waver.

And so Ouroboros once more closes its mouth on its tail, the cycle resumes, and the world begins again. This time, in rude, hilly Macedonia, from which isolated land the West would launch another attack on the East in the footsteps of Achilles, and led by a young man who saw himself as that great hero's re-embodiment and known to us today as Alexander III of Macedon—the Great.

---

18. Composer of *Dido and Aeneas* (1689), one of the earliest operas in English, and still performed today.

Three

ALEXANDER AT GAUGAMELA

"There is a further tradition that, fully armed, he was the first to leave the ship and set foot upon the soil of Asia, and that he built an altar on the spot where he left the shore of Europe and another where he landed on the other side of the strait, both of them dedicated to Zeus, the Lord of safe landings, Athena, and Heracles."

—ARRIAN, *THE CAMPAIGNS OF ALEXANDER*

WE VIEW ALEXANDER OF MACEDON (356–323 B.C.) THROUGH THE wrong end of a very long telescope. The first of Western history's mighty conquerors and field marshals, he's a hard man to get to know. There are no extant or significant epic poems about him, nor prominent dramas, nor important operas from music's classical period, when so much of the source material originated in the ancient world.[1] Aside from *Alexandre le Grand* by Jean Racine (1665), and a series of novels by Mary Renault, Alexander largely figures as a secondary or offstage character, and sometimes even a ghost, as in part 3 of Swift's *Gulliver's Travels* during the trip to Glubbdubdrib.[2]

---

1. Mozart, for example, wrote operas featuring Idomeneus, the Greek general from the Trojan War; Mithridates of Pontus, one of the early Roman Empire's most formidable foes; and *Ascanio in Alba,* about the son of Aeneas.

2. "And because my first inclination was to be entertained with scenes of pomp and magnificence, I desired to see Alexander the Great at the head of his army, just after the battle of Arbela: which, upon a motion of the governor's finger, immediately appeared in a large

The closer we look, the farther away he appears to be, remote, hard to humanize and, despite his achievements, almost impossible to warm to. Julius Caesar we can not only understand but also sympathize and even identify with (Napoleon and Patton certainly did). Ditto Mark Antony, whose all-too-humanity eventually brought him to grief in the embrace of Cleopatra. But Alexander, driven by visions of glory to rival and surpass the achievements of Achilles—the man who thought himself the son of Zeus and who, in his rage to conquer, died just a month short of his thirty-third birthday, having no worlds left to subdue—remains a cipher.

And yet he still stalks the pages of our shared history, chiefly for his blitzkrieg conquest of the most powerful nation on earth at the time, the Achaemenid Empire of Persia. It was the Achaemenids, under the command of their king, Xerxes, who had first pushed westward, crossing from Asia Minor to Europe, massacring the Spartans at Thermopylae in 480 B.C. and subsequently sacking Athens before being defeated at Salamis at sea and at Plataea by land by Greek forces in 479 B.C. In this sense, 'twas East that fired the first shot against the West, and the humiliation of having to have abandoned Athens and the loss of other major cultural and population centers rankled Greek pride for a century and a half thereafter.

Such considerations may seem trivial and unimportant in the modern age of "globalism," which, however, is itself a Western construct, derived from the mature mercantilism of the eighteenth century and its obsession with international trade. Although trade with the East (which at that time included Egypt, the principal source of wheat) was an important part of the Roman economy, it came into full flower at the dawn of the Renaissance—itself a rediscovery of classical Greek and Roman culture. The Age of Exploration was powered by it, as European navigators sought to open up new trade routes and find new lands both to exploit their unused natural resources and—in the case of China

---

field, under the window where we stood. Alexander was called up into the room: it was with great difficulty that I understood his Greek, and had but little of my own. He assured me upon his honour "that he was not poisoned, but died of a bad fever by excessive drinking." Jonathan Swift, *Gulliver's Travels*, chapter 7.

and India—to obtain luxury goods (silk, spices, tea) unavailable in their homelands.

To look at a modern map, it might appear impossible that tiny Portugal, the old Roman province of Lusitania, should have acquired an international commercial and political empire, but it did; just ask the Brazilians and the Goans. The British launched their conquest of India via the East India Company, a stock (and later joint stock) company founded in 1600 in the wake of the defeat of the Spanish Armada twelve years before. The elimination of Spain as a potent naval force opened up the seaways to Britain, and by 1612, after their defeat of the Portuguese in India, they were trading with the Mughal Empire. The company was an enthusiastic slaver until the middle of the eighteenth century, impressing black African labor from Mozambique and Madagascar. The company also expanded its sphere of influence to China, financing tea with opium exports and provoking the first Opium War from 1839 to 1842.

The explosion in European wealth, and the extension of European values and culture around the globe, was a uniquely Western idea. Neither the Chinese nor the Japanese were explorers; the Chinese experience with Westerners came via the historic trade routes across Persia to Cathay that delivered Marco Polo to their door, while the Japanese confined themselves to their island kingdom, with only a single trading port at the artificial island Dejima, off the coast of Nagasaki, and executed any foreigners unlucky enough to land on their shores. Arab vessels had long plied the Mediterranean, but sub-Saharan Africa, with no seafaring tradition, remained largely a mystery aside from coastal trading ports established by the Europeans and Arabs. This is often described as "colonialism," as if the word were self-evidently pejorative, but in reality the colonial aspects of European exploration were primarily an outgrowth of curiosity, technology, a thirst for knowledge, and the economic imperatives of mercantilism, and not a malevolent desire to arbitrarily subjugate strange lands and peoples in the name of various gods, whether Christian, Muslim, or simply monetary. To insist otherwise is to put the Marxist cart of oppression before the capitalist horse of inquisitiveness and greed.

Alexander's impulse, however, was not trade but conquest. His father, the assassinated Philip II, had made Macedon into the dominant power in Greece. Although the classical Greeks regarded the Macedonians as little better than barbarians who spoke a mangled version of the Greek language, Philip understood the importance of the higher civilizational values of the Athenians and engaged no less a personage than Aristotle for a princely sum to tutor Alexander in politics and morals and gnostic mysteries available only to the initiated. (Plutarch reports that Philip had "captured and destroyed Aristotle's native city of Stageira; but now he rebuilt it, and repeopled it, ransoming the citizens, who had been sold for slaves, and bringing back those who were living in exile.") One of the things Aristotle taught the young man was to love the *Iliad,* which Alexander regarded as "a complete manual of the military art"; throughout his life, he carried Aristotle's edited edition of the text and slept with it under his pillow, along with a dagger.[3] In every way, Alexander the Great was the Platonic form of the Aristotelian man, and the highest expression of Greek philosophy.

Far overshadowed later by his glorious son, Philip was nevertheless a formidable man in his own right. From his capital in Pella, he had taken over a weak, fractious kingdom and promptly set about transforming its army into a first-rate fighting force. One of his innovations was the *sarissa,* a pike up to twenty-one feet long that became the deadliest feature of the bristling phalanx that so bedeviled Greece's foes until the Battle of Cynoscephalae in 197 B.C., when the Roman legions finally solved the problem of defeating the porcupine by means of the maniple. Armed with *sarissas,* the Macedonian had a distinct advantage over other Greek hoplite armies, whose spears were generally seven to ten feet in length.

Philip also bequeathed to his son the classic Greek battle formation that was to serve Alexander so well: a central phalanx preceded by a rank of *psiloi,* or light skirmishers, including archers; a center mass

---

3. Plutarch, in *Parallel Lives,* relates that when Alexander discovered a priceless casket, "the most valuable of all the treasures taken from Darius, he asked his friends what they thought he should keep in it as his own most precious possession." After a few suggestions, he replied: the *Iliad.* "The poems of Homer were far from idle or useless companions to him, even when on a campaign."

made of up heavily armed *hoplites*; and a rear or flanking guard of highly mobile *peltasts* armed with javelins, which they could fling as far as twenty-five yards. The wedge-shaped cavalry formations were divided between the left and right flanks and employed as a devastating offensive weapon that probed the enemy lines looking for an opening before striking like vipers. Philip also created an early form of military intelligence and a corps of engineers that eventually developed the first catapults—an invention his son would later put to good use.

Philip's goal of uniting all of Greece was constantly frustrated by Athens, with its powerful navy and its dexterous diplomacy and knack for alliance-building. Desirous (as were other Greek city-states) of starting an expansionary war against the powerful Achaemenid Empire just across the Aegean Sea to the east, Philip decided to gamble everything on one smashing, definitive victory against the Athenians and their Theban allies. Then he could get on with his real work.

Moving south, Philip found the way blocked by the Thebans at Thermopylae and rather than relearn the hard lesson of Xerxes he sought another path through the mountains. But the passes, too, were cordoned by Theban and Athenian troops. Feigning retreat, Philip pulled back, and the news spread that the Macedonians were giving up and going home. Their guard thus relaxed, Thebes and Athens reasserted their old animosity. Philip then struck quickly, across a broad front, heading through Phocis, a Greek swing state as we might call it today, alternately allied with Persia, Athens, and Sparta as circumstances dictated. In short order, he found himself facing the allied armies of Thebes and Athens at Chaeronea in the summer of 338 B.C.

It was an ideal battlefield from the allies' point of view: an open plain below the city, bounded by the foothills of Mount Thurion on the south and on the north by the Kephisos River, it was a natural funnel that gave the Athenians and Thebans protection on both flanks and would force Philip to attack the allied center. Further, the allied line was stretched obliquely, forestalling a direct, head-on attack.

Unfazed, Philip took up his customary position at the head of his right flank, and entrusted the cavalry on his left to the command of his son, Alexander, then about seventeen or eighteen years old. His force has been estimated at thirty thousand infantry and about two thousand cavalry, ranged against some thirty-five thousand allied Greek troops, some of them mercenaries, and many hitherto untested in combat. The elite Theban troops, stationed on the right flank, included the Sacred Band, which consisted of one hundred and fifty pairs of male lovers fighting side by side, the older *erastês* paired with their younger *erômenos*. The Thebans prized their devotion to one another, harnessing the power of homoeroticism with raw male strength to create one of the ancient world's most potent fighting forces.

But not on this day. On this day, Philip had ordered Alexander not to strike until the moment was right—and trusted that his son would know the moment when it came. Accounts of the battle are relatively sketchy, but it appears that Philip moved his right wing forward to attack the Athenian left, engaged, and then suddenly withdrew in a feigned retreat.[4] The inexperienced Athenians responded just as he had hoped and moved forward to give chase but in doing so separated themselves from their own line. This provoked the allied center to shift leftward to plug the gap, which, however, created a corresponding gap in the Athenian-Theban center.

The trap was now sprung. Young Alexander, leading Philip's Companion Cavalry, instantly charged diagonally across the field and through the gap, getting behind the Thebans, attacking them from the rear and slaughtering the Sacred Band to the last man[5] while the out-of-position Athenians were mopped up by Philip. As a twelve-year-old boy, Alexander had tamed the fearsome stallion Bucephalus, the horse that would carry him all the way to India; at Chaeronea he rode him to victory. Writing from earlier sources, the Greek historian Diodorus of Sicily (died c. 30 B.C.) attributes the Macedonian victory primarily to Philip's superior *sarissa*-armed phalanxes, which gave them a distinct advantage in reach over the more traditionally armed Athenians. But Alexander's contribution cannot be overlooked. Indeed, it became his

---

4. One of the earliest examples of this tactic, which would later serve the Crusaders under Bohemond so well at the Battle of the Iron Bridge near Antioch in 1098.

5. In 1878, archaeological excavations near the battle site revealed some 254 paired skeletons, buried in seven rows, some with arms interlinked and others holding hands. They are believed to belong to members of the Sacred Band.

signature move throughout his career, and one that opponents could never figure out how to stop. Chaeronea was the making of Alexander.

That was the end of resistance to Philip. The following year, he founded the League of Corinth with himself as *hegemon*, effectively uniting all of Greece except Sparta as he prepared for his upcoming campaign against the Persians. But he was never to lead it; in October of 336 B.C. he was assassinated by the captain of his bodyguards, a man named Pausanias,[6] while celebrating the wedding of his daughter Cleopatra of Macedon to Alexander of Epirus. Cleopatra, like Alexander the Great, was the daughter of Olympias (one of Philip's many wives), and Alexander of Epirus was Olympias's brother; he thus became Alexander the Great's brother-in-law as well as his uncle.

Olympias, one of the progenitors of the Monster Mother, was more than suitable as the woman who gave birth to a god. Plutarch, in his *Parallel Lives* chapter on Alexander and Julius Caesar, relates that the young Philip and Olympias, an orphan, met during a religious ritual in Samothrace and married soon thereafter. "The bride, before she consorted with her husband, dreamed that she had been struck by a thunderbolt, from which a sheet of flame sprang out in every direction, and then suddenly died away. Philip himself some time after his marriage dreamed that he set a seal upon his wife's body, on which was engraved the figure of a lion. When he consulted the soothsayers as to what this meant . . . Aristander of Telmessus declared that she must be pregnant, because men do not seal up what is empty, and that she would bear a son of a spirited and lion-like disposition."

Philip was afraid of his wife. One time he found her asleep with a tame serpent stretched out beside her. Another story relates that Macedonian women were given to Bacchic frenzies; "Olympias, it is said, celebrated these rites with exceeding fervour, and in imitation of the Orientals, and to introduce into the festal procession large tame serpents, which struck terror into the men as they glided through the ivy wreaths and mystic baskets which the women carried on their heads."

---

6. The motive remains unclear, although multiple theories have been expounded, including a frustrated homosexual love affair, a Persian plot, and the machinations of Olympias and Alexander himself.

And, the story goes, Philip lost the sight in one of his eyes because, through a crack in a half-opened door, he had seen Zeus, in the form of a serpent, copulating with Olympias.

On the day of Alexander's birth, the temple of Artemis at Ephesus[7] (in modern-day Turkey) was destroyed by fire, leading the Persian magi there to announce that a worse disaster for Persian Asia Minor would be coming, for "on that day was born the destroyer of Asia."

> Philip, who had just captured the city of Potidæa, received at that time three messengers. The first announced that the Illyrians had been severely defeated by Parmenion; the second that his race-horse had won a victory at Olympia, and the third, that Alexander was born. As one may well believe, he was delighted at such good news and was yet more overjoyed when the soothsayers told him that his son, whose birth coincided with three victories, would surely prove invincible.

Upon Philip's death, young Alexander, twenty, fair-skinned, and, by tradition, fair-haired, was suddenly king of Macedon and lord of Greece. Initially his position was insecure. Shortly before his death, Philip had taken a new wife, Cleopatra Eurydice of Macedon, his seventh, and Alexander and his mother had temporarily fled the capital. Olympias was born a Molossian, not a Macedonian, whereas any son of Cleopatra Eurydice would be a full-blooded Macedonian and would thus outrank him in the line of succession. Not without reason, Alexander suspected that his life might be forfeit.[8] However, Philip apparently had no intention of replacing him as his heir and after six months in Illyria

---

7. Later to become one of the centers of early Christianity, as St. Paul's epistle to the Ephesians (c. 62 A.D.) attests. The authenticity of the letter is, however, disputed, and it more likely was written by one of Paul's disciples.

8. There was trouble at the wedding when Attalus, the uncle of the bride, got roaring drunk and called upon the assembled Macedonians to pray that the union of Philip and Cleopatra Eurydice would produce a "legitimate" heir to the Macedonian throne. There were words, then swords as Philip tried to intervene, but, also drunk, he tripped and fell. Alexander mocked his father: "This is the man who was preparing to cross from Europe to Asia, and has been overthrown in passing from one couch to another."

Alexander returned home. Alexander moved quickly to liquidate any possible claimants to the royal titles, including a cousin and very possibly Cleopatra Eurydice's infant son, Caranus, while Olympias, without his knowledge, had Cleopatra Eurydice and her daughter, Europa, burned alive, just to make sure.

Philip's assassination was momentous, comparable in its effect upon history to the death of Julius Caesar three centuries later. Plutarch tells us that Alexander resented his father's skill at conquest, complaining to his friends, "Boys, my father will forestall us in everything; he will leave no great exploits for you and me to achieve." He had no desire for a life of luxury and peace and worried that Philip would leave nothing for him to do and no worlds to conquer.

While there is no question that Philip was prepared to invade Asia Minor and slice off as much of the Achaemenids' western empire—where there were many Greek cities—as he could, there is no indication that he would dare embark on a history-changing campaign that would take the Macedonian armies all the way to Afghanistan and India. Had Philip lived and Alexander never succeeded to the throne, the enormous expansion of Greek and Hellenistic culture that followed in his wake might never have occurred. The future Seleucid and Ptolemaic empires never would have been created, Egypt might have become a Roman province far earlier than it actually did, and the Byzantine Empire, the eastern half of the Roman Empire, might never have achieved either the status or the longevity that it did. And all because of an assassin's dagger.

The Battle of Chaeronea was where Alexander's particular genius first exhibited itself, the prologue to his brilliant career and characteristic of his tactics in most of his principal battles. The sweeping charges of the heavy Companion Cavalry, cutting across the field with the king at their head, turned the tide again and again against numerically superior forces. Recall that his father Philip had told him to wait for the right moment to strike and, what's more, had told him that he would know when that moment came. Diagrammed battles may resemble chess games, but in reality they are swirls of motion, constant confusion, punctuated by the clash of arms and the screams of wounded and dying men. Whether the fight is waged with swords, spears, pikes, axes, lances, bows and arrows, crossbows, muskets, rifles, cannons, big guns, aerial bombardment, or even missiles, it is never static.

This kineticism is part of what Clausewitz called *Friktion,* and the ability to slow it down, to visualize the immediate tactical future toward which it points, and to act on it is the hallmark of every great military commander. Alexander took that preternatural ability into every fight. It gave him the confidence to wait, wait . . . wait until the time was right to strike the one decapitating blow that would end the conflict before fatigue and injuries began to wear on his troops. Such judgment cannot be taught, although it can be retrospectively analyzed and explained. We might perhaps be surprised to find such a talent in one so young as Alexander because it implies a mature knowledge not only of battlefield tactics and the enemy's capabilities but of human nature as well.

But many men of genius have such insight into the human condition and often do their best work when they are young, younger even than Alexander, and die young as well. As we'll see in the case of Napoleon, there is an art to war—indeed, however sanguinary, war is an art form unto itself, and the comparison of genius in both fields is not inapt. John Keats died at twenty-five, Mozart at thirty-five, Rimbaud at thirty-seven. Would any of them have produced greater work had they lived longer? Impossible to know. Prodigies are hardly unknown in the world of the arts, and they appear throughout history, able to penetrate the heart with insight and wisdom far beyond their years. So it can be with generalship as well—as Alexander proved.

To recount the extent of Alexander's conquest and, even greater, his ambition, has taken up many an entire volume. For our purposes, we will concern ourselves with his three great battles against the armies of Darius III Codomannus, the last of the Achaemenid "King of Kings," a rising succession of victories against the Persians that began at the river Granicus, continued at Issus, and culminated in 331 B.C. with the smashing rout at Gaugamela, a small village near what is today called Arbil in Kurdistan.[9] From that moment on, the course of the rest of Alexander's short life was set. He had achieved the destiny of Achilles but on a far

---

9. And therefore sometimes called the Battle of Arbela.

greater scale; his name has become a household word; and the resonances of his short-lived empire but everlasting renown are with us still.

Upon arrival in Anatolia, the first thing he did was make obeisance at the tomb of Achilles: "When he had crossed the Hellespont he proceeded to Troy, offered sacrifice to Athena, and poured libations to the heroes who fell there," writes Plutarch. "He anointed the column which marks the tomb of Achilles with fresh oil, and after running round it naked with his friends, as is customary, placed a garland upon it, observing that Achilles was fortunate in having a faithful friend while he lived, and a glorious poet to sing of his deeds after his death." That done, he was ready to conquer the world.

Alexander set out on what was, in his mind, a journey unlimited by time, space, or objective—endless conquest was the sum and substance of it, although he never told his men that. In numbers, he seems to have had about thirty thousand foot soldiers and five thousand cavalry, but these do not include his additional retinue of scientists, historians, engineers, mapmakers, bureaucrats, and camp followers.

His first test came quickly, at the Granicus in 334 B.C., where Persian troops and Greek mercenaries blocked his entrance into Asia Minor. Despite a slight numerical superiority, his task was not going to be easy. The river ran rapid; the enemy was arrayed on the other side, atop a steep bank. In order to get at them, Alexander would have to have his thirteen squadrons of cavalry ford the river, take a muddy shore on which the steeds would be slipping, vulnerable, then climb the bank to get at the main body of the enemy. That would, naturally, play havoc with the central Macedonian phalanx's order and hamper its initial effectiveness.

His best general, Parmenion, older and wiser (he had served Philip), advised caution,[10] but Alexander dismissed his concerns: "I should be ashamed of myself if a little trickle of water like this (a very derogatory way of referring to the Granicus!) were too much for us to cross without further preparation, when I had no difficulty whatever in crossing the Hellespont" (Arrian). To show hesitation in the face of danger, said

---

10. This becomes a common trope in the ancient accounts: Parmenion suggests a cautious approach but Alexander immediately takes the opposite course and, naturally, is always right.

Alexander, would be to give the Persians confidence, "and they would begin to think they were as good soldiers as we are."

As would become his custom, Alexander put Parmenion's son, Philotas, in command of the central infantry, while the Companion Cavalry was split between the flanks, with Alexander, conspicuous by his regalia,[11] taking the place of honor on the right. Parmenion was in command on the left. The infantry moved first, crossing the river in the teeth of Persian archers. Shortly thereafter, both wings of the cavalry swung into action. Parmenion charged straight forward, but Alexander naturally took a sharp diagonal to his left, avoiding the Persian cavalry ready to meet him and instead assaulting the Persian center directly. In short order, he and his Companions were the foxes in the hen house, wreaking havoc and spreading panic in the center of the Persian line.

It turned into hand-to-hand combat, the men on horseback effectively immobilized, hacking away at their enemies. A javelin struck Alexander but bounced off his corslet.[12] Two of the Persian generals, Rhœsakes and Spithridates, set upon him; Alexander broke his spear against Rhœsakes's breastplate and reached for his sword. At that moment, Spithridates smote him on his helmet with a battle-axe, splitting the protective headgear and severing one of the plumes; Plutarch tells us the blow reached "his hair with the edge of the axe." Just as his enemy was preparing to strike another, surely fatal, blow, Spithridates was run through by his friend Cleitus's lance as Alexander dispatched Rhœsakes.

Alexander's men quickly formed a protective square around their dazed and perhaps briefly unconscious king, but at this point the central phalanx had made its way across the river and up the hill. At the same time, Parmenion brought his cavalry into play, getting behind the Persian center and sending them fleeing in disarray. As the Persian army broke and ran, the Macedonians found themselves opposed

---

11. Plutarch: "Alexander . . . made a conspicuous figure by his shield and the long white plume which hung down on each side of his helmet." Caesar, Napoleon, George Armstrong Custer, Patton, and Douglas MacArthur made themselves conspicuous on the battlefield as well, consciously or unconsciously following in Alexander's footsteps.

12. Body armor, covering his trunk.

by some eighteen thousand Greek mercenaries, who had been held in reserve and were now leaderless. Although they begged for mercy, a recovered Alexander had many of them butchered as traitors and sent the rest back to Greece as slaves. Meanwhile, the bulk of the Persian forces escaped. Casualties were relatively light on the Macedonian side, while Plutarch estimates that the Persian/Greek losses numbered about twenty thousand, although that number—like all ancient battle figures—is disputed by scholars.

Needing fungible assets back home, Alexander sent what military spoils he grabbed back to Greece, with this inscription: "Alexander, the son of Philip, and the Greeks, all but the Lacedæmonians [Spartans], won these spoils from the barbarians of Asia." The rest, Plutarch tells us, including golden drinking cups and "purple hangings," he sent back to his mother. The pickings were relatively slim because there were no regal personages on the Persian side at the Granicus. But that would change at Issus the following year.

Rather than continuing east, however, Alexander decided he needed to secure his supply and communications lines first. Accordingly, he set off down the Levantine coast in order to liberate it from the Persian navy, which was controlling access to the ports in Asia Minor. He conquered Ephesus, Miletus, and Halicarnassus, then moved to the east, rolling up victories as he went. Along the way, according to legend, in Phrygia he solved the problem of the Gordian Knot—a huge, entangled mess of rope that fastened a sacred ox-cart to a post; an oracle had predicted that the man who could untie the knot would become king of Asia—by the simple expedient of drawing his sword and slicing it in two.[13] He was also, for a time, seriously ill, and his life was even despaired of. It would not be the last time.

The Battle of Issus was the first of two direct confrontations between Alexander and the King of Kings, Darius. Although the Achaemenid Empire was on its last legs, this would have been news to Darius, a canny political operator who had been installed on the throne by a

---

13. Other sources say the solution was more prosaic: Alexander pulled the linchpin from the pole and, with both ends of the knot now accessible, simply untied it. In any case: problem solved.

manipulative eunuch, Bagoas, who had poisoned its previous two royal occupants. With Darius showing distressing signs of becoming his own man, Bagoas went for the hat trick, but Darius was on to him and forced Bagoas to drink the poison himself.

After learning of his army's defeat at the Granicus, Darius resolved to meet Alexander in the field himself, and was considering forcing the issue in the hilly country of Cilicia. A Macedonian-born spy informed the Great King that Alexander's relatively small force would be best met on an open plain, where the Persians' superior numbers could be used most effectively against the Macedonians, and so Darius, raising a huge force, marched west in search of the impertinent Greeks.

As *Friktion* would have it, however, the two armies passed each other in the night; Alexander had left a garrison force under Parmenion at Issus, on the southern coast of Anatolia, to dissuade the Persian navy, and moved away from the dangerous topography of Cilicia, on the southeastern Anatolian coast, into Syria. Meanwhile, Darius had marched eagerly toward Issus in the hopes of recovering his lost territory and goading Alexander to come out and meet his force of one hundred thousand men on favorable terrain. The Persians there encountered the remains of the garrison, mostly wounded men unfit for combat, and slaughtered them—but unknown to them, Parmenion had already rejoined Alexander, whose main force was now to the Persian south.

Too late, Darius realized his error of geography: "He already had perceived the mistake which he had committed in entering a country where the sea, the mountains, and the river Pyramus which ran between them, made it impossible for his army to act, while on the other hand it afforded great advantages to his enemies" (Plutarch). Alexander could thus turn the liability of the terrain to his own advantage: Darius, meanwhile, had entered the trap he had hoped to spring on Alexander.

At this point in his chronicle, Arrian gives Alexander a stirring speech, evoking the memory of the Ten Thousand in Xenophon's *Anabasis*,[14] and indicative of the Macedonian morale. The Macedonians,

---

14. Recounting the march of the Greek mercenaries in 401–300 B.C., returning home after fighting the Battle of Cunaxa on the wrong side of a Persian civil war—an extraordinary tactical retreat in hostile terrain that remains unequaled in Western military history. The

Alexander foremost among them, thought the Persians dandified voluptuaries, spoiled by long-unchallenged hegemony. Reminding his troops that they had already defeated the Persians once before, Alexander said:

> God himself, moreover, by suggesting to Darius to leave the open ground and cram his great army into a confined space, has taken charge of operations in our behalf. We ourselves shall have room enough to deploy our infantry, while they, no match for us either in bodily strength or resolution, will find their superiority in numbers of no avail. Our enemies are Medes and Persians, men who for centuries have lived soft and luxurious lives; we of Macedon for generations past have been trained in the hard school of danger and war. Above all, we are free men, and they are slaves. There are Greek troops, to be sure, in Persian service—but how different is their cause from ours! They will be fighting for pay—and not much of it at that; we, on the contrary, shall fight for Greece, and our hearts will be in it. . . . And what, finally, of the two men in supreme command? You have Alexander, they—Darius!

As indeed they did. Darius suddenly found himself squeezed between the mountains and the Gulf of Issus, with the river Pinarus between his army and the Macedonians, where his army's superior size was now neutralized by the topography. It's hard for a large army to fight in a box. Accordingly, the small coastal plain north of the river was his best option, so he deployed his cavalry on his right, nearest the sea, and arranged his infantry forces, which included the famous Immortals as well as some Greek mercenaries, in the center. There, he awaited Alexander, now moving swiftly northward.

Alexander arranged his troops in his customary formation, with Parmenion's cavalry on the left, opposite his mounted Persian counterparts, and leading the Companion Cavalry himself on the right. The center was formed by the *sarissa*-armed phalanx and other troops. Darius sent his elite cavalry charging across the river to engage the

---

closest modern comparison might be the U.S. Marines' "advance to the rear" after fighting their way out of the Chinese ambush at the Chosin Reservoir in late 1950.

outnumbered Parmenion, while Alexander's phalanx advanced across the Pinarus in the other direction, under heavy archery fire as well as potent pushback from the well-trained Greek mercenaries. Things were not going well for the Macedonians until Alexander and the Companions charged the weak left side of the Persian infantry line (most of the Persian cavalry was fighting Parmenion) and broke through. He wheeled and attacked the Persian center from the rear, pushing it into the teeth of the phalanx. It was the classic Alexandrine right hook, delivered at the precise, dispositive moment.

Now Alexander spotted Darius himself and his command post behind the Persian center, and made straight for him. As his line collapsed, Darius turned and fled, and the rout was on; seeing their imperial commander leaving the field, the Persian cavalry, which had been getting much the best of poor Parmenion, also wheeled and ran. The victorious Macedonians mopped up what was left of the Persian army while Alexander personally chased Darius, but night was falling and so Alexander returned to the battlefield, but not before collecting Darius's abandoned chariot, his shield, his kingly mantle, and his bow. During the course of the fighting Alexander had also received another war wound, this one minor—a sword thrust to the thigh that some said was caused by Darius himself, although Alexander himself refuted that in one of his letters, now lost but cited by Plutarch, who had access to them.

Darius had left most of his treasure behind in Damascus for safekeeping, so Alexander sent Parmenion off to secure it as he returned to the battlefield. In Darius's own pavilion, Alexander disarmed himself to settle into Darius's royal tub for a nice hot bath. "When he entered the bath and saw that all the vessels for water, the bath itself, and the boxes of unguents were of pure gold, and smelt the delicious scent of the rich perfumes with which the whole pavilion was filled; and when he passed from the bath into a magnificent and lofty saloon where a splendid banquet was prepared, he looked at his friends and said, 'This, then, it is to be a king indeed.'"

Plutarch goes on to relate that more surprises were awaiting Alexander in the Persian camp: Darius's mother, his wife (who was also his sister), and his daughter Stateira, along with, literally, a king's ransom in plunder. It was not unusual for monarchs to bring their families to the battlefield and at least part of their treasuries with them for safekeeping. Alexander informed the fearful women that he meant them no harm, that they would be treated with respect, and that his fight with Darius was not personal but "a legitimate war for the sovereignty of Asia." In his mind, however, that objective could only mean one thing: the annihilation of Darius and the conquest of the Achaemenid Empire.

As keen as Alexander was to finish the job, however, following the Battle of Issus he did exactly what a smart general should do. He called off the pursuit, and instead of chasing Darius into the interior strongholds of his vast empire, he headed for the Levantine coast in order to shore up his supply lines by continuing to neutralize the Persian fleet in the eastern Mediterranean. Accordingly, he made his way down the Syrian and Phoenician littorals, picking off its principal cities without resistance, thus denying the ports of Biblos and Sidon to the Persians, and then moved on to the biggest and most formidable prize of all, the Phoenician-held city of Tyre,[15] the only thing standing between him and his proximate goal: the fertile lands of Egypt—nominally a Persian possession, but one weakly held and ripe for expropriation. The rule of the Achaemenids there had been overthrown in 404 B.C. but reestablished by them in 343, and by the time of Alexander's arrival in the region, the unhappy Egyptians were ready to welcome him as a liberator and even pharaoh.

With Persian power in the eastern Mediterranean now effectively destroyed—Alexander controlled most of Anatolia at this point—it was vital to ensure that he could not be attacked from his rear. Nor could he have his sea lanes from Macedon and Greece threatened, nor have Darius's fleet launch an attack on the Greek homeland—perhaps even allying with a truculent Sparta, which remained stubbornly outside the Panhellenic League of Corinth. Accordingly, he had rolled up the coastal cities, helping himself to their ships and tribute as he went.

---

15. A city that continued to loom large for more than a millennium, as Muslims and Crusaders warred over it in 1187; the weakened Crusaders, stunned by their disastrous defeat at Hattin in July of that year and the loss of Jerusalem, held off Saladin's siege, puncturing the Muslim commander's aura of invincibility and leading to the partial success of the Third Crusade under Richard the Lionheart two years later.

Neutral Tyre, however, was the crown jewel of the Levantine ports, a citadel with walls that rivaled Troy's, stretching down to the sea. It could not be left in his rear on his march toward Egypt and the delta of the Nile, where Persian power was ripe for toppling and some much-needed respite for his battle-weary troops beckoned.

The siege of Tyre was one of Alexander's most brilliant campaigns but can only be treated briefly here. First he created a *casus belli* for himself by demanding to be able to offer sacrifice in the temple of Heracles[16] in New Tyre, the walled island city less than a mile from Old Tyre on the mainland. The Phoenicians replied that they were happy to allow Alexander to worship, but it would have to be in Old Tyre on the mainland, not New Tyre, to which neither Persian nor Macedonian could gain admittance. The Phoenicians knew such a refusal meant war and evacuated most of their women and children to their sister city of Carthage on the North African coast, leaving about forty thousand inhabitants to defend the city.

Under the rules of siege warfare, besieged towns had two choices: either open their gates in surrender and hope for the best or fight to the death in the certain knowledge that if conquered their inhabitants would be put to the sword or sold into slavery. They chose to fight.

This, actually, was just what Alexander wanted; his demand to visit the temple was a mere pretext. By taking Tyre, formidable as it was, he could wrest command of the Phoenician navy—the best in the Mediterranean—from Persian oversight and capture or otherwise control the island of Cyprus. "With the accession of Cyprus and the united fleets of Macedon and Phoenicia, our supremacy at sea would be guaranteed," Arrian quotes him as saying, "and the expedition to Egypt would thus be a simple matter, and finally, with Egypt in our hands we shall have no further cause for uneasiness about Greece: we shall be able to march on Babylon with security at home, with enhanced prestige,

---

16. Confusingly, not the Heracles of Greek myth but a major Phoenician god known as Melqart, who sometimes demanded human sacrifice in times of war or natural disaster; from about the sixth century B.C., the Greeks adopted him and identified him with the legendary strongman. Herodotus mentions a visit he made to the temple of Melqart in the fifth century B.C.

and with Persia excluded not only from the sea, but from the whole continent up to the Euphrates." Tyre was the strategic key to his whole campaign of conquest.

Even if this speech is wholly invented by Arrian, writing hundreds of years later,[17] it depicts Alexander's remarkable grasp of both military and geopolitical realities, clearly marking him as the first modern Western supreme commander of both land and naval elements. As much in a hurry as the young Macedonian king was, he had restrained himself from haring after the fleeing Darius, and thus had not only secured his position and diminished his opponent's but also enhanced both his forces and his territorial possessions while at the same time damaging Persian morale. The Achaemenids were not used to losing, but suddenly they had been humiliated on the battlefield in two separate encounters with the Macedonians and had lost the western parts of their empire almost overnight. Furthermore, the great King of Kings was now essentially a fugitive in his own land and, as every failing monarch understood, ripe for replacement by one of his satraps or subordinates even before the invaders got to him.

The siege of Tyre was no easy victory. The Phoenician position was strong, not only with the city's near-impregnable walls but two natural harbors facing the coast that could be stoutly defended and even blockaded to prevent a Macedonian landing. Undaunted, Alexander immediately ordered construction of a causeway, or mole, between the old city (which he of course promptly razed) and the island. Fortunately, the waters were not terribly deep, and so, in part using the rubble from Old Tyre, Alexander's engineers gradually created a pathway in order to move his catapults close enough to begin pounding New Tyre's walls. Accordingly, he even built two giant siege engines, rolling them along the causeway as he prepared his assault.

The Tyrians, however, demolished both of them by loading up a cattle boat, filling it with combustibles, setting it aflame, and crashing it into Alexander's forward position on the mole. The Tyrians also used

---

17. The noble speeches earlier historians invented and put into the mouths of their characters were interpretations, not falsifications, fabricated in the interests of emotional accuracy and narrative drive.

their fleet to good effect, harassing the Macedonians working on the causeway and raising such Cain that work on it had to be discontinued. It was then that Alexander marched back up to Sidon to commandeer about eighty Phoenician vessels that had fallen into his hands during his drive south. At this point even the Cypriots, having heard of Alexander's smashing victory at Issus, decided to get with the program and chipped in some 120 ships.

Gathering reinforcements, he boarded his new fleet and sailed for Tyre, once again positioning himself on the right flank of his attacking forces, now afloat. The Tyrians were caught by surprise at the sudden appearance of a hitherto unsuspected Macedonian navy, and blocked their harbors with their own ships. To conceal their maneuvers, they even rigged sails across the northern harbor entrances to prevent the Greeks from peeping in.

Rather than attacking, Alexander bottled up the Phoenicians with some of his ships, then retreated to the mole, where construction of new siege engines had been completed in safety. Even under renewed and effective assault, however, the resourceful Tyrians poured down fire-arrows on the attackers as they came close and hurled giant stone blocks into the waters to prevent the ships from closing in. When Alexander attempted to anchor his ships and use them as fighting platforms, Tyrian divers cut their anchor cables and sent them floating unsteadily on the tides. As a counter move, Alexander substituted chains for ropes, and hauled away the stone blocks, dumping them farther out to sea.

Next the Tyrians tried a surprise attack, sending their best ships, crews, and marines out of the north harbor and attacking the Cypriot squadron, sinking some ships and sending the rest reeling. Roused from his customary afternoon meal and about to take a nap, Alexander immediately counterattacked, sinking several ships and routing the others. The sortie turned out to be a fatal error for the Tyrians, as the Macedonians quickly resumed their artillery barrage both from the causeway and from specially outfitted ships with catapults on board. Turning his attention to the narrow south end of the island, Alexander concentrated his forces and, landing, finally forced a breach. Into the gap poured the

Macedonians, led by Alexander himself at the head of his Guards.[18] Overwhelmed, the city fell.

The ancients put great store in dreams, and viewed them as windows into the future, or another plane of existence. Dreams were the realm of the gods and dead ancestors. Dreams were private omens, whose interpretations were crucial to future success or failure. True, there was hardly a dream or an omen that could not admit of at least two different and often contradictory explanations, but successful men invariably chose the more favorable, especially in hindsight and in the retelling. When Alexander, in the midst of the siege, was told by his soothsayer, Aristander, that according to the animal sacrifices they had just made, Tyre would fall that very month:

> All who heard him laughed him to scorn, as that day was the last of the month, but Alexander seeing him at his wits' end, being always eager to support the credit of prophecies, gave orders that that day should not be reckoned as the thirtieth of the month, but as the twenty-third. After this he bade the trumpets sound, and assaulted the walls much more vigorously than he had originally intended. The attack succeeded, and as the rest of the army would no longer stay behind in the camp, but rushed to take their share in the assault, the Tyrians were overpowered, and their city taken on that very day.

Herodotus also tells us that during the siege—history's first recorded amphibious landing under fire[19]—Alexander dreamed that Heracles himself had appeared to him "in a friendly manner," calling to him from the city walls. He also relates another dream, this one involving a satyr, who taunted Alexander and dared him to catch him. After a chase, Alexander finally ran the creature down and later, when awake, he asked his prophets and soothsayers to explain the dream's

---

18. Elite, mobile infantry troops, handpicked for speed, strength, courage, and stamina.

19. The Trojans never tried to prevent the Greeks from landing. Instead, they allowed the Greeks to beach their ships and chose to fight them on the plain in front of the city.

meaning. "This was very plausibly explained by the prophets to mean 'Sa Tyros'—'Tyre shall be thine,' dividing the Greek word Satyros[20] into two parts."

And so it was. As the Macedonians ran rampant through the city, Azemilcus, the king of Tyre, took refuge in the temple of Heracles; he and all those who sheltered with him, Alexander spared. The rest met the usual fate of unsuccessful defenders. For his part, Alexander offered sacrifice to the god in the once-forbidden temple, then staged a series of games on the site. He even, according to Arrian, brought the siege engine that had first breached the city's walls, and dedicated that to Heracles as well.

Now emissaries from Darius arrived, offering Alexander a fortune for the release of the Persian monarch's mother, wife, and children, whom Alexander had captured at Issus, as well as all the Achaemenid territory between the Aegean Sea and the Euphrates River. The deal would be sealed by the marriage of his captured daughter Stateira (also known as Barsine) to Alexander. Alexander's captains, among them Parmenion, advised him to take the deal and go home, but naturally he refused. According to Herodotus, Alexander replied, "That is what I should do were I Parmenion; but since I am Alexander, I shall send Darius a different answer."

His offer to Darius was this: nothing. He, Alexander, was already in control of all of Asia Minor, its treasures, and its inhabitants, and he would do as he pleased with them; if it suited him to marry Stateira, he would, whether Darius liked it or not. Finally, if Darius wished to parley, he would have to come to Alexander. Having lost to the *wunderkind* twice now—once in person—Darius surely now understood there could be no haggling or bargaining with the Macedonian upstart, and so he rejected the non-terms. He was going to have to fight.

With Tyre secure, Alexander headed for Egypt and took possession of it without so much as a by-your-leave from Darius. There would be a hard-fought battle at Persian-controlled Gaza, that he knew, but he needed the town not only for military reasons but for morale as well;

---

20. Satyrs—the Greek word for imaginary male creatures with a horse's ears and tail and a permanent, prominent erection.

the loss of Gaza would yield yet more proof that Darius was incapable of holding on to anything Alexander wanted to take from him.

The official commanding Gaza, a eunuch named Betis, had raised a contingent of Arab troops to help him fend off the Macedonians and he had every confidence that the well-fortified town could withstand anything Alexander threw at him. As with Tyre, Gaza presented an engineering problem. Alexander's solution was to build up the ground around the base of its walls and then put the siege engines he had used at Tyre atop the new elevation. Just as he was about to launch the fighting with a ceremonial offer of sacrifice, another omen, this time not a dream: a bird of prey flew over the altar and dropped a rock on Alexander's head, conking him badly.[21] The ever-helpful Aristander assured his lord that he would take the town, but he must take care about his own personal safety.

As it happened, Alexander was in fact wounded during the assault. One of the Arab defenders, pretending to be a deserter, got close enough to Alexander to attack him with a concealed sword. Alexander dodged the strike aimed at his neck and with his own sword lopped off the man's hand. But Fate wasn't about to be put off so easily: an arrow struck Alexander in the chest, penetrating his cuirass[22] (which he rarely wore but had donned that day in fear of the omen) and lodging in his shoulder. The wound was treated and Alexander feigned indifference to it, but the blood loss was substantial and he had to be carried back to his camp. Betis saw him fall and rejoiced, believing he was dead.

Alexander, his shoulder wound far from healed, was injured again the following day when he was hit in the leg by a rock, which wobbled him and forced him to lean on his spear as a crutch. Infuriated at the physical price he had to pay for victory, the triumphant Alexander vented his ire on the defiant Batis by treating him the way Achilles treated Hector at Troy. According to the Roman senator, consul, and historian Quintus Curtius Rufus[23] in his *History of Alexander the Great,*

---

21. Gaza, it seems, has been a troublesome place for more than two thousand years.

22. Armor that protects both the chest and the back.

23. A brief account of his life is given by Tacitus in *The Annals of Imperial Rome,* book 11,

written in Latin at some point in the first century A.D., but which has come down to us from a ninth-century codex:

> Betis was brought before the young king, who was elated with haughty satisfaction, although he generally admired courage even in an enemy. "You shall not have the death you wanted," he said. "Instead you can expect to suffer whatever torment can be devised against a prisoner." Betis gave Alexander a look that was not just fearless, but downright defiant, and uttered not a word in reply to his threats. "Do you see his obstinate silence?" said Alexander. "Has he knelt to me? Has he uttered one word of entreaty? But I shall overcome his silence: at the very least I shall punctuate it with groans." Alexander's anger turned to fury, his recent successes already suggesting to his mind foreign modes of behaviour. Thongs were passed through Betis' ankles while he still breathed, and he was tied to a chariot. Then Alexander's horses dragged him around the city while the king gloated at having followed the example of his ancestor Achilles in punishing his enemy.

After Gaza, Egypt was almost a holiday for both Alexander and his Macedonians. The Egyptians did indeed welcome him as a liberator. Mazaces, the Persian commander, met him at the coastal town of Pelusium and immediately folded, handing over his treasure rather than fighting. In November of 332 B.C. Alexander was proclaimed pharaoh at Memphis—then Egypt's principal city—and deemed a "son of the gods." And why not? His scheming mother, Olympias, had always told him he was the son of Zeus. And wasn't the Egyptian god Ammon Zeus's functional equivalent? Indeed, the Greeks had been calling their deity Zeus-Ammon for more than a century.

It was probably at this point that Alexander, all of twenty-four years old, began to believe in his own divinity. Who but a god could have accomplished the things he already had? He had always been a

---

chapter 21. There is some question among scholars whether this particular Curtius Rufus is the same man who wrote the Alexander biography, although it seems likely.

dutiful adherent to the Greek gods and customs, offering sacrifices, staging games. We have seen how important the *Iliad* was to him, both as a religious text and as a Boy's Own adventure story he strove to live up to. It is also likely that it was here, in Egypt, that Alexander formed his own notions of uniting disparate cultures and faiths under one Hellenistic banner, a new world in which the races would freely mingle, creating a new people under Greek cultural and political hegemony. He adopted Egyptian dress (as he would later do with Persian), studied Egyptian laws and customs, restored temples. In short, he went native.

Sailing down the Nile toward the sea, he founded the city of Alexandria (the first, and greatest, of the many he named after himself). Choosing a site near the Homeric island Pharos, mentioned in the *Odyssey*, Alexander immediately got to work planning his new town. Notes Arrian, "He was immediately struck by the excellence of the site, and convinced that if a city were built upon it, it would certainly prosper. Such was his enthusiasm that he could not wait to begin the work; he himself designed the general layout of the new town, indicating the position of the market square, the number of temples to be built, and what gods they should serve—the gods of Greece and the Egyptian Isis—and the precise limits of its outer defences. He offered sacrifice for a blessing on the work; and the sacrifice proved favourable."

To ensure the success of his new urban venture, Alexander needed—of course—the approval of the gods. Hunches were always improved when they were backed up by favorable omens and a little help from the folks upstairs. And a friendly soothsayer was already to hand in the form of Aristander: as Alexander was laying out his envisioned city of Alexandria, he was forced to use barley flour to mark the locations of various streets, avenues, and principal buildings—flour that was quickly snatched up by the birds and devoured. Not to worry, Aristander assured him: this was indeed a sign that his new city would flourish and create an abundance of resources, here at the fertile mouth of the Nile, which would be a wonder of the world.[24]

---

24. As indeed it did, becoming an unrivaled center of scholarship, the locus of Greco-Jewish religious disputation and Greco-Roman learning, and the glory of Ptolemaic Egypt.

Accordingly, he undertook an arduous desert pilgrimage to the shrine of Ammon in Siwa, a nearly inaccessible oasis far from the Nile delta near what today is the Libyan border. It was not a journey undertaken lightly. Nearly two hundred years earlier, the Persian king Cambyses II, the second "King of Kings" of the Achaemenid Empire, had sent an army of fifty thousand men to raze its temple and put down a rebellion of the newly conquered Egyptians; they vanished in the inhospitable desert and a blinding sandstorm without a trace.[25]

Alexander and his retinue ran out of water and were on the verge of perishing themselves when a violent rainstorm miraculously arrived, which was instantly attributed to divine intervention by the Greek historian Callisthenes, a great-nephew of Aristotle, who was accompanying the expedition. Next came a sandstorm akin to the one that had wiped out Cambyses's army, but the gods came through once more, sending a pair of ravens (some said snakes) to guide them safely to Siwa. Arrian, in his telling of the story, can't choose between the two accounts, but does say, "I have no doubt whatever that he had divine assistance of some kind—for what could be more likely? But precisely what form it took we shall never know because of the disparity in the various records."

In any case, Alexander was hailed by the high priests upon arrival as the son of Ammon, and his future as a conqueror dutifully foretold what Alexander wanted to hear: that he would rule over all the world and remain undefeated in battle until the time came for him to rejoin his divine ancestors.

These prophecies, and Alexander's response to them, were not an unalloyed good. As Curtius notes, "So Alexander did not just permit but actually ordered the title 'Jupiter's [Zeus's] son' to be accorded to himself, and while he wanted such a title to add lustre to his achievements he really detracted from them. Furthermore, although it is true

---

25. Or so Herodotus tells us. In 2009, Italian archaeologists discovered human remains and weapons dating back to the early Achaemenid period in Egypt near Siwa. Others more recently have discounted the sandstorm theory and instead speculated that Cambyses's army was ambushed and destroyed by resistance forces under Petubastis III, who were put down by Darius I (550–486 B.C.).

that the Macedonians were accustomed to monarchy, they lived in the shadow of liberty more than other races, and so they rejected his pretensions to immortality with greater obstinacy than was good either for themselves or their king." The grumbling in the ranks over Alexander's ambition and willingness to adopt foreign ways, customs, and dress, which would last all the way to India, had begun.

The only thing left for Alexander to do now was finish off the only man who stood between him and universal acknowledgment of both his kingship and his divinity. And so the stage was set for one of the pivotal battles of history: Gaugamela—Alexander's tactical masterpiece, and the last stand of the Achaemenids. Also known as the battle of Arbela (the name was deemed more euphonious by early historians), it was the turning point in the military balance of power between East and West and the battle that won the ancient world for Hellenism and ensured the primacy of the West for the next two millennia.

Let us first set the stage. From Egypt, Alexander began his pursuit of Darius by heading north along the Levantine coast, the easier to keep his troops supplied by sea in light of his command of the Mediterranean. He then cut eastward, heading for the Euphrates River, causing the Persian spies tailing him to assume that his goal would be the city of Babylon, where the Great King had been raising yet another army, drawn from all quarters of his empire. This was in fact just what the Persians were hoping for: a repeat of the stinging defeat suffered in 401 B.C. by Greek mercenaries on the wide plain at Cunaxa, ideal for cavalry, and their subsequent perilous fighting retreat back to Hellas, immortalized in the *Anabasis*.

But Alexander kept going, crossing the Euphrates—where Hephaestion had already constructed a pontoon bridge with his advance guard—and eluding a small Persian force under Mazaeus, one of Darius's satraps and senior military officers. Alexander was also familiar with the *Anabasis* and wasn't about to make the same mistake. Instead, he kept going east-northeast to the Tigris River, the other Mesopotamian boundary. Accordingly, Darius marched his army north, hoping at last to find a sympathetic battlefield upon which he could deploy his superior numbers, including his fearsome scythed chariots, and await Alexander's arrival. He found it outside the small village of Gaugamela.

Darius wasted no time in sculpting the wide field according to his needs. He flattened as much of it as he could, the better to suit his two hundred chariots and his cavalry, not to mention a small contingent of Indian war elephants. The expanse of the field would also allow him to take advantage of his huge numbers (between 100,000 and 150,000 men), creating a battle line that could outflank Alexander's smaller force (estimated at just under 50,000, although all such numbers are speculative) at both ends, putting the Macedonians at a severe tactical disadvantage. Darius was not going to repeat his error at Issus: an out-flanked army was a dead army—unless it could strike a fatal blow to its opponent's heart first.

Knowing this made Alexander all the more keen to engage—was he not the son of a god, and a god himself? He had already taken the measure of his man and found him wanting: Darius was a quitter and a coward. Alexander gradually moved into position near the battlefield, driving Mazaeus off a lightly held redoubt in some low hills about ten miles from Darius's army, behind which Alexander could encamp and scout the enemy.[26] He took careful note of Darius's earth-moving ac-tivity along with his disposition of forces, drew up his battle plans, and went serenely to bed. Before he retired, Parmenion, who surely must have suspected by this time that he and his left flank were going to take the brunt of the Persian attack during the course of the fighting, advised a bold night attack, but Alexander dismissed it as dishonorable. Still, the prospect of such a thing froze Darius and his men, keeping them up all night in battle array, waiting for an assault that never came.

But not all was well in the Macedonian camp, either. There had been an eclipse of the moon a few days earlier, which had spooked the already restive Macedonians. "Right on the brink of a decisive battle the men were already in a state of anxiety, and this now struck them with a deep religious awe which precipitated a kind of panic," writes Curtius. "They complained that the gods opposed their being taken to the ends of the earth, that now rivers forbade them access, heavenly bodies did not maintain their erstwhile brightness, and they were met everywhere by

---

26. To the Greeks, the Persians advertised their presence by their body odor; Alexander's men joked that they would easily beat them because they smelled like goats.

desolation and desert. The blood of thousands was paying for the grandiose plans of one man who despised his country, disowned his father Philip, and had deluded ideas about aspiring to heaven."

To put down any thoughts of mutiny, Alexander summoned his Egyptian seers, who explained that the eclipse was a portent of doom for the Persians, and cited prior examples of Persian losses in such celestial circumstances, which heartened the men; "nothing exercises greater control over the masses than superstition."

As it happened, Darius's wife, one of Alexander's captives, died at this point, and the news was brought to the Persian king by one of her attending eunuchs, who had slipped away from the Macedonian camp. Alexander lamented her death, but Darius was convinced the Greek interloper had raped and killed her, wailing, "Alexander, what is the great crime I have committed against you? Which of your relations did I kill that my cruelty should merit such punishment? Your hatred of me is unprovoked, but even supposing the war you have started is just, should you have fought it with women?" Warfare, then as now, was personal.

Eventually, Darius came to believe the eunuch that she had died of natural causes, and, as Curtius reports—very likely unreliably, but it makes a good story—"Darius covered his head and wept for a long time. Then, with tears still streaming from his eyes, he uncovered his face and held his hands up to the sky. 'Gods of my country,' he said, 'before all else make firm my rule; but my next prayer, if my career is at an end, is that Asia find no other ruler than this just enemy, this merciful victor.'"

Before the two sides engaged, Darius tried other stratagems, including an attempt to infiltrate assassins into Alexander's camp, and offered large sums of money to the Greek soldiers to desert. Always the foil, Parmenion observed that the ransom of the remaining women in Darius's family—the king's mother and his two daughters—could bring a handsome sum, thirty thousand gold talents (roughly twenty-five years' worth of Athenian income and the city's total current wealth), but Alexander dismissed the notion: "Yes, I too would prefer money to military glory if I were Parmenion. As it is, I am Alexander."

On the day of the battle, October 1, 331 B.C., Alexander slept late that morning, rising about noon. An alarmed Parmenion finally shook him awake: "What has happened to your old alertness?" he barked. Replied Alexander: "Do you think I could have fallen asleep before easing my mind of the worries that kept me from resting?"

Unperturbed by the size of Darius's army, Alexander had every confidence in his battle plan. The enemy was beaten even before the first arrows had been fired. He split his cavalry between his flanks and bowed them and their accompanying infantry inward, the better to defend against encirclement should things go badly against a numerically superior foe. He also obliquely angled his entire line rather than squaring up against the Persians, with his right wing slightly forward and his left wing under Parmenion held a bit back. In the center was the *sarissa*-bristling phalanx, reinforced in the rear by mobile hoplite infantry, who could support the phalanx or turn and fight any Persians who had gotten into the Macedonian rear.

Alexander thus began the battle in his customary position, at the head of the Companion Cavalry on the right, but gradually feinted even farther right, toward some higher and rougher turf, causing the Persians to move their left flank under Bessus outward as well, to prevent him both from flanking them and moving the center of the battle away from the prepared ground. Rising to the bait—which was, after all, Alexander himself, splendidly visible as ever—Bessus pulled more forces away from the Persian line and engaged Alexander in a fierce battle.

Meanwhile, the right side of the Persian line under Mazaeus headed straight for Parmenion's customarily outmanned forces, flanking them in what amounted to a second separate engagement. Finally, in the middle, Darius unleashed his chariots straight at the Macedonian phalanx, scythes whirring. But the Greeks were ready for the onslaught, deftly parting ranks to allow the chariots through, then closing suddenly and swallowing them up and annihilating them. This discomfiture only provoked Darius into launching more units at the Macedonian center, including his elite Immortals. It was a fatal error.

With Darius's forces yanked apart, the Great King a sitting duck at his left-center, the time had come for the death blow. Outnumbered ten to one on the right, and taking a hellacious beating, Alexander suddenly withdrew elements of the Companion Cavalry along with some hypaspists[27] and a few unengaged phalanx units and delivered his trademark right cross to Darius's glass jaw. Cutting diagonally to his left across the field, Alexander headed straight for Darius's command and control center; in especially fierce fighting, Alexander had several horses killed beneath him, but kept on coming, implacable. True to form, Darius ran.

In ancient warfare the flight of the commander was a signal for a general breakdown. As Bessus withdrew from his engagement on the Persian left, the center completely collapsed as the Great King hightailed it away, with Alexander in hot pursuit. Only an urgent message from the beleaguered Parmenion, who had all he could handle from Mazaeus (who was ignorant of Darius's rout) on the Greek left, got Alexander to turn around and send the remaining Persians scattering, but at the loss of sixty members of the Companion Cavalry.

Still, Darius's fate was sealed. After stopping to secure Babylon (where he appointed the defeated Mazaeus as satrap) and Persepolis, the Persian capital (which he burned in long-delayed revenge for Thermopylae and the subsequent destruction of Athens), Alexander would pursue Darius to the east, into Media (the land of the Medes, today's Azerbaijan and Iranian Kurdistan) and Bactria,[28] near the Hindu Kush, where Darius was eventually betrayed, taken prisoner by his former commander Bessus, and, with Alexander hot on his heels, murdered in 330 B.C. "In military matters he was the feeblest and most incompetent of men," writes Arrian, "in other spheres his conduct appears to have been moderate and decent." He was about fifty years old at the time of his death.

Alexander was furious at this act of regicide. When he finally caught up with Bessus, Alexander ordered him stripped naked, fitted with a dog collar, and made to stand by the side of the road until Alexander passed by, and which point he was scourged and then executed. The prodigy from Macedonia had crushed the mighty Achaemenid Persian Empire in less than five years. But he only had a few more years to live.

---

27. Formidable soldiers trained to guard the exposed flanks of the phalanx and experts in hand-to-hand combat.

28. Present-day northern Afghanistan.

Would Alexander have become an even greater conqueror had he lived as long as, say, Philip, who died at the age of forty-six? Unlikely. For one thing, where would he have gone? He had just begun to engage the Indians around the Indus River basin in present-day Pakistan—then nominally part of the Achaemenid Empire—when his long-suffering soldiers finally dug in their heels and demanded that he turn back. Might Alexander have lost a battle had he continued fighting his way across the Asian subcontinent? Given his insistence on leading from the front, would he have been killed?

Further, his makeshift empire was vastly overextended; each new land he conquered had to be garrisoned, costing him valuable manpower. His supply lines were now beyond the logistical capabilities of the era. Worse, his men were growing resentful of his pretensions to godhood, finding them unseemly, barbaric, "oriental." He was thus forced into a strategy of co-opting the locals into the administration of his territories—Alexander was, willy-nilly, a proponent of what today we might call "diversity." This included marrying their princesses. He himself led the way by marrying Stateira, the captive daughter of the departed Darius, during a mass wedding at Susa in 324 B.C. upon his return from the East. His goal was to blend the bloodlines of the Macedonians and the Persians, and so he ordered his men to take Persian wives:

> Similarly, the other officers—to the number of eighty all told—were given as brides young women of the noblest Persian and Median blood. The marriage ceremonies were in the Persian fashion: chairs were set for the bridegrooms in order of precedence, and when healths had been drunk the brides entered and sat down by their bridegrooms, who took them by the hand and kissed them. The King, who was married just as the others were, and in the same place, was the first to perform the ceremony—Alexander was always capable of putting himself on a footing of equality and comradeship with his subordinates, and everyone felt that this act of his was the best proof of his ability to do so. After the ceremony all the men took their wives home, and for every one of them Alexander provided a dowry. There proved to be over 10,000 other Macedonians who had married Asian

women; Alexander had them all registered, and every man of them received a wedding gift. (Arrian)

It was also for political reasons that he had earlier acquired another wife, the Bactrian princess Roxana, in order to protect his flanks and secure his lines of supply and communication. Battling the army—which included rampaging war elephants—of King Porus at the Battle of the Hydaspes, near present-day Lahore, Alexander was once again victorious, but causalities were high, and by then his men had had enough. The Indian warlords were powerful, their troops good fighters. The Macedonians, what was left of them, had taken a thrashing in their victory at the Hydaspes, and probably no amount of further improvisation, however flecked with genius, would have served their leader well enough to keep fighting all the way to East Asia. Not even a spirited pep talk by Alexander could convince them. "Sir," retorted Coenus, one of his officers, "if there is one thing above all others a successful man should know, it is when to stop."

The long-suffering men applauded, even wept, at the thought of finally returning home. A resentful Alexander withdrew to his tent to sulk for three days. He consulted the omens: bad. Finally, he gave in. The men cheered. Arrian calls it "the only defeat he had ever suffered." Cementing the peace, Alexander left the defeated Porus in charge of his new satrapy and headed for home. He never made it back to Macedonia.

Alexander died in Babylon on June 13, 323 B.C., of causes still debated. Certainly he had pushed his body to its utmost physical limits. The boy who had shown little interest in athletics had been transformed into the ideal lead-from-the-front commander, wounded, sometimes seriously, on multiple occasions, including an arrow to the lung. This was hardly surprising since, much to the chagrin of his advisors, he was always the most visible target on the field, leading the Companion Cavalry in charge after charge, scrambling up mountainsides, climbing over fortified walls, always in the thick of things. Further, the punishing march back to Mesopotamia across the Gedrosian desert he inflicted on himself and his men affected all of them; at one point Alexander refused a helmet full of water because there wasn't enough for the troops to share.

He had begun to drink heavily, even more than usual. In a drunken fit, he had killed his trusted friend Cleitus, who had saved his life at the Battle of the Granicus. He had suspected a treasonous plot against him, led by Philotas—the son of his most reliable general, Parmenion, who had bravely and faithfully served not only Alexander but Philip before him—and had him executed on the flimsiest of evidence. For good measure, he even had Parmenion murdered and his men liquidated. He purged his own officials left and right while appointing Persians to the satrapies, something his Macedonians came to resent bitterly. He had gone mad.

These and other irrational actions began to turn his men against him: dressing himself in the high Persian style, he was accused of orientalism, of turning into a voluptuary. He sent some ten thousand of his veterans back to Macedon, leading his army to suspect that his attempt to fuse Macedonians and Aryans into one master race under his control would not end any time soon. The death in 324 B.C. at Ecbatana (in modern-day Iran) of his closest companion, Hephaestion, drove him wild with megalomaniacal grief; already identified in his own mind as the reincarnation of Achilles, Alexander took his friend's death as hard as Achilles had the death of Patroclus. He staged an elaborate funeral, with an expensive pyre upon which to cremate his dearest Companion; in its wake, he proclaimed himself divine to his men.

And then he died. We're not sure why. Certainly, he had lived his brief, Achilles-like life to the fullest, and as we look ahead through history, men may not be finished with war but when war is finished with them, their lives are for all practical purposes over. One thinks of Napoleon wasting away on St. Helena for six years after Waterloo to die at fifty-one, or Patton, killed in a minor traffic accident just seven months after the end of the war in Europe, his services no longer needed. Alexander's time had come.

Naturally there were omens. On the march to Babylon from the east, the Chaldeans had warned him that their god, Bel, had prophesied doom for Alexander should he enter the city. Occupying the palace of the great Babylonian king Nebuchadnezzar II, Alexander rose from the royal throne to get some water, attended by his courtiers and leaving only the eunuchs to guard the throne. Someone—it might have been a prisoner, says Arrian, "under open arrest"—impudently and brazenly took Alexander's seat. Instead of chucking him out, the eunuchs, emasculated males, could only beat their breasts and wail. A few days later, a late-night feast turned into a marathon drinking session. Alexander rose to leave, intending to sleep, but ran into his closest Companion at that point, a man named Medius, who persuaded him to keep the party going. He continued drinking the next day. A fever came upon him as he bathed and went to bed that night.

Despite his illness, he was determined to go on an expedition to Arabia, by sea. His men managed to ferry him across the Euphrates to a park on the other side of the river, where he again bathed[29] and rested—something he characteristically did after a drinking bout. This time, though, there was no restorative effect. Rapidly failing, he was still issuing orders, offering sacrifices to the gods, and making preparations for the trip, but it was no use. He was brought back to his palace chambers, his commanders waiting just outside the door. Arrian tells us he recognized his officers but could no longer speak, and died about twenty-four hours later. He was thirty-two years old.

Various explanations have been suggested: he died of malaria or typhoid fever. He was poisoned with strychnine, perhaps by Antipater, Alexander's regent in Greece. Others said he died of acute alcoholic liver disease. We'll never know. Arrian offers this obituary:

Alexander died in the 114th Olympiad, in the archonship of Hegesias at Athens. He lived, as Aristobulus tells us, thirty-two years and eight months, and reigned twelve years and eight months. He had great personal beauty, invincible power of endurance, and a keen intellect; he was brave and adventurous, strict in the observance of his religious duties, and hungry for fame. Most temperate in the pleasures of the body, his passion was for glory only, and in that he was insatiable. . . . When risks had to be taken, he took them with the utmost boldness, and his ability to seize the moment for a swift blow, before his enemy had any suspicion of what was coming, was beyond praise.

---

29. He had always said he would die in his bath, not on the battlefield.

On his deathbed, Alexander was supposed to have been asked to whom he bequeathed his empire. "To the strongest," he is said to have replied. But his minions soon fell to squabbling and fighting, his wives and heirs were murdered, and the Alexandrian realm quickly broke up into its various component parts, the most notable of which became the Seleucid empire, consisting of Mesopotamia and central Asia; and the Ptolemaic kingdom of Egypt, of which Cleopatra VII was the last queen.

Even had Alexander lived, it couldn't have lasted. His handful of fidgety Macedonians, who had been with him so long and had come so far and at such great personal and physical cost, saw no point in going any farther. What, after all, was left either for Alexander or them to prove? They had conquered the known world and parts of the unknown world as well. They had covered themselves in glory. They had seen and done things that no men of Europe had ever done before, or ever dreamed of. But the world was so vast, and there were so few of them.

Alexander's solution had been to do away with the concept of tribe and race altogether, which is why he had come to adopt the Persian manner of dress and other cultural customs. He was the original integrationist and miscegenist. Facing desertion and even a rebellion from his Macedonians, he had plunged into their midst, arrested the ringleaders, and had them executed. The next day, according to Curtius, he met with his "Asiatic" soldiers, Persians, Bactrians, Parthians, Assyrians, Medes, and addressed them thus:

When I was crossing from Europe to Asia, I hoped to annex to my empire many famous peoples and large numbers of men. I was not wrong in believing the reports I had heard of these men. But there is more than that: I am looking upon brave soldiers of unfailing loyalty to their kings ... I took Darius' daughter as a wife and saw to it that my closest friends had children by our captives, my intention being that by this sacred union I might erase all distinction between conquered and conqueror. So you can believe that you are my soldiers by family, not conscription. Asia and Europe are now one and the same kingdom. I give you Macedonian arms. Foreign newcomers though you are, I have made you established members of my force: you are both my fellow-citizens and my soldiers. Everything is taking on the same hue: it is no disgrace for the Persians to copy Macedonian customs nor for the Macedonians to imitate the Persians. Those who are to live under the same king should enjoy the same rights . . .

However invented, this speech faithfully represents his beliefs and speaks to his ineradicable importance in both Western and world history. On the road to the European nation-state, it was the path not taken. We know he lived for the joy of combat; we know he was compelled by sex; we know of his conspicuous bravery on the field; we can see the number of trophies and scalps on his walls. And yet he effectively died in his tub—a death worthy of Agamemnon perhaps, but not the reincarnation of Achilles, much less the son of a god and a god himself.

Alexander is history's golden boy, a man eclipsed by his own glory. Despite his wounds, we don't feel his pain. We don't see him bleed. At every critical moment on the field, he knew what was going to happen, not only because he could see it happening but because he was *making* it happen. He could not lose. The gods would not let him. Besides, he was a god, and a god cannot allow himself the luxury of defeat. Like Achilles, he lived fast and died young; it was a bargain he was fully prepared to accept. He was, after all, Alexander the Great.

Four

CAESAR AT ALESIA

Vercingetorix, having convened a council the following day, declares, "That he had undertaken that war, not on account of his own exigencies, but on account of the general freedom; and since he must yield to fortune, he offered himself to them for either purpose, whether they should wish to atone to the Romans by his death, or surrender him alive." Ambassadors are sent to Cæsar on this subject. He orders their arms to be surrendered, and their chieftains delivered up. He seated himself at the head of the lines in front of the camp, the Gallic chieftains are brought before him. They surrender Vercingetorix, and lay down their arms.

—JULIUS CAESAR, *THE GALLIC WARS*

IN HIS EFFECT ON HISTORY, GAIUS JULIUS CAESAR WAS THE GREATEST man of his age and likely of any age. Caesar took up the profession of arms relatively late in life. He was already in his early forties when he launched his conquest of Gaul. He then not only conquered Celtic France but invaded Britain as well, in addition to scoring major victories in Italy, Greece, Spain, Egypt, and North Africa. Like some rogue Samson, he crossed the Rubicon (forbidden to Roman generals under arms) and shoved the tottering pillars of the Roman Republic onto an ash heap, defeated the famous general Pompey Magnus in the Roman civil war, wooed and won Cleopatra and her kingdom and sired an heir, created the embryonic Roman Empire, and finally had himself declared dictator for life, which led directly to his assassination in 44 B.C. in a coup led by several men to whom he had offered mercy after Pompey's final defeat at Pharsalus four years earlier.

But that wasn't enough for a man of his ambition. He reformed the Roman calendar by adding a couple of months and introducing the idea of a leap year. An accomplished writer, he chronicled his conquest of Gaul and his victory over Pompey in *De bello Gallico* and *De bello civili*, which are among the first readings set before the beginning student of Latin. He also somehow found time to write speeches, plays, and poetry as well as several works of history, all now unfortunately lost, as well as two books on the Latin language, dedicated to Cicero, the greatest orator of his day, of which fragments remain.[1] Unlike many of the Roman strongmen who seized power both before and after him, his road to the top was at first not via the military but via the bureaucracy, following the prescribed political path up the ladder of mandatory Roman offices on his way to consul. So mighty did he become, however, that his very cognomen, Caesar, entered the lexicons as a synonym for supreme ruler: *Kaiser* in Germany, for example, and *tsar* or *czar* in Russia.

It is one of history's supreme ironies that, by his own account in his *Commentaries*, Caesar had mercilessly slaughtered hundreds of thousands of Gauls, Germans, and others during his military campaigns, only to be brought low by his clemency toward Brutus, Cassius, and others—men he had trusted until they suddenly drew concealed daggers and stabbed him to death on the Ides of March.[2] Shakespeare, in *Julius Caesar*, gives him the famous last words, *Et tu, Brute?* but historians such as Plutarch and Suetonius record his final utterance upon seeing Brutus readying the last, fatal blow, as (in Greek): Καὶ σύ, τέκνον (*Kaì sý, téknon?*). "You too, child?"[3] And drawing his bloodied toga across his

---

1. *De analogia libri II ad M. Tullium Ciceronem.*

2. The middle of the month: the fifteenth in March, May, July, and October, the thirteenth otherwise. The *calends* were the first of every month; the *nones* coming nine inclusive days—eight days by our modern reckoning—before the *ides*. Thus the *nones* of March and the three other listed months would fall on the seventh while the *nones* of, say, November would fall on the fifth.

3. In his 2007 study of the Kennedy assassination and its aftereffects on American liberalism,

face so he could die with some dignity, he fell at the base of the statue of Pompey, his former son-in-law and the man he had defeated for control of Rome.

As befits a complex man of his stature, Caesar (of the *Julii,* or *Iulii*) was a man of many contradictions. His patrician family was not of the highest caliber, and he had to make his way through Roman society on the strength of his wits and his personal bravery, threading the deadly needle between the partisans of Sulla and Marius (his uncle by marriage to his aunt Julia) during their bloody civil war from 83 to 82 B.C., with Sulla emerging the victor, after which he was made dictator (a constitutional office). One false step, one foot put wrong, could mean immediate execution or banishment. Julius Caesar, as the son-in-law of Lucius Cornelius Cinna, the populist Marius's ally, thus came under possible proscription.

We know Caesar was brave, and willing to risk everything when he thought he was right. When ordered by Sulla to divorce his wife, he simply refused. As the Roman historian Suetonius writes in the opening chapter of *The Twelve Caesars* (121 A.D.): "He then married Cornelia, the daughter of Cinna, who was four times consul; and had by her, shortly afterwards, a daughter named Julia. Resisting all the efforts of the dictator Sylla to induce him to divorce Cornelia, he suffered the penalty of being stripped of his sacerdotal office [a high priest of Jupiter called the *Flamen Diali*],[4] his wife's dowry, and his own patrimonial estates; and, being identified with the adverse faction, he was compelled to withdraw from Rome."

Camelot and the Cultural Revolution, James Piereson relates John Wilkes Booth's assassination plot against Lincoln to Brutus's. Like Brutus, Booth had expected to be welcomed as a liberator in the just-defeated Confederacy, only to find himself instead a hunted animal. Booth had planned the assassination for April 13, the ides of that month, but had to delay it until the following day, which was Good Friday. He quotes from Michael W. Kaufmann's *American Brutus* (2004): "Booth had hoped to kill Lincoln on the Ides and highlight his resemblance to Caesar, but instead he shot him on Good Friday, and the world compared him to Christ."

4. The officeholder could not ride a horse or spend a single night away from the city. Nor could he divorce his wife, which certainly must have figured into Caesar's political calculations. Refusing to divorce Cornelia cost him the position anyway.

Caesar, however, eluded the fate of others, cultivated the right mentors, allied himself with the powerful Pompey Magnus via his daughter's marriage to the great general, studied voraciously, watched others with a keen eye to advancement, borrowed money liberally when he had to, paid back enormous sums when he could, and learned that the surest way to wealth was to conquer and take it.

Most historians pass lightly over Caesar's religious offices, but this is a confirmation bias most likely born of agnosticism or atheism. Caesar's faith may have been superfluous, formal, and careerist, or it may have been deep and heartfelt; just because we no longer believe in the Greco-Roman gods doesn't mean the men and women of the time didn't. Like any good Roman official, Caesar was punctilious about observing the formalities[5] of the Roman state religion, which accompanied every office. There was no separation of church and state in ancient Rome. The Romans wanted nothing to do with kings, but gods they had aplenty, and it was mandatory for a Roman citizen to offer them sacrifice and obeisance when the tenets of the religion mandated such.

In the prologue (often omitted in performance) to *Caesar and Cleopatra* by George Bernard Shaw (1899), the Irish playwright's characteristically sardonic account of the world's most famous May-December romance, the Egyptian god Ra addresses the audience and declaims: "Ye shall marvel, after your ignorant manner, that men twenty centuries ago were already just such as you, and spoke and lived as ye speak and live, no worse and no better, no wiser and no sillier. And the two thousand years that have past are to me, the god Ra, but a moment; nor is this day any other than the day in which Caesar set foot in the land of my people." More recently, Mary Lefkowitz writes in *Greek Gods, Human Lives*: "Modern writers and readers often find it hard to imagine that the ancient Greeks [and, by extension, the Romans who worshipped the same gods] could have believed in their own very different gods. The ancient Greek notion of divinity is very different from that of the modern monotheistic religions."

To what extent, if any, Caesar was motivated by religious fervor in

---

5. Unlike the Abrahamic faiths, there was no "holy book" or dogma. The Roman religion was primarily petitionary or propitiatory.

his conquests or whether the preponderance of his activity was driven by a lust for power and glory remains moot. We cannot know what's in the hearts of our contemporaries, much less those of the past. Caesar remained, as was customary, *pontifex maximus* until his death, when the office went briefly to Lepidus, the forgotten member of the Second Triumvirate, and ultimately devolved upon Augustus, Caesar's adopted son and heir. The *pontifex maximus* was the highest rank of the Roman priesthood, in charge of the entire state-sanctioned cult, including the supervision of the eighteen Vestal Virgins—a position taken very seriously. Indeed, the *pontifex*'s official residence, the *domus publica*, was adjacent to the Vestals' nunnery, and it was there it is said that Caesar spent his last night on earth.

Among his duties was the recording of various signs and omens, and what occurred subsequently, so that his successors might interpret them more accurately. Given Caesar's (like Alexander's) pronounced interest in omens, the job must have meant *something* to him, and as the chief administrator of the *jus divinum*, or "divine law," the position also gave him a great deal of temporal authority: he could proclaim divine laws and postpone elections if the signs from the gods were not propitious.

In our era, in which the trappings of Christianity are dropping away and traditional Christian dogma is under both secular and religious assault, and the Protestant churches no longer seem to stand for anything that smacks of political incorrectness, especially former religious prohibitions against homosexuality and abortion, it is easy for us to underestimate and therefore dismiss the extent and importance of Caesar's faith, and that of the rest of the Romans. It seems too ridiculous for words, all these signs and portents and entrails, these necessary oblations and ablutions. Gods coming down from heaven to, at least temporarily, become mortal; mortal men being elevated to the status of gods; gods and mortals having invisible or miraculous sexual intercourse and producing demigods. Who could possibly believe such things?[6]

Romans attributed both the Republic's and the Empire's successes not only to military prowess but also to religious piety, especially that of

---

6. Both "monotheistic" Jews and Christians, as we shall see.

their women. Cicero, in *De Natura Deorum,* observed that "if we care to compare our national characteristics with those of foreign peoples, we shall find that, while in all other respects we are only the equals or even the inferiors of others, yet in the sense of religion, that is, in reverence for the gods, we are far superior."

Something that particularly strikes the modern student of classical history is the sheer number of objects of veneration, to each of whom some respect and offering must be paid. Big gods, little gods, public gods, private gods; there was a god or goddess for literally every occasion. It was almost impossible to keep track of them all, and yet each was best propitiated whenever possible.[7] You couldn't be too careful. Almost every public space was also a sacred space, and the reading of omens, including the flights of birds, was an important factor in daily decision-making.

The Numidian Lucius Apuleius,[8] in his treatise *The Florida,* noted of the Romans that "it is the usual practice of wayfarers with a religious disposition, when they come upon a sacred grove or holy place by the roadside, to utter a prayer, to offer an apple, and pause for a moment from their journeying"—a practice that Christianity later adopted, as any traveler in Europe or Ireland will soon note. Celsus, the second-century Greek philosopher, and no friend of Christianity, noted that an essential element of Roman religious ritual was "to give thanks to the gods who control earthly things, to render them the first fruits and prayers, so that they will befriend us while we live."

The bargain was simple: Romans prayed and sacrificed to the gods, and in return they had reasonable expectations that their prayers and offerings would be rewarded with favorable outcomes. It was petitionary prayer at its most transactional. Pilate prayed to his personal gods, his *lares* and *penates,* before trying Jesus. Sacrifices could be something as simple as a few drops of wine, or something as grand as hundreds of head of cattle or, when necessary for statecraft, human beings. Despite

---

7. "The Romans assigned particular gods to particular spheres and to almost every single moment," wrote St. Augustine in *The City of God.*

8. Of *The Golden Ass* fame, also known as the *Metamorphoses,* the only novel written in Latin to survive in full.

their reputation for ruthlessness, Romans prized life; sacrificing it was therefore the highest form of religious observance.

"Cult" is the word that comes to mind—but we forget that all religions begin as cults. Further, the word "*cultus*" for the Romans lacked the modern connotations of crackpot extremism in its English cognate. A "cult," as Cicero defined it, was the "cultivation of the gods," a series of religious practices akin to the nurture of plants. There was nothing wrong in being a member of a cult: even Christianity was called, in its earliest years as a Jewish breakaway sect, the "Jesus Cult"; Catholics also subscribe to the "cult of the Virgin." Alexander believed he was directly descended from Zeus, and before his death declared himself divine; Caesar was divinized after this death. Almost to the end, the Romans believed that their ancient rituals had saved the Capitol during the Celtic sack of Rome in 387 B.C. and kept Hannibal at bay during the Second Punic War, even after their disastrous defeat at the Battle of Cannae in 216 B.C.

From the very beginnings of Western religious history, the characteristics of the gods have remained remarkably steady. The Jews and the Christians replaced the many gods of the Greco-Romans with two similar but conflicting deities—the mercurial, minatory, self-imposed ("I am the Lord thy God"), demanding deity of the Jews, and the more loving but still remote and distant God the Father of the Christians—who somehow were deemed by some (not all) early Christians to be the same entity.[9] Indeed, Zeus/Jupiter resembles in some particulars the irascible One God of the Torah and the modified Christian Old Testament, while more ameliorative divinities were grafted together to create the sympathetic God the Father of Christianity, which gradually but steadily supplanted the "Eastern" faith of the Jews as it became gentilized, Europeanized, and Westernized. Even then, the Christians eventually adopted the doctrine of the Trinity in order to account for both the divinization of Jesus and the evangelizing impulse, called the Holy Ghost or Spirit.

---

9. As we shall see, the conflict between these two irreconcilable deities would come to define the first and second centuries A.D.

The Greco-Roman religious tradition lasted thousands of years. It is already in evidence in the pages of Hesiod and Homer, and antecedes both the *Iliad* and the *Odyssey*. It is thus roughly contemporaneous with the traditional origins of Judaism, another Bronze Age faith. Judaism, however, has some roots in the ancient Canaanite[10] polytheism, itself an outgrowth of the Babylonian/Sumerian deities; rabbinic Judaism only dates from around the time of Christ. The Moses story, for which modern scholars believe there is scant if any historical evidence, dates from around 1280 B.C., or around the time of peak Mycenaean Greek civilization.

The syncretic Romans, in conquering Greece, folded the Greek gods into their own systems of observance and belief, and maintained at least the letter of the law until the reign of Constantine the Great in the fourth century A.D., when Christianity at first became decriminalized and then supplanted the old faith as the official cult of the Empire. Christianity, as it evolved, was a *political* faith first and foremost. It was the lever and fulcrum with which the locus of the Empire was moved, beginning with Constantine's Council of Nicaea in 325 A.D. From that point on, it gradually took on the trappings of the western Roman Empire itself, which withered away in the aftermath of Constantine's establishment of the new imperial city in Greek Byzantium in 324, and its renaming as Constantinople six years later.

Suffice it to say that Caesar left us no ruminations on his inner beliefs, nothing after the manner of his imperial successor, Marcus Aurelius, in his *Meditations,* written in Greek during his reign from 161 to 180 A.D.—most of it conducted from the Empire's Germanic frontiers. What Caesar did leave us, however, is one of the foundational literary and historical classics of Western history—letters from him to the

---

10. The early Hebrews worshipped multiple gods, including Baal of the Canaanites, Phoenicians, and the Carthaginians, and bits of each found their way into the synthetic Yahweh-Adonai/Elohim—who, according to some scholars of religion, are actually two different gods with distinctive, different personalities in Jewish scripture; indeed, the word "Elohim" is plural although used in the singular. Mormons, for example, view Jehovah and Elohim as separate entities. More on this in chapter 5.

Senatus Populusque Romanus and thence to us. In the not-so-distant past, the *Commentaries* were required reading for every schoolboy afforded a proper education. *Gallia est omnis divisa in partes tres* went the famous opening, as each student set to work translating a "dead" language into living history.

There is nothing "dead" about the *Commentaries,* Caesar's personal account of the Gallic and the Civil Wars, written dispassionately in the third person, with three later sections on the wars in Egypt, Africa, and Spain contributed by others in his service. In these, Caesar's most salient characteristics, including his sheer unflappability, his bounding ambition, his pride, and his personal indifference toward his men are revealed unflinchingly. Although they loved him, Caesar holds them at arm's length throughout the *Commentaries* and never shies from an opportunity to ascribe any military failure to them and not to himself.

Indeed, they allow us history's first window into the mind of a commander, a kind of template for every conqueror who came after him. It is one of the theses of this book that the great commanders of history are remarkably similar in their traits, even while they may and do differ in particulars. We can trace a straight line from the volatile Achilles to Alexander to Caesar to Constantine to Aetius to Bohemond of Taranto to Napoleon and Patton. What they all share is supreme confidence in their own abilities, indifference to their personal safety, and an ability to see the strategic picture while in the midst of tactical battle. They also have outsized egos, almost limitless resourcefulness, and a profound sense of their place in history. They often even wear distinctive dress, from Alexander's plumes to Caesar's cloak to Douglas MacArthur's scarf and aviator sunglasses.

Like Alexander, Caesar was not an innovator. Alexander had taken what his father Philip had bequeathed him and perfected it. Although he had lost the civil war against Sulla, Marius—Caesar's uncle—had nevertheless transformed the legions into the most potent fighting forces in the known world, and Caesar, upon inheriting them, made the best of them. For it was Marius who created the notion of a standing army, permanent legions who did not disperse after every campaign.

It was Marius who created the idea of the *century,* a hundred fighting men, headed by a *centurion.* It was he who opened the ranks of the military to the poorer classes, men who couldn't afford their own weapons and armor (helmets, the *gladius* and the *scutum*), much less the horses of the equestrian class.

Finally, it was Marius who promised his veterans that most valuable of commodities in the ancient world, land of their own upon the conclusion of successful campaigns and terms of service. The generals were on the hook for these expenses, of course, but the need to pay their troops in money, accoutrements, slaves, women, and land created a better and more motivated class of commander as well. And the fact that generals, not civilian consuls, could reign supreme in the increasingly shaky Republic made the career of conqueror all the more enticing, not to mention profitable.

Romans had long since abjured any thoughts of a king—with the expulsion of the Tarquins in 509 B.C., in which a Roman by the name of Lucius Junius Brutus[11] led the revolt, no Roman had dared utter or even bruit the title—but emperor . . . ? The honorific *Imperator* was awarded to victorious generals. Further, the notion of a *Dictator* was part of the Roman constitution, a temporary office enabled in times of national emergency, with power reverting to the consuls once the crisis was past, but no later than six months. Before Sulla, the last time it had been invoked was 202 B.C. during the Second Punic War. By the time Sulla held it, it was essentially open-ended until the "restoration of the Republic" had been achieved. He kept it for three years before relinquishing it voluntarily in 79 B.C.

Caesar, in embarking upon his military and political career, surely had these two possible offices in mind. And why wouldn't he? The teetering Republic had already been through one vicious civil war, and another was brewing. In an effort to head off complete disaster, Caesar had in 60 B.C. formed the so-called First Triumvirate with Pompey and Marcus Licinius Crassus, and had cemented his alliance with Pompey by marrying his daughter, Julia (his only legitimate child), to the general the following year. Her death in childbirth at the age of twenty-two in

---

11. The forebear of Marcus Junius Brutus who struck the final blow against Caesar.

54 B.C., while Caesar was in the midst of his Gallic campaigns, turned out to be the death blow of the Republic.

What effect Julia's death had on her father, now in his mid-forties (Pompey was six years older than his father-in-law), we can only speculate. Certainly it put Caesar in a tough spot, which got even tougher the following year when one of his partners in the triumvirate, Crassus, seeking military glory for himself instead of resting on his riches, undertook a disastrous, unprovoked expedition against Rome's perennial *bête noire*, Parthia, and was killed there, along with his son and most of his men at the Battle of Carrhae (Harran in modern Turkey) in 53 B.C. Crassus, by repute the richest man in Rome, had been instrumental in putting down the Spartacan slave revolt in 71 B.C. and was a two-time consul of Rome, both times serving alongside Pompey. Now proconsul[12] (governor) in Syria, notorious for his greed, he decided that the riches of the East could be his.

Carrhae ranks with the Battle of the Allia,[13] Cannae, and the Teutoburg Forest near the top of Roman military disasters. Confronting the mobile Parthian archers, nine thousand strong, who would ride their horses near the Roman infantry lines, then wheel in their saddles and, while retreating fire a volley of "Parthian shots,"[14] Crassus led the Romans ever deeper into hostile Mesopotamian territory. The heavily armored Parthian cataphracts (armored horses), about a thousand of them, also terrified the legions, their horses and riders the nearest equivalent in the ancient world to tanks and against which the Romans had no defense.

When the seven legions under his command had finally had enough of these tactics, they begged Crassus for a negotiated peace. That turned out to be his last, best, and final mistake. Crassus led an embassy to Surenas, the Parthian commander. Things quickly went sideways. A

---

12. An office that could be awarded to former consuls after their one-year term as consul was up. They could be reelected consul again, but not consecutively.

13. Fought between the Romans and the invading Gauls under Brennus c. 387 B.C., resulting in the first sack of Rome. Livy records the debacle in his *History of Early Rome*.

14. Linguistically corrupted to "parting shots" in modern parlance.

fight broke out, and Crassus and his men were killed. All seven legion-ary eagles were lost, a humiliation almost without equal in Roman his-tory up to this point.[15] There are conflicting accounts of how Crassus died, but the most piquant one is related by the Roman historian Cas-sius Dio (c. 155–c. 235 A.D.), which goes like this: "Not only the others fell, but Crassus also was slain, either by one of his own men to prevent his capture alive, or by the enemy because he was badly wounded. This was his end. And the Parthians, as some say, poured molten gold into his mouth in mockery; for though a man of vast wealth, he had set so great store by money as to pity those who could not support an enrolled legion from their own means, regarding them as poor men."

Caesar, then, had many good reasons to be cautious as his cam-paign in Gaul began to wind down, with Crassus dead and Pompey increasingly estranged after Julia's death. Political alliances in Rome, from which Caesar had been absent for years, were shifting and un-steady. News traveled slowly to and from the wild battlefields of Celtic Gaul, and spies and enemies were everywhere. To that end, in moments of high crisis he developed his own secret code in order to send secure messages to his subordinate commanders in Gaul, such as Quintus Tul-lius Cicero, the besieged commander of the Fourteenth Legion during the battles with Ambiorix of the Eburones.[16] As Cassius Dio writes:

> [H]e sent a horseman of the allies who knew the dialect of Ebu-rones and was dressed in their garb. And in order that even he might not reveal anything, voluntarily or involuntarily, he gave him no verbal message and wrote to Cicero in Greek all that he wished to say, in order that even if the letter were captured, it should even so be meaningless to the barbarians and afford them no information. In fact, it was his usual practice, whenever he

---

15. Caesar's planned campaign against the Parthians in 44 B.C. was meant to avenge Crassus and recover the eagles. It was canceled by his assassination.

16. Caesar alludes to this episode in chapter 45 of book 5 of the *Commentaries*. Ambiorix was the leader of the Belgae, one of the most fearsome confederations of the Celtic/Gallic tribes. Their territory included modern Belgium.

was sending a secret message to any one, to substitute in every case for the proper letter of the alphabet the fourth letter beyond, so that the writing might be unintelligible to most persons.

To keep up his profile in Rome, despite his increasing defiance of the Senate (which had never authorized the conquest of Gaul), Caesar hit upon the idea of sending dispatches back from the front, giving us history's first surviving battlefield memoirs—a genre that would be burnished by such later additions as the *Personal Memoirs of U.S. Grant,* written after Grant's wartime service and his presidency and finished just before his death in 1885. Caesar's annual summaries of his (under Roman law quite illegal) campaigns in Gaul are written in excellent Latin, coolly observant, and as objective as he could make them. They were not apologias for his actions; rather they were reports—"sitreps," in contemporary military jargon—on the theory that it was better to ask for forgiveness (or simply demand it) later than to ask for permission beforehand.

Caesar's role model, to use a modern term, was Alexander. This is not conjecture: Plutarch, in *Parallel Lives,* makes the similarity explicit, twinning the two leaders, Macedonian and Roman, in his seminal work of historical biography. Plutarch's account of Caesar begins with his hegira to the Sabine countryside, trying to avoid the wrath of Sulla, who saw the youthful Gaius of the Julii as suspiciously Marian in his political affinities. Although Sulla had pardoned Caesar in 82 B.C., he later regretted allowing him to live, noting his boundless ambition: "in this Caesar, there are many Mariuses." How right he was. Encountering some of Sulla's soldiers c. 80 B.C., Caesar managed to bribe his way out of possible trouble and, using his connections, protectively set sail for the kingdom of Bithynia (in western Anatolia, directly across the Bosphorus from Byzantium and running along the northern coast of what today is Turkey—as it happens, near the site of ancient Troy). He was acting as an ambassador of Rome to King Nicomedes,[17] on the staff of

---

17. Where it was whispered he became the king's catamite—the Queen of Bithynia. "A man to every woman," they said, "and a woman to every man." The subordinate position in sodomy was considered disgraceful for a man.

the Roman praetor, Marcus Minucius Thermus. Thus began his career as a politician.

His subsequent travels took him all over the Roman sphere of influence. Plutarch tells us that in Spain, "when he was at leisure and was reading from the history of Alexander, he was lost in thought for a long time, and then burst into tears. His friends were astonished, and asked the reason for his tears. "Do you not think," said he, "it is matter for sorrow that while Alexander, at my age, was already king of so many peoples, I have as yet achieved no brilliant success?" Suetonius describes this moment of self-actualization thus: "As quaestor it fell to his lot to serve in Further Spain. When he was there, while making the circuit of the assize-towns, to hold court under commission from the praetor, he came to Gades,[18] and noticing a statue of Alexander the Great in the temple of Hercules, he heaved a sigh, and as if out of patience with his own incapacity in having as yet done nothing noteworthy at a time of life when Alexander had already brought the world to his feet, he straightway asked for his discharge, to grasp the first opportunity for greater enterprises at Rome." That would make him about thirty-three years old, just a year older than Alexander was when he died.

Weeping, however, was not generally Caesar's wont. He was by all accounts a man of steady, even steely demeanor, who rarely got rattled even in the most dangerous circumstances. Consulting Suetonius[19] once more, we find this famous anecdote about the young Caesar:

> While crossing to Rhodes, after the winter season had already begun, he was taken by pirates near the island of Pharmacussa and remained in their custody for nearly forty days in a state of intense vexation, attended only by a single physician and two body-servants; for he had sent off his travelling companions and the rest of his attendants at the outset, to raise money for his ransom. Once he was set on shore on payment of fifty talents, he did not delay then and there to launch a fleet and pursue the

18. Modern Cádiz.

19. *The Lives of the Twelve Caesars,* 121 A.D.

departing pirates, and the moment they were in his power to inflict on them the punishment which he had often threatened when joking with them. . . . Even in avenging wrongs he was by nature most merciful, and when he got hold of the pirates who had captured him, he had them crucified, since he had sworn beforehand that he would do so, but ordered that their throats be cut first.

The modern reader may not at first understand why this was considered merciful. Thanks to the triumph of Christianity starting in the fourth century A.D., and continuing more or less to the present, the presence of the cross is a familiar sight. It is, in fact, one of the holiest symbols of the Roman Catholic Church, in part because it has taken the most feared and agonizing punishment of the tormentor and turned it into the triumph of the tormented. Under Roman law, no Roman citizen could be executed via crucifixion. That was reserved for the lower orders, slaves, rebels, criminals.

While Judaism was peaceably tolerated by the Romans, as were most other faiths, politically rebellious Hebrews were given no special consideration in the Roman province of Judaea, and thus the Roman provincial governor, Pontius Pilate, had no qualms about sentencing to death by crucifixion a particular troublemaking, miracle-working rabbi called Jesus of Nazareth—one of several[20] at a time when rabbinic Judaism was struggling to form itself—in part because he preached a gospel of a new kingdom of God that would replace Rome, and that it was imminent. In a rare instance of New Testament concordance, all four canonical gospels (the three synoptic[21] gospels of Mark [the earliest and shortest], Matthew, and Luke, and the more rhapsodic outlier of John,[22] in which Jesus makes claims to divinity nowhere present in the three

---

20. The Hebrew prophet Elijah was also said to be able to raise the dead, while Hanina ben Dosa, a contemporary of Jesus, could heal the sick and control the weather.

21. Synoptic = "to be seen together." All three gospels share the same stories about the life and sayings of Jesus, although none is identical with the others, and indeed they differ in many particulars.

22. Written last, c. 90–100 A.D.

earlier gospels) agree on Jesus's fate. It was the most painful, literally excruciating death possible—which is why Caesar's throat-cutting of the Cilician pirates who had kidnapped him was deemed an act of mercy.

Caesar, in fact, was renowned for his clemency. He often forgave rebels, whether Gauls or Romans, in order to advance his political and strategic interests. Not raised in the military, he remained in many ways a bureaucrat rather than a butcher, although he didn't hesitate to kill large numbers of people, including women and children, when he deemed it necessary. Indeed, Caesar in his personal and administrative life seemed to foreshadow a famous maxim, attributed to Stalin, that one death was a tragedy but a million deaths were a statistic: he himself estimated that some one million Gauls died during his eight years in the field, although like many such body counts from ancient sources, this is almost certainly an exaggeration.

Caesar's most important Gallic victim, one who emphatically did not benefit from his famous clemency, was Vercingetorix, the most effective leader of the largely disunited Gauls, who gave Caesar and the Romans all they could handle in the fateful year of 52 B.C., when the last major revolt against Roman rule there broke out.

In his *Commentaries,* Caesar never makes explicit why, exactly, he wanted to conquer Gaul, nor Britain for that matter. The Gauls were not wilding savages. They had significant settlements and towns of their own, highly developed forms of art, and technological skills, mining being one of them. Parts of Gaul routinely conducted trade with the Romans. Like the Germans across the Rhine—another part of the ancient world the Romans had thus far treated gingerly—they had a well-established culture, military traditions, and social mores. Like the Germans, who frankly terrified the much smaller Romans, the Celts fought with a berserker ferocity, often to their tactical detriment.

The battle for Avaricum (modern Bourges, in central France), the first of the three great clashes between Vercingetorix and Caesar, was fought in the late winter and early spring of 52 B.C.[23] It was a battle

---

23. Like Alexander, Caesar fought his principal adversary three times, winning twice. Caesar, however, had to face Vercingetorix in person thrice, whereas Alexander only met Darius on the field twice.

Vercingetorix did not initially want to fight, preferring to destroy the town as part of his scorched-earth guerilla campaign against the invading Romans. Vercingetorix's strategy from the start had been sound: to lure the Romans deeper and deeper into increasingly hostile and unfriendly territory, raze his own Gallic villages and burn their cropland, and thus stretch the Roman supply lines to the breaking point.

In the far-distant future, such a strategy would work spectacularly well for the Russians under Kutuzov after the battle of Borodino against Napoleon in 1812. There, however, the Russians were prepared to cede Moscow, firing the city as the French arrived, and ultimately forcing the Grande Armée into a catastrophic retreat back to central Europe—the pivotal moment in the Napoleonic Wars, after which the French defeat at Leipzig during the Battle of the Nations was inevitable. The Gauls had no single principal city, no capital, which meant that the war against them had to be conducted on multiple fronts, employing a combination of military might, shock and awe, diplomacy, hostage taking, and canny diplomatic horse trading. Caesar's Gallic campaigns, in fact, fully embody the truth of Clausewitz's maxim that war is merely the continuation of policy *with* other means. Caesar's policy objective was the complete subjugation of Gaul, and he used whatever means to hand to accomplish it. All of it was in the service of his larger political ambitions.

Caesar instinctively grasped the highest principles of leadership, which included seizing command in a vacuum (something Napoleon would emulate nearly two millennia later with even greater élan and bravado), remaining undaunted in the face of challenges, instilling absolute trust in your men, and never showing hesitancy or weakness at moments of crisis. *Alea iacta est,* Caesar was supposed to have said as he crossed the Rubicon in the fateful year of 49 B.C. to launch the Roman Civil War. Dice were rolling, knives were out; Caesar welcomed them.

Unlike Alexander, Caesar generally did not fight in the front lines of the armies[24] he commanded but nonetheless inspired fierce loyalty

---

24. One notable exception was the Battle of Munda, in Spain, in 45 B.C., the final clash in the civil war against Pompey's forces, now led by one of the late general's sons. "Then [Caesar] sprang forward in advance of his line of battle toward the enemy so far that he was only ten feet distant from them. Some two hundred missiles were aimed at him, some

among his legions (literally "his"—Roman generals usually raised, organized, and paid their legions out of their own pockets), often turning
up on the line at critical moments, dressed in his distinctive red cloak
for maximum visibility. Caesar was generally not one to put steel into
the bellies of the foe but rather put steel into the backbones of his men;
they rewarded him with feats of endurance and courage that were the
wonder of the ancient world. Indeed, the famous Tenth Legion Equestris
was known as "Caesar's own" and, along with the Thirteenth, was among
his most loyal units, acutely aware they were legionaries of Rome fighting
under the standards of her greatest commander. Even at their unhappiest
and most mutinous (conditions largely triggered by tardy pay), he could
silence them with a gesture and a word. As Suetonius writes:

> Again at Rome, when the men of the Tenth clamoured for their
> discharge and rewards with terrible threats and no little peril to
> the city, though the war in Africa was then raging, he did not
> hesitate to appear before them, against the advice of his friends,
> and to disband them. But with a single word, calling them "cit-
> izens," instead of "soldiers," he easily brought them round and
> bent them to his will; for they at once replied that they were his
> "soldiers" and insisted on following him to Africa. . . . Even then
> he punished the most insubordinate by the loss of a third part of
> the booty and of the land intended for them.

This is a familiar story, but one important element that is generally omitted is Caesar's use of the word "citizens." Facing down this
potential mutiny in 47 B.C. by restive, unpaid legions, including the
loyal Tenth, Caesar merely held up his hand and addressed his troops
as *Quirites* (citizens), not *Romani* (soldier-citizens). Generally unre-
marked, however, is the humiliation attendant upon the word *Quirites*.

---

of which he evaded while others were caught on his shield. Then each of the tribunes ran
toward him and took position by his side, and the whole army rushed forward and fought
the entire day, advancing and retreating by turns until, toward evening, Caesar with difficulty won the victory. It was reported that he said that he had often fought for victory, but
that this time he had fought even for existence" (Appian, *The Civil Wars*, book 2).

First, it implied that they had all just been fired, summarily reduced in rank from legionaries to nobodies. Second, more stinging, *Quirites* was the name the Romans had given to the forcibly cuckolded and absorbed Sabine men. From Livy's *The History of Early Rome,* book 1, chapter 13: "In this way the population was doubled, and that some concession might after all be granted the Sabines, the citizens were named *Quirites,* derived from the name of a Sabine god, Quirinus"—"wardsmen," with perhaps an underlying sense of subordination, although the word eventually came to mean simply "citizen." Faced with such disgrace, the rebellion promptly ended.

Caesar had set out on the wars of political and mercenary conquest that would make him immortal as a thickening, balding, middle-aged man—a canny populist politician who had wisely made common cause initially with two men more famous, important, and rich than himself. Politics was an expensive business in the late Roman Republic, and Caesar, chronically broke, needed a wealthy patron to help ensure his election to various civic and religious offices, including quaestor (the first rung on the ladder to consul); aedile and *pontifex maximus*; praetor (which gave a man the *imperium,* or authority of the Roman state, wherever he served, usually in a judicial capacity); governor of Spain; consul, in 59 B.C.; and then terms as proconsul of two of Rome's northwestern provinces, Transalpine Gaul and Cisalpine Gaul.[25] It was from this power base that he launched the Gallic Wars from 58 to 50 B.C.

Having been given the two provinces he most wanted, Caesar saw a mighty opportunity. Allied with Crassus and Pompey, he left Rome in their hands as co-consuls, with the proviso that his posting in Gaul would be extended by five years beyond the customary one-year terms allotted to proconsuls. As Suetonius notes:

Presumptuous now from his success, he added, at his own private charge, more legions to those which he had received from the republic; among the former of which was one levied in Transalpine

---

25. Mediterranean France and northwestern Italy today.

Gaul, and called by a Gallic name, Alauda,[26] which he trained and armed in the Roman fashion, and afterwards conferred on it the freedom of the city. From this period he declined no occasion of war, however unjust and dangerous; attacking, without any provocation, as well the allies of Rome as the barbarous nations which were its enemies: insomuch, that the senate passed a decree for sending commissioners to examine into the condition of Gaul; and some members even proposed that he should be delivered up to the enemy. But so great had been the success of his enterprises, that he had the honour of obtaining more days (seventeen) of supplication, and those more frequently, than had ever before been decreed to any commander.

The proximate cause of the Gallic wars was the desire of the Helvetii in what is today central Switzerland to migrate from their mountain fastness westward. The tribes through whose lands the Helvetians wished to pass, or grab, appealed for help to Rome, with whom some had cordial diplomatic and economic relations. Caesar magnanimously played peacekeeper and promptly went to war with the Swiss, whom he regarded as among the most formidable Celtic warriors: "the Helvetii also surpass the rest of the Gauls in valour, as they contend with the Germans in almost daily battles, when they either repel them from their own territories, or themselves wage war on their frontiers" (*Commentaries*, chapter 1).

Caesar then proceeded to bring the rest of the Gallic tribes to heel, fully intending to bring all of Gaul (divided into three parts—the Belgians, the Aquitani, and the Celts) into Rome's official orbit. Aside from an occasional foray across the Rhine, Caesar gave the formidable Germans a wide berth, but essayed two raids on Britain in in 55 and 54 B.C. The first was an inconsequential and nearly disastrous landing in what is now Kent, but during the more extensive second invasion he managed to cross the Thames and planted the seeds for what would become Roman Britain under the emperor Claudius in 43 A.D.

---

26. The Fifth Legion, raised by Caesar and the first legion to include non-Romans.

Gaul had been largely pacified by 53 B.C., with Caesar, now aided by an ambitious staff officer named Mark Antony, snuffing out a few minor revolts. He seemed to have accomplished his mission. But then, the following year, Vercingetorix, a young chieftain of the Arverni, a proud and ferocious warrior, arrived on the scene.

We don't know very much about Vercingetorix.[27] We don't know, for example, his real name: "Vercingetorix" means "Victor of a Hundred Battles"; the Gauls generally kept their family names private. Statuary depicts him as a handsome man, tall and strong, with long flowing hair and a luxuriant mustache, often brandishing a large sword. He was the son of a tribal noble, Celtillus, and a natural leader, well-spoken and inspiring. Based on his military record against Caesar, we know that his people—not just the Arverni but members of other tribes yearning for freedom after a brief taste of the Roman yoke—loved him. We also know that the Arverni were the mortal enemies of the Aedui, who'd been under the protection of Rome for more than sixty years. In fact, it was the Aedui's defeat by a rival tribe, the Sequani, who were led by a German general named Ariovistus, that also had in part justified Caesar's Gallic incursion in 58 B.C. Finally, we know that Vercingetorix and his tribesmen had initially joined Caesar in his fight to keep the Germanic tribes out of Celtic territory, so he had some experience with the Roman way of warfighting and tactics, later to be put to good use.

Hitherto, the Romans and the European Celts had observed a rough balance of power and nonaggression. The Celts, while quarreling among themselves, enjoyed what we might term today ethnic or even racial autonomy. They were free to observe their own customs, habits, and rules for living and dying. Still, after the Battle of the Allia the early Roman kingdoms and later the Republic regarded them warily and steadily pushed the Celts out of Italy and north and west during their conquest of the peninsula. Seen in this light, Caesar's Gallic intrusion, an act of pure opportunism in the service of his own military and political career, can be considered a war of aggression. In part thanks

---

27. The Gallic suffix "rix" means "king," cognate with the Latin *Rex*.

to Vercingetorix and his rebellion—which came as Caesar's long run as proconsul was ending—he used the ends (the neutralizing of the Celts) to justify the means.

But Caesar's martial successes in the first years of the war, and his brutal subjugation of the hitherto unaffiliated tribes, also made the Celts suddenly understand what it was they had lost. To become—at spearpoint—a Roman ally at this time was essentially a protective bargain for the Gauls. It meant they would have to supply troops, especially cavalry and auxiliaries, upon demand, and provide important hostages to be taken to Rome to ensure their continued cooperation. While they could appeal to Rome for military assistance—as some had done versus the Helvetii and the Sequani—it was not necessarily guaranteed, and generally came with a heavy premium.

Caesar's campaign against the Gauls resembles in many particulars the American government's prolonged campaign against the American Indians. It was a strategy of divide and conquer, of subornation, of the enlistment of collaborators and spies, of economic and territorial bribery, of shifting alliances, occasional uprisings, and an inevitable conclusion. Except for the Battle of the Little Bighorn, the native tribes had the added disadvantage of almost always being outnumbered by the *wasichus,* whereas the Gauls had superior numbers, not only in aggregate but tactically on the battlefield most of the time as well. What neither tribal society could overcome was their opponents' superior armaments, technical skills, military theory and discipline, and superior command of logistics.

Napoleon, at leisure in his final exile at St. Helena, explored Caesar's campaigns in his *Commentaries on the Wars of Julius Caesar (Précis des Guerres de César),* dictated to his secretary and published in 1836, fifteen years after his death. He points out that it was the very success of the standard Roman procedure of taking hostages among the locals in order to ensure the safety of the administrators and garrison legionaries that in part led to Vercingetorix's uprising.[28] The Romans, well established in the Celtic towns of Gaul, were very vulnerable:

---

28. Further payback came later in the form of the German Hermann, called Arminius, a former hostage, a man raised in the Roman military tradition, and a Roman citizen, who

Caesar . . . had taken large numbers of hostages, a largely ineffective policy since the needs of the service brought many Roman legionary officers into the towns, and at the moment of insurrection they became hostages themselves. . . . Vercingetorix, a young lord of Clermont, placed himself at the head of the rebels. At first he was driven out of the town as a young fool who was putting everyone's safety at risk; but soon after he raised an army, returned in force to Clermont and was proclaimed king.

This brought Caesar on the run from Cisalpine Gaul, where he had been wintering with his troops. (The ancients rarely fought in winter, preferring instead to hole up in camps and await the coming of spring, and thus of the "fighting season.") Napoleon describes the siege of Avaricum, noting with admiration the Romans' ability to construct fortifications on the spot, as well as their vengeful nature when frustrated.

Caesar invested the place, protecting his camp with double lines of circumvallation and contravallation in the part of the town not covered by marshes, and began siege operations. . . . In twenty-five days, the Romans constructed a terrace 330ft wide by 80ft high, which dominated the walls of the town. Vercingetorix sent in across the marshes a reinforcement of 10,000 men and advanced with his cavalry to support a sortie by those besieged. Caesar thought this a favourable opportunity to capture the Gaulish camp, and marched to it. The soldiers demanded the order to attack, but it was too well fortified by nature and by artifice. Caesar returned to his lines, having achieved nothing. Meanwhile, the besieged, supported by Vercingetorix, made a sortie; they fought with fury but were driven back.

Soon after, Caesar mounted an assault, entered the place, burnt it, pillaged it and slaughtered 40,000 men. Only 800

---

annihilated several Roman legions at the Battle of the Teutoburg Forest in 9 A.D. See also the chapter on the battle in *Last Stands* (St. Martin's Press, 2020).

escaped. This success seemed likely to bring about the collapse of the Gaulish resistance, but it proved otherwise; it raised their spirits and the resistance was entirely united. Vercingetorix was accused of treason in the national assembly, but defended himself with success. He argued that he had advised that Bourges be burnt because it was impossible to resist the Roman prowess at siege warfare. He emerged from this dispute more powerful and more respected than ever. (Translation by R. A. Maguire)

Caesar, extremely chary with praise in the *Commentaries*—humility was never one of his strong suits—mentions Vercingetorix several times in chapter 7, which is largely devoted to the unexpected rebellion. In one memorable scene, Caesar even fashions a speech for his antagonist as Vercingetorix articulates his theory of guerilla war and why some of the Gallic towns and villages should be destroyed in order to save them:

The interests of private property must be neglected for the sake of the general safety; that the villages and houses ought to be fired, over such an extent of country in every direction from Boia, as the Romans appeared capable of scouring in their search for forage. That an abundance of these necessaries could be supplied to them, because they would be assisted by the resources of those in whose territories the war would be waged: that the Romans either would not bear the privation, or else would advance to any distance from the camp with considerable danger; and that it made no difference whether they slew them or stripped them of their baggage, since, if it was lost, they could not carry on the war. Besides that, the towns ought to be burnt which were not secured against every danger by their fortifications or natural advantages; that there should not be places of retreat for their own countrymen for declining military service, nor be exposed to the Romans as inducements to carry off abundance of provisions and plunder. If these sacrifices should appear heavy or galling, that they ought to consider it much more distressing that their wives and children should be dragged off to slavery, and themselves slain; the evils which must necessarily befall the conquered.

It's an extraordinary speech, and a philosophy that has been adopted by resistance fighters ever since, from the Gauls of the first century B.C. to the Viet Cong[29] and beyond. That Vercingetorix ultimately failed in his resistance to Roman power, as so many others did, does not invalidate the sentiments. As it turned out, though, he was right: the locals (in Caesar's telling) pleaded with their chief not to destroy their homes. The town, they pointed out, was well sited defensively:

> The Bituriges threw themselves at the feet of all the Gauls, and entreat that they should not be compelled to set fire with their own hands to the fairest city of almost the whole of Gaul, which was both a protection and ornament to the state; they say that "they could easily defend it, owing to the nature of the ground, for, being enclosed almost on every side by a river and a marsh, it had only one entrance, and that very narrow." Permission being granted to them at their earnest request, Vercingetorix at first dissuades them from it, but afterward concedes the point, owing to their entreaties and the compassion of the soldiers. A proper garrison is selected for the town.

With Vercingetorix in the field with his troops, however, the Romans took the town and, as was their custom, massacred most of the inhabitants for their act of *lèse-majesté*. They were angry at the Gauls for making them work; rampaging Roman legions furious at their own losses were an unholy terror to all who defied them.

The legions at this period were nearly always on offense, and would be for the next two centuries. Only later, as the borders of the Empire reached their farthest limits under Trajan in 117 A.D. did the legions molt into frontier garrisons and sentinels. Defensive warfare was

---

29. "Don't these people ever give up?" wonders Lieutenant Colonel Kilgore in *Apocalypse Now*.

something they hadn't had to practice for nearly a century; already by the time of Marcus Aurelius (d. 180 A.D.), the legions were struggling to hold back the Germans and, as always, the ever-troublesome Parthians in the east.

Not that they had contempt for their enemies. Romans rarely underestimated their foes, especially the valiant, crazy-brave Celts. "They are a nation of consummate ingenuity, and most skillful in imitating and making those things which are imparted by any one," writes Caesar in the *Commentaries,* taking admiring note of Celtic courage:

Then there occurred before our eyes a thing which, as it seemed worthy of record, we have not thought it right to omit. A certain Gaul before the gate of the town was hurling into the fire over against a turret lumps of grease and pitch that were handed to him. He was pierced by a dart from a "scorpion"[30] in the right side and fell dead. One of the party next to him stepped over his prostrate body and went on with the same work; and when this second man had been killed in the same fashion by a scorpion-shot, a third succeeded, and to the third a fourth; and that spot was not left bare of defenders until the ramp had been extinguished, the enemy cleared away on every side, and a stop put to the fighting.

Once broken, however, Gallic resistance quickly turned into a rout. What they lacked was Roman discipline and, even more (as they themselves admitted), Roman command of construction and siege warfare. The Romans were master builders and could create a walled encampment to protect their forward positions literally overnight. They could cross rivers with pontoon bridges, or ring an enemy redoubt with a wall. Or, if he was holding out in a fortified position, they could erect siege engines and move them right up to the enemy's defenses. The Roman legions were a formidable fighting force, to be sure, the best in the world, but they were also a mobile corps of engineers who could

---

30. A kind of field artillery crossbow, very powerful.

overcome nearly any physical obstacle. Above all, they had tremendous physical fortitude and regarded their enemies as comparatively indolent and disorganized.

Although they suffered a tremendous loss at Avaricum, including many of their women and children, the Gauls' faith in their charismatic commander remained unshaken. At a pow wow, Vercingetorix reminded the survivors that he had advocated the abandonment and firing of the town in order to deny the Romans sustenance and draw them deeper into his trap while he was raising manpower from other tribes. The Gallic chieftain attributed the defeat not to any want of courage on the part of the Celts but to the Romans' technological superiority. But never mind, said Vercingetorix: "He would soon compensate it by superior advantages; for that he would, by his exertions, bring over those states which severed themselves from the rest of the Gauls, and would create a general unanimity throughout the whole of Gaul, the union of which not even the whole earth could withstand, and that he had it already almost effected; that in the meantime it was reasonable that he should prevail on them, for the sake of the general safety, to begin to fortify their camp, in order that they might the more easily sustain the sudden attacks of the enemy."

At the Battle of Gergovia (52 B.C.), Caesar mounted another assault on a Gallic town, this one the capital city of the Arverni, from which Vercingetorix had once been expelled by his own people. But this time Vercingetorix was ready for Caesar and his six legions. With the river Allier between them, the Gauls mirrored the Romans' movements, destroying the bridges as they went. Caesar, however, resorted to characteristic subterfuge. He sent the larger part of his force ahead, but kept a couple of legions behind. Vercingetorix took the bait and followed the main cohort, giving Caesar's rump legions a chance to rebuild a bridge and then link up with the others. Once he'd realized his error, Vercingetorix hastily made his way into Gergovia, arriving before the reassembled Romans.

Gergovia was especially well situated defensively on a twelve-hundred-foot mountain rising above a wide plain, with only one way into the town. A frontal assault was out of the question. The Romans quickly captured a smaller hill, which supplied the Gauls with grain, forage, and water, and then, entrenching as was their wont, they cut it off from the town itself, intending to starve the Gauls out.

But things quickly went wrong. Caesar had been relying on his old allies, the Aedui, to act as auxiliaries, defending the Roman supply lines. But the Aedui went over to Vercingetorix, and attacked the Romans instead. Caesar snuffed out the mutiny, and the Aedui once again switched sides. Caesar, however, was still faced with the intractable problem of storming Gergovia. Once again he resorted to a feint; after taking a few outlying Gallic camps, he pretended to withdraw, hoping the Gauls would think he was abandoning the siege. Some of his forces, including the Tenth Legion, played along—but those who had captured the camps didn't hear the order. With the wind still up, they continued their advance on the town, throwing themselves at its walls to no avail except exhaustion. As Caesar later noted, "Being animated by the prospect of speedy victory, and the flight of the enemy, and the favourable battles of former periods, they thought nothing so difficult that their bravery could not accomplish it."

The Gallic women in the besieged town, however, were terrified, throwing their clothes and silver over the walls to the attacking Romans and "bending over as far as the lower part of the bosom, with outstretched hands beseech the Romans to spare them, and not to sacrifice to their resentment even women and children, as they had done at Avaricum." Some even climbed down from the walls and into the arms of the waiting Roman soldiers, begging for mercy.[31]

At this point, Roman lines of communication completely broke down. The reoriented Aedui arrived in support, but some of the legionaries reasonably still took them for enemies and started fighting with them. Hearing the wailing of the women, Vercingetorix led a ferocious cavalry charge that broke the Roman lines and turned the battle into a rout; the victorious Gauls even dismounted and joined their infantry brethren in order to kill more Romans. It was left to the Tenth and part of the Thirteenth Legions to hold them off as the Romans withdrew.

---

31. As both prior and subsequent female behavior during wartime demonstrates, this is entirely characteristic of women, with their keen instinct for self-preservation and protection. We will see it again during the Battle of Dorylaeum in 1097.

Never one to accept blame for a loss if he could roll it off on his soldiers, Caesar upbraided his men for their "rashness and avarice . . . he censured their licentiousness and arrogance, because they thought that they knew more than their general concerning victory, and the issue of actions: and that he required in his soldiers forbearance and self-command, not less than valour and magnanimity." Caesar began a tactical retreat in the direction of Cisalpine Gaul.

Thinking he had Caesar on the run, Vercingetorix pursued. The time to attack Caesar was now, he argued, with his defeated forces in retreat. What he didn't know was that Caesar had been reinforced with the arrival of one of his principal lieutenants in Gaul, Titus Labienus, who brought four legions, as well as German auxiliaries. Also arriving was Mark Antony, who had joined Caesar's staff in 54 B.C. The Gauls, themselves reinforced by other Gallic tribes, caught up with the Romans at the Battle of the Vingeanne River, a cavalry clash in July of 52 B.C. in which the Celts were badly mauled. Now it was their turn to retreat. They decided to take shelter in the fortified hilltop town of Alesia, which could only be taken by siege.[32]

This, the battle that doomed a free Gaul to Roman rule for the next five hundred years or so, was a triumph of Roman engineering ingenuity over Gallic gallantry, the *ne plus ultra* of Caesar's inventive approach to siege warfare: his masterpiece. With Vercingetorix and his eighty thousand men ensconced inside Alesia's walls, with only enough rations to last about thirty days, Caesar's men first constructed their own wall around the town, a *circumvallation* designed to prevent the Gauls from escaping. This wall encircled Alesia for a distance of more than sixteen kilometers, dotted with more than twenty-three guardhouses or watchtowers.

Before the wall could be completed, Vercingetorix sent the remainder of his cavalry into the surrounding countryside to raise a relief force. Unfazed, the Romans promptly built a second wall, known as a *contravallation*, four and half kilometers beyond the first wall, and running more than twenty-one kilometers in length. Thus, not only

---

32. The 2005 HBO series *Rome* opens with the surrender of Vercingetorix to Caesar in the battle's immediate aftermath.

were the remaining Gauls contained inside the first wall, but any reinforcements were walled out, with the Romans in between. Now all they
had to do was wait the Gauls out—and given the implacable nature of
the Romans under Caesar, this would not be a problem.

The Roman fortifications bring to mind the *Todesstreifen* of the
Berlin Wall during the Cold War—deadly obstacle courses filled with
wooden blocks studded with iron hooks (*stimuli*), sharpened stakes in
sunken pits (*lilia*), immovable wooden blocks called "tombstones," and
trenches. Even should the Gauls breach the contravallation at its weakest point in the northwest, they would have to come at the Romans
across this lethal no-man's land.

Vercingetorix's embassies were successful, raising a force estimated
at 250,000 men, drawn from several tribes, including the fickle Aedui.
They vastly outnumbered the Romans and were confident of victory. As
Caesar notes in chapter 76 of book 7, "All march to Alesia, sanguine and
full of confidence: nor was there a single individual who imagined that
the Romans could withstand the sight of such an immense host: especially in an action carried on both in front and rear, when [on the in-
side] the besieged would sally from the town and attack the enemy, and
on the outside so great forces of cavalry and infantry would be seen."

That was the plan; the practice was something else. Inside the besieged town, the Celts were running out of food and uncertain whether
help would ever come. Things were growing desperate. A tribal elder,
one Critognatus, rose to propose cannibalism:

> What, therefore, is my design? To do as our ancestors did in the
> war against the Cimbri and Teutones, which was by no means
> equally momentous; who, when driven into their towns, and op-
> pressed by similar privations, supported life by the corpses of
> those who appeared useless for war on account of their age, and
> did not surrender to the enemy: and even if we had not a prec-
> edent for such cruel conduct, still I should consider it most glo-
> rious that one should be established, and delivered to posterity.

Caesar, in recording this probably imaginary oration by a defiant
Gaul, observes: "After various opinions had been expressed among them,

some of which proposed a surrender, others a sally, whilst their strength would support it, the speech of Critognatus ought not to be omitted for its singular and detestable cruelty." Hoping, futilely, for Roman mercy, Vercingetorix and the defenders of Alesia decided to expel the civilians, including the women and children, in order for the warriors to have enough food to continue the fight until help arrived. Making their way to the initial Roman fortifications, weeping piteously, "they begged of the soldiers by every entreaty to receive them as slaves and relieve them with food. But Caesar, placing guards on the rampart, forbade them to be admitted," and left them to starve in plain sight of the warriors inside the town. Pleas for mercy or offers of sexual slavery fell on deaf ears.

Romans were notorious for their cruelty, but the deaths from starvation and exposure of the women, children, and the weak of Alesia strikes us today as especially bestial. But given that the Romans were in effect surrounded by the Gauls, only the hastily erected fortifications on both sides of their forces offered any protection; further, the Romans were as hungry as the Gauls trapped inside the city. There was no food to give the noncombatants, and to allow the most vulnerable through the inner walls and into the Roman encampments was unthinkable. A Roman must do as he always did in the past, and would do for hundreds of years into the future; harden his heart, stuff up his ears to mute the cries, and avert his gaze from the pleading victims as they died before him.[33]

Fierce fighting ensued, including a midnight attack with the relief force gallantly charging the Romans from the outside, scaling the outer wall, and knocking off the Roman guards atop them with slings, arrows, and stones. Meanwhile, Vercingetorix sallied forth from within the town, hoping to catch the outnumbered Romans in a pincer movement and annihilate them. But the Romans, in the superior defensive position as long as their walls held on both sides, pushed back the Gallic reinforcements with the help of their German auxiliaries, and Vercingetorix retreated back into the town at daybreak.

---

33. In the 2003 film *Julius Caesar,* a boyish Caesar visually associates a dying Gallic mother and her baby with the death of his own daughter two years earlier. The two-part miniseries also affords Vercingetorix a soldier's death in the Tullianum prison by the sword instead of being strangled like a common criminal.

On the final day of the battle, the Arvernian Gallic commander Vergasillaunus, one of Vercingetorix's close relatives, led a force of sixty thousand of his bravest warriors to attack the Roman camp at its weakest point, while Vercingetorix again charged from the town. This put the Romans in an especially difficult position, for while the Gauls could concentrate their forces at a few spots, the Roman legions were dispersed all along both walls, unsure of from which direction an attack might come. It was the crucial moment and both sides knew it.

"The idea uppermost in the minds of both parties is, that the present is the time in which they would have the fairest opportunity of making a struggle," writes Caesar in book 7 of *The Gallic Wars*; "the Gauls despairing of all safety, unless they should succeed in forcing the lines: the Romans expecting an end to all their labours if they should gain the day." Both sides threw everything they had into the fight; the slightest bit of high ground could be not only advantageous but dispositive. The Romans at one point went into their *testudo* formation, the centuries arranging their shields as a protective carapace, like the shell of a turtle. The battle raged around the position of Vergasillaunus, where the Romans were on the verge of collapse—"our men have no longer arms or strength"—and at the inner wall, where the Gauls under Vercingetorix were attempting to penetrate the circumvallation, knocking the defenders from their turrets, filling in the trenches with clay, tearing down the ramparts and breastworks with hooks.

Caesar drafted four cohorts (about 420 men, the rough equivalent of a battalion) and sent them *behind* the contravallation to attack Vergasillaunus from the rear. At this point, according to the *Commentaries,* Caesar himself entered the fray, conspicuous by his red robe[34] and the cavalry and soldiers following him. With the Gauls now attacked from all sides, the fight became a rout:

> Our troops, laying aside their javelins, carry on the engagement with their swords. The cavalry is suddenly seen in the rear of the Gauls: the other cohorts advance rapidly; the enemy turn their

---

34. Some accounts say it was purple, but Caesar seems quite clear on this point.

backs; the cavalry intercept them in their flight, and a great slaughter ensues.

That was the end. Trapped behind the circumvallation, Vercingetorix convened his last war council the next day. Declaring he had fought the war in the interests of Gallic freedom, he asked whether he should be executed on the spot or surrendered to the Romans. The Gauls opted for surrender, and the chieftains delivered him unto Caesar.

The episode is depicted in the famous 1899 painting by Lionel Royer. However romantically inaccurate it might be in its rendering of the scene it captures the gallant sweep of the moment, with Vercingetorix, still mounted on his horse, throwing down his arms while Caesar, on a dais, looks on with a mixture of both impassivity and disdain, wrapped in his red cape and wearing a golden laurel wreath on his head. Plutarch records the moment this way: "But those who held Alesia, after giving no small trouble to themselves and to Cæsar, at last surrendered; and the leader of the whole war, Vergentorix [sic], putting on his best armour, and equipping his horse, came out through the gates, and riding round Cæsar who was seated, and then leaping down from his horse, he threw off his complete armour, and seating himself at Cæsar's feet, he remained there till he was delivered up to be kept for the triumph."

Considering this epic struggle from a distance of more than eighteen hundred years, Napoleon had a few very practical questions for Vercingetorix. "Can it be true that Vercingetorix shut himself up in the town, which was not large, with 80,000 men? When he sent away his cavalry, why did he not also send away three-quarters of his infantry? Twenty thousand men would have been more than sufficient to reinforce the garrison of Alesia, which stood on a hill 3 miles in perimeter, and which besides was inhabited by a numerous and warlike population. There was only enough food in the place for thirty days, so why shut in so many men who could not contribute to the defence but must hasten the surrender? Alesia was strongly defended by its position; it had nothing to fear but hunger. If instead of 80,000 men, Vercingetorix had only had 20,000, he would have had food for 120 days, while 60,000 men taking the field would have troubled the besiegers. It took more than fifty days to assemble a new Gaulish army and for it to arrive to relieve the place."

Further: "And with 80,000 men, how could Vercingetorix let himself be shut up in the town? He should have taken position outside, halfway up the hill, and encamped there, surrounded by fortifications, ready to sally out and attack Caesar. Caesar tells us that the relief army amounted to 240,000 men. But it did not encamp, and did not manoeuvre like an army so superior to its enemy, but like one of equal size. After two attacks, it detached a force of 60,000 men to attack the high point in the north. This attack failed, but that should not have caused the entire army to retreat in disorder." Hindsight may be 20/20, but Napoleon's observations are spot on.

Thus, for all practical purposes, ended the Gallic Wars, although sporadic resistance continued for another couple of years. Vercingetorix was brought to Rome in chains, incarcerated in an underground oubliette of the Carcer Tullianum[35] for almost six years, exhibited to the Roman people during one of Caesar's four staged triumphs in 46 B.C., and then strangled.

It was an ignoble end for a noble foe, but the Gallic hero has been memorialized in French history with great statues; he is for the French what Arminius, the victor of the Battle of the Teutoburg Forest, is for the Germans. He is also the inspiration for the popular *Asterix* series of comic books, known to every schoolchild in France and Germany. The main character is the leader of a small village of Gauls holding out against the mighty Romans in 50 B.C. through the means of a special magic potion.

In the largest historical sense, the loss of Gaul was the final and most important defeat in the rollback of Celtic culture across what is today

---

35. Located at the foot of the Capitoline, near the Forum and known today as the Mamertine; the site contains two superimposed holy sites, the church of San Giuseppe dei Falegnami, built above the old prison and now called the Chapel of the Crucifix. The former prison below is called San Pietro e Paolo in Carcere; tradition has it that the early Christian saints Peter and Paul were held there before their executions by Nero between 64 and 67 A.D.

Western Europe. Where once the Celts had sacked Rome early in her history, the loss of Gaul found them pushed back even farther, into the outer reaches of their former territory: Britain, Ireland, the Isle of Man, and the peninsula of Brittany ("Land of the Britons"), where the Celtic language known as *Breton* is a member of the Brythonic family, which also includes Welsh and Cornish. (The other branch, Goidelic/Gaelic, is the starting point of the Irish, Scots Gaelic, and Manx tongues.)

And while Alesia was the last stand of the Celts in Western Europe, it was very nearly Caesar's last stand as well. Had he lost at Alesia—indeed, had he been crushed, as he well might have been—it would have been the end of him. Even had he somehow struggled back to Transalpine Gaul, much less to Italy, he would have been hauled back to Rome in disgrace as an enemy of the Republic, certainly imprisoned, and probably executed.

It was a fight he had to win. Caesar was lucky that the crucial spot in the battle for Alesia came at the battlefield's narrowest possible point, where the Gauls' overwhelming numerical superiority went for nothing, and their lack of fortitude and discipline sent them scattering at the pivotal moment of Roman tactical cunning and, most of all, heart. The Romans were like the Spartans at Thermopylae, the topographical circumstances of the fight giving the advantage to the numerically inferior side—at least temporarily, as in the case of the Greeks against the Persians. But as we'll see throughout these pages, taking full advantage of the physical circumstances of the battlefield is generally the key to victory for the undermanned side.

Absent the victory at Alesia—had the Celts crushed Caesar as the Germans would crush Varus at the Teutoburg Forest sixty-one years later, thus discouraging Augustus from further adventurism in the German heartland—Western Europe as we know it today might never have come into being. France became Romanized; Germany largely did not. France adopted Latin as its *lingua franca*; Germany never did. Romanized France emerged as the heart of modern Europe, a blending of Celtic and Mediterranean influences, yanking Rome's attention for the first time to the north and west, and not to the south and east. Indeed, had not Caesar pushed the limits of Roman power all the way to the English Channel and, for a few hundred years, beyond into Britannia, the linguistic history of the Continent would have been very different. The Latinate languages would have been confined to Italy, Romania, and perhaps—but not assuredly—parts of Spain, while the Celtic and Germanic languages would continue to hold sway north of the Pyrenees and the Alps. And what would have become of English absent its Norman/French overlay?

None of these considerations was in Caesar's thoughts as he pushed toward victory in the pursuit of political power. Anticipating Clausewitz, Caesar employed war as a continuation of policy *with* other means: operating far from home, with uncertain supply lines, living off the land as much as possible, the object of increasing agitation back in Rome as he prosecuted a war for his own financial and political ends. *Alea iacta est,* indeed. Caesar, by now the leader of the *Populares* faction in Rome thanks to his military successes, had bet everything, including his life, on a successful outcome in Gaul, teaching himself how to become one of history's greatest generals as he went. Suetonius, in *The Lives of the Twelve Caesars,* sums up Caesar's achievements in Gaul:

> During nine years in which he held the government of the province, his achievements were as follows: he reduced all Gaul, bounded by the Pyrenean forest, the Alps, mount Gebenna, and the two rivers, the Rhine and the Rhone, and being about three thousand two hundred miles in compass, into the form of a province, excepting only the nations in alliance with the republic, and such as had merited his favour; imposing upon this new acquisition an annual tribute of forty millions of sesterces. He was the first of the Romans who, crossing the Rhine by a bridge, attacked the Germanic tribes inhabiting the country beyond that river, whom he defeated in several engagements. He also invaded the Britons, a people formerly unknown, and having vanquished them, exacted from them contributions and hostages. Amidst such a series of successes, he experienced thrice only any signal disaster; once in Britain, when his fleet was nearly wrecked in a storm; in Gaul, at Gergovia, where one of his legions was put to the rout; and in the territory of the Germans, his lieutenants Titurius and Aurunculeius were cut off by an ambuscade.

He couldn't stop there, of course. Crassus was dead from his mis-adventure in Parthia. His familial alliance with Pompey was buried with Julia. At the instigation of Cato the Younger and Cicero, who both correctly feared the emergent strongman as a mortal threat to the frac-tious and decaying Republic, the Senate was roiling. The experience of the Sulla-Marius civil war thirty years earlier had scarred the senators, and the prospect of another one, this time between Pompey and Cae-sar, terrified them. Their worst fears were realized when, in January of 49 B.C., Caesar—threatened by Cato with impeachment (arrest) if he didn't disband his army, and declared an enemy of Rome by the Senate—marshaled his Thirteenth Legion in secret and approached a small river in northern Italy near Ravenna, at the limit of the Roman homeland, called the Rubicon. "I, Caius Caesar, after all the great achievements I had per-formed, must have been condemned, had I not summoned the army to my aid!" he is supposed to have said in justifying his action.

This moment has been mythologized down through the ages, even entering the language as the decisive, risk-everything instant in a man's life. According to Suetonius, Caesar almost lost his famous nerve:

He set forward on his journey with all possible privacy, and a small retinue. The lights going out, he lost his way, and wandered about a long time, until at length, by the help of a guide, whom he found towards day-break, he proceeded on foot through some narrow paths, and again reached the road. Coming up with his troops on the banks of the Rubicon, which was the boundary of his province, he halted for a while, and, revolving in his mind the importance of the step he was on the point of taking, he turned to those about him, and said: "We may still retreat; but if we pass this little bridge, nothing is left for us but to fight it out in arms."

While he was thus hesitating, the following incident occurred. A person remarkable for his noble mien and graceful aspect, ap-peared close at hand, sitting and playing upon a pipe. When, not only the shepherds, but a number of soldiers also flocked from their posts to listen to him, and some trumpeters among them, he snatched a trumpet from one of them, ran to the river with it, and sounding the advance with a piercing blast, crossed to the other side. Upon this, Caesar exclaimed, "Let us go whither the omens of the Gods and the iniquity of our enemies call us. The die is now cast."

So he crossed the river and thus toward his rendezvous with history—twenty-three thrusts of dagger and sword—and so into immortality five years later.

He came, he saw, he conquered.[36] It was a trade-off that, one suspects, even had he known the outcome in advance he, like Achilles and Alexander before him, would willingly have made. Brutus may have been, in the words Shakespeare gave to Mark Antony, "the noblest Roman of them all," but Caesar was the greatest. It would not be for 350 years that another conqueror would come along to alter the course of history just as spectacularly. His name: Constantine.

---

36. Deathless words, made more potent by their brevity, uttered after Caesar's easy victory over Pharnaces II of Pontus at Zela in 47 B.C. while on leave from his amorous duties in Egypt with Cleopatra.

Five

CONSTANTINE AT THE MILVIAN BRIDGE

A CANDID but rational inquiry into the progress and establishment of Christianity may be considered as a very essential part of the history of the Roman empire. While that great body was invaded by open violence, or undermined by slow decay, a pure and humble religion gently insinuated itself into the minds of men, grew up in silence and obscurity, derived new vigour from opposition, and finally erected the triumphant banner of the Cross on the ruins of the Capitol . . .

The theologian may indulge the pleasing task of describing Religion as she descended from Heaven, arrayed in her native purity. A more melancholy duty is imposed on the historian. He must discover the inevitable mixture of error and corruption which she contracted in long residence upon earth, among a weak and degenerate race of beings.

—EDWARD GIBBON, *THE HISTORY OF THE DECLINE AND FALL OF THE ROMAN EMPIRE* (1776)

CHRISTIANITY, IN ONE FORM OR ANOTHER, HAD BEEN AROUND SINCE shortly after the death of an itinerant, apocalyptic[1] Jewish rabbi, known to us today as Jesus of Nazareth, or Jesus the Christ, sometime around 30 A.D. In Jerusalem for the religiously mandatory annual Passover feast, he was arrested, brought before the Roman governor of Judea,

---

1. The word "apocalypse" simply means "revelation," not the End Times.

Pontius Pilate, passively condemned as an enemy of the state at the behest of the Jewish Sanhedrin for various religious and political offenses
against both Judaism and the state, and executed by crucifixion—an
indication that Jesus was not a Roman citizen since citizens could not
be crucified; that punishment was reserved for foreigners and slaves,
especially seditionists. All this occurred during the reign of Tiberius,
Augustus's stepson, and a successful general and diplomat in his own
right before succeeding the *Princeps* as the second Roman emperor in
the year 14 A.D.

Jesus's short life marks a turning point in the history of civilization, as is signified by how we in the West indicate dates: "B.C." for
Before Christ and "A.D."—*anno Domini*—thereafter.[2] This convention
first came into common European usage via the Venerable Bede, an
English monk who lived between c. 673 and 735, and was cemented in
place with the coronation of Charlemagne by Pope Leo III on Christmas Day in the year we now call 800 A.D. Up to then, monks, courtiers,
and scholars had dated documents in a wide variety of ways, generally
by indicating the regnal year of the local potentate, or even the reign
of the emperor at Constantinople. The neat division of history with
Christ as the fulcrum also reflected the triumph of Roman Christianity
in the West, a point emphasized by the establishment of what came
to be known as the Holy Roman Empire under Charlemagne and the
Carolingians.

As historian Tom Holland notes in *The Forge of Christendom* (2008):
"Monks both in Francia itself and in the British Isles, looking to cali-
brate the mysterious complexities of time, had found themselves arriving at a framework that was as practical as it was profound. From whose
accession date, if not that of some earthly emperor or king, were years

---

2. A convention retained here. As the Western world dechristianizes, the expressions
"Common Era" (CE) and "Before Common Era" (BCE) have come into use; they were initially adopted by some Jewish writers in the mid-nineteenth century. The Jewish calendar
differs from the Christian, and today some Jewish scholars continue to reject even "CE,"
since the term "Common Era" still reflects its Christian origins. The term "common"
or "vulgar" era seems to have originated in seventeenth-century and early eighteenth-
century England. In any case, BCE and CE are identical in meaning with B.C. and A.D.

to be numbered? The answer, once given, was obvious. Christ alone was the ruler of all mankind—and His reign had begun when He had first been born into the world. It was the Incarnation—that cosmos-shaking moment when the Divine had become flesh—that served as the pivot around which all of history turned. Where were the Christians who could possibly argue with that? Not at the Frankish court, to be sure. Clerics in Charlemagne's service had accordingly begun to measure dates from 'the year of our Lord'—'*anno Domini.*'"

As we approach Constantine—the most consequential leader in Roman history, after Caesar and the divine Augustus himself, and the monarch who finally made explicit the historic connection between the Greece of Alexander and the Rome of Julius Caesar by moving the capital to the Greek city of Byzantium—it's important to keep this in mind. All this might well be moot had it not been for the momentous events of the early fourth century, when, after a prolonged struggle, a Roman military leader named Constantine, raised in the Eastern Empire's capital at Nicomedia but at that point based in Britannia, succeeded to the imperial purple in the year 306 A.D. upon the death of his father and then set out on a campaign of conquest to reunite the two halves of the Roman Empire under a single ruler. Of all the pivotal battles in Western history, that of Constantine's victory over a rival Western emperor named Maxentius (who also happened to be his brother-in-law) just outside Rome at the Milvian Bridge may at once be the least known and the most important. For on that date, October 28, 312 A.D., the fates of both the Western and Eastern Roman Empires were settled, and the nearly two-thousand-year-long triumph of Christianity in the West was assured.

For such an important figure in Western history, Constantine to most remains an obscure figure. Compared with Caesar, say, there are relatively few books written about him, fewer still movies made. He does not cut a heroic figure like Achilles or Alexander, nor was he notorious for sexual excess as were Caligula or Nero. In fact, he seems colorless when compared with his predecessors, in large part because his early biographer, Eusebius, was utterly devoted to the sanctity of his memory.

A more gimlet-eyed Gibbon writes, "His stature was lofty, his countenance majestic, his deportment graceful; his strength and activity were displayed in every manly exercise, and from his earliest youth to a very advanced season of life, he preserved the vigour of his constitution by a strict adherence to the domestic virtues of chastity and temperance. . . . In the field, he infused his own intrepid spirit into the troops, whom he conducted with the talents of a consummate general; and to his abilities, rather than to his fortune, we may ascribe the signal victories which he obtained over the foreign and domestic foes of the republic. He loved glory, as the reward, perhaps as the motive, of his labours. The boundless ambition, which, from the moment of his accepting the purple at York, appears as the ruling passion of his soul, may be justified by the dangers of his own situation, by the character of his rivals, by the consciousness of superior merit, and by the prospect that his success would enable him to restore peace and order to the distracted empire."

Toward the end of his reign, it seems he succumbed to the same temptations as had Alexander, a love of Eastern finery and luxury. The almost Spartan warrior who cut his teeth against the barbaric Britons became a big-spending edifice builder:

The dress and manners, which, towards the decline of life, he chose to affect, served only to degrade him in the eyes of mankind. The Asiatic pomp, which had been adopted by the pride of Diocletian, assumed an air of softness and effeminacy in the person of Constantine. He is represented with false hair of various colours, laboriously arranged by the skilful artists of the times; a diadem of a new and more expensive fashion; a profusion of gems and pearls, of collars and bracelets, and a variegated flowing robe of silk, most curiously embroidered with flowers of gold. . . . We are at a loss to discover the wisdom of an aged monarch and the simplicity of a Roman veteran. A mind thus relaxed by prosperity and indulgence was incapable of rising to that magnanimity which disdains suspicion and dares to forgive.

For his part, Eusebius—the early Christian historian and Constantine hagiographer known today as the "Father of Church History"; he was the bishop of Caesarea in Roman Palestine—draws an explicit analogy with the biblical Moses in his *Life of Constantine*, citing scripture as he goes. Like Moses, Constantine had been raised by his enemies in a foreign court. Like Moses, he did battle with a tyrant on the order of Pharaoh, and led his Christian people to the Promised Land of Constantinople and empire. Eusebius (d. 339), who also wrote a history of the early Church, was less interested in either Constantine the man or Constantine the warrior; his panegyric was intended *pour encourager les autres*, offering a quasi-religious figure of international renown to make the case for the still-nascent faith—the only thing, in his estimation, that offered a way out of the crisis that was engulfing the Empire.

What we can say, however, is that Constantine was a warrior-diplomat in the Clausewitzian sense, the genius who took a persecuted faith and made it a tool of diplomacy *with* other means and, in so doing, ruled the world.

It was a turbulent time in Roman history, and had been for more than a century; indeed, historians refer to the events of that era as the "Crisis of the Third Century." We might also term it the "Christian Crisis." Following the death in 180 of Marcus Aurelius, the last "good emperor," the imperial throne fell to his most unworthy son, Commodus. After Commodus was assassinated in 192, Rome was plunged into the succession wars of the Year of the Five Emperors (Pertinax, Didius Julianus, Pescennius Niger, Clodius Albinus), which ended when an African[3] general named Septimius Severus, the commander of the Danube army, was proclaimed emperor by his own troops, marched on Rome, and seized power.

Rome, as we have seen, had long tolerated other faiths as long as they did not conflict with the Roman state religion and its formalities were observed. From the divinization of Julius Caesar and Augustus as Republic was transformed into Empire, that faith included a form of emperor worship (both Vespasian and his son Titus would be similarly honored, as eventually would Severus after his death in 211). While

---

3. Born near Carthage in 145 in Roman Libya, Septimus Severus was of Roman colonial equestrian descent. He was neither black, Berber, nor Arab. The term "Africa" pertained to the coastal areas of the southern Mediterranean, and was only later applied to the entire continent once its extent was understood.

Christians had been scapegoated as far back as Nero during the Great Fire of 64 A.D., they had not been formally persecuted. But as their numbers steadily grew, Rome demanded that they, too, offer public offerings to the gods, including blood sacrifices of animals, on various state occasions. This, however, the Christians would not do: like the Jews, they had one god, not many, and Jesus Christ had already made the only sacrifice necessary for salvation.[4]

This identification with Judaism was protective, for one of the problems Christianity had early on was its novelty. One of the conditions of Roman religious tolerance was pedigree. Judaism had stood the test of time; its very antiquity gave it legitimacy. At first Christianity was regarded by the Romans as merely another dispute among the perennially squabbling Jews, among whose number had been and were to be numerous "messiahs" of a generally political bent, arrived to declare the imminent restoration of the Kingdom of Israel in the face of Roman oppression.

Christianity had not begun as a gentile faith; it was as Jewish as any other interpretation of the Torah, and indeed many of the early members of the Palestinian[5] Jesus Cult (in the nonpejorative, original sense of the word) were otherwise orthodox Jews, such as the Ebionites, who arose and flourished around the time of the destruction of the Second Temple by the Roman general Titus, later emperor, in 70 B.C. during the First Jewish War. Indeed, one had to first be or become Jewish in order to become a Christian. The Ebionites, who disappeared around the fourth century at a time when Christianity had become

---

4. The Romans cared neither for "salvation" or "messiahs." As long as Rome continued to propitiate its gods, all would be well. Gibbon, therefore, is at least partially correct in his view that Christianity was a leading cause of the fall of the western empire; certainly, the Romans of Caesar's time would have interpreted it that way.

5. A word that is the source of much disputation today, some variation of "Palestine" was the Roman name for the general area. It first appears in Herodotus referencing a district of Syria "called *Palaistinê.*" In the year 135 A.D., the Romans merged Judea and their province Syria and called them "Syria Palaestina." It persisted under the Arab and Muslim occupation and remained in common parlance during the British mandate after the collapse of the Ottoman Empire. It is thought to be derived from "Philistine," which of course redirects to the Hebrew scriptures.

canonical and its break from rabbinic Judaism was complete, accepted Jesus as the Messiah prophesized in Deuteronomy 18:15,[6] but rejected the Virgin Birth. Think of them as the original Jews for Jesus. The Ebionite writings and teachings have been lost/purged, and, as with other early Christian "heretical" sects, what we know of them and their beliefs comes from the writings of their ideological and religious foes, in this case Irenaeus,[7] the archenemy of heretics, including not only the Ebionites but also the followers of Marcion of Sinope and the Gnostics.

At the same time, Judaism itself was undergoing its own internal sectarianism, primarily over the issue of messianism and the apocalyptic literature of the period, with its emphasis on "prophecy." That was something the early Christians eagerly seized upon and adopted as a hallmark of their developing new faith, going so far as to rearrange the books of the Jewish Tanakh for their own Old Testament to place the prophets at the end, with the implication that such "major" (as opposed to the "minor") prophets as Isaiah and Jeremiah directly foretold the arrival of the *Mosiach,* the Messiah, the Christ.[8]

Christianity, however, was something new, like Mormonism or Scientology to us. The early Christians, therefore, needed the protective coloration of their Jewish roots as proof of their claim to historical validity. And while Judaism and the Greco-Roman faith differed in one important respect, the unity of the deity, in many others they were not dissimilar.

The Hebrew Bible is startlingly bloodthirsty (one might say "pagan") in its celebration of death; Abraham was perfectly willing to cut the

---

6. "The Lord thy God will raise up unto thee a Prophet from the midst of thee, of thy brethren, like unto me; unto him ye shall hearken." Hardly very specific.

7. St. Irenaeus (c. 120/140–203 A.D.), the bishop of Lugdunum (modern Lyon, France), born of Greek parents in Asia Minor. He could trace his spiritual lineage from St. John the Apostle to St. Polycarp of Smyrna, who when very young had encountered St. John in Ephesus; Irenaeus, as a boy, was said to have heard Polycarp preach. Irenaeus was instrumental in the formation of what ultimately became the canonical scriptures more than a century later, at the Councils of Hippo (393) and Carthage (397).

8. And understood initially to be a temporal leader who would restore the Kingdom of Israel/Judah, with the apostles as subsidiary monarchs. That, too, changed over time as Christ failed to return and the restoration was put off well into the indefinite future.

throat of his son, Isaac, and make of him a "burnt offering" (the literal meaning of the word "holocaust" in Greek) in response to a command from Yahweh, the tetragrammatonic,[9] Baal-derived god of the Hebrews, and a self-proclaimed rival of many of the other gods of the region.[10] Furious at the "stiff-necked" Israelites for worshipping the Golden Calf while Moses was up on Mount Sinai receiving the Ten Commandments, Elohim sends a deadly plague to kill many of them. Indeed, from time to time the Jewish god considers wiping them out entirely, as he had earlier done to humanity with the Flood, when he rebooted the species with Noah. "How long will this people spurn Me, and how long will they have no faith in Me despite all the signs that I have performed in their midst?" the Lord God complains to Moses in Exodus. "I will strike them with pestilence[11] and disown them . . ."

The god of the Torah does not stop there. Remorseless, he gives the land of the innocent Canaanites to the Hebrews and commands them to exterminate its occupants. God's way of war, described in the Deuteronomic Code that updated the covenant code between God and Israel, explicitly includes slavery, rape, and genocide:

---

9. The name, consisting of the consonants YHWH, eventually morphed into Jehovah in the Christian versions of the Pentateuch, using the vowels available from the alternative names of God, *Adonai* and *Elohim,* which when translated into Greek, turned to *Kyrios.* Yahweh was the god of Existence, the creator god. As we shall see, this notion of a stern creator/warrior god as opposed to a loving, paternal god would become a particularly divisive and nearly irreconcilable issue among the early Christians.

10. "The relationship between the plot of the Bible and the character of monotheism's God, a deity who was, historically, a precipitate of Semitic polytheism, is thus intricate but coherent," writes Jack Miles in *God: A Biography* (1995). "The unity of the Bible was not imposed entirely after the fact by clever editing. That unity rests ultimately on the singularity of the Bible's protagonist, the One God, the *monos theos* of monotheism. This God arose as a fusion, to be sure, but not of all prior gods, only of several . . . The equation is creator (yahweh/telohim) + cosmic destroyer (Tiamat) + personal god (god of . . .) + warrior (Baal) = GOD, the composite protagonist of the Tanakh." The "personal god" element was echoed in the Roman household gods, specific to each home, the *lares* and the *penates.*

11. Worth recalling that at the opening of the *Iliad* (contemporaneous with much of Hebrew scripture) the gods—in this case Apollo, the sun god—strike the besieging Greeks with the plague because Agamemnon has at first refused to return the captive maiden Chryseïs to her father.

When you approach a town to attack it, you shall offer it terms of peace. If it responds peaceably and lets you in, all the people present there shall serve you at forced labor. If it does not surrender to you, but would join battle with you, you shall lay siege to it; and when the Lord your God delivers it into your hand, you shall put all its males to the sword. You may, however, take as your booty the women, the children, the livestock, and everything in the town—all its spoil—and enjoy the use of the spoil of your enemy, which the Lord your God gives you. (Exodus 20:10–18)

For his part, Moses howls gigantic threats and curses upon his people should they refuse to shape up:

Because you would not serve the Lord your God in joy and gladness over the abundance of everything, you shall have to serve—in hunger and thirst, naked and lacking everything—the enemies whom the Lord will let loose against you. He will put an iron yoke upon your neck until He has wiped you out. The Lord will bring a nation against you from afar, from the end of the earth, which will swoop down like the eagle[12]—a nation whose language you do not understand, a ruthless nation, that will show the old no regard and the young no mercy. It shall devour the offspring of your cattle and the produce of your soil, until you have been wiped out, leaving you nothing of new grain, wine, or oil, of the calving of your herds and the lambing of your flocks, until it has brought you to ruin. It shall shut you up in all your towns throughout your land until every mighty, towering wall in which you trust has come down. (Exodus 28:47–52)

Note in its ethos the similarity to the Roman way of siege warfare, itself a variation on that of the earlier Greeks. A city or town under siege had to first be given the opportunity to surrender by opening its gates

---

12. The symbol of Rome, as it happened.

to the attackers and throwing itself upon the clemency of the besieger. If, however, the inhabitants refused, then the investors were entirely within their rights to deal with the inhabitants as outlined above. And even if the defenders did surrender, everything within the walls, including the men, women, and children, became the property of the victors. None of this strikes us today as "fair," and certainly not as "Christian." Political and military struggles were not for the squeamish, and were played out to the bitter end. Combat in the ancient world was existential, a zero-sum game.

Under Trajan, emperor from 98 to 117, Christians were ordered to observe the pieties of the Roman religion, but under a condition of benign neglect they were not to be sought out for non-compliance. Severus changed that. In the year 202, he issued an edict that forbade Roman citizens to convert to either Judaism or Christianity. By this time, there was no love lost between the sects that had often battled each other in the streets of such prominent Roman cities as Alexandria, where they took theological disputation to sometimes murderous heights. (To the Romans they both were irrational troublemakers.) Thus began the persecutions, which would last on and off, in increasing ferocity, throughout the reign of Diocletian in 284–305.

Eusebius remarks that "when Severus, in his turn, was instigating persecution of the churches, the champions of true religion achieved glorious martyrdoms in every land. These were most numerous at Alexandria, to which, as to a huge arena, God's noble champions were conducted from the whole of Egypt and the Thebaid. There, by their heroic endurance of every kind of torture and every form of death, they were wreathed with the crowns laid up with God." He noted that "sometimes they were killed with the axe, sometimes their legs were broken. Sometimes they were hung up by the feet head down over a slow fire; sometimes noses, ears, and hands were severed."

We don't really know how many martyrs there eventually were. The hostile Gibbon, however, asserted the number of Christian martyrs was far overestimated by the divines of the nascent church, likely for propaganda reasons: "The frequent instances which might be alleged of holy martyrs, whose wounds had been instantly healed, whose strength had been renewed, and whose lost members had miraculously been re-stored, were extremely convenient for the purpose of removing every difficulty and of silencing every objection . . ."; but:

> The vague descriptions of exile and imprisonment, of pain and torture, are so easily exaggerated or softened by the pencil of an artful orator that we are naturally induced to inquire into a fact of a more distinct and stubborn kind; the number of persons who suffered death. The multitude of Christians in the Roman empire on whom a capital punishment was inflicted by a judicial sentence will be reduced to somewhat less than two thousand persons . . . it must still be acknowledged that the Christians, in the course of their intestine dissensions, have inflicted far greater severities on each other than they had experienced from the zeal of infidels.[13]

Still, one martyr who had an electric effect on the subsequent history of Christianity—and its widespread adoption throughout the Empire—was Vibia Perpetua, a well-bred, well-educated young married Roman woman of Carthage, a new mother, who was a Christian catechumen[14] when Severus's edict came down. In 203, she was arrested, tried, and sentenced to death in the arena as part of a birthday celebration for Severus's son Geta.[15] In many respects, she was just another of the Christian martyrs of the period, fanatics (as many today might see them) who willingly went to their deaths and transfigurations hopefully singing hymns of praise to a god who had—on earth, at least—so publicly abandoned

---

13. A sentiment echoed 120 years later by another eloquent anti-Christian, George Bernard Shaw: "It must be a constant puzzle to many of us that the Christian era, so excellent in its intentions, should have been practically such a very discreditable episode in the history of the race."

14. A postulant.

15. Named a co-successor to the throne along with his brother Caracalla, he survived the death of his father in 211 by only a few months, when Caracalla treacherously had him killed in their own mother's arms. Severus's parting advice to his heirs, unheeded, was, "Be harmonious, enrich the soldiers, scorn all others."

them. But she did something no other martyr did: during her imprisonment she kept a diary, which recounts her ordeal practically up to the moment of her death. (It was later completed by a fellow Christian, name unknown, with firsthand knowledge of the events.) Known today as *The Passion of Saints Perpetua and Felicity,* the diary provides us vivid insight into the white heat of philosophical religiosity boiling in the heart of empire.

Perpetua refused to recant her apostasy from Roman orthodoxy—which was, keep in mind, a political act—and so was condemned along with the pregnant Felicity and a few others to *damnatio ad bestias*: death by wild beasts in the arena. The night before their execution, they presented a calm demeanor to the curious spectators who had come to see them die the next day:

> On the day before, when they had their last meal, which is called the free banquet, they celebrated not a banquet but rather a love feast. They spoke to the mob with the same steadfastness, warned them of God's judgment, stressing the joy they would have in their suffering, and ridiculing the curiosity of those that came to see them. Saturus said: "Will not tomorrow be enough for you? Why are you so eager to see something that you dislike? Our friends today will be our enemies on the morrow. But take careful note of what we look like so that you will recognize us on the day." Thus everyone would depart from the prison in amazement, and many of them began to believe.

That night she had a dream in which she was transformed into a man and fought and defeated a terrifying Egyptian. "We drew close to one another and began to let our fists fly. My opponent tried to get hold of my feet, but I kept striking him in the face with the heels of my feet. Then I was raised up into the air and I began to pummel him without as it were touching the ground. Then when I noticed there was a lull, I put my two hands together linking the fingers of one hand with those of the other and thus I got hold of his head. He fell flat on his face and I stepped on his head." But that was just a dream. The reality was far grislier:

For the young women, however, the Devil had prepared a mad heifer. This was an unusual animal, but it was chosen that their sex might be matched with that of the beast. So they were stripped naked, placed in nets and thus brought out into the arena. Even the crowd was horrified when they saw that one was a delicate young girl and the other was a woman fresh from childbirth with the milk still dripping from her breasts. And so they were brought back again and dressed in unbelted tunics. First the heifer tossed Perpetua and she fell on her back. Then sitting up she pulled down the tunic that was ripped along the side so that it covered her thighs, thinking more of her modesty than of her pain. Next she asked for a pin to fasten her untidy hair: for it was not right that a martyr should die with her hair in disorder, lest she might seem to be mourning in her hour of triumph. Then she got up. And seeing that Felicitas had been crushed to the ground, she went over to her, gave her hand, and lifted her up. Then the two stood side by side. But the cruelty of the mob was by now appeased, and so they were called back through the Gate of Life.

That, however, was not a reprieve. Those who had survived the beasts would now be dispatched by the sword of a gladiator. Normally, this was done out of sight of the crowd, but the mob wanted to see them die—not necessarily out of blood lust but to learn whether these Christians were truly as fearless and even joyous in death as they professed to be.

Perpetua, however, had yet to taste more pain. She screamed as she was struck on the bone; then she took the trembling hand of the young gladiator and guided it to her throat. It was as though so great a woman, feared as she was by the unclean spirit, could not be dispatched unless she herself were willing. Ah, most valiant and blessed martyrs! Truly are you called and chosen for the glory of Christ Jesus our Lord!

The choice of how to live one's life, and how to die—critically important in the Roman moral scheme—wasn't simply between traditional, agglutinative Greco-Roman faith and Christianity. Marcus Aurelius, only recently dead, had famously espoused Stoicism; Epicureanism and Platonism had their adherents as well. Judaism remained a minority but potent force, and also provided a focal point for continuing anti-Roman and sometimes violently anti-Christian sentiment. While Rome, even after dispersing the rebellious Jews from the biblical Land of Israel in the years 70 and 135 A.D., mostly continued her policy of religious toleration, Jewish hostility toward the Romans remained unremitting: the "Kingdom of the Wicked" was the name they gave to Rome. Gibbon was even more contemptuous of the Jews than he was of the Christians,[16] for what he regarded as their adamant refusal to extend to others the religious courtesies others extended to them:

> A single people refused to join in the common intercourse of mankind. The Jews, who, under the Assyrian and Persian monarchies, had languished for many ages the most despised portion of their slaves, emerged from obscurity under the successors of Alexander; and, as they multiplied to a surprising degree in the East, and afterwards in the West, they soon excited the curiosity and wonder of other nations. The sullen obstinacy with which they maintained their peculiar rites and unsocial manners seemed to mark them out a distinct species of men, who boldly professed, or who faintly disguised, their implacable hatred to the rest of human kind. Neither the violence of Antiochus, nor the arts of Herod, nor the example of the circumjacent nations, could ever persuade the Jews to associate with the institutions of Moses the elegant mythology of the Greeks. According to the maxims of universal toleration, the Romans protected a superstition which they despised.

There were also stresses with Christianity itself. The new faith was just beginning to develop its own set of scriptures, and various factions differed on such fundamentals as which gospels to accept or reject,

---

16. The neologism "anti-Semitism" was not coined until 1879, and has no meaning in assaying European or even nominally Christian society toward Jews. It does no one credit to retroactively apply terms of modern opprobrium to the past, and only colors any issue that needs to be discussed rationally and dispassionately.

which of the letters of St. Paul were to be considered authentic and then, later, canonical. And so it was that somewhere in the middle of the second century, from the Euxine (Black) Sea town of Sinope in the region of Pontus, on the northern coast of what is today Turkey, to Rome had come one Marcion, a wealthy ship owner and son of the local bishop, preaching a radical notion: that the god of Israel and the Christian god were two entirely different entities.

The proto-gnostic Marcion therefore rejected the Old Testament completely, unable to reconcile the irascible Yahweh with the loving God the Father of the Christians. A dualist, he believed in an evil creator god, termed the Demiurge, who had fashioned the world, and a benevolent, superior Supreme Being, who sent Jesus to mankind as its savior. Marcion regarded St. Paul as the only true apostle (although Paul was not one of the twelve), the Hellenized Jew who had popularized Christianity by opening it up to the gentiles, and even prepared his own New Testament, the first of its kind, which consisted of a shortened version of Luke and ten of the Pauline letters. In effect, he created an entirely Christ-originated and -centered faith, and one that needed no reliance on selective prophecy[17] to establish its bona fides. For this he was later dubbed by Polycarp "the first-born of Satan."

At first Marcion was welcomed in Rome, largely on the strength of a sizable gift of two hundred thousand sesterces (as much as half a million dollars in today's currency). He may in fact have already become a bishop and might have had his eye on the *sede vacante* of St. Peter, Pope Hyginus having recently died.[18] But he soon ran afoul of the influential Carthaginian church father Tertullian (155–220 A.D.), who denounced

---

17. "When they would demonstrate the divine origin of Christianity, they insist much more strongly on the predictions which announced, than on the miracles which accompanied, the appearance of the Messiah," writes Gibbon. "But this mode of persuasion loses much of its weight and influence, when it is addressed to those who neither understand nor respect the Mosaic dispensation and the prophetic style." A point about the logical fallacy of the "appeal to authority" entirely lost on those who insist on both the validity of prophecy and the presumed divine authority of scripture.

18. Thus the origin of the term "sedevacantism"—the seat is empty—which today holds that the Vatican II council of 1962–1965, which drastically revised the liturgy and drove millions of cradle Catholics from the Church, has rendered the chair of St. Peter empty

Marcionism in a five-volume series of hostile philippics, masterpieces of *ad hominem* argumentation, called *Contra Marcion*. Tertullian hated everything about Marcion, beginning with his birthplace:

> The Euxine Sea, as it is called, is self-contradictory in its nature, and deceptive in its name. As you would not account it hospitable from its situation, so is it severed from our more civilised waters by a certain stigma which attaches to its barbarous character. The fiercest nations inhabit it, if indeed it can be called habitation, when life is passed in waggons. They have no fixed abode; their life has no germ of civilization; they indulge their libidinous desires without restraint, and for the most part naked. Moreover, when they gratify secret lust, they hang up their quivers on their car-yokes, to warn off the curious and rash observer.
>
> Thus without a blush do they prostitute their weapons of war. The dead bodies of their parents they cut up with their sheep, and devour at their feasts. They who have not died so as to become food for others, are thought to have died an accursed death. Their women are not by their sex softened to modesty. They uncover the breast, from which they suspend their battle-axes, and prefer warfare to marriage.
>
> In their climate, too, there is the same rude nature. The daytime is never clear, the sun never cheerful; the sky is uniformly cloudy; the whole year is wintry; the only wind that blows is the angry North. Waters melt only by fires; their rivers flow not by reason of the ice; their mountains are covered with heaps of snow. All things are torpid, all stiff with cold. . . . Marcion is more savage than even the beasts of that barbarous region. . . . Verily, O Euxine, thou hast produced a monster.

Tertullian's animus toward Marcion may well have been exacerbated by the increasing Hellenization of Christianity, which made him uncomfortable: "What has Athens to do with Jerusalem?" he famously

---

and thus the current Argentine-born Pope Francis—referred to derisively as "Bergoglio" (his Italian surname) or "Pope Pancho"—as an imposter.

asked. But Christianity's transformation from a Levantine religion into a Greco-Romanized one was inexorable.

Marcion's money was returned, and he was condemned as a heretic[19]—in other words, one who did not accept the emerging orthodoxy—and excommunicated from the Roman Church. His expulsion triggered a serious push for the idea of incorporating a version of the Hebrew scriptures into the as-yet-nonexistent Christian Bible. Later, all his writings, including his magnum opus, the *Antitheses* (the Contradictions), were apparently destroyed during the religious equivalent of the Roman *damnatio memoriae,* in which everything about the victim was expunged so that he might disappear from the historical record. What we know about Marcion's teachings derives largely from what enemies such as Tertullian[20] said about him. Still, his particular sect found wide favor and was for centuries a serious rival to the emerging orthodox consensus, lasting in the East for hundreds of years after his death in Asia Minor in 160 A.D.

How very different the history of both Judaism and Christianity might have been had Marcion's views about the fundamental, irreconcilable differences between the two religions been adopted. The prolonged antagonism between Jews and Christians might well have been ameliorated by a frank admission of the doctrinal disparity between them, and much subsequent animosity averted. For one thing, the issue of whether Christianity is a "fulfillment" of the Hebrew scriptures—insulting to believing Jews, as many have recognized—would disappear. For another, the notion of Jews as "Christ killers" would have no sting, since the two faiths would be properly seen as entirely separate, the way Islam is from both Christianity and Judaism, although all three are "Abrahamic" in the broadest allegorical sense.

As Christianity became increasingly Europeanized—beginning in

---

19. "The appellation of heretics," observes Gibbon, "has always been applied to the less numerous party."

20. Tertullian later became a Montanist, believing that the Holy Spirit was revealing new truths through new prophets and prophecy, and that the Second Coming was imminent. Later still, he founded his own sect. He thus became what he had beheld in Marcion: an apostate if not an actual heretic.

the ninth century with the advent of the Holy Roman Empire under Charlemagne and punctuated by the conquest of Constantinople (the "second Rome") by the Muslim Turks in 1453, which destroyed the seat of the eastern Church—there might, would, have been no residual resentment, and a great deal of human misery could have been avoided. After all, what are the odds that three versions of monotheism arose in the same part of the world within a few hundred years[21] of one another, each one claiming to be the One True Faith?

The doctrinal chaos in the Church mirrored the political and social chaos in the Empire as the Crisis of the Third Century got fully underway with the accession of Caracalla, Severus's son, to the throne. There followed a full century of transitory rulers, each unable to wrap his arms around the collapsing political entity of the Roman Empire. Territorial loss, pandemics of deadly diseases, naturally occurring changes in the climate, the weakening of the currency, encroachment of the barbarian hordes such as the Goths against the shrinking perimeters of Roman rule . . . there were huge movements of peoples, with exotic tribes sweeping in from the east and, for a time, a total loss of control of some territory in both the West and in the East. The end, while not quite near, was approaching.

There was a long series of inadequate emperors—some of their reigns lasting mere months—including the freakish Elagabalus, an Arab who at the age of fourteen had effectively succeeded Caracalla in 218 and lasted until his well-deserved demise at the hands of his Praetorian Guard in 222. A member of the cult of Baal, Elagabalus was also a high priest of the sun god, worshiped a piece of meteorite, had an insatiable sexual appetite for both men and women, and finally attempted to turn himself into a transsexual—the last straw. In *Roman History,* the Roman historian Cassius Dio tells us:

> He married many women, and had intercourse with even more without any legal sanction; yet it was not that he had any need

---

21. Although Judaism is as old as if not older than the Greco-Roman faiths, the emergence of Rabbinic Judaism is roughly contemporaneous with that of Christianity and the Roman Empire, and in its modern form only a century or so older than Islam.

of them himself, but simply that he wanted to imitate their actions when he should lie with his [male] lovers and wanted to get accomplices in his wantonness by associating with them indiscriminately. He used his body both for doing and allowing many strange things, which no one could endure to tell or hear of; but his most conspicuous acts, which it would be impossible to conceal, were the following. He would go to the taverns by night, wearing a wig, and there ply the trade of a female huckster. He frequented the notorious brothels, drove out the prostitutes, and played the prostitute himself. Finally, he set aside a room in the palace and there committed his indecencies, always standing nude at the door of the room, as the harlots do, and shaking the curtain which hung from gold rings, while in a soft and melting voice he solicited the passers-by. . . . He carried his lewdness to such a point that he asked the physicians to contrive a woman's vagina in his body by means of an incision, promising them large sums for doing so.

Today, of course, he is hailed by some as the first transgender emperor. Elagabalus was succeeded by a parade of nonentities. It was not until Valerian (reigned 253–260) that some stability in succession returned, and it was Valerian who recognized the Empire had become too large for one man to handle; he appointed his son Gallienus to protect the West against the incursions of the Goths and the Alemanni[22] along the Rhine and in northern Italy while he dealt with the eternally recrudescent Persian threat in the East. His defeat by the Sassanids at the Battle of Edessa in the year 260 and death in captivity a few years later was a stunning blow to Roman pride. For a time, the Empire had even split apart into a Gallic Roman Empire from 260–274 (France, Britain, and Spain) and the Palmyrene Empire in 271 (Egypt, the Levant, Syria, and parts of Asia Minor, briefly ruled by a woman, Zenobia). Imperial Rome was reunited in 274, after a series of military victories by the emperor Aurelian, who was assassinated the following year.

---

22. Whence comes the Romance languages' word for Germans.

It was going to take a strong imperial hand in order to salvage the collapsing realm. That hand ultimately belonged to Diocletian. The Dalmatian-born Diocletian (ruled 284–305, d. 316) is notable for a number of reasons—he was the first emperor to voluntarily abdicate, for one thing—but he's primarily remembered today as the military man who bifurcated the Empire, with himself reigning in the East and an old comrade named Maximian handling the West. Dubbing himself the *Augustus*, Diocletian made his capital in the city of Nicomedia (the capital of the Roman province of Bithynia, in northwestern Asia Minor), while Maximian, dubbed *Caesar*, ruled from Trier, in what is today Germany.[23]

Diocletian, a soldier who never lived in Rome and only visited the city once, took the throne in 284, having arrived by administrative and not lineal means. A consummate bureaucrat, he was an activist, reformer, and reactionary. Rome, for all her past glory, had become greatly reduced in cultural and political stature. As the Empire gradually contracted, it could conquer no more new territory to increase revenues, and yet its bureaucratic costs had not decreased. The legions had in large part become border garrisons (when they were not in active revolt or engaged in successional fighting), and they still had to be paid, booty or no booty. Ambitious military men were preying on the rotting carcass of the Western Empire from the inside, while German barbarians were increasing in size and strength, both outside the borders and also within, where they were becoming more and more important both militarily and administratively. Effectively, the Eternal City was being abandoned; it was only a matter of time before the word "Rome" became attached to other principal cities of the Empire, closer to and more involved with the East.

Most important, inland Rome was no longer where the international action was. Her geographical position was now working against her. The riches of the Empire were in the East, as were the more dangerous of the Empire's enemies. The West, including Gaul and Germania, was still flush with natural resources, such as timber and mining, but the

---

23. Celebrated for its Roman ruins.

East glittered seductively, perhaps even more brightly than it had at the time of Caesar and Cleopatra; gold, silver, and precious jewels seemed to adorn the homes and bodies of every foreign potentate, their wives, their mistresses, and their catamites. The East, still dominated culturally by the sophisticated, cultivated Greeks, was the commercial and intellectual center of the Roman world.

Diocletian's first orders of business were the restoration of civil order, removing the army from politics insofar as possible, suppressing internal revolts and fending off external invasions, and getting inflation under control (via wage and price controls, which naturally failed). In 286 Diocletian went one step further and elevated Maximian to co-emperor; Diocletian and Maximian now both took the titles *Augustus*—the top job was too big for one man. In 293, he further subdivided command, adding two subordinates each with the title of *Caesar*: Constantius in the West and Galerius in the East. This novel arrangement, which went a brief way to stabilizing the collapsing Roman Empire, is known today as the Tetrarchy. It couldn't last, and of course it didn't.

Notoriously, Diocletian was responsible for the last major persecution of the Christians, in which he was enthusiastically joined by his *Caesar*, a former herdsman turned military man named Galerius, who divorced his wife and married Diocletian's daughter in order to cement his position. Although the proscriptions against Christianity were eventually eased (Galerius issued an Edict of Toleration from his deathbed in 311), Galerius's spectacularly agonizing death was seen by Christian apologists such as Eusebius in his *History of the Church* and Lactantius in *De mortibus persecutorum* as God's righteous vengeance. It's not for the squeamish:

And now when Galerius was in the eighteenth year of his reign, God struck him with an incurable disease. A malignant ulcer formed itself in the secret parts and spread by degree. The physicians attempted to eradicate it. . . . But the sore, after having been skimmed over, broke again; a vein burst, and the blood flowed in such quantity as to endanger his life. . . . The physicians had to undertake their operations anew, and at length they cauterized the wound. . . . He grew emaciated, pallid, and feeble, and the bleeding then stanched. The ulcer began to be insensible to the remedy as applied, and gangrene seized all the neighboring parts. It diffused itself the wider the more the corrupted flesh was cut away, and everything employed as the means of cure served but to aggravate the disease. The masters of the healing art withdrew.

Then famous physicians were brought in from all quarters; but no human means had any success . . . and the distemper augmented. Already approaching to its deadly crisis, it had occupied the lower regions of his body, his bowels came out; and his whole seat putrefied. The luckless physicians, although without hope of overcoming the malady, ceased not to apply fermentations and administer remedies. The humors having been repelled, the distemper attacked his intestines, and worms were generated in his body. The stench was so foul as to pervade not only the palace, but even the whole city; and no wonder, for by that time the passages from waste bladder and bowels, having been devoured by the worms, became indiscriminate, and his body, with intolerable anguish, was dissolved into one mass of corruption. (Lactantius)

Gibbon—customarily dispassionate but, one senses, with descriptive relish—describes the end of Galerius in a memorable passage: "His death was occasioned by a very painful and lingering disorder. His body, swelled by an intemperate course of life to an unwieldy corpulence, was covered with ulcers, and devoured by innumerable swarms of those insects who have given their name to a most loathsome disease; but, as Galerius had offended a very zealous and powerful party among his subjects, his sufferings, instead of exciting their compassion, have been celebrated as the visible effects of divine justice."

Not fully understood at the time, the death of Galerius effectively marked the end of the Tetrarchy, although it was to stagger on for a few years, at one time numbering as many as seven competing emperors, Augustuses and Caesars alike. Curiously the man who emerged triumphant was not at first among any of them. In 305, after the joint abdication of Diocletian and Maximian, their *Caesars* Galerius and Constantius, both successful generals, were elevated to first position in East and West, respectively. Much to everyone's surprise, especially his own, Constantius's[24] son, Constantine, was passed over to replace him as *Caesar*: Maximinus II and Severus II were named the two subordinate rulers in the East and the West.

Constantine, however, moved expeditiously to stake his claim to the throne. At his father's behest, and at considerable personal risk, he eluded the forces of Severus to join Constantius in the field in Gaul to put down a rebellion led by a rogue Roman commander named Carausius, and then traveled with him to Britain to war against the Picts north of the Antonine Wall.[25] There, in what is now the English city of York, Constantius died on July 25, 306, at about the age of fifty-six.

Since the prolonged Crisis of the Third Century, the men of the legions had once again grown increasingly politically powerful. With the Senate now vestigial, with the Eternal City having waned considerably as anything other than the tattered symbol of Roman glory, with the frontiers besieged on all sides, and with the center of economic gravity steadily moving eastward, the legionaries' first devotion was no longer to Rome but once again to their commanders, just as it had been under Pompey and Caesar. Then as now, a successful general could not only make himself rich but his soldiers men of property and coin themselves.

It was little wonder, therefore, that the legionaries should want a say in their leadership. Constantius had been especially beloved by his troops, and so upon his death the men immediately hailed his strapping son Constantine as their new leader. Sometimes men have the right fathers, with Clio as their mothers. Constantine was one of them. Just as the birth of the Empire had happened simultaneously with the birth of Christianity, so now were their fates intertwined again, and as the Empire was coming apart, Christianity was struggling toward a coherent and unified theology. Just as emperors were multiplying in response to the Crisis of the Third Century, so was the Christian faith comprising

---

24. An Illyrian-born soldier who had risen through the ranks to become an honored officer in Emperor Aurelian's legions and, later, governor of Dalmatia. He had left Constantine's mother, Helena, for a daughter of his patron, the *Augustus* Maximian, in 289, calling into question the eldest son's legitimacy for a time.

25. A lesser fortification than Hadrian's Wall, about a hundred miles to the north, running roughly between the modern-day cities of Glasgow and Edinburgh.

multiple versions of Christianity, each competing with the other to attain the status of orthodoxy. And, of course, state and church were pitted against one another.

Constantine was the solution. For one thing, he had Christians in his family, including his own mother, today known to Christians as St. Helena. True, his father had divorced her—she may have simply been a concubine—in order to marry the stepdaughter of the western *Augustus*, Maximian, for political reasons. But Constantine remained devoted to his mother and had her elevated to the rank of dowager empress in the year 306, immediately after his father Constantius's death at York. Possibly under her son's influence, in the year 312 she professed Christianity and, three years later, made a pilgrimage to the Holy Land, during which, it is said, she discovered the True Cross buried under Constantine's Church of the Holy Sepulcher at Golgotha, the site of the Crucifixion, and later built churches of her own in Bethlehem (the Church of the Nativity) and on the Mount of Olives in Jerusalem (the Chapel of the Ascension).

For another, during his personal crusade to unite all the thrones into one, Constantine found Christianity to be increasingly useful as a tool of state. Not for him were the Persecutions of Diocletian, which had caused great turmoil and amounted to nothing: there were Christian functionaries across the Empire, their numbers increasing yearly. While Constantine himself cannily hedged his religious bets, remaining partial to the sun god, Sol Invictus, throughout his life, he understood the value of having the Christians on his side, with him rather than against him.

Finally, at thirty-four, the man was a born commander. In many ways, he was a throwback to the days of Alexander: a general who fought from the front instead of from behind the lines, who engendered fierce personal loyalty in the hearts of his men. As the distinguished military historian John Keegan asks in his seminal 1987 study of military leadership, *The Mask of Command*, the question is: In front always? Sometimes? Never? There are arguments for each. Alexander never lost a battle, but he put himself at terrible risk—he was almost killed at the Granicus—and his body had the scars to show for it. At any point during his campaign against the Persians his death would have meant the end of the enterprise, and yet you can't argue with his undefeated record. A front-line commander has a way of inspiring his troops as no mere appeals to patriotism or even greed can.

Wellington, the second object of Keegan's study, was present at the Battle of Waterloo with bullets and cannon fire rattling all around him, but he was not an active combatant; Grant, the third, was similar, always in the thick of the action, often disregarding his own personal peril—bullets bouncing off his saber at Shiloh—to get a better look at the field, or riding from one beleaguered unit to another. But generally he commanded from his headquarters slightly behind the lines. The last of Keegan's subjects was Adolf Hitler; although he had served bravely during World War I as a signals runner, he never saw the twin fronts during the Second World War until the Soviets brought the Eastern Front to him in Berlin during the closing days of the war. And yet, until the catastrophic decision to launch Operation Barbarossa in June 1941—one might have thought that, having experienced a two-front war in 1914–1918, he would naturally have shied away from such a blunder—Hitler was an effective commander, correctly gauging weaknesses in Poland, Czechoslovakia, the Low Countries, and France but critically underestimating the industrial might of the United States in the west and the Russians' will to survive in the east.[26]

(One might add to this list Napoleon, whom we shall consider in detail in a subsequent chapter, very much a fighting soldier in his youth as an artillery officer, but emerging as a kinetic strategist of genius at Austerlitz until the disaster not only at Waterloo but two years earlier at Leipzig during the "Battle of the Nations." Still, Napoleon understood better than any major general since Caesar the importance of being visible to his men during the thick of battle, if not actually fighting beside them.)

True, the Empire had had mixed experience with the sons of beloved commanders. Germanicus (15 B.C.–19 A.D.), probably the ablest man never to become emperor during the Julio-Claudian period, bequeathed to posterity both his son, Caligula,[27] and his grandson, Nero. Bad they were; even worse in many respects was Commodus, the natural son of

---

26. A lesson well worth remembering.

27. The name means "Little Boot," given to Gaius Julius Caesar Augustus Germanicus as he tromped around in small *caligae*, the sandals the legionaries wore while in the field.

Marcus Aurelius, a cowardly libertine who betrayed his father's legacy in every way possible. He abandoned Marcus's war against the Germans on the Danube frontier, took little interest in intellectual or philosophical pursuits, and executed ministers on a whim. He changed the name of Rome to *Colonia Commodiana* (the colony of Commodus), began to fancy himself the reincarnation of Hercules, and entered the ring as a gladiator. On the last day of 192, just before he was to announce a new title for himself—consul of Rome—he was strangled and drowned in his bath by his trainer, a wrestler named, appropriately, Narcissus.

Constantine, on the other hand, proved an inspired choice. He wasted no time in striking, setting off a series of complex civil wars, marked by near-constant shifting of alliances of convenience among the competing members of the Tetrarchy, and in short order the entire unwieldy edifice was on the verge of collapse. First to go was Severus (the western *Caesar*), the victim of a rebellion led by Maxentius, with the help of his father Maximian (the former *Augustus,* who had earlier abdicated along with Diocletian). As these things often go, father and son fell out and Maximian fled to Gaul to join Constantine, who had married his daughter Fausta in 307; after then plotting against Constantine, he was murdered or committed suicide in 310.

Constantine moved into Italy and marched on Rome, where Maxentius had been ruling since 306, with the help of his Praetorian Guard. According to Constantine's hagiographer Eusebius—hardly a disinterested source—Maxentius was not beloved by his people: "Indeed, the one who had thus previously seized the imperial city was busily engaged in abominable and sacrilegious activities, so that he left no outrage undone in his foul and filthy behaviour." Maxentius was a notorious persecutor of Christians, the scribe tells us (although in fact he appears to have stopped the persecutions, but Eusebius found him a useful enemy). He turned his guards loose on the populace in random orgies of wanton murder, assassinated senators, and confiscated their property. "At their peak the tyrant's crimes extended to witchcraft, as for magical purposes he split open pregnant women, sometimes searched the entrails of newborn babies, slaughtered lions, and composed secret spells to conjure demons and to ward off hostilities." Disinformation was a useful tool even in ancient Rome.

He was also by repute a sex addict, who used women of all social ranks profligately and shamelessly; Eusebius relates the story of the Christian wife of one of the senators who, with the procurers at her door, "having requested a little time to put on her customary attire, went into her room and once alone plunged a dagger into her breast. Dying at once, she left her body to the procurers, but by her actions, which spoke louder than any words, she shewed to all mankind both present and future that the only thing that is invincible and indestructible is the chastity acclaimed among Christians. Such then did she prove to be." That, at least, was the beleaguered Christian view.

Gibbon notes, "The virtue of the primitive Christians, like that of the first Romans, was very frequently guarded by poverty and ignorance. The chaste severity of the fathers, in whatever related to the commerce of the two sexes, flowed from the same principle; their abhorrence of every enjoyment which might gratify the sensual, and degrade the spiritual, nature of man. It was their favourite opinion that, if Adam had preserved his obedience to the Creator, he would have lived for ever in a state of virgin purity, and that some harmless mode of vegetation might have peopled paradise with a race of innocent and immortal beings."

Constantine took Taurinorum (Turin) and the Western imperial capital at Mediolanum (Milan), to which it had been moved in the year 286. There was a necessary diversion at Verona, in northern Italy, during which Constantine displayed his military skills against a Maxentian garrison during a tricky siege. Sieges are always a test of a commander's capabilities, and this one was no different. Verona was naturally well fortified, being surrounded on three sides by the waters of the Adige River and accessible otherwise only across a narrow peninsula. Constantine managed to force his way into the city, but the commander—Pompeianus, Maxentius's ablest—escaped and returned with a sizable force to turn the besieger into the besieged.[28] In the ensuing fight, in which Constantine himself took part,[29] Pompeianus was killed, and resistance in northern Italy ceased.

---

28. As we shall see, the same thing happened to the Crusaders under Bohemond of Taranto at Antioch in 1098, with the same result. Alesia also comes to mind.

29. Writes Gibbon: "When the officers of the victorious army congratulated their master

By October of 312, his forces were just north of Rome and itching for a decisive fight. Victory against Maxentius would mean control of the Western Empire; the surviving Eastern potentates, Licinius (who had replaced Galerius) and Maximinus, would have to wait their turn. Constantine, however, was confident of victory. Maxentius (like Augustus, but absent the political savvy) was another Roman lover, not a fighter. He had no taste for combat, especially not against Constantine and his battle-tested army, but the direness of the situation would brook no refusal by the "effeminate" Maxentius to put on his armor and take up his arms. But something singular—miraculous, even—happened before the battle.

As we have noted earlier, dreams, signs, visions, and omens played an outsized part in the decisions of commanders in the ancient world. Several dreams had factored into Alexander's successful assault on Tyre; Calpurnia's nightmare that Caesar would be assassinated on the Ides of March if he went to the Senate house proved to be true. Yet Constantine's vision beat them all: it is the most potent and important dream in Western history. Eusebius tells the story:

> Knowing well that he would need more powerful aid than an army can supply because of the mischievous magical devices practised by the tyrant, he sought a god to aid him . . . his own father had throughout his life honoured the God who transcends the universe, and had found him a saviour and guardian of his Empire and a provider of everything good. . . . He decided he should venerate his father's God alone.[30]
>
> About the time of the midday sun, when day was just turning, he said he saw with his own eyes, up in the sky and resting over

---

on this important success . . . they represented to Constantine that, not contented with performing all the duties of a commander, he had exposed his own person with an excess of valour which almost degenerated into rashness; and they conjured him for the future to pay more regard to the preservation of a life in which the safety of Rome and of the empire was involved." Perhaps they had the lessons of Alexander in mind.

30. There is little evidence that Constantius was a Christian, but Eusebius was an advocate as well as a historian.

the sun, a cross-shaped trophy formed from light, and a text attached to it which said, "By this conquer."[31]

He was, he said, wondering to himself what the manifestation might mean; then, while he meditated, and thought long and hard, night overtook him. Thereupon, as he slept, the Christ of God appeared to him with the sign which had appeared in the sky, and urged him to make himself a copy of the sign which had appeared in the sky, and to use this as protection against the attacks of the enemy.

In hoc signo vinces. Eusebius's account of the famous vision identifies it as a cross, but later in his narrative he relates that Constantine showed him a standard from the battle, which he describes: "A tall pole plated with gold had a transverse bar forming the shape of a cross. Up at the extreme top a wreath woven of precious stones and gold had been fastened. On it two letters, intimating by its first characters the name 'Christ', formed the monogram of the Saviour's title, *rho* being intersected in the middle by *chi*." This symbol, known as the Christogram, or Chi-Rho, became synonymous with Christianity, and it seems clear that while Constantine saw something resembling to the Cross of Christ in the sky, his troops fought under the Chi-Rho and kept the image as his standard throughout the rest of his life, appearing on many of the coins of the realm during his reign.

With the Lord on his side, Constantine and his men believed there was no way they could lose. They had hailed him on his father's death as the new *Augustus* and together they had fought their way south from remote Britain, through hostile Gaul, and into Maxentius's Italian stronghold. Constantine was ready to lay siege to the Eternal City herself if need be, but public pressure forced Maxentius's hand and, to Constantine's surprise, he led his legions out of Rome and headed northward to accept battle. Gibbon:

---

31. The message, written in Greek—a language in which Constantine was not fluent (he spoke Latin)—was Ἐν τούτῳ νίκα.

Constantine had always apprehended that the tyrant would obey the dictates of fear, and perhaps of prudence; and that, instead of risking his last hopes in a general engagement, he would shut himself up within the walls of Rome. . . . It was with equal surprise and pleasure that, on his arrival at a place called Saxa Rubra, about nine miles from Rome, he discovered the army of Maxentius prepared to give him battle. Their long front filled a very spacious plain, and their deep array reached to the banks of the Tiber, which covered their rear, and forbade their retreat . . . Constantine disposed his troops with consummate skill, and that he chose for himself the post of honour and danger. Distinguished by the splendour of his arms, he charged in person the cavalry of his rival; and his irresistible attack determined the fortune of the day.

Of course, he would do that. He had not come this far to lose, and in fact he had no intention of stopping in Rome for long: there was still the conquest of the East to come, the end of the Tetrarchy, and the reuniting of the Empire under a single ruler.

The field Maxentius had chosen for his confrontation with Constantine on October 28, 312, was at the Ponte Milvio, about seven kilometers north of central Rome. It was certainly defensible, located on a loop of the Tiber, thus affording the partial protection of water across the battlefront. All Maxentius—who had been assured by Sibylline augurs and prophecy that victory was surely to be his on this, the sixth anniversary of his accession to the throne of the West—had to do was to allow Constantine to cross the bridge and then fall upon him at the choke point on the other side. But, in preparing for the siege that he had thought he was going to face, it seems (the historical sources are unclear) that the militarily inexperienced Maxentius had already partially destroyed part of the old stone bridge and had assembled either a makeshift wooden bridge or a pontoon bridge next to it. To top things off, instead of waiting for Constantine's forces to make the first crossing, in his lust to get at his enemy, Maxentius decided to make the first move and take a position across the Tiber, with his back now to the river. The result was disaster.

Constantine probably couldn't believe his good fortune when he saw

Maxentius's forward equestrians and legionaries squeezing their way across the river and right into his approaching arms. As the Persians had discovered at Thermopylae, and Darius at Issus, numerical superiority counts for little when the battlefield is constricted or your troops lack full mobility; Maxentius's initial development of his wide front line was quickly halted by Constantine's cavalry attacks on his flanks, led by Constantine himself. Stripped of its protection, the Maxentian center quickly broke, but Maxentius's men had nowhere to which to fall back: they were caught between the river and the full weight of Constantine's forces, which pushed them back toward the water; they had neither time nor space in which to reform their already shattered lines.

At this point, Maxentius—who had unwisely ridden out onto the bridge in full armor—did the only thing he could: he ordered a retreat back across the rickety bridge in order to regroup where he had started. This put his front lines, which included his Praetorian Guard, in an impossible position. Their unit cohesion had already been destroyed on the far bank, his attack cavalry had been rendered useless, and a panicked, retreating army is prey for an aggressive attacker—which Constantine had already proven himself to be. The Praetorians, unable to retreat and knowing that their fate was inextricably bound to that of their boss, made a stand and were shredded.

In his haste, or perhaps his terror, Maxentius had made every mistake possible. In a solid defensive position behind the river, all he had to do was wait for Constantine to come to him. By attacking first, across a damaged or makeshift bridge, he immediately forfeited all his advantages, hanging his cavalry and his Praetorian Guard out to dry while blocking whatever path he had hoped to carve into Constantine's front lines.

Fate played the final card against Maxentius. The bridge wobbled under the crush of desperate men trying to shove their way back to their lines on the opposite bank. Then it broke, depositing men and horses alike into the Tiber. Weighted down by his armor, Maxentius floundered and drowned, along with many of his men. The rest fled, and the battle for Rome was over almost as soon as it had begun. For Constantine, it was a stunning, utterly dispositive triumph.

Christians, naturally, saw Constantine's triumph as not only his but God's—and theirs. "God himself drew the tyrant out, as if with chains, far away from the gates . . ." noted Eusebius, "just as once in the time of Moses and the devout Hebrew tribe 'pharaoh's chariots and his force he cast into the sea, and picked rider-captains he overwhelmed in the Red Sea' (Exodus 15:5), in the very same way Maxentius and the armed men and guards about him 'sank to the bottom like a stone.'"

Constantine's men spaded Maxentius's body out of the mud, stripped it of its armor, decapitated it, and paraded the head through the city the next day. Writes Gibbon, "The sight of his head, when it was exposed to the eyes of the people, convinced them of their deliverance, and admonished them to receive with acclamations of loyalty and gratitude the fortunate Constantine, who thus achieved by his valour and ability the most splendid enterprise of his life."

Constantine was hailed as a liberator. Maximian was given the *damnatio memoriae*, his laws invalidated, his images effaced, his memory expunged. Constantine appropriated his many building projects and disbanded what was left of the Praetorian Guard. He promised the Senate that it would be restored to its ancient privileges and prestige, but that never happened. In 315, the Arch of Constantine was dedicated in honor of his victory, but such was the sorry state of Roman craftsmanship that many of the figures on it were cannibalized from earlier triumphal monuments, including Trajan's, Hadrian's, and Marcus Aurelius's. There is no Chi-Rho on the arch, nor indeed any reference to Christianity. Snorts Gibbon:

> The triumphal arch of Constantine still remains a melancholy proof of the decline of the arts, and a singular testimony of the meanest vanity . . . curious antiquarians can still discover the head of Trajan on the trophies of Constantine.

As great conflicts and epic struggles go, the Battle of the Milvian Bridge doesn't appear to have been much. In fact, it may be the shortest yet most consequential engagement in Western military history. It was the midpoint, not the climax, of a long campaign, as was Alexander's long pursuit of Darius, or Caesar's decade-long conquest of Gaul. Once the troops clashed, the outcome was never really in doubt, and it was over in a matter of hours. Constantine would briefly enter Rome, and then return only twice in his life, to celebrate various anniversaries of his succession. By rights, it should be no more than a footnote, like Verona, in the tale of Constantine's rise to power.

But the injection of the Christian faith into the equation literally changed everything. Before the Milvian Bridge, Christianity was still nominally under the Diocletian persecution; after it the persecutions stopped, Christianity was legalized by the Edict of Milan a year later, and, in 380 under the emperor Theodosius I, it was declared the official religion of the Empire. The small subsect of Judaism, known initially as the "Jesus Movement" or the "Jesus Cult," had gradually muscled its way up through the bowels of the Empire, its message of divine forgiveness, eternal salvation, and life everlasting backed by a fanatical proselytizing zeal, iron political discipline, and the examples of wondrous miracles in its early days—not to mention the fearlessness with which the Christian martyrs such as St. Perpetua had embraced their deaths in the arena, cannily exploited by the early Church fathers as models of effective passive aggression against the pagan Romans.[32]

The final collapse of the Western Empire in 476 A.D.—with the seat of government now located in Ravenna—is attributed to many causes, including falling Italian birthrates, increased immigration, and the political shift to the East. Gibbon, in the controversial fifteenth and sixteenth chapters of his magisterial *Decline and Fall of the Roman Empire,* lays a good deal of the blame for the corruption of Roman morals, ethics, and societal norms on the rise and ultimate triumph of Christianity. And this observation leads us into the thorniest part of this book.

For Christians, the eventual adoption of the faith by the Empire is seen in many ways, few of them historical and fewer indeed even factual. The triumph of Christianity is, however, seen as *inevitable,* something that, after the birth of Jesus of Nazareth and the death and reported resurrection of the man who came to be called the Christ, was fated to happen. Indeed, it was "prophesied" in the Hebrew scriptures, and the entire history of Christianity is a fulfillment of those prophecies, liberally interpreted.

---

32. Gandhi would learn from them, as would later adherents of the various antiwar movements.

Problems arise, however, with the birth of Christ itself. According to the Gospel of Luke 2:1–7 in the King James Bible translation from Greek into English:

> And it came to pass in those days, that there went out a decree from Caesar Augustus that all the world should be taxed. (And this taxing was first made when Cyrenius was governor of Syria.) And all went to be taxed, every one into his own city. And Joseph also went up from Galilee, out of the city of Nazareth, into Judaea, unto the city of David, which is called Bethlehem; (because he was of the house and lineage of David) to be taxed with Mary his espoused wife, being great with child. And so it was, that, while they were there, the days were accomplished that she should be delivered. And she brought forth her firstborn son, and wrapped him in swaddling clothes, and laid him in a manger; because there was no room for them in the inn.

But was that true? Judea only became a Roman province in the year 6 A.D. Further, there is no historical record that Augustus ordered an empire-wide census around the time of the birth of Christ, or any other time for that matter. There was, in the year 6, the Census of Quirinius— Publius Sulpicius Quirinius was the governor of the Roman province of Syria—which functioned as a property tax for residents of the newly declared province of Judea, so it makes little practical sense that Joseph and Mary would have to schlep to Jerusalem when whatever real property Joseph had was in Nazareth.

Another problem is that the Gospel of Matthew, written before Luke, and the most Jewish of the traditional Christian gospels, places the birth of Jesus squarely during the reign of Herod, the last king of Judea (a puppet, installed on the throne by the Romans), who died in the year 4 B.C.[33] Here is the episode of the Slaughter of the Innocents as it reads in the King James Version:

---

33. If true, the biblical story of the murders of the firstborn in Bethlehem had nothing to do with the coming of the messiah but was rather indicative of the mental deterioration of Herod, who also killed his own firstborn son, Antipater. After a good deal of fussing about

Then Herod, when he saw that he was mocked of the wise men, was exceeding wroth, and sent forth, and slew all the children that were in Bethlehem, and in all the coasts thereof, from two years old and under, according to the time which he had diligently inquired of the wise men.

So, from the beginning, contradictions.[34] The four canonical gospels—three of them (Mark, Matthew, and Luke) referred to as the "synoptic" or biographical gospels, each a variation and in some cases a repetition of the others, and the fourth the more spiritual narrative of John—taken together with the letters of St. Paul, became the foundation of the Christian narrative, the "origin story." What would eventually come to be the Christian canon was subject to enormous disputation that often had less to do with doctrine than with political usefulness.

Indeed, it was not until the accidental discovery of a buried trove of early Christian noncanonical manuscripts by an Arab boy named Muhammed Ali at Nag Hammadi in Egypt in 1945 that we were able to obtain a more accurate idea of the principal strains of early Christianity, and of what had been rejected—and expunged—by the Church fathers in the fourth century. These writings, thirteen leather-bound papyrus codices buried in a sealed amphora, written in, or at least translated into, Coptic, give us a radically different view of early Christianity. In gospels such as the reportorial Gospel of Thomas (a "sayings" gospel, made up of purported quotations from Jesus) we see and hear Jesus,

---

his will, divvying up his Augustan-approved kingdom, he died. Judea became a Roman province in the year 6 A.D., after which the provincial capital was moved to Caesarea. After the Jewish Wars of 65–73 and 132–135, the Jews were expelled from Jerusalem, and the city was largely razed. Its name was then changed to Aelia Capitolina. The claim therefore that Jerusalem has always been a Jewish city is demonstrably false. But neither was it an Egyptian, Babylonian, Persian, Arab, or Turkish Muslim city, or a Christian city, except sporadically. The truth is, it has almost always been an international city, currently sacred to all three Abrahamic faiths.

34. Faith, however, is faith, and it can be argued that to truly *have faith,* one must be prepared to accept historical inaccuracies or contradictions. It's a fool's errand to try and "prove" the truth of the Bible.

not the Son of God (as he was later made out to be, although he never claimed the title[35]) but Jesus the Rabbi. Its opening:

> These are the secret sayings that the living Jesus spoke and Didymos Judas Thomas[36] recorded.
>
> **1.** And he said, "Whoever discovers the interpretation of these sayings will not taste death." **2.** Jesus said, "Those who seek should not stop seeking until they find. When they find, they will be disturbed. When they are disturbed, they will marvel, and will reign over all. [And after they have reigned they will rest.] . . ."
>
> **5.** Jesus said, "Know what is in front of your face, and what is hidden from you will be disclosed to you. For there is nothing hidden that will not be revealed. [And there is nothing buried that will not be raised.]"

And so on. The Gospel of Thomas has been dated by biblical scholars as early as the first century, making it roughly contemporaneous with the nonapocalyptic canonical synoptic gospels, or perhaps even older, relating to the putative "Q" (for *Quelle*, or "source" or "wellspring" in German) gospel thought to be an as-yet-undiscovered sayings-gospel urtext from which Matthew and Luke sprang. The Nag Hammadi writings also include the Gospel of Philip, the Gospel of Truth, the Apocalypse[37] of Peter, and the Sophia (Wisdom) of Jesus Christ. They mostly date from the second to the fourth century A.D. The books

---

35. Despite Matthew 16:15–17, Jesus never utters the words. The closet he comes is this lawyerly response: "He saith unto them, But whom say ye that I am? And Simon Peter answered and said, Thou art the Christ, the Son of the living God. And Jesus answered and said unto him, Blessed art thou, Simon Bar-jona: for flesh and blood hath not revealed it unto thee, but my Father which is in heaven."

36. The Greek word "Didymos" means "twin." Many early Christians believed that Jesus had a non-divine brother, similar to the Greek siblings, the divine Castor and the mortal Pollux, the Gemini—which is probably where the belief originated.

37. Peter's *Apocalypse* revealed Heaven to be "a great garden, open, full of fair trees and blessed fruits, and of the odor of perfumes."

were buried in order to keep them from destruction by the early Christian censors, especially active after the codification of the New Testament. In his Festal Letter of 367, the highly influential St. Athanasius of Alexandria, a participant in the Council of Nicaea spoke with finality: "These [the twenty-seven canonical books of the New Testament] are fountains of salvation, that they who thirst may be satisfied with the living words they contain. In these alone is proclaimed the doctrine of godliness. Let no man add to these, neither let him take ought from these."

Christianity grew up along with the Roman Empire. Both were in need of, and in pursuit of, gods. Caesar had been in effect canonized after his death,[38] ascending from mere mortal to godhood. After a long reign as both Caesar Augustus and *pontifex maximus,* the deceased Augustus was also declared divine by the Senate, marking his transition from man to god. Following Gibbon's "melancholy duty," therefore, it is instructive to note how much the turmoil inside the early Church paralleled the turmoil of the Empire. If the Prince of Peace's mission was a reduction in bloodshed, it was a mission not accomplished. But the early Church fathers weren't at all interested in that. Their mission was to spread the faith across the Empire.

But first they had to define precisely what that faith was. Jesus had left behind no writings; accounts of his life and ministry were oral. It took hundreds and hundreds of years of discussion, argumentation, anathemas, and outright conflict for the principal elements of what became Christianity to develop, and one of the most important was the very nature of Christ himself. God? Man? Both?

In the early second century, St. Ignatius, bishop of Antioch, was condemned to death by wild beasts in the arena, as Perpetua was later to be. Unusually, he was transported all the way to Rome to meet his fate—a fate he welcomed in a series of seven letters to his coreligionists that have come down to us. In the ongoing argument about the nature

---

38. The process by which a mortal human becomes a god is known as *divinization.* It was adopted by the Christians to claim divinity for Jesus of Nazareth, something that evolved over time.

of Christ, Ignatius came down squarely on the side of "fully God and fully man." The suffering Christ was no simulacrum of a divine being but a genuinely suffering human being, and a good Christian follows his path. In his epistle to the Traillians, Ignatius asks, "Why am I in bondage, and why also do I pray to fight the wild beasts? I am then dying in vain and am, even more, lying about the Lord." Elsewhere, as the Bible scholar Bart D. Ehrman notes in his 2003 book, *Lost Christianities,* Ignatius pleads:

> Allow me to be bread for the wild beasts; through them I am able to attain to God. I am the wheat of God and am ground by the teeth of the wild beasts, that I may be found to be the pure bread of Christ. . . . Fire and cross and packs of wild beasts, cuttings and being torn apart, the scattering of bones, the mangling of limbs, the grinding of the whole body, the evil torments of the devil—let them come upon me, only that I may attain to Jesus Christ.

The suicidal ecstasy of these sentiments may seem extreme to us today, but blood, torture, and death were commonplaces of the time; they were something to be expected in the course of life, and to embrace them in the name of the Lord was a path to eternal life. In this respect, Christianity gave as good as it got, promising hellfire and damnation to all who rejected the meaning and mission of Christ: deny Him and be condemned for all eternity. The message of Christian love and everlasting life in paradise was balanced against the richly satisfying certainty of the heathens and deniers getting what was coming to them. Eternal torture was to be the fate of those who rejected a loving God. Revenge in the afterlife would be sweet.

At the epicenter of this spiritual and political turmoil stood Constantine. As he continued stitching the Empire back together after the Milvian Bridge, he solidified the position of Christianity in 313 with the Edict of Milan, signed jointly by Constantine and his co-emperor (for the moment), Licinius, in partial celebration of the wedding of Constantine's half-sister, Flavia Julia Constantia, daughter of Constantinius, to Licinius. The edict,[39] one of the earliest official statements of the principle of religious tolerance, read in part:

> It was proper that the Christians and all others should have liberty to follow that mode of religion which to each of them appeared best; so that that God, who is seated in heaven, might be benign and propitious to us, and to every one under our government. And therefore we judged it a salutary measure, and one highly consonant to right reason, that no man should be denied leave of attaching himself to the rites of the Christians, or to whatever other religion his mind directed him, that thus the supreme Divinity, to whose worship we freely devote ourselves, might continue to vouchsafe His favour and beneficence to us.
>
> And accordingly we give you to know that, without regard to any provisos in our former orders to you concerning the Christians, all who choose that religion are to be permitted, freely and absolutely, to remain in it, and not to be disturbed any ways, or molested.

For Constantine, however, there were still military victories to be won. The balance of power between Constantine and Licinius was inherently unstable; there could be only one emperor. His campaign moved eastward. In 324, Constantine defeated his rival at the battles of Adrianople (present-day Edirne in western Turkey, near the border with Greece) and again a few months later at Chrysopolis (just across the Bosphorus, east of Byzantium), the twin climaxes of Constantine's struggle with his brother-in-law. Chrysopolis followed on the heels of the Battle of the Hellespont, a naval battle in which Licinius's fleet was destroyed; at Chrysopolis, Constantine eschewed the niceties of strategy in favor of a frontal assault that overwhelmed and routed his rival.

In 325, Constantine had the exiled Licinius executed (despite a promise not to do so), and his memory was officially damned; the same thing happened to Licinius Junior, killed the following year. Constantine may

---

39. As recorded by Lactantius in *Liber de Mortibus Persecutorum, XLVIII*. Eusebius also recorded it in Greek.

have had Christian inclinations, but his pragmatic, Roman approach to leadership would brook no resistance: in 326 he had his own son Crispus—the naval hero of the Hellespont—executed along with Constantine's second wife, Fausta. One story goes that the pair was having an illicit sexual affair, although scholars have come to doubt that. We likely will never know, but in any case both were not only killed, but their memories were expunged as well. Constantine was hell-bent on a new beginning for everything he touched.

The year 325 also marked the epochal Council of Nicaea, convened by the emperor to resolve the doctrinal problem posed to the emerging orthodox Christianity by a bishop called Arius, and his teaching that Jesus Christ was not "one in being with the Father" but rather a kind of subordinate God, created by his father at some distant point in the past.[40] The distinction was critical to an early Christianity riven with alternative and sometimes antithetical understandings of Christ. There were multiple sects trying to make sense of Jesus's history and message. There were conflicting sets of scriptures and, as yet, no official Christian canon called the New Testament.

In his 2014 book and television series *How Jesus Became God*, Bart Ehrman examines the gradual evolution of Jesus of Nazareth from a holy man and miracle worker, similar to his near contemporary the Greek Apollonius of Tyana[41] (c. 15–100), to divinized mortal and, after the Resurrection, to God incarnate—the Word made flesh. One clearly sees the Roman influences on Christology, right down to the Virgin Birth; in Roman mythology, for example, demigods could have one immortal parent and another one mortal, viz: Hercules and Achilles; in

---

40. Gibbon: "Arius was supported by the applause of a numerous party. He reckoned among his immediate followers two bishops of Egypt, seven presbyters, twelve deacons, and (what may appear almost incredible) seven hundred virgins." He was no renegade but, like Marcion, a dissenter and original thinker.

41. Who shares many biographical details with Jesus: his mother had a dream that she would give birth to a divine son, he became an itinerant preacher extoling spiritual values, he healed the sick and raised the dead, his followers believed him to be divine, he defied an emperor (Domitian), he ascended bodily into heaven, he appeared to his followers after his death. These may well be back-formations, Greek reactions to the Judeo-Christian gospels—the pagan Jesus—but they were widely credited.

Christianity's case, the immortal parent was Mary, who was conceived without original sin (the Immaculate Conception) and was assumed bodily into heaven (the Assumption.) Gods could and often did take human or animal incarnations in order to interact with human beings. Zeus could impregnate mortal women, such as Danaë, in the form of golden raindrops.

Ehrman notes, "The time when Christianity arose, with its exalted claims about Jesus, was the same time when the emperor cult had started to move into full swing, with its exalted claims about the emperor. Christians were calling Jesus God directly on the heels of the Romans calling the emperor God. Could this be a historical accident? How could it be an accident? These were not simply parallel developments. This was a competition. Who was the real god-man? The emperor or Jesus?"

To make matters worse, in addition to the conflict between Christians and Romans, there was an ongoing battle between the Jews and the Greeks, two older faiths, literary traditions, and civilizations that had been superseded by momentous events that included the birth of Jesus and the foundation of the Empire. Politically, the Jews were in constant revolt against the Romans. But culturally and philosophically, their real enemies were the Greeks. Greek theology was essentially as old as Jewish monotheism; Greek military might under Alexander had conquered the known world, while Jewish militarism had lasted only a short while, before being overwhelmed by the superior martial prowess of the Assyrians and Babylonians; Greek philosophy formed the foundation of Western philosophy and drama and literature—the essential elements of civilization, while the fables of the ancient Hebrews that became the Tanakh bespoke a people in near-constant mourning for lost military and political glory, and which eventually, via Christianity, found their way into Western art forms as shared morality tales, iconography, and theatrical drama.

This rivalry has often been glossed over in the wake of the triumph of more feminine Judeo-Christian devotional ethics over the masculinity of Greco-Romanism, which in part accounts for the conflicted nature of Christianity that Constantine and all subsequent Christian rulers have not only faced but had to embrace. Gibbon, who had even less love for the Jews than he did for the Christians, notes:

> From the reign of Nero to that of Antoninus Pius, the Jews discovered a fierce impatience of the dominion of Rome, which repeatedly broke out in the most furious massacres and insurrections. Humanity is shocked at the recital of the horrid cruelties which they committed in the cities of Egypt, of Cyprus, and of Cyrene, where they dwelt in treacherous friendship with the unsuspecting natives; and we are tempted to applaud the severe retaliation which was exercised by the arms of the legions against a race of fanatics, whose dire and credulous superstition seemed to render them the implacable enemies not only of the Roman government, but of human kind. [*Gibbon's footnote*: 'In Cyrene they massacred 220,000 Greeks; in Cyprus, 240,000; in Egypt, a very great multitude. Many of these unhappy victims were sawed asunder, according to a precedent to which David had given the sanction of his example. The victorious Jews devoured the flesh, licked up the blood, and twisted the entrails like a girdle round their bodies.']⁴²

"I have described the triumph of barbarism and religion," observed Gibbon about his magnum opus. "It has been observed, with truth as well as propriety, that the conquests of Rome prepared and facilitated those of Christianity."

Gibbon has been dismissed, even excoriated, by Christian apologists (in the sense of "one who offers a defense of," not of "one who makes

---

42. Contemporary scholarship is at odds over the question of Gibbon's apparent anti-Semitism (a term that as noted did not exist in the eighteenth century). The problem arises when one considers that Gibbon often uses the Jews—"a barbarous and superstitious people"—as a foil for his derision of Christianity, which as a Greco-Romanist he holds in equal cultural contempt. Gibbon may well have been a closet Marcionite, minus the Gospel of Luke and the Pauline letters. In other words, a Deist; in this, he would not be unlike, say, his contemporary Thomas Jefferson.

excuses for"). But Gibbon was a man of the Anglo-French Enlightenment, who had lived through the French Revolution: reason was his god, not the god of Abraham. Still, his analysis of the political triumph of Christianity was spot on. The Council of Nicaea, supervised by the emperor Constantine himself, ended with the victory of the proto-orthodox position and the condemnation of Arius of Alexandria and Arianism as heretical. The Council also finally resolved the question of when the moveable feast of Easter should be celebrated; previously the date had simply been proclaimed annually by the pope, but the Empire had grown too large for the message to reach the hinterlands, and so the date was decided to be the first Sunday after the paschal full moon on or after the March solar equinox.

In the history of both the rise of Christianity and the decline of the Roman Empire (the two are practically coterminous), events in one mirror inversely events in the other. Instinctively, Constantine grasped this. With paganism waning and the Empire fracturing, he saw waxing Christianity as one element that would help preserve the imperium. When Constantine embraced a form of Christianity at the Milvian Bridge, already some 5 percent of the Empire's population of sixty million souls were Christians, and their numbers were growing rapidly; during the first three hundred years of Christianity, its numbers are said to have grown by 40 percent every decade.

Through force of will and arms, Constantine had eliminated the Diocletian experiment with co-emperors and lesser emperors. So now too did the Christians, under his watchful eye, do the same thing with dogma. The consubstantiality of the Father and the Son was affirmed, and "begotten not made"—*homoousianism*—became doctrinal, and both were incorporated into the orthodoxy of the Nicene Creed. Although Arianism persisted, especially in the East, by the time of the Council of Constantinople in 381 the internal argument was over, and with the Councils of Hippo (393) and Carthage (397), orthodoxy reigned supreme. Marcion, the Gnostics, Arius, and other "heretics" were consigned to the dustbin of history.

Meanwhile, life in Rome continued to deteriorate, the city's descent into irrelevance and indeed ruin hastened by Constantine's triumphs and his strategic foundation of his new imperial capital—a "New Rome."

Rome was old, inland, not on the principal trade routes, oriented west instead of east. The new city of Constantinople would be at the confluence not just of rivers but of seas—the Black Sea and the Sea of Marmara, which itself opens into the Aegean and thus into the Mediterranean. Its location, on the western side of the Bosphorus, was ideally situated for defense, being surrounded by water on three sides and commanding vital commercial and military passageways.

On the other side of the world, the Western Empire had begun a final descent that would end at the hands of Christianized barbarian emperors; it would be briefly reconquered by the Byzantine emperor Justinian and his general Belisarius, symbolically revived by Charlemagne in the year 800, and finally reborn as the modern states of Europe and the European Union. The Eternal City had become a *memento mori,* viewed by subsequent generations, beginning with the Romantics of the nineteenth century, as a tourist destination along the Grand Tour and, as a magnificent ruin, an artistic rather than a religious inspiration.

Despite his partiality to Christianity, Constantine had never been baptized. Indeed, throughout his reign, the image of Sol Invictus was a signature icon. The question naturally arises, then, how dedicated was Constantine to the new faith? True, he built churches, statues, shrines aplenty—but how different was that in petitionary intent from erecting temples to the earlier gods, which emperors did as a matter of prudent course? To the end of his life he played both hands with consummate political and tactical genius.

At last, he was forced to choose. In early 337, around Easter, he was stricken by a serious illness and traveled eastward from Constantinople to seek treatment in the hot baths of his mother's hometown of Helenopolis, in Bithynia, but he never made it. Deathly ill, he became a catechumen, having previously expressed the hope to be baptized in the Jordan River, and tried to return to Constantinople. He got as far as Nicomedia, where he was baptized by its Arian bishop. Writes Eusebius, "When the due ceremonies were complete, he put on bright imperial clothes which shone like light, and rested on a pure white couch, being unwilling to touch a purple robe again. Then he lifted up his voice and offered up a prayer of thanksgiving to God, after which he went on to say, 'I know that now I am in the true sense blessed, that now I have been shown worthy of immortal life, that now I have received divine light.'" He died on May 22, 337.

His unification of the throne didn't survive him. His three surviving sons, each named some variant of "Constantine," fought it out, disastrously. Three decades after his death, in 361, the throne went to a nephew, Julian, known today as Julian the Apostate, the last pagan emperor. Julian, named for Caesar, rejected Christianity in an essay titled "Against the Galileans" and attempted to restore the old Greco-Roman gods via Neoplatonic Hellenism, a syncretic faith that also incorporated Egyptian and Syrian deities. While battling the Sassanid Persians, he was killed at the Battle of Samara in 363.

The centuries-old contest between emperor and king was over. Julian's last words were *Vicisti, Galilaee,* "You have won, Galilean."

Six

AETIUS AT THE CATALAUNIAN PLAINS

*The victory which the Roman general Aetius, with his Gothic al-
lies, had then gained over the Huns, was the last victory of Imperial Rome. But among the long Fasti of her triumphs, few can be
found that, for their importance and ultimate benefit to mankind,
are comparable with this expiring effort of her arms. It did not,
indeed, open to her any new career of conquest; it did not con-
solidate the relics of her power; it did not turn the rapid ebb of
her fortunes. The mission of Imperial Rome was, in truth, already
accomplished. . . . For no beneficial purpose to mankind could the
dominion of the seven-hilled city have been restored or prolonged.
But it was all-important to mankind what nations should divide
among them Rome's rich inheritance of empire . . .*

—Sir Edward Creasy, *The Fifteen Decisive Battles of the
World* (1851)

With Constantine's establishment of the New Rome at Constantinople, the Empire's center of gravity moved sharply east, to a spot
that was highly defensible and made doubly so by its magnificent fortifications, which were to last a millennium. As we have seen, from the
time of Augustus onward, the East had been the more desirable half of
the Roman imperium. It was where the money and foodstuffs were, in
rich provinces such as Syria and Egypt, the breadbasket. It was also the
tip of the Greco-Roman spear, positioned at the gateway to Europe and
thrusting into the heartland of the West's ancient enemies, the Persians,

the Parthians and other Iranian peoples and, with the coming of Islam in the seventh century, Arab and Turkish Muslims.

Rome, by contrast, was already widely viewed as a spent force. The forced subdivisions of the Tetrarchy had taken their toll on the very idea of Rome, and Romans had begun to get comfortable with the idea of Romanism without Rome. The emperors in the East continued to style themselves as "Romans,"[1] but Greek had supplanted Latin as the language of both the elite (it had always been thus[2]) and the citizenry. The virtues of the old Republic as limned by Livy, if they ever really existed as a rule instead of an exception, were long in the past, a past as ancient to the Romans as the voyages of Columbus are to contemporary Americans.

Constantine, born in the Balkans, had begun his rise to power in Roman Britain and had cemented it with his Italian campaign against Maxentius. He owed nothing to the Eternal City, rarely visited it after his triumph at the Milvian Bridge; for him, Rome had served its purpose. Further, the Goths and other barbarians were pushing closer, steadily eroding the frontiers from the days of Trajan, when the Empire was at its territorial height. In 378, at the Battle of Adrianople in what is today European Turkey near the Greek and Bulgarian borders, the eastern Roman forces under the emperor Valens were annihilated in one of the worst defeats in imperial history, and Valens himself killed, by a combined force of Goths and Alans.

In 402, the western emperor Honorius moved his capital from Milan to Ravenna, a city on the Adriatic, with a strong natural defensive position and a sea lane to Constantinople, on which he was by now almost entirely dependent. Under pressure in Italy from the Visigoths and dealing with increasing domestic civil strife, in the year 410 Honorius told his garrisons in Britain to look to their own defenses; no further help would be forthcoming. Roman Britain withered away. That same year,

---

1. Indeed, even after the Muslim Turks had conquered western Anatolia, they called the territory the Sultanate of Rum (Rome).

2. Constantine was something of an exception. He spoke in Latin and had to have his speeches translated into Greek.

the Christianized Visigoths under Alaric (an Arian, as it happened)—themselves under pressure in their traditional homeland from the Huns arriving from central Asia—sacked Rome. Rome was being eaten alive.

Without the legions to provide stability and territorial integrity, restive populations were on the move. Caesar had rounded up the Helvetians and sent them back to what's now Switzerland. But not even Caesar could have stopped the Great Migration that was now underway. After centuries of the stability of the *pax Romana,* the world was awash in the movement of peoples from east to west. Unlike today's wave of economic migrants, mostly coming from the global South, they did not come "in search of a better life"; they came because they had been forced by superior arms and ruthless butchery out of their homelands.

The ripple effects were first experienced in China and the Far East, far beyond the steppes of central Asia, then gradually swept westward, challenging the stability of dynasties everywhere. It was not a sudden, massive invasion of the European continent but a continuous flow of displaced humanity, bumping one another out of the way. The Celts had been pushed to the fringes of the British Isles by both the Romans and the Germanic tribes; the Germans and Slavs in central Europe in turn came under pressure from ravaging nomads to their east. Some of the names remain familiar even today, but others—the Suebi? The Pannonian Avars? The Gepids?—have vanished into history. As Sir Edward Creasy, a mid-nineteenth-century Briton very much of his own chauvinistic time and place, notes in *The Fifteen Decisive Battles of the World: From Marathon to Waterloo,* "Keep in mind, that the Roman empire in the West was not crushed by any sudden avalanche of barbaric invasion. The German conquerors came across the Rhine, not in enormous hosts, but in bands of a few thousand warriors at a time. The conquest of a province was the result of an infinite series of partial local invasions, carried on by little armies of this description." But it was relentless, nearly irresistible, and carried most everything before it.

Longstanding legend held that twelve vultures had circled the skies as Romulus founded the city of Rome, each one representing a century of power: therefore, Rome would survive for some twelve hundred years.

Given that the accepted date for the founding of the city by Romulus was 753 B.C., it seemed clear that time was running out.[3] The power vacuum in the west had given rise to all manner of ambitious men—and, behind the scenes, women—in the mad scramble to prepare for whatever came next. Terror made for strange bedfellows and even stranger alliances as various warlike peoples jousted for control of the Empire's husk by means both fair and foul. Even now, in its throes, the old Roman practice of hostage-taking came back into play one more time to set up one of history's unlikeliest confrontations: Attila the Hun versus the last of the great Roman generals, Flavius Aetius.

The biggest threat to Rome came from the Huns who—likely expelled from Kazakhstan by the invading Mongols—had crossed the Volga in 370 A.D., pushed the Alans (another nomadic tribe) out of the way, and made for Europe. The equestrian Huns, who sometimes even slept on horseback, were nothing like anything anyone in the West had ever seen. Appearing out of nowhere, merciless, pitiless, wielding their composite, curved bows that were deadly within a range of about eighty yards, they were practically infernal; a Hunnish horseman could lasso a mounted enemy in full gallop and drag him off his mount and to his death. They were also, according to Western accounts, spectacularly ugly, demonic. Their swarthy physiognomy terrified: "They are short in stature," observed the Gothic historian Jordanes, who wrote in Latin, "quick in bodily movement, alert horsemen, broad-shouldered, ready in the use of bow and arrow, and their firm-set necks are ever erect in pride . . . though they live in the form of men, they have the cruelty of wild beasts." Not for nothing would Attila come to be called "the Scourge of God." As Creasy notes:

> The armies of the Roman emperor that tried to check their progress were cut to pieces by them; and Panonia and other provinces

---

3. Creasy adds, "If to the twelve centuries denoted by the twelve vultures that appeared to Romulus, we add for the six birds that appeared to Remus six lustra, or periods of five years each, by which the Romans were wont to number their time, it brings us precisely to the year 476, in which the Roman empire was finally extinguished by Odoacer." Prophecy is a wonderful, flexible thing.

south of the Danube were speedily occupied by the victorious cavalry of these new invaders. Not merely the degenerate Romans, but the bold and hardy warriors of Germany and Scandinavia were appalled at the numbers, the ferocity, the ghastly appearance, and the lightning-like rapidity of the Huns. Strange and loathsome legends were coined and credited, which attributed their origin to the union of "Secret, black, and midnight hags" with the evil spirits of the wilderness.

Failures in battle are often attributed to insufficient piety, no matter the faith. "Sacrifice harder" was a belief fervently held by pagans, Christians, and later Muslims alike. The Semitic monotheist religions seem especially vulnerable to this misapprehension of the wheel of Fortune: the people were not up to the demands of their God, therefore that god is personally punishing them with defeat, humiliation, subjugation, misery. In the Jewish bible, the confident assurances of the prophets concerning the restoration of the Kingdom of Israel go unfulfilled, and gradually peter out until, after Yahweh's discomfiture at the hands of both Job (whose faithfulness he challenges in the most sadistic book in scripture) and Satan (who goads the weakening deity into it), he vanishes from the Jewish scriptures as an active character in the narrative.[4] By rearranging the sequence of the books of the Tanakh after the failure of the world to end and the heavenly kingdom to arrive shortly after the death of Jesus, Christianity put a forward spin on "prophecy" to explain away its failure; eventually, the promise of a heavenly if indefinite future became part of the religion's appeal.

Prophecy is best viewed in a rearview mirror: *post hoc, ergo propter hoc.* It has been the hallmark—and perhaps the defect—of all Christian denominations from the start. Both Judaism and early Christianity needed something upon which to found, justify, and/or support their

---

4. "God's last words are those he speaks to Job, the human being who dares to challenge not his physical power but his moral authority," writes Jack Miles in *God: A Biography.* "Reading from the end of the Book of Job onward, we see that it is Job who has somehow silenced God. God never speaks again, and he is decreasingly spoken of."

faiths, and they found it in "prophecy," primarily via the simple expedient of reverse-engineering it so that present-day occurrences could be explained and justified by appeals to an exasperatingly unspecific past authority.

Prayers to deities, however, rarely if ever demonstrably work, and in any case there's no earthly way to prove it one way or the other. Churches are burned with the faithful inside; pilgrims and penitents are slaughtered, Holocausts happen; the gods remain silent. As we shall soon see, the Mohammedans ascribed their calamities in the rollback of the *ummah* at the hands of the Franks during the First Crusade and throughout the Spanish *Reconquista* not to the Westerners' superior size, physical strength, armor, and steeds but to a paucity of Islamic piety. Religion is often the all-purpose excuse for defeat.

Of the beliefs of the Huns, we know comparatively little, largely because they were illiterate, but their practices were likely shamanistic. Temporal fidelity was given to charismatic warlords like Attila—which may also account for the rapid collapse of the Hunnish empire within a few years after Attila's death; even imaginary gods are generally made of sterner stuff. In any case, the Huns drove all before them: Ostrogoths and Visigoths alike; Romans and Byzantines. With their unfamiliar cavalry tactics (somewhat akin to those of the Plains Indians in North America millennia later) and consummate skill as riders, raiders, and fighters, they couldn't be beaten. When Constantinople was threatened, the eastern emperor Theodosius II bought them off with tribute (a practice that was to become habitual with the Byzantines) rather than engage them in battle. The poor hunkered down and prayed.

Improbable as it seems, it was at this moment in Western history that a man arose who actually *could* beat them, because he knew them, practically from childhood: Flavius Aetius, the Last Roman. Needless to say, his coming was not prophesied. By this time, both the Empire and the legions had long since ceased to be Roman, or even Italian. Their equipment and weapons were a poor imitation of what the legionaries once wielded. Their tactical skills had atrophied, and their ranks consisted largely of foreigners and foreign allies, called *foederati*.

Aetius himself was born c. 390 A.D. in what is today Bulgaria; his father, Gaudentius, was a Scythian provincial Roman general, his mother likely an Italian.[5]

An early fifth-century historian named Frigeridus described him: "Of middle height, he was manly in appearance and well made, neither too frail nor too heavy; he was quick of wit and agile of limb, a very practiced horseman and skilled archer; he was indefatigable with the spear. A born warrior, he was renowned for the arts of peace.... Undaunted in danger, he was excelled by none in the endurance of hunger, thirst, and vigil."

As a boy, under the imperial aegis, he was given as a hostage to Alaric, the barbarian king of the Visigoths and, later, to the Hunnish kings Uldin and Charaton. Living among the Huns, he learned their arts of war, including how to ride the way they did, how to shoot from horseback, and most of all, their battlefield tactics. Think of him as the Roman version of Arminius.

The Western emperor Honorius died in 423;[6] there was an eighteen-month struggle for power in the west between relatives of the eastern emperor, Theodosius II (who reigned for forty-two years in the east), and an elevated bureaucrat named Joannes, who was finally captured and executed by Theodosius, who then placed the youthful Valentinian III on the western throne; he therefore succeeded Julian the Apostate and the short-lived Jovian. Back among his people, Aetius, who as a fast-rising military figure had supported Joannes and was given the title of *curopalates* ("master of the palace"), had been sent into Hunnish territory to raise an army of Hun mercenaries to defend Joannes at Ravenna but returned with his troops to find that Joannes had already

---

5. None of these terms of what we today would call "ethnicity" or even "race" meant much. Even at this late stage, you were either a Roman or you weren't. Aetius was a Roman. Another danger of "presentism."

6. "During a long and disgraceful reign of twenty-eight years, Honorius, emperor of the West, was separated from the friendship of his brother, and later of his nephew, who reigned over the East; and Constantinople beheld, with apparent indifference and secret joy, the calamities of Rome" (Gibbon).

been deposed and killed. Thus was the origin of the bad blood between him and Valentinian, which eventually had fatal consequences for both of them.[7]

By this point the territorial integrity of what had been the Roman Empire for nearly half a millennium was an impolite fiction. In 439, the Vandals conquered what had been the Roman province of Africa, with Carthage as its capital, as well as parts of Numidia and Mauretania. Visigoths had taken northern Spain and southern Gaul. The Suebi[8] (a Germanic tribe that had once battled Caesar) occupied their own kingdom in Spanish Galicia, and one of their number, Ricimer, eventually became the de facto ruler of the Empire as the power behind the throne of various puppet emperors from roughly 456 to 472.

Most important of all were the Visigoths (western Goths, as distinct from the eastern Goths, called Ostrogoths), a Christianized tribe. The Visigoths had sacked Rome in 410 and eventually went into an uneasy coexistence with the Romans under Honorius after Alaric's death in 411; in 418 Theodoric I took over as the Visigothic king. Then in 451 Attila invaded Gaul. Now all the players were in place.

As it happens, one of the principal players was a woman, the princess Honoria, daughter of the redoubtable Placidia, and elder sister of Valentinian III. Placidia herself was the daughter of the emperor Theodosius (Roman regal bloodlines had become no less tangled than they had been in the days of the Julio-Claudians, nor power machinations less deadly), and she effectively acted as the power behind the throne of the childish Valentinian. Like other embarrassing Roman maidens—Augustus's trampy daughter Julia comes to mind—Honoria appears to have been a frisky lass who like so many Roman women deployed her sexuality as a weapon. Although given the exalted title of *Augusta*, she is supposed to have had an affair at sixteen with her chamberlain, one Eugenius, which resulted in pregnancy and her banishment to

---

7. Think of their poisonous relationship as akin to the that of General Maximus and the emperor Commodus in Ridley Scott's 2000 film *Gladiator*.

8. The name lives on today as Swabia/Schwabenland, a state in southern Germany. The Swabian dialect is one of the foundations of the High German language.

Constantinople, there to live alone among the sisters of the eastern emperor Theodosius and their virgin attendants. What was a girl to do?

She offered herself to Attila. By means of a eunuch, she boldly sent a kind of engagement ring to the Hunnish chieftain, who was even then preparing an attack on the Western Empire, having scourged the eastern half after the discovery of a plot by Theodosius to assassinate him. His plan was to saw off the Visigothic forces from their alliance of convenience with Valentinian via diplomacy and then destroy them before gobbling up Rome, but the Visigoths were holding firm. Honoria's precipitous offering of herself in marriage was at first rejected—Attila had plenty of wives with whom to indulge his ferocious sexual appetites—but then he realized Honoria's presumption had given him the perfect *casus belli*. When the horrified Romans disavowed the "engagement," the fierce Hun played the wronged lover and promptly struck out for Gaul. With the aid of some Frankish and other vassal allies, Attila assembled an enormous army, crossed the Rhine, and, after defeating several minor powers, made his way into what today is modern France.

In raising a force to confront Attila, Aetius had to concentrate on first winning the direct conflict and then winning the peace. He had to ensure that his alliance with the Visigoths under Theodoric would hold, given that the effete young men of Italy (Gibbon's characterization) "trembled at the sound of the trumpet" and had no desire to experience bloodshed. This he did via the embassy of one Avitus,[9] a retired Roman senator living in the Auvergne, who went directly to the fence-sitting Visigothic king and passionately explained that if he did not join Aetius in the defense of Gaul, his territory would be next on Attila's list of conquests. This was no easy task, since Aetius had earlier frustrated Theodoric's expansionist desires at the Battle of Arelate (modern Arles) using Hunnish allies to turn back the Visigoths.

Now the tables were turned, and Aetius needed his former enemy to help fight off his former friends. "The lively eloquence of Avitus

---

9. Who later briefly ruled the Western Empire between July 455 and October 456. After he was deposed by the forces of Ricimer, he was forced to become the bishop of Piacenza, and died shortly thereafter. Thus were church and state freely mixed in the late Roman Empire—a sign of the increasing ascendancy of the former over the latter.

inflamed the Gothic warriors, by the description of the injuries which their ancestors had suffered from the Huns; whose implacable fury still pursued them from the Danube to the foot of the Pyrenees. He strenuously urged that it was the duty of every Christian to save from sacrilegious violation the churches of God and the relics of the saints; that it was the interest of every Barbarian who had acquired a settlement in Gaul to defend the fields and vineyards, which were cultivated for his use, against the desolation of the Scythian shepherds." The aging Theodoric (he was about sixty) not only agreed to join the fight but to lead his troops personally, assisted by his two sons, Thorismond and Theodoric.

Even as the battle loomed, Aetius was already looking beyond the immediate outcome to the larger picture: To the preservation of at least those bits of the Western Empire in Italy and parts of Gaul, and to a practical working partnership with the east. To the maintenance of the Roman alliances with the Christianized barbarians and the establishment of what we might today term "common ground" for the evolution of the entire Empire. To the full integration of the Goths and other tribes into the Roman customs, laws, and now religion. And to his place in this new world order.

Aetius knew the fight to preserve Rome as she once had been was long lost. Nothing lasts forever; the vultures that were feeding on Rome had been circling since the baby's birth. Now they were thick in the lowering sky. As Aetius saw it, a victory against Attila would benefit Rome but even more would benefit the Visigoths; Theodoric had brought his sons along for reasons of state as well as military necessity. Even in triumph, Aetius would have trouble down the line controlling his Visigothic allies. But that was a price he was prepared to pay, given the immediate objective.

Further, what in the end would victory gain him, politically? Valentinian would always hate him, for both personal and professional reasons. Both men knew Aetius, like every other ambitious general—most far less distinguished than he, the *Magister Militum*—had his eyes on the prize, and that Valentinian was a most unworthy Caesar. A triumphant Aetius might easily sweep away the Valentinian dynasty. Failing that, Aetius was even entertaining thoughts of arranging a political marriage between his son Gaudentius and Valentinian's daughter

Placidia.[10] And there remained still, even in the wake of the Council of Nicaea, a ferocious and ongoing theological battle between the orthodox Christians (Jesus, fully God and fully Man) and the Arians (fully God, but not fully Man) that was now being fought at the imperial level. Internecine warfare among the Christians was gnawing on the entrails of the dying Empire when it could least afford it.

Finally, he and Attila had been friends of a sort, not that that would mean anything in battle. As the Roman Civil War showed, warriors put their personal feelings aside when it came to conflict and combat; there was no room for sentimentality on the battlefield, no time to weep ("like a woman"), no time to mourn. No time for magnanimity, no time for mercy. War is compartmentalization, a virtue much disparaged in an age of "intersectionality" that elevates victimhood above all else. Even at the end, a true Roman refused to be a victim, and in fact had contempt for them. Of one thing we can be certain: he wasn't afraid. The last of the Romans would do his duty and, if necessary, *pro patria mori*.

A word about the battlefield. As noted, ancient commanders spent a great deal of time choosing the right battlespace whenever possible—one that suited their troops and tactics while putting the enemy at as much of a disadvantage as possible. Making the enemy fight you on the turf of your choice could be critical to success or failure. The champagne country east of Paris and south and west of the modern border regions of Belgium, Luxembourg, and Germany, flat and open, with few hills, is among the most fought-over pieces of land on earth. The Battle of the Catalaunian Plains, sometimes called the battle of Châlons, is the second notice Western history takes of this region; in the year 274, the emperor Aurelian defeated the Gallic chieftain Tetricus I there to regain control over that part of Gaul. Centuries later, the general area would become the principal warring ground between France and Germany during the Franco-Prussian War (the pivotal Battle of Sedan); World War I (St.-Mihiel), and World War II (the Bulge). Entering Gaul, Attila and his troops went on a rampage; with the legions gone, the countryside was very nearly defenseless.

The battle was precipitated by Attila's attempted siege of Aurelianum

---

10. This betrothal was actually contracted in 454 but never enacted, as we shall see.

(modern Orleans). Leading his hastily assembled army (with very few actual Romans), Aetius got there ahead of the Hun and, entrenched, scared Attila off. Presenting himself to the other peoples of Gaul (Celts, Alans, Franks, Suebians, Germans, Sarmatians), Aetius managed to cobble together a kind of coalition in opposition to Attila and force the Hun, now checked, away from Orleans. The steppe barbarians were not especially skilled in siege warfare or even pitched, set-piece battles; hit and run was more their style.

And so when Attila heard of the approach of a combined Roman-Visigothic army, which included a large contingent of Alans who had settled in and around Orleans, he prudently withdrew to the north and east. He could not afford a defeat this deep into Gaul, far from home, with no hope for reinforcements and living off the land. His entire army, and thus his whole rationale for trying to conquer Gaul, would go up in the smoke of battle. He decided to retreat to the relative safety of the stretch of open country between Troye and Châlons, where his cavalry (largely useless in a siege) could be most effective. It was the only move he could make. The Huns, after all, were offensive, not defensive, warriors. At the Battle of the Catalaunian Plains, that would be their downfall.

Attila moved north and east, trailed by Aetius and his Visigothic allies, and took up a position on the west bank of the River Seine for a decisive confrontation. A wide-open plain was highly prized by commanders who could make effective use of cavalry and who had a huge infantry force that could be strung out widely to prevent flanking and envelopment by a numerically inferior adversary—and cavalry, of course, was the source of the Hun's overwhelming blitzkrieg power.[11] With the river at his back, it would act as a barrier to any pursuing Romans should the battle go sideways.

Arriving from the west, threading his way through some hills, Aetius arranged his men across the plain from the Huns. He was not at the disadvantage one might have suspected. Aetius had cavalry too, both in

---

11. Scholars and historians have attempted for centuries to place the battle exactly, with little or no success. "The vast plains of Châlons-sur-Marne," says Creasy. Gibbon identifies it as "Catalaunian fields [which] spread themselves round Châlons."

his center and on his right flank, where he stationed the Visigoths under Theodoric, but his forces were also partially protected by the treed hills to his flanks and rear that would make it tough for the Hunnish horsemen to get behind them.

To say the stakes were high on both sides is an understatement. Of Attila's frame of mind, we can reasonably expect that while confident of victory—when had he ever failed?—he was far from home, his forces partly ad hoc and of uncertain loyalty. Further, he knew that in Aetius he faced his most formidable opponent, a man who could equal him in bravery and fortitude, both a supreme commander and a consummate politician; here, at the end of Empire, Rome sent forth her last great son to show the world, for the final time, what it meant to be a Roman. Finally, a defeat here would shatter the myth of Hunnish invincibility; having clawed his way to the top over the bodies of his father and his brother, Bleda (whom he probably murdered), Attila—like Alexander before him—could not afford a single loss.

The Hun gave an address to his troops, practically Alexandrine in nature. He reminded them of their past victories over foes from central Asia to Gaul. This would be the culmination of everything they had fought for, and achieved. No one could defeat them, certainly not the dissipated, earthbound Romans, with their cowardly shield walls and close formations and manifest physical and moral weakness. "I myself will throw the first javelin, and the wretch who refuses to imitate the example of his sovereign is devoted to inevitable death," Gibbon reports.

The result was, according to the sixth-century Ostrogothic historian Cassiodorus, "a conflict fierce, various, obstinate and bloody; such as could not be paralleled either in the present or in past ages." All Europe and parts of central Asia were represented on the field that day. A conflict that had arisen as an inevitable byproduct of the Great Migration and its concomitant violent displacement (for such displacement is rarely if ever ameliorated by good will, a *Willkommenkultur,* or international peacekeeping agencies) was about to take place, and would decide the fate of the European continent for centuries to come. As Gibbon notes: "The nations from the Volga to the Atlantic were assembled on the plain of Châlons; but many of these nations had been divided by faction, or conquest, or emigration; and the appearance of similar arms and ensigns, which threatened each other, presented the image of a civil war."

As for Aetius . . . what was he thinking? Did he understand the significance of what was about to happen? In hindsight, it's tempting for us living in the world that Aetius in part made, and which is even now undergoing the same internal and external stresses that were then tearing the Roman world asunder, to see the Battle of the Catalaunian Plains in modern terms: as a social problem to be solved peacefully, or as ethnic conflict (it was no such thing, as the passage quoted above from Gibbon clearly indicates) suitable for amelioration.

Such options, however, were not available to the ancients, who much preferred force to reason when diplomacy had failed; long before Clausewitz, they understood that violence really was diplomacy *with* other means. There were no fleets of diplomats or lawyers to gad about, flinging writs, resolutions, and white papers in all directions; the world was not that of *Jarndyce and Jarndyce*. Intelligence was mostly rudimentary, although it did exist, and had for thousands of years; think of book 10 (possibly a later interpolation) of the *Iliad,* called the *Doloneia,* in which Odysseus and Diomedes undertake to scout the Trojan position, encounter Dolon (a Trojan spy coming to snoop on them), promise him safety, interrogate him, kill him,[12] wreak havoc behind the Trojan lines, and then return to the Greek camp for a ritual, purifying bath. Indeed, a large element of ancient warfare involved simply finding the enemy—a problem that persisted beyond the age of aviation during World War I and into the Second World War.

And so it was that a Gallo-Roman Christian Western army now faced off against the largely but not entirely pagan Hunnish-Ostrogothic forces from the East. One of the recurring themes of European history—one dating back to the Trojan War—was about to be reenacted. Both sides needed a decisive battle: Attila, in order to break his most formidable opposition and thus clear the way for his continuing conquest of Gaul; and Aetius, because if Rome lost today there would be no tomorrow, since

---

12. For which war crime Dante placed both Greek heroes in the eighth circle of Hell.

his fickle Visigothic allies would quickly scatter, leaving the Empire defenseless.

The Hun had already gone into fortified camp as he watched Aetius and Theodoric arrive. The Visigothic forces were largely on horseback, while Aetius's troops were mostly infantry (standard Roman practice right to the end). In classic battle formation, each side divided into three sections. counterintuitively, the canny Aetius put the Alans under their king Sangiban, the least trustworthy of his allies, in the center; at the siege of Orleans, the story went, Sangiban had offered to open the gates of the city to Attila—treachery that was prevented by Aetius's timely arrival. Accordingly, Aetius flanked the Alans with his own forces on the left and put the Visigoths on the right.

As June 20, the day of the battle, dawned, a comet flew across the sky. Attila, meanwhile, had been consulting his soothsayers and haruspices, who could read the future in entrails and burnt bones. The omens were not good: the Huns would be defeated, but at least the opposing commander would be killed. We may suppose that Attila believed that would be his old friend and now archenemy (on this day, at least) Aetius. The shamans, notes Gibbon, "reported that, after scrutinizing the entrails of victims and scraping their bones, they revealed, in mysterious language, his own defeat, with the death of his principal adversary; and that the Barbarian, by accepting the equivalent, expressed his involuntary esteem for the superior merit of Aetius." The divines were correct, but it wasn't Aetius who would die.

Earlier, while awaiting Aetius's arrival, Attila had noted the presence of the small ridge on the left of the battlefield as he faced it and, correctly, sent a small detachment of cavalry to occupy it—likely not for offensive reasons, but to disrupt Aetius's deployment and string out his right flank. Aetius, with a superior tactical sense, took the bait and sent a detachment of cavalry under King Theodoric's son Thorismond to take the ridge, driving off the Huns, even though it meant a nearly four-hour delay in his positioning. This textbook move, however, would prove critical later in the day.

Aetius thus anchored his right flank on the ridge while on his left he was shielded by a thick forest; meanwhile, behind him was a sloping upland that would afford him some measure of protection against

Attila's cavalry should he be forced to beat a defensive retreat. He had no intention of moving out onto the plain where Attila's slightly superior numbers and greater mobility could flank him. He would force Attila to come to him, crashing head-on into his shield walls and stronger infantry. Aetius knew there was no way Attila could resist; never defeated, on a battlefield of his own choosing, at the head of the greatest cavalry force on the continent, and determined never to retreat . . . Attila was now right where Aetius wanted him.

Thus was the battle joined. To the east, Attila took the leader's customary place in the center, at the head of his unbeatable cavalry. On his left, he deployed his Ostrogoths, directly opposite their Visigothic counterparts, while on his right, confronting Aetius and his Romans, he placed his Gepid allies.[13] Whereas Aetius and Theodoric shared command, Attila was supreme and personally led the opening charge of the Hunnish cavalry against the Roman center's weak spot, the Alans. By rights, this gambit should have given Attila an immediate, possibly dispositive, advantage. The centers generally were the strongest part of an army's formation, and in the bloody chess match of warfare, to command the center was to hold the upper hand. But Aetius, making a virtue out of necessity, gambled that the lure of the Alans in the center would suck Attila's blunt force into the same kind of trap in which the Romans had found themselves more than six hundred years earlier at Cannae: a double envelopment.

And so it was directly at the center that Attila charged, his Huns swooping down in bunches, loosing volleys of arrows, then wheeling, turning, and charging again. Frozen in place, the mounted Alans and the Roman foot soldiers to their immediate left remained steadfast, absorbing the punishment for hours; it was no mean feat for men on horseback to stand in place. But they did not, would not, break: an unhorsed or dismounted cavalryman is soon a dead cavalryman.[14]

---

13. The Gepids were an eastern Germanic Arian Christian tribe that had been swallowed up by the Huns and absorbed into their empire in 375. After Attila's death in 453, they took a leading role in the revolt against the Huns.

14. As both George Armstrong Custer and Major Marcus Reno discovered at the Battle of the Little Bighorn in 1876. See chapter 10 of *Last Stands* for the gruesome details.

At this point, it appears that Attila ordered a general charge, with the tip of the spear again heading straight for the Roman center. This time, the weakened Alans finally broke, splitting the center line. The Roman allies moved some of their cavalry into place to plug the gaps, but now Attila unleashed his Gothic infantry, who came running across the plain at full tilt, colliding with both wings of Aetius's overall forces. It was now hand-to-hand combat with spear and sword at its most elemental, a throwback to the glory days of the legions who, even at this late stage, knew how to fight this kind of war. Meanwhile, Aetius continued to hold his left flank ready.

On the right, it was a different story. The Visigoths were hard-pressed as it was, but then King Theodoric went down while rallying his men. Some say he was killed by a spear; others, that he was unhorsed and trampled to death in the melee. Attila didn't realize it at the time, but half of the prophecy was fulfilled. Now for the other half. Aetius signaled to Thorismond and his cavalry, largely forgotten by the Huns on the ridge at the far right of the allied flank, to enter the fray. Charging down the slope, he quickly flanked the Ostrogoth infantry—the men who had just killed his father—and cut them down. What was left of the Ostrogoths fled the field.

Now, for the first time in his military career, Attila was in trouble. Aetius and the Romans had steadied the center against which Attila had expended so much energy and so many men; and the Visigoths under Thorismund were now threatening to get behind him. Aetius had been proven right: a double envelopment—nonsurvivable—loomed. Before he could be surrounded, Attila broke off and ordered a general retreat back to his fortified camp at the far side of the battlefield near the river. Thorismund pressed his advantage, getting so far ahead of his allies that he charged right into the Hunnish camp and was even thrown from his horse. With the help of some of his men, he cut his way out. In the chaos, Aetius became separated from his troops and camped that night with the Goths, protected as best they could behind a makeshift shield wall in case the Huns struck again.

Meanwhile, in Attila's camp, nobody knew what to do. That the Huns had failed was beyond question. Still, they were safe, couched behind strong fortifications. None of Attila's allies, no matter how bloodied, thought of slipping away during the night. Instead, martial music sounded defiantly, and those of Aetius's forces who approached were turned away by a shower of arrows. Attila, no doubt, brooded over this strange and abrupt change of fortune. For the first time in his life, his gods had forsaken him.

The allies decided not to force the issue but to besiege Attila in his camp by isolating him and preventing reprovisioning. They would starve him out and force a humiliating and costly peace upon him and then send him packing, because even had Aetius wanted to keep fighting he was in no position to do so. The Alans had taken up to 70 percent causalities by some estimates. His Visigoths had also taken a beating, as had the Huns, with casualty rates of up to 40 percent.[15] There wasn't much fight left in anybody.

The body of Theodoric was found the next day, and was buried where he fell. The Huns failed to sally forth that morning in an attempt to break the siege lines, but in fact Aetius had gambled that they would not and instead counseled Thorismond to return to the Visigoth's seat of power in Toulouse and protect his interests there. Thorismond lusted to avenge his father, but he knew that Aetius was right, and so he and his men departed to assert and defend his claim to the throne. (This was wise, as his brothers were itching to succeed Theodoric; two years later, in 453, Thorismond was murdered and succeeded by his brother Theodoric II, who reigned for thirteen years.) In any case, the last thing a weakened Aetius needed at this moment was for the angry Visigoths to now turn on *him*.

For his part, Attila fully expected an assault on his camp. When he saw Thorismond's Visigoths ride off, he assumed it was a feint, another Roman trick. He was not about to fall into two of Aetius's traps in the same fight. And so he barricaded himself inside his camp, ready to go down fighting and taking everybody and everything with him.[16] Notes Creasy:

---

15. To allow his Germanic allies to take the brunt of the casualties might have been Aetius's plan as well. Notes Gibbon, "The Imperial general was soon satisfied of the defeat of Attila, who still remained inactive within his intrenchments; and, when he contemplated the bloody scene, he observed, with secret satisfaction, that the loss had principally fallen on the Barbarians."

16. As we have seen, as far back as Darius, kings often brought all their valuables with

Expecting an assault on the morrow, Attila stationed his best archers in front of the cars and waggons, which were drawn up as a fortification along his lines, and made every preparation for a desperate resistance. But the "Scourge of God" resolved that no man should boast of the honour of having either captured or slain him; and he caused to be raised in the centre of his encampment a huge pyramid of the wooden saddles of his cavalry: round it he heaped the spoils and the wealth that he had won; on it he stationed his wives who had accompanied him in the campaign; and on the summit he placed himself, ready to perish in the flames, and baulk the victorious foe of their choicest booty, should they succeed in storming his defences.

The combatants eyed each other warily across the field for two days. Although the battle at this point was technically a draw, Aetius's objectives had been satisfied. The Hunnish invasion of Gaul had been stopped cold, and Attila had suffered heavy losses, in large part thanks to the unsung bravery of the underestimated Alans, who at this point largely vanish from the history books, but with honor. Worse, his prestige had suffered a blow from which it never recovered. The Christian God had stopped the Scourge of God.

In hindsight, Attila lost because Aetius forced him to fight a Roman battle, not a Hunnish one. Additionally, several hundred years of living in and in proximity to the Roman Empire had taught the once-undisciplined Germans that individual courage on the *Schlachtfeld* was not enough to defeat a more militarily disciplined and tactically more sophisticated enemy, and they had learned from the Roman example. From the time of the Greeks, the Western way of war had proven superior to the Eastern, and it now had done so once more.[17]

The aftermath is quickly told. Attila withdrew under cover of darkness.

---

them to the battlefield, including their wives, children, and treasury, on the theory that if they were killed, it didn't matter, but if victorious, they wanted to make sure their possessions were intact upon their return home.

17. Gibbon: "Attila was compelled to retreat. He had exposed his person with the rashness of a private soldier; but the intrepid troops of the centre had pushed forwards beyond the rest of

He wasn't finished with the Romans yet, though. He wanted revenge, and besides, there was still that business with Honoria, which he hoped would gain him access to Constantinople. He crossed the Alps into Italy and sacked Aquileia, then considered one of the great cities of the world along with Rome, Constantinople, Alexandria, and Antioch. Located at the head of the Adriatic, Aquileia was so thoroughly raped and ravaged that it was unrecognizable. Attila's further predations in northeastern Italy, combined with earlier Gothic invasions, so terrified the residents of the area that the inhabitants of cities around the lagoon fled to the nearby islands, thus establishing the city of Venice.

Attila continued south, heading for Rome, but his weakened army was nowhere near the invincible force it once had been. Illness, perhaps plague, had ravaged his troops, he was short on supplies, and back home, the Romans under the eastern emperor Marcian (ruled 450–457) were launching attacks into Hun territory. In 452, Pope Leo I ("the Great") traveled north from Rome to meet Attila in his camp, somewhere near Mantua, where he dissuaded the Hun from sacking the Eternal City; the meeting is commemorated by a great fresco in the Apostolic Palace of the Vatican executed c. 1514 by Raphael and some of his acolytes.

Leo was the first great political Pope, a worthy successor not to St. Peter but to the Good Emperors such as Antoninus Pius and Marcus Aurelius a couple of hundred years earlier, whose offices and authority the popes were now attempting to claim. The seat of temporal power was in Ravenna; into the power vacuum moved the popes in Rome, signifying the imminent triumph of the Church as the true successor to Augustus and Tiberius, in whose reigns the faith had begun. It was also at this point that Christianity shed the last of its Jewish roots, especially since they were no longer needed as a protective cover for the new faith. The Jesus Cult had now become a European faith, with its moral center in Rome—"the Kingdom of the Wicked"—not Jerusalem. The son had outgrown the father and was now prepared to make his own way in the world. What had Athens—or Rome—to do with Jerusalem, indeed?

Leo's ascendance also marked the triumph of what Christian scholars

---

the line; their attack was faintly supported; their flanks were unguarded; and the conquerors of Scythia and Germany were saved by the approach of the night from a total defeat."

refer to as the "proto-orthodox" wing of Christianity, the Nicaeanists who believed as a matter of dogma in the dual nature of Christ as both God and man. This was codified at the Council of Chalcedon in 451 (making it contemporaneous with the battle of the Catalaunian Plains), which also dogmatized the Nicene Creed. Additionally, Leo codified proto-orthodox Christian belief in his great *Tome* of 499, which categorically rejected Monophysitism.[18] Ultimately, the Council of Chalcedon's dictates led to the Great Schism of 1054 between Roman Catholicism and Eastern Orthodoxy; the mutually excommunicative break over whether the third person of the Trinity, the Holy Spirit, proceeds from both the Father and the Son (Catholic) or from the Father *through* the Son (Eastern). Ironically, the schism occurred during the reign of Pope Leo IX (1049–1054) and, as we shall soon see, contributed to the launching of the First Crusade in 1095.

We don't know what transpired between the Hun and the *pontifex maximus.*[19] The story goes like this: Leo knelt before the barbarian and pleaded with him to spare Rome: "The people of Rome, once conquerors of the world, now kneel conquered. We pray for mercy and deliverance. O Attila, you could have no greater glory than to see suppliant at your feet this people before whom once all peoples and kings lay suppliant. You have subdued, O Attila, the whole circle of the lands granted to the Romans. Now we pray that you, who have conquered others, should conquer yourself. The people have felt your scourge. Now they would feel your mercy." At that moment Saints Peter and Paul appeared by his side, wielding flaming swords at the head of an enormous host of Christian soldiers. The Hun, terrified, swore eternal peace and withdrew.

Everything went downhill for Attila from there. The emperor Marcian stopped paying tribute and continued to harass him militarily, across the Danube, with a Byzantine force under the command of a general also named, of all things, Aetius. Plague broke out among the

---

18. The belief that Jesus's true nature was fully divine and his human body merely a carapace.

19. Leo may have been the first pope to adopt the religious title that had belonged to both Caesar and Augustus, although most scholars believe it didn't come into regular use until the Renaissance.

Huns. Furious, Attila was plotting a strike against Constantinople to reclaim his tribute and to demand the hand of the renegade princess Honoria when, in March of 453, he died. The night before, he had added a new wife ("Ildico," probably a German girl) to his collection and celebrated uproariously, drinking in a way to make Alexander the Great proud. He was found the next morning, covered in blood but with no signs of wounds, his new bride weeping over his dead body. Most likely, it was some kind of esophageal hemorrhage, brought on by a lifetime of excessive bibulation. In any case, he died as he had lived—in the saddle.

As per the Hunnish custom, his men mourned him by slashing their faces—no weeping for them—riding their horses wildly around his tent, and then burying him in a triple coffin of gold inside silver inside iron along with his most precious possessions. Then they killed every man involved in the preparation of the body, so that his secrets and his wealth would die with him, safe from predators. According to legend, that same night the emperor Marcian had a dream in which a god appeared to him holding Attila's broken bow as proof of his death.

Aetius, whose courage, experience, fortitude, and tactical genius had not only saved Rome one last time but assured that the future of Europe for the next two thousand years would be Christian, succeeded in betrothing his son Gaudentius to Valentinian's daughter Eudoxia, thus hoping to ensure his own safety in the collapsing empire while positioning himself within striking distance of the throne. But the jealous, suspicious Valentinian was too quick for him. He summoned his hero general to a private meeting with himself and his attendant eunuch, Heraclius, who had inflamed the thirty-five-year-old emperor against the man who had saved his throne. Suspecting nothing—Aetius disdained personal protection against a man he despised as a weakling and a coward—he entered the palace alone. Gibbon describes what happened next:

Whilst he urged, perhaps with intemperate vehemence, the marriage of his son, Valentinian, drawing his sword, the first sword he had ever drawn, plunged it in the breast of a general who had saved his empire; his courtiers and eunuchs ambitiously struggled to imitate their master; and Aetius, pierced with an hundred wounds, fell dead in the royal presence. Boethius, the Prætorian præfect, was killed at the same moment; and, before the event could be divulged, the principal friends of the patrician were summoned to the palace, and separately murdered.

Thus, the last of the great Romans died the way one of the first of the great Romans had: by treachery and perfidy and the sword. Julius Caesar's death had sealed the end of the Roman Republic. Now Aetius's told the death of the Empire.

Fate soon enough caught up with Valentinian. By subterfuge, he raped the virtuous wife of a wealthy senator, Petronius Maximus. As luck would have it, Valentinian had imprudently placed a couple of Aetius's loyalists among his palace guard, and this enormity was all they needed. While Valentinian was observing some Roman soldiers at sport at the Campus Martius, these men, at Petronius's behest, drew their swords, cut down the eunuch, and, unopposed, stabbed Valentinian III through the heart. The date was March 16, 455. History rhymes.

The Western Roman Empire lasted twenty-one more years, during which time it went through nine more emperors, among whom was the wronged Petronius (whose reign lasted two months) and Majorian, who reconquered some lost territory before being outmaneuvered by Ricimer and executed, and concluding with the boy Romulus Augustulus, deposed by the barbarian general Odoacer in 476. The final years were marked by increasingly punitive taxation, economic irresponsibility, and a vast gulf between rich and poor, one exacerbated by the open contempt the upper classes felt for the lower. The people fled the cities, preferring life among the encroaching barbarians. The last few provinces broke away as the ruling class issued more and more proscriptive laws against their former countrymen. A dispirited populace "abjured and abhorred the name of Roman citizens, which had formerly excited the ambition of mankind." They were ashamed of themselves, and of Rome. There's a lesson to be learned here.

Let us conclude this part of our story by giving the last word to Gibbon. Referring to the prophecy of the twelve vultures, he writes:

This prophecy, disregarded perhaps in the season of health and prosperity, inspired the people with gloomy apprehensions, when the twelfth century, clouded with disgrace and misfortune, was almost elapsed; and even posterity must acknowledge with some surprise that the arbitrary interpretation of an accidental or fabulous circumstance has been seriously verified in the downfall of the Western empire. . . . If all the Barbarian conquerors had been annihilated in the same hour, their total destruction would not have restored the empire of the West; and, if Rome still survived, she survived the loss of freedom, of virtue, and of honour.

Rome was dead. The crucified Galilean had indeed won, his appointed heirs now ruling with the barbarians among the ruins, but keeping the memory of empire alive in their religious rituals, their dress, their borrowed titles and trappings of office, and their inexorable extension of temporal and spiritual power to encompass what once had been the realm of both Jupiter and the Caesars. As the skeptical Gibbon notes: "The church of Rome defended by violence the empire which she had acquired by fraud."

What if Attila had won, killed Aetius and the Visigothic king, seized their possessions in Gaul? Certainly, it would have hastened the end of the Western Empire. Emboldened and undefeated, Attila would have had the wind in his sails as he swooped down on the Italian peninsula with Rome in his sights. Would Pope Leo, aided by Saints Peter and Paul, have stopped him? Doubtful. The long-suffering cities of the West would have absorbed another sacking, their walls razed, their valuables plundered, and their women and children carted off to sexual and actual slavery.

But the savage Huns would still have fallen apart after Attila's death, and their empire still would have collapsed. The Huns offered nothing to replace Christianity as the glue holding the West together in the absence of Rome, no civilizational ethos, no moral code, no intellectual achievements, no reason, no art, no beauty. Only savagery. In the end, the result would have been more or less the same, but with this difference: the men of the West had fought the barbarians to their last breath, and not surrendered in terror.

And so Europe entered a period that has come to be known as the Dark Ages. The embryonic nation-states began to coalesce. In the absence of central authority, warlords in the form of princes and dukes created their own fiefdoms on the Continent. In Gaul, Clovis of the Franks established the first French monarchy. In far-off Britain and Ireland, almost as isolated as they had been at the time of Julius Caesar, Christian monks nursed the remnants of classical civilization as best they could. In the sixth century, the emperor Justinian in Constantinople managed to reconquer parts of Italy and North Africa under general Belisarius.[20] But those gains were quickly frittered away.

And then, starting around 622, a militarized prophet arose in obscure Arabia, one Muhammad, preaching at sword point a new form of monotheism called Islam. Within ten years he had captured the Arabian peninsula. After his death in 632, his ferocious votaries swarmed across the remnants of dying empires, conquering Persia and destroying the Sassanids and their Zoroastrian faith. Roman Syria fell, and Egypt, and all of North Africa. Arab armies crossed the Strait of Gibraltar and conquered formerly Roman Spain and Lusitania, and, as the English historian Henry Hallam noted, "within about two years the name of Mohammed was invoked under the Pyrenees."

Arab raiders scourged the Mediterranean coasts, carrying off thousands, perhaps millions of slaves, many of the women and boys destined for the harems and the armies of the caliphs, a crime completely forgotten today. Italians in the coastal cities moved inland, erecting towns on rocky outcrops to escape Muslim depredation. The Greco-Romans of Constantinople now had to factor in a new opponent, one less inclined to accept financial blandishments in lieu of rapine and religious conquest. There was no god but Allah, they proclaimed, and Muhammad was his Prophet—the last in the line of Semitic prophets that had begun with the Hebrews and continued through the early Christians, including Jesus of Nazareth. His, they averred, was the final revelation. The history of man's interaction with the One God was now over. All that remained was for the true faith of the Believers to be accepted worldwide.

What would come next? It would take six hundred years to find out, in a strange place at the other end of the world the Europeans would come to call *Outremer*.

---

20. For more details on Belisarius, see *The Savior Generals* by Victor Davis Hanson (2014).

Seven

BOHEMOND AT DORYLAEUM
AND ANTIOCH

The sacred armies, and the godly knight,
That the great sepulchre of Christ did free,
I sing; much wrought his valor and foresight,
And in that glorious war much suffered he;
In vain 'gainst him did Hell oppose her might,
In vain the Turks and Morians armed be:
His soldiers wild, to brawls and mutinies prest,
Reduced he to peace, so Heaven him blest.
—TORQUATO TASSO, *LA GERUSALEMME LIBERATA* (JERUSALEM
DELIVERED), TRANSLATED BY EDWARD FAIRFAX

IN THE HISTORY OF WESTERN WARFARE, THERE'S NEVER BEEN ANY-thing to equal it: fired by religious zealotry and lured by a lust for com-bat and conquest, in just four years an unorganized group of squabbling petty noblemen, united not by race[1] or lineage or language but by a shared faith, raised their own private armies, transported them by land or ship or some combination of both across two thousand miles of often hostile and inhospitable territory, provisioned them on the fly, and fought their way—sometimes through nominal friend, most often

---

1. The word is used in the ancient, not the contemporary sense; today we might call it "ethnicity," a word unknown to the residents of medieval Europe.

through dedicated religious foe—all the way from France, Germany, and Italy to Constantinople and Jerusalem. And won.

Although often ritualistically (and retrospectively) condemned today as prima facie evidence of European colonialism, racism, anti-Semitism, territorial aggression, and other assorted modern evils, the Crusades as a whole and the First Crusade in particular must be assessed reasonably, rationally, and, above all, dispassionately within their historical context. This has been a challenge facing historians practically from the time of the Crusades—extraordinarily well-chronicled by both Christian and Muslim writers at the time and the subject of historical inquiry and interrogation ever since. Called everything from "iniquitous and unjust" to "the greatest event since the Resurrection," the Crusades and their theological foundations have served as a touchstone for scholars—religious, agnostic, atheist, or otherwise—since the first histories were first compiled in the very last year of the eleventh century for Pope Urban II, the man who had launched the First Crusade with an inspiring address at Clermont in the year 1095.[2]

Writes Crusades scholar Christopher Tyerman in his *Chronicles of the First Crusade 1096–1099*: "However viewed, the crusades constitute one of the great subjects of European history. They conjure issues of the manifestation of systems of transcendent belief; cultural and religious identity; economic and political expansion; imperialism and colonisation; the ideology, legitimacy and pathology of public violence; the experience of war; the impact of militarism on non-combatants, host societies and victim communities; inter-ethnic and inter-faith relations; the nature of popular political and religious action; state-building; and the use of propaganda. The crusades remain one of the few subjects of professional history that carry wide popular recognition even if little serious understanding."

No matter one's political stance, one thing is immediately clear. The Crusades, which lasted from 1096 until the failure of the Ninth Crusade in 1292, were an epochal event in world history. With the collapse of the Western Roman Empire in 476, Europe entered the period colloquially

---

2. The idea was not original with Urban, but with his predecessor, Gregory VII, who had briefly entertained such a venture.

known as the Dark Ages, exacerbated by the Arab conquests of the Levant, North Africa, Syria, and Anatolia during the seventh and eighth centuries, which cut the West off from its civilizational and religious moorings in ancient Greece, the Holy Land, and the eastern Byzantine Empire. The Latin language—the *lingua franca*—fractured into the multiple Romance languages of the emerging nation-states, including French, Italian, Portuguese, Spanish, and Romanian; via the Normans, it even found its way into what became English by blending with the Anglo-Saxon and Celtic tongues of the British Isles.

The logistical requirements of such a vast undertaking as the Crusades had the knock-on result of reopening contact and trade with the East, especially as the maritime Italian city-states such as Genoa, Amalfi, Pisa, and Venice emerged as formidable commercial seagoing powers. The entrepenurial wealth of Italy made possible the Renaissance as early as the fourteenth century, beginning in Florence and spreading up and down the Italian peninsula and then northward and over the Alps. Technological advances in shipbuilding and navigation expanded trade and led directly to the fifteenth-century voyages of discovery to the New World, which were spearheaded by a Genoese Italian, Christopher Columbus, on behalf of Spain, newly reconquered from Muslim Moorish overlords.

The Crusades also had the effect of encouraging the strengthening of the emerging monarchies of Europe. Since the withering of Carolingian authority after the death of Charlemagne, the Holy Roman Empire had ceased to be supreme. Instead, members of the nobility began to jockey for position as *primus inter pares*. By the middle of the tenth century, the Capetians had ceded much of their land to their nominal vassals and the writ of Philip I, the King of the Franks, extended not much farther than Orleans, Paris, and their urban environs. The First Crusade partially solved that problem, as the principal nobles (generally but not exclusively lacklands and younger brothers) signed up for the quest and thus took themselves out of contention with the nominal sovereign. "The crusade," writes the mid-nineteenth century French historian Joseph-François Michaud in his magisterial *Histoire des croisades* (1840), "removed far from Europe all who could have taken advantage of the unhappy situation in which the kingdom was placed; it saved the country from a civil war, and prevented such sanguinary discords as had broken out in Germany under the reign of Henry and the pontificate of Gregory."

Literature, poetry, music, and the pictorial arts were all inspired by the Crusades and their leaders. Befitting the nature of the First Crusade, and its remarkable military success, many of these men have entered legendary status, celebrated for hundreds of years later in poetry, stories, songs, plays, and operas. Most important of these "afterlives" (to use the term coined by the late Jonathan Miller in his 1986 book, *Subsequent Performances*) is the Italian epic poem *La Gerusalemme liberata*, published in 1581 by Torquato Tasso,[3] and later extensively rewritten by the emotionally unstable poet, much to the poem's detriment.

Seeking a world-historical subject that would rival Virgil's *Aeneid*, Tasso fell eagerly upon the First Crusade for his epic poem, written in *ottava rima* (eight lines with a rhyme scheme of ABABABCC, in iambic pentameter). Although half a millennium in the past, the topic had contemporary resonance, since the Turks were still a potent threat to Europe in the late sixteenth century: the pivotal naval battle at Lepanto had been won by the West just ten years earlier and the long conflict would continue for nearly another century until the Ottoman invasion was turned back at Vienna in 1683.

Tasso, half-mad at the best of times, had deliberately sought the comparison with the great poet of the imperium of Augustus and, even farther back, with Homer himself. In the *Divine Comedy* of 1321, Dante had completed the transformation of Latin into Italian; now it would be up to Tasso to perfect it. *Jerusalem Delivered* was greeted at first with puzzlement at its mixture of martial ferocity and courtly love, all happening at the same time and on the same battlefield; he rewrote the poem as *La Gerusalemme conquistata* near the end of his life, stripping it of its amours. But the unique original quickly found favor with readers across Europe and inspired multiple variations, spinoffs, and homages for centuries.

Tasso invented and immortalized the love stories of Tancred and

---

3. Although largely neglected today, Tasso (1544–1595) was one of the most important figures in European literary history, and he had a powerful influence on subsequent generations of artists well into the nineteenth century.

Clorinda,[4] and Rinaldo and the witch Armida; limned the martial exploits of both Christian and Muslim warriors; and sang the praises of his main character, Godfrey of Bouillon, the noblest of God's holy warriors. Tancred and Tasso enter the history of the stage in Monteverdi's great dramatic madrigal *Il combattimento di Tancredi e Clorinda* of 1624, followed by Voltaire's tragedy *Tancrède* (1760); Goethe's play *Torquato Tasso* (1790); Byron's poem *The Lament of Tasso* (1817); and Liszt's tone poem, written in honor of both Goethe and Byron, *Tasso: lamento e trionfo* (1849–1854), depicting the love-stricken poet's seven years in the insane asylum of St. Anna.

Dozens of operas have taken characters from the poem as their principal subjects, including Handel's *Rinaldo*[5] (1711), Rossini's *Tancredi* (1813), based on Voltaire; Armida became the heroine of operas by composers as disparate as Gluck (1777), Haydn (1784), and Dvorak (1904). Painters such as Poussin, Delacroix, Tiepolo, and Tintoretto found resonance and inspiration in the stories. And where would Sir Walter Scott—whose two most popular novels are *Ivanhoe* and *The Talisman*—be without the Crusades? Even as recently as the year 2000 the great American author Evan Connell tackled the thorny subject from the perspective of one of the Crusades' actual chroniclers, Jean de Joinville, in his historical novel *Deus lo Volt!*

But their most potent effect came in the field of religion. In the absence of a western emperor, the pope in Rome assumed both temporal and spiritual territories and duties. The Church grew immensely wealthy, its pomp and license evoking in many aspects the grandeur and excess that had once been Rome. The struggle between religious and political authority, so starkly revealed by the conflict between

---

4. A fearsome and beautiful Muslim warrior woman who dresses in male armor. At first sight, she falls in love on the battlefield with the Christian knight Tancred, and he with her. When they later meet in hand-to-hand night combat, Tancred doesn't recognize her, and so slays her. Mortally wounded, she converts to Christianity and dies in his arms.

5. One of whose tunes was pirated by John Gay and Johann Pepusch as "Let Us Take the Road" for their 1728 ballad opera, *The Beggar's Opera;* that work itself was later transformed by Bertolt Brecht and Kurt Weill into *Die Dreigroschenoper* (*The Threepenny Opera*) in 1928.

Henry IV and Pope Gregory VII just before the start of the First Crusade, only intensified until it finally provoked the Reformation in the sixteenth century. The Church's unease about its Jewish patrimony—so useful to it when as a fledgling faith it avoided the Roman Empire's deep suspicion of religious novelty by grandfathering itself in under the aegis of Judaism—now broke into the open, and was reflected in the gratuitous massacres of the Jews of the Rhineland as the unsanctioned Peoples' Crusade got underway.

One thing no scholar can ignore, however, is the animating primacy of faith held by the warriors on both sides and their intimate relationships with their respective deities. In every battle fought from Dorylaeum to Jerusalem during the period of July 1097 to July 1099, success or failure was ascribed either to sinfulness or virtue, and outcomes were determined by the level of fidelity to the faith even more than to bravery, tactical skills, or force of arms. The power of prayer was given the highest rank in the military lexicon, although one suspects that to men like Bohemond[6] of Taranto, a ferocious Norman warrior, his huge stature, his strong right arm, and his lust for power and turf counted for more. Victory was proof of God's favor, defeat of his displeasure.

One of the principal attractions of the First Crusade was Urban's promise of the complete remission of sins for those who took part in the march on Jerusalem. Given the state of morals during that period, this was no mean thing. Rome's old provinces may have cast off centralized imperial rule along with her pagan gods, but murder was as much a tool—*policy with other means*—of political pole-climbing as it had been for the ancients. Also, sex was as popular then as it is today; among the gentry, infidelity was unremarkable, while the lower orders, if clerical accounts are to be credited, rutted like farm animals. Seduced maidens were a *sou* a barrel, while mistresses shuttled regularly between and among masters' bedchambers. Nor was the clergy, then as now, immune from enthusiastically embracing and enjoying the pleasures of the flesh.

In addition, there was the assurance by the Church—the only supranational authority—that while on Crusade, participants' property and

---

6. Baptized Mark, he was nicknamed by his father after a mythical giant, and lived up to his name in every way.

families would be under its temporal protection, debts would be forgiven, and pilgrims would have immunity from litigation back home. In an age of extreme religiosity these were no small enticements. Whether duke or commoner, a man was not about to head off to war lightly. Or a woman, for that matter: the numbers of wives and female camp followers during the Crusades was surprisingly large, and while women did not actively fight (except on rare, exigent occasions), they would provide valuable battlefield services such as bringing water to the parched knights, sweltering in their armor in the desert heat; and dragging away the bodies of the dead and the wounded to clear the fighting spaces.

Crusading, notes Tyerman, "appeared to embrace some of the constant and dangerous issues facing Western European Christians: how to earn salvation in a sinful world; how to lead a strenuously active, not just passive, good and faithful life; how to measure God's approbation of individuals and society on the gauge of physical victory and defeat; even how to ensure the political survival of their entire religion." These considerations were among the most important motivations of the entire enterprise—some of the things that make the First Crusade seem unintelligible to us at a remove of nearly a millennium. But as Tyerman also notes, "The plundering of history to pronounce modern indictments serves no rational purpose and merely clouds understanding of a distant actuality whose interest lies as much if not more in its uniqueness and difference from other times, and especially from today. To observe the past through the lens of the present invites delusion."[7] The Crusades, in other words, must be judged by the standards, morals, and beliefs of their time, not ours.

Another important factor in Urban's machinations was the doctrinal and political split in 1054 between the Roman Catholic and the Eastern Church centered in Constantinople—a rupture that, as we have seen in the preceding chapter, had been some seven centuries in the making. The theological and liturgical differences, over which the leaders of Roman and Byzantine Christianity excommunicated one

---

7. The very definition of "presentism."

another, included clerical celibacy, the wording of the Nicene Creed, and whether it was permissible to use unleavened bread for the Eucharist. The deal-breaker, however, concerned papal authority over all Christianity, something the Greeks rejected then and continue to reject now.[8]

To make matters more complex, the struggle over lay investiture[9] between the reformist Pope Gregory VII and the Holy Roman Emperor, Henry IV, resulted in Henry's excommunication and temporary capitulation to spiritual authority in the snows of Canossa in 1077; a German civil war over Henry's throne (won by Henry); and the deposition of Gregory by Henry's choice of an antipope, Clement III, as well as the capture of Rome by Henry's troops in 1084—during which much of the Church hierarchy went over to the German side. Pope—now Saint—Gregory died in Salerno in May 1085. His successor, Pope Victor III, strove unsuccessfully to unseat the antipope, a battle that was still ongoing at his death in 1087, when Victor was succeeded in the eyes of the Church by Urban II (born in the Champagne region of France as Odo of Châtillon-sur-Marne). Urban, a reformer in the Gregorian spirit, conducted the most significant years of his papacy on the fly, in Piacenza, Clermont, and Bari, before returning to Rome, where he died on July 29, 1099, just before the electrifying news of the Crusaders' capture of Jerusalem two weeks earlier could reach him.

The trigger for the whole enterprise was a renewed appeal from the recently crowned emperor of the East, Alexios I Comnenus, for help in combating the Muslim armies who were rolling up the Byzantines in Asia Minor and once again threatening Constantinople itself, as they had been doing off and on since 668. Most recently, and ignominiously, the Seljuks under the command of their brilliant sultan, Alp Arslan, had routed a combined Byzantine-mercenary force at Manzikert in Asia Minor in 1071, crushing the Empire's forces and capturing the emperor,

---

8. The mutual excommunications were finally lifted in 1965 by Pope Paul VI and the patriarch Athenagoras I.

9. The practice of having religious offices filled by appointment by kings and civil potentates rather than by Church leaders. One hears echoes of Julius Caesar's long reign as *pontifex maximus* of Rome during his rise to political power.

Romanos IV Diogenes. To emphasize the humiliation, Arslan forced Romanos to the ground and put his foot on his neck before allowing the noble warrior, who had fought fiercely to the end, to rise. There are conflicting accounts of how he was treated during his eight-day captivity, after which he was ransomed and returned to Constantinople. The Greek nobles were not pleased to see him: he was deposed, blinded, and sent into exile, and soon died of his wounds. In the ensuing palace intrigue for power, Alexios, a military man who had served under Romanos, came to the throne in 1081.

As it happens, Alexios quickly found himself embroiled in a war against an invading force of Normans under Robert Guiscard (c. 1015–1085). The rumbustious Normans had conquered southern Italy by the year 1040, and Guiscard had acquired a dukedom in Apulia, the heel of the Italian peninsula, Calabria, and Sicily.[10] The weakening Eastern Empire's regional provinces, however, were too juicy a target for a freebooter like Guiscard to ignore, and so he set out upon a campaign of constant harassment, which won him the undying loathing and enmity of the Byzantines. Even worse, in Byzantine eyes, Robert was the sire of Bohemond of Taranto, who had fought with his father in the western Balkans and with him had captured the Byzantine city of Dyrrachium[11] in a pitched battle against Alexios in 1081, before finally ceding back the territory as a result of the Battle of Larissa, in Thessaly, in 1083.

Finally, there had long been a steady stream of Western mercenaries heading to Constantinople in search of action with the famed Varangian Guard—the emperor's personal bodyguards, mostly Scandinavians and Germans. Indeed, after the Norman Conquest in 1066 the Byzantines actively solicited them in Britain: the Greeks maintained a bureau in London to recruit the disaffected, leaderless Anglo-Saxon *ronin* who had recently lost to the Normans and were only too happy to have a chance to fight them again.

---

10. The native Sicilians' rebellion in 1281 against the Normans was commemorated by Giuseppe Verdi in his 1855 opera, *Les vêpres siciliennes*.

11. Site of a critical battle in the Roman Civil War between Caesar and Pompey in 48 B.C., won by Pompey in a rare, and temporary, defeat for Caesar.

Why was the Holy Land so important to the Christians? The Western Empire had fallen six centuries earlier, and over that time span Roman Christianity had increasingly taken on the character of the peoples of the West: Celts, Normans, Anglo-Saxons, Germans, Hungarians, Slavs, and Italians. Its Semitic roots were long obscured. But the pull of the homeland of the faith remained strong, thanks not only to the prophetic readings from the Old Testament that had become part of the Christian Bible but also to their incorporation into the symbolism of Western art—pictorial at first, and later in music and song. Jerusalem was a long way off, on the other side of the sea, *Outremer*. Yet it remained in the hearts of the faithful, in large part owing to Constantine the Great and, even more important, to his mother, St. Helena. Indeed, Michaud opens his three-volume account of the Crusades with her invocation:

From the earliest ages of the Church, a custom had been practised of making pilgrimages to the Holy Land. Judea, full of religious remembrances, was still the promised land of the faithful; the blessings of heaven appeared to be in store for those who visited Calvary, the tomb of Jesus Christ, and renewed their baptism in the waters of the Jordan. Under the reign of Constantine, the ardour for pilgrimages increased among the faithful; they flocked from all the provinces of the empire to worship Jesus Christ upon his own tomb, and to trace the steps of their God in that city which had but just resumed its name, and which the piety of an emperor had caused to issue from its ruins.

The Holy Sepulchre presented itself to the eyes of the pilgrims surrounded by a magnificence which redoubled their veneration. An obscure cavern had become a marble temple, paved with precious stones and decorated with splendid colonnades. To the east of the Holy Sepulchre appeared the church of the Resurrection, in which they could admire the riches of Asia, mingled with the arts of Greece and Rome. Constantine celebrated the thirty-first year of his reign by the inauguration of this church, and thousands of Christians came, on occasion of this solemnity, to listen to the panegyric of Christ from the lips of the learned and holy bishop Eusebius.

St. Helena, the mother of the emperor, repaired to Jerusalem, at a very advanced age, and caused churches and chapels to be built upon Mount Tabor, in the city of Nazareth, and in the greater part of the places which Christ had sanctified by his presence and his miracles. From this period, pilgrimages to the Holy Land became much more frequent. The pilgrims, no longer in dread of the persecutions of the Pagans, could now give themselves up, without fear, to the fervour of their devotion; the Roman eagles, ornamented with the cross of Jesus Christ, protected them on their march; they everywhere trampled under-foot the fragments of idols, and they travelled amidst the abodes of their fellow Christians.

This, then, is the backdrop of the First Crusade. Despite the fall of Jerusalem to the Arabs of the Rashidun Caliphate in 638—who wrested it from the Zoroastrian Sassanid Persians before the Muslims' subsequent conquest of Iran, complete by 654—Christian pilgrims had continued for centuries to make the journey to the Holy Land, with only occasional interruptions. Under the caliph, Umar (Muhammed's father-in-law), Christians were free to practice their religion upon payment of the *jizya* tax, while the Jews—who had been expelled and banished from the city by the Romans under Hadrian after the bloody and costly Bar Kokhba Revolt in 135 A.D. that unleashed the diaspora—were finally permitted a return to the city. But the treatment of pilgrims was subject to the whims of whichever Muslim ruler currently controlled Jerusalem: for some, the money to be made from the Christians was too good to pass up. Others were more concerned with Islamic dogma. Still, a certain *modus vivendi* largely prevailed.

The liberation of the Christian Holy Land, therefore, was a relatively new objective. It was Urban's genius to combine his religious and political concerns into one grand gesture, something given inflammatory, even sexual urgency by Alexios's appeal, which Urban received via a Byzantine embassy to Piacenza during the council there in March of 1095. "Every day and without interruption, came reports from the emperor, countless Christians were being killed; boys and old men, nobles and peasants, clergymen and monks were suffering the terrible sin of

sodomy at the hands of the Turks; others were being forcibly circum-
cised, while aristocratic ladies and their daughters were being raped
with impunity."[12] In his *Historia Hierosolymitana*, written in the early
twelfth century, Robert the Monk recounts the fate of some of the
Christian women who fell into Muslim hands in a letter from Alexios
to Count Robert of Flanders, one of the leaders of the First Crusade:

> The aim of this letter is to alert you, in your wisdom, to just how
> hard the most holy Greek Christian Empire is being pressed by
> the Pechenegs[13] and Turks, pillaged daily and constantly raided,
> with Christians being murdered and mocked in various inde-
> scribable ways. The evils are many and, as we said, indescrib-
> able. . . . For instance they circumcise Christian boys and youths
> above Christian baptismal fonts, pour the blood from the cir-
> cumcision into the fonts in mockery of Christ, force them to
> urinate on it, and then drag them round the church and force
> them to blaspheme the name and faith of the Holy Trinity. Those
> who refuse are subjected to various punishments and eventually
> killed.
>
> Meanwhile they rob and mock noble women and their daugh-
> ters, taking turns to defile them like animals. Others again as
> part of their corruption set virgins up in front of their mothers
> and force them to sing wicked and lustful songs until they have
> finished their foul acts. . . . But this pales into insignificance
> compared to the worse things to come. They force men of all
> ages and stations into the sin of sodomy—boys, adolescents,
> young men, old men, nobles and servants and worse still and
> more terrible priests and monks; and—woe is me! The shame of
> it!—something which has never yet been told or heard of, bishops
> as well. . . . Therefore, you should make every effort to stop them

---

12. Cited by Peter Frankopan in *The First Crusade: The Call from the East* (2012).

13. A central Asian, seminomadic Turkic people, much given to fighting the *Kievan Rus*
for control of what became the Russian homeland, although founded by Varangians from
Sweden.

capturing Constantinople, thus ensuring that you will gain the joy of glorious and ineffable mercy in Heaven.[14]

The sexuality of the enterprise should not be underestimated, on either side. Rape, torture, and sexual humiliation had long been part of the attractions of warfare: the ancient and medieval battlefields were a sexual sadist's paradise. There was no more effective way to humble and humiliate an enemy than to sodomize his youths and defile his women. Indeed, among the many collateral benefits on this first major meeting between West and East since the time of Alexander (who himself fell victim to the loucheness of "oriental" Persian culture) was the erotic exoticism of the Arab and Turkish sexual practices, against which the Christian ideal of the pure and sinless knight errant could be developed and contrasted.[15] Combining the cult of the Virgin Mary with newly discovered narrative literary techniques and strange musical sounds and sonorities, European poetry and song blossomed with ballads and lays as the new figures of the trouvères and troubadours began to flower. Now the knights were not only fighting for the Holy Virgin but for their own wives and daughters as well. Chivalry (from *chevalerie,* applied to mounted warriors) was being born.

The speed of the Arab conquests had come as a shock. "When the Arabs issued from the desert, they must have been surprised at the ease and rapidity of their success," notes Gibbon. "But, when they advanced in the career of victory to the banks of the Indus and the summit of the Pyrenees, when they had repeatedly tried the edge of their scymetars and the energy of their faith, they might be equally astonished that any nation could resist their invincible arms, that any boundary should confine the dominion of the successor of the prophet."

As with the Huns six hundred years earlier, there seemed no way

---

14. *Robert the Monk's History of the First Crusade* (Crusade Texts in Translation), by Carol Sweetenham (Taylor and Francis, 2005).

15. Even a cursory glance at an unexpurgated translation of the Arabian Nights—*The Book of a Thousand Nights and a Night*—will startle a Western reader used to the sanitized version of Scheherazade's bedtime stories with its descriptive eroticism and obsession with copulation. See also this author's *The Fiery Angel* (Encounter Books, 2018) for more details.

to stop them. Like the Huns, they were swift and extremely mobile, eschewing set-piece battles in favor of a proto-blitzkrieg that overwhelmed their enemies (who in many cases didn't even know the Arabs were coming until it was too late), and gave their conquered foes the simple choice of conversion, submission, or death. They appeared to materialize out of thin air, swarming and swooping, killing everything in their path. The brunt of the shock was borne by the Byzantines and their ancient enemies, the Sassanid Persians—a continuation of the centuries-old contests between the Romans and the Parthians—now weakened and caught off-guard and undermanned.[16] Both civilizations were old and weary; Islam, just a few years after the death of Muhammad, was young and hungry. The Persians fell quickly, surrendering their former territories and suzerainty up and down the Levant, across North Africa, and into Byzantine territory in Asia Minor.

Encountering the nomadic Turks, arriving from the steppes via the former lands of the Persians, the Arabs converted them by means of missionaries and military example and quickly turned them into neighbors and coreligionists beginning in the late seventh century; by the middle of the eighth century, they were military allies as well. At the Battle of Talas in 751 in present-day Kyrgyzstan, a combined Abbasid Arab, Tibetan, and Turkish army demolished the Tang Chinese under general Kao Hsien-chih (an ethnic Korean, since the Chinese nobility regarded military careers as beneath them) and their dreams of expansion into central Asia. The crushing defeat set the tone for Chinese military futility against foreign armies that has persisted to this day.

As it happened, the Turks were even more fearsome warriors than the Arabs, on whom they quickly turned in a struggle for Islamic supremacy. Like the Huns, the Turks were superb horsemen and expert bowmen; their hit-and-run tactics were predicated on near-constant shock and awe, pinning their enemies down in a rain of arrows, never coming close enough to fully engage and forcing their opponents into a defensive circle that slowly narrowed until it collapsed and they were overrun.

---

16. "Forty-six years after the flight of Mahomet from Mecca, his disciples appeared in arms under the walls of Constantinople," notes Gibbon.

For militant Islam, however, the principal and most desirable targets for conquest were not the Sassanids and the Byzantines but the Christianized West and the historic strongholds of Christianity. Antioch and Jerusalem fell in 637, Alexandria in 641. Those were just warm-ups. The next obvious target was Constantinople, the "New Rome," and after that, Rome herself. In the meantime, the short hop from North Africa to the Iberian Peninsula gave the Umayyad Muslims and later Islamic dynasties a foothold on the European continent that lasted from the early eighth century until 1492, when the Spanish monarchs Ferdinand and Isabella, uniting the kingdoms of Aragon and Castile, drove the last of the Moors from Spain, for the first time establishing a "Spanish" identity for the nation.[17]

As we've seen, both Alexander and the Roman legions employed cavalry, but in different ways and to different effect. Not everyone could be an equestrian; for one thing, you had to have your own horse, which meant that cavalrymen were men of property. For the Macedonians, the cavalry were Companions, Alexander's most elite troops, and they went into the battle with their youthful general always in the front and in the lead. The Romans used their heavy infantry as the heart of the legions, with flanking cavalry providing support but rarely figuring decisively in the outcome. After the collapse of the Western Empire and the loss of central authority and supply, the emerging European nations had fought most local battles as the various dukes and princes struggled for supremacy. In those battles, however, a thunderous cavalry charge by heavily armed knights[18] often spelled the difference between victory and defeat. Therefore, the European uses of cavalry, especially

---

17. The so-called golden age of Al-Andalus is mostly illusory. In 711, the Arabs defeated the Visigoths, who had been instrumental in turning back Attila at the Catalaunian Plains; six years later the Christians had already started the rollback at the Battle of Covadonga in 722, the culmination of a rebellion that had begun four years earlier. In the early ninth century the Holy Roman Emperor, Charlemagne, recaptured much of northern Spain near the Pyrenees, including Barcelona, and thereafter followed a long, slow, steady push of the Moors to the south and then out of the peninsula entirely. Muslim scholars, however, did loom large in the revival of Greek learning and its retransmission to the West, among them Averroes (1126–1198).

18. Now outfitted with stirrups, which had come into use in the West around the eighth or ninth centuries.

heavy cavalry, were more along Roman lines than Alexandrine—as deal clinchers that, at the end of a long day of infantry combat, could smash through weakened lines and so win the field. There was little guerilla warfare: the surprise attack by the Basques on the rear column of Charlemagne's army at the Roncevaux Pass in 788, which formed the basis for what became the French epic poem *La Chanson de Roland* several hundred years later,[19] was a notable exception.

The first major clash between specifically Christian and Muslim armies had occurred at the Battle of Tours on October 10, 732,[20] when Frankish forces under Charles Martel turned back a Muslim invasion under the command of Abd al-Rahman, expelling Islam from what would become France and establishing the Carolingian dynasty. Ever on the lookout to demonstrate the superiority of British Anglo-Saxon culture to all others, Creasy in *The Fifteen Decisive Battles of the World* characterizes the battle thus: "This region has been signalized by more than one memorable conflict; but it is principally interesting to the historian, by having been the scene of the great victory won by Charles Martel over the Saracens, A.D. 732, which gave a decisive check to the career of Arab conquest in Western Europe, rescued Christendom from Islam, preserved the relics of ancient and the germs of modern civilization, and re-established the old superiority of the Indo-European over the Semitic family of mankind." Gibbon, more soberly, says that "by his signal victory over the Saracens, [Charles Martel] saved his country, and perhaps Europe, from the Mahometan yoke."

In what in retrospect might be seen as a harbinger of the battles of the First Crusade—which were at first fought against the Turks but, in the latter half of the campaign in Jerusalem and Ascalon, were won against the Fatimid Muslims of Egypt—Abd al-Rahman's Arabs were principally light mounted cavalry, while Charles Martel's soldiers were heavily armored infantry. As was typical of the nomadic warriors, Abd al-Rahman

---

19. Nearly contemporaneous with the First Crusade, and replacing the Basques of the actual battle with Muslims as the villains. Covered in detail in *Last Stands*.

20. Exact location uncertain; somewhere between Tours and Poitiers in west-central France. Military history buffs will note its relative proximity to the Catalaunian Plains and to Alesia; as we shall see, history was not yet finished with this part of France.

ibn Abd Allah Al-Ghafiqi (to give the Arab commander his full name) had not only brought a large army but also a host of camp followers, including multiple wives, children, their treasury, plundered booty, and most of their belongings, which they left behind in the camp before the battle.

Al-Rahman, however, was outmaneuvered by Charles, who interposed his army between the mobile Arabs and the rich city of Tours. As Aetius had been at the Catalaunian Plains, Charles was wise in his choice of a battlefield: defending the end of a long field, where his attackers would have to charge across an open plain and expend their energy on his shield walls, manned by tall, strong Frankish-German veterans. In addition, Charles had positioned himself near the confluence of two rivers and in front of a small, elevated forest, which both gave him a clear view of the battlefield and protected him from being outflanked and surrounded by the Arab cavalry. It also allowed him to conceal much of his troop strength in the trees behind his front line.

The two sides skirmished cautiously for about six days. But as the days shortened, the clock was running down on al-Rahman's logistical situation. The Arabs had no supply lines but instead lived off the land, but that would soon no longer be possible. Al-Rahman had to gamble on a decisive strike, which came on the seventh day. The Arab cavalry repeatedly crashed against the brawny infantry's front line, whose broadswords and superior physical strength cut them to pieces; even when the Arabs briefly penetrated the line, they were driven back by the reinforcements just behind the Frankish front.

At last, some of the cavalry under Charles's ally, Odo of Aquitaine, broke out and got behind the Saracens, heading for the Arab camp. Seeing this, the rear echelon of the Arab force broke off the battle and began to rush back to protect their belongings; this, however, looked like a disorganized retreat to their compatriots on the front line, who also scattered in confusion and were quickly surrounded by Charles's counterattack. Al-Rahman was killed in the ensuing melee, and that, characteristically, broke the spirit of his troops, who turned tail and fled as nightfall approached.

The next days the Franks braced for resumption of hostilities but, as at the Catalaunian Plains, discovered that the enemy had abandoned the field and retreated during the night. The Frankish victory at Tours halted Muslim expansionism in Western Europe, although it would take hundreds of years before they were completely driven back beyond the Strait of Gibraltar; it also dealt a serious blow to Muslim confidence that, as their prophet's holy warriors, they were invincible. The Battle of Tours also alerted the Franks to the danger of weaponized religious fanaticism on their southern borders, helping to propel cultural unification.

The Western armies that set out for Jerusalem in the wake of the pope's call to arms and action, therefore, were slow and solid, even stolid: strength and sinew were prized over mobility in both horse and man. But in fact the first wave of Crusaders to reach the strait of the Bosphorus in 1096 was a largely disorganized rabble of pious peasants led by a preacher named Peter the Hermit, a charismatic French monk who habitually went barefoot and rode upon a donkey. He claimed to have made the pilgrimage to Jerusalem on a previous occasion and was still seething with anger about the difficulties with the Turks he had encountered along the way.

Urban's exoration found in Peter a willing listener.[21] He gathered a sizable cohort of mostly commoners, some twenty to forty thousand pilgrims, with only a relative handful of knights as their leaders (among them Walter Sans-Avoir, a minor French aristocrat), and many of them without weapons of any kind, and, amazingly, managed to lead them all the way to Constantinople, which they reached on August 1. En route they had looted their way across Europe, caused the deaths of thousands of innocent Jews in the Rhineland and elsewhere and forcibly converted others, and scourged a path through Hungary and into Byzantine territory. A contemporary Jewish chronicler, Soloman bar Samson, of whom little is known, described the scene in Mainz on May 27, 1096. The echoes of Masada are unmistakable:

The foe Emico[22] proclaimed in the hearing of the community that the enemy be driven from the city and be put to flight. Panic

---

21. Some of the later accounts of the origin of the Crusades attribute the entire venture to Peter who, in their telling, personally convinced Urban to make his speech. This is incorrect.

22. Count Emicho of Flonheim, whose troops worshipped a goose they believed to be filled with the Holy Spirit.

was great in the town. Each Jew in the inner court of the bishop girded on his weapons, and all moved towards the palace gate to fight the crusaders and the citizens. They fought each other up to the very gate, but the sins of the Jews brought it about that the enemy overcame them and took the gate.

When the children of the covenant saw that the heavenly decree of death had been issued and that the enemy had conquered them and had entered the courtyard, then all of them—old men and young, virgins and children, servants and maids—cried out together to their Father in heaven and, weeping for themselves and for their lives, accepted as just the sentence of God. One to another they said: "Let us be strong and let us bear the yoke of the holy religion, for only in this world can the enemy kill us— and the easiest of the four deaths is by the sword. But we, our souls in paradise, shall continue to live eternally, in the great shining reflection [of the divine glory]."

With a whole heart and with a willing soul they then spoke: "After all it is not right to criticize the acts of God—blessed be He and blessed be His name—who has given to us His Torah and a command to put ourselves to death, to kill ourselves for the unity of His holy name. Happy are we if we do His will. Happy is anyone who is killed or slaughtered, who dies for the unity of His name so that he is ready to enter the World to Come, to dwell in the heavenly camp with the righteous—with Rabbi Akiba and his companions, the pillars of the universe, who were killed for His name's sake."

As soon as the enemy came into the courtyard they found some of the very pious there with our brilliant master, Isaac ben Moses. He stretched out his neck, and his head they cut off first. The others, wrapped by their fringed praying shawls, sat by themselves in the courtyard, eager to do the will of their Creator. They did not care to flee into the chamber to save themselves for this temporal life, but out of love they received upon themselves the sentence of God. . . . The women there girded their loins with strength and slew their sons and their daughters and then themselves. Many men, too, plucked up courage and killed their wives, their sons, their infants. The tender and delicate mother slaughtered the babe she had played with, all of them, men and women arose and slaughtered one another. The maidens and the young brides and grooms looked out of the Windows and in a loud voice cried: "Look and see, O our God, what we do for the sanctification of Thy great name in order not to exchange you for a hanged and crucified one. . . ."

As with St. Perpetua and the early Christian martyrs, we see again the deleterious effects of intense religiosity on the instinct for self-preservation: the Jews, noncombatants, accepted this war crime as punishment for insufficient fidelity to the god of Abraham and killed themselves both in expiation and to signify their rejection of the pilgrims' Jesus as the Messiah.

Arriving in Constantinople, Peter's forces were now much reduced after repeated battles with the Hungarians and Byzantines on their march. They were initially well received by Alexios, who was both surprised and appalled by the size and nature of Peter's army and wished to hasten them across the water to Asia Minor as quickly as possible. But the emperor's fears were justified once the main force was admitted to the city and conflicts immediately broke out among the Crusaders and local merchants.

Alexios was in a tricky position, trying to defend an empire that was simultaneously being attacked at its western and eastern extremities, so while he welcomed the aid from the west, no matter how strange in form, he could not let the arrival of the Europeans—some of whom he had only recently been at war with—destabilize his position any further. Anna Comnena, his daughter, describes the arrival of Peter and his troops in the *Alexiad,* drawing upon her recollections as a fourteen-year-old princess at the court:

Before he had enjoyed even a short rest, he heard a report of the approach of innumerable Frankish armies. Now he dreaded their arrival for he knew their irresistible manner of attack, their unstable and mobile character and all the peculiar natural and concomitant characteristics which the Frank retains throughout; and he also knew that they were always agape for money, and seemed to disregard their truces readily for any reason that cropped up. For he had always heard this reported of them, and found it very true. However, he did not lose heart, but prepared himself in every way so that, when the occasion called, he would be ready for battle . . .

Those Frankish soldiers were accompanied by an unarmed host more numerous than the sand or the stars, carrying palms and crosses on their shoulders; women and children, too, came away from their countries. And the sight of them was like many rivers streaming from all sides . . .

The Emperor, knowing what Peter had suffered before from the Turks, advised him to wait for the arrival of the other Counts, but Peter would not listen for he trusted to the multitude of his followers, so crossed and pitched his camp near a small town called Helenopolis.[23]

Once on the other side, the Crusader forces at first based themselves in the old imperial capital of Nicomedia, now abandoned. Their plan was to make an assault on the ancient Roman city of Nicaea, one of the most important sites in the history of early Christianity and the location of Constantine's Council in 325. Accordingly, they then divided themselves between Nicomedia, where the Norman contingent remained, and Civetot, on the Sea of Marmara and thus easily supplied, where Peter and the rest of his troops now encamped. With grain shipments from Alexios running low, Peter returned to Constantinople.

At the same time, the German and Italian forces at Nicomedia decided to attack Nicaea, located at the eastern edge of the inland Sea of Ascanius.[24] Initially successful, they sent the Sultan of Rum, Kilij Arslan, fleeing from his capital, but the Turkish commander quickly counterattacked and destroyed the Germans who had holed up in the nearby fortress of Xerigordos after their attack had stalled. What the

---

23. Originally called Drepana. Constantine renamed it in her honor in 318.

24. The name of a Greco-Roman river and lake god of western Bithynia. It was also the name of the son of Aeneas in the *Aeneid*.

Turks knew but the Crusaders did not was that the water supplies lay outside the castle and at a fair distance from the walls. In a few days, the soldiers were reduced to drinking the blood of their horses and their own urine. Their leader, a knight named Reynald, rode out and surrendered, renouncing Christianity in favor of Islam. A few others did so as well, and were promptly sent into slavery. The rest were massacred.

The Turks then spread a rumor at Civetot that Nicaea had fallen and was even then being looted by the other Crusaders. With Peter absent, the leaderless forces at Civetot moved out but were immediately ambushed by Arslan's mobile Turks and destroyed. The camp followers at Civetot were largely sold into slavery all over the Seljuk Empire. Only a few survived. Writes Anna:

> As they journeyed neither in ranks nor in squadrons, they fell foul of the Turkish ambuscades near the river Dracon and perished miserably. And such a large number of Franks and Normans were the victims of the Ishmaelite sword, that when they piled up the corpses of the slaughtered men which were lying on either side they formed, I say, not a very large hill or mound or a peak, but a high mountain as it were, of very considerable depth and breadth—so great was the pyramid of bones.

And that was the end of the Peoples' Crusade.

The crusade envisioned and ordered by Pope Urban, however, was now underway. It was led neither by charismatics nor, at this stage, kings—later crusades were in fact led by kings, such as Richard the Lionheart and, at the end of the series, Louis IX of France—but rather dukes and counts of various duchies and principalities. Just thirty years earlier, the Normans of northern France under Duke William— once known as William the Bastard and now dignified as William the Conqueror—had crossed the English Channel and defeated Harold Godwinson at the Battle of Hastings; William was now a king. But at the end of the eleventh century, kings were still a relative rarity; the First Crusade is therefore known as the Princes' Crusade.

Numbering some seventy thousand strong at the outset, its principal leaders were—with a few notable exceptions—noblemen of both piety and property. Mobilizing between December of 1095 and August 1096, with the goal of assembling in Constantinople, there to join forces with the Byzantine emperor Alexios, they were:

- **Godfrey of Boullion**, Duke of Lower Lorraine, and his brothers **Eustace III** and **Baldwin** of Boulogne. Godfrey, an older man much celebrated for his piety, became the moral leader of the crusade. Tall, strong, blond, and bearded, this "perfect Christian knight" had previously opposed Urban II in his battle with the Holy Roman Emperor, Henry IV, but unhesitatingly had answered the call to the Cross. Baldwin, the youngest, with no lands of his own, eventually became Count of Edessa and King of Jerusalem. With Godfrey came his kinsman **Robert II,** Count of Flanders, who led a strong detachment from what are now the Low Countries.

- **Bohemond** of Taranto. Encountering warriors on their way to the Holy Land, Bohemond had broken off a siege of Amalfi against Italian enemies, taken the Cross, and made a vow never to fight fellow Christians again. The Norman leader was an experienced military commander, and, like his father Robert Guiscard, a scourge of the Byzantines. Ambitious, avaricious, quarrelsome, libidinous—and totally mistrusted by Alexios—Bohemond would be instrumental in the Crusaders' first victories at Dorylaeum and Antioch but, distracted by his overweening ambition, did not take part in the siege of Jerusalem and thereby seriously crippled the entire enterprise.

- **Tancred**, Bohemond's nephew, was a fearless warrior whose place was ever in the forefront of battle. "He was always ready, always armed, and took pleasure in being exposed to danger," wrote his biographer Ralph of Caen, in the contemporaneous *Gesta Tancredi,* a panegyric. "He refused to say anything about himself, but had an insatiable longing to be talked about. He disregarded sleep in favor of watchfulness, quiet in place of labor, satiety in place of hunger, leisure in favor of work, and indeed everything that was superfluous in favor of what was needed. It was only the glory of praise that moved the spirit of this young man. But in regularly pursuing glory he brought frequent suffering on himself, for he did not spare his own blood or that of his enemy."

- **Raymond de Saint-Gilles**, Count of Toulouse, and **Adhemar** de Monteil, bishop of Le Puy, the papal legate with the expedition. The most highly esteemed of the Franks, Raymond, who headed a force of Provençals, seemed the natural leader of the expedition, but his modesty forbade him from ever claiming the title. His friendship was prized by Alexios, and the two appeared to have become friends, although unlike the other Crusader leaders, Raymond declined to swear an oath of allegiance to Alexios after the emperor refused to lead the assault on the Holy Land in person, and instead insisted upon staying behind in the safety of Constantinople to administer his empire. Adhemar, a man of God who was also handy with the sword,[25] was Urban's personal representative.
- **Robert Curthose** (Short Pants), Duke of Normandy, eldest son of William the Conqueror, and his brother-in-law, **Stephen of Blois**. Curthose, as his derogatory nickname implies, was the odd man out in the complex politics that followed in the wake of the Norman Conquest; the Count of Blois would later disgrace himself by abandoning the crusade, only to be shamed into returning by his termagant wife. He was killed at the Second Battle of Ramla in 1102, after the capture of Jerusalem in 1099.

They did not march as one body but as separate regional units, sometimes in alliance with one or more of the others. (The lack of a centralized command would eventually spell the doom of the entire crusading enterprise.) They did not think of themselves as men of the West marching off to do battle with a foe from the East but as Christians, answering the call of their coreligionists to liberate the Holy Land from the Arab and the Turk. They raised their own funds, mortgaged or sold their lands, bid their loved ones farewell, and headed off into an uncertain future in an unknown place, marching under their own standards and the banners of their lords and the Cross. Whether they traveled overland

---

25. He is the real-life counterpart to the character of Bishop Turpin in *La chanson de Roland*.

or by sea, their first stop was the New Rome, the city of Constantine, whose troops had also marched under the Cross and the Chi-Rho: Constantinople.

Naturally, there were signs in the sky as the great armed pilgrimage got underway. Like their Roman forebears, the Europeans put considerable store in portents. "Historians inform us," writes Michaud, "that whilst the barons were assembled, the moon, which was in eclipse, appeared of the colour of blood. When the eclipse was over, its disc was surrounded by an unprecedented splendour. Some weeks after, says the Abbé Guibert, the northern horizon was seen to be all on fire, and the terrified people rushed from the houses and cities, believing that the enemy was advancing, fire and sword in hand. These phenomena, with several others, were regarded as signs of the will of God, and presages of the terrible war about to be made in his name. They everywhere redoubled the enthusiasm for the crusade. Men who had hitherto remained indifferent now partook of the general delirium. All Frenchmen called to the profession of arms, and who had not yet taken the oath to fight against the infidels, hastened now to take the cross."

Reigning there in Constantinople in sybaritic eastern splendor was the *Basileus*,[26] Alexios I, military parvenu, and founder of the Comnenian dynasty, which, over the course of its 104-year existence, managed to restore many of the lands and territories of the Eastern Roman Empire. Largely Greek in language and customs, the Byzantines nevertheless called themselves Romans, used Latin as their official language, and were acutely conscious of their status as heirs of the Roman Empire, even if its western half no longer existed.

The emperor's daughter, Anna, has in her hagiography of her father, the *Alexiad*, left us a rich and exotic, even perfumed, account of life at the court. The opening of her memoir is one of the most evocative and memorable in world literature:

Time in its irresistible and ceaseless flow carries along on its flood all created things, and drowns them in the depths of obscurity,

---

26. The word, meaning monarch or king, is Greek: βασιλεύς.

no matter if they be quite unworthy of mention, or most note-worthy and important, and thus, as the tragedian[27] says, "he brings from the darkness all things to the birth, and all things born envelops in the night."

Writing from a distance of half a century and certainly unreliable in many of its particulars, owing to her hero-worship of her father and the fact that much of her information was necessarily secondhand, Anna's work nevertheless is our most direct line into the heart and soul of the period. The other chroniclers, Latins who followed the princes on their way to Constantinople and Jerusalem, wrote from a masculine perspective; theirs are largely stories of battle and heroes: the saga of (as they were called), the Men of Iron, the Right Arms of God. The highly educated and sophisticated Anna, by contrast, provides a distinctly feminine insight into the characters and motivations of her subjects, both Byzantine and Frankish. After her arresting opening, she continues:

But the tale of history forms a very strong bulwark against the stream of time, and to some extent checks its irresistible flow, and, of all things done in it, as many as history has taken over, it secures and binds together, and does not allow them to slip away into the abyss of oblivion. Now, I recognized this fact. I, Anna, the daughter of two royal personages, Alexius and Irene, born and bred in the purple. I was not ignorant of letters, for I carried my study of Greek to the highest pitch, and was also not unpractised in rhetoric; I perused the works of Aristotle and the dialogues of Plato carefully, and enriched my mind by the "quaternion"[28] of learning.

However, to resume—I intend in this writing of mine to recount the deeds done by my father so they should certainly not be lost in silence, or swept away, as it were, on the current of time into

---

27. Sophocles, *Ajax*.

28. A group or set of four persons or things. She refers to the *quadrivium,* the study of music, mathematics, poetry, and astronomy, which was studied after the student had mastered the *trivium*: grammar, logic, and rhetoric.

the sea of forgetfulness, and I shall recount not only his achievements as Emperor, but also the services he rendered to various Emperors before he himself received the sceptre. These deeds I am going to relate, not in order to shew off my proficiency in letters, but that matters of such importance should not be left unattested for future generations. For even the greatest of deeds, if not haply preserved in written words and handed down to remembrance, become extinguished in the obscurity of silence.

Spoken like a true historian. Anna was present as the Crusaders passed through Constantinople, and she has left us striking portraits of some of them, particularly Bohemond, with whom she has a palpably erotic fascination:[29]

Now the man was such as, to put it briefly, had never before been seen in the land of the Romans, be he either of the barbarians or of the Greeks (for he was a marvel for the eyes to behold, and his reputation was terrifying). Let me describe the barbarian's appearance more particularly—he was so tall in stature that he overtopped the tallest by nearly one cubit, narrow in the waist and loins, with broad shoulders and a deep chest and powerful arms. And in the whole build of the body he was neither too slender nor overweighted with flesh, but perfectly proportioned and, one might say, built in conformity with the canon of Polycleitus. He had powerful hands and stood firmly on his feet, and his neck and back were well compacted. An accurate observer would notice that he stooped slightly, but this was not from any weakness of the vertebrae of his spine but he had probably had this posture slightly from birth. His skin all over his body was very white, and in his face the white was tempered with red. His hair was yellowish, but did not hang down to his waist like that

---

29. Some historians have speculated about a possible sexual relationship between Bohemond and Anna. Although she was young by modern standards, aristocratic young women of that age were routinely betrothed and married off. If there was a sexual relationship, however unlikely, it would have been an act of *lèse-majesté* and even a *casus belli*.

of the other barbarians; for the man was not inordinately vain of his hair, but had it cut short to the ears.

Whether his beard was reddish, or any other colour I cannot say, for the razor had passed over it very closely and left a surface smoother than chalk, most likely it too was reddish. His blue eyes indicated both a high spirit and dignity; and his nose and nostrils breathed in the air freely; his chest corresponded to his nostrils and by his nostrils . . . the breadth of his chest. For by his nostrils nature had given free passage for the high spirit which bubbled up from his heart. A certain charm hung about this man but was partly marred by a general air of the horrible. For in the whole of his body the entire man shewed implacable and savage both in his size and glance, methinks, and even his laughter sounded to others like snorting. He was so made in mind and body that both courage and passion reared their crests within him and both inclined to war. His wit was manifold and crafty and able to find a way of escape in every emergency. In conversation he was well informed, and the answers he gave were quite irrefutable. This man who was of such a size and such a character was inferior to the Emperor alone in fortune and eloquence and in other gifts of nature.

The Franks, she notes, were not at all like the refined Byzantines. They grasped instruments of war while also holding sacred objects, with no moral compunctions. "The Latin barbarian will simultaneously handle divine things, and wear his shield on his left arm, and hold his spear in his right hand, and at one and the same time he communicates the body and blood of God, and looks murderously and becomes 'a man of blood,' as it says in the psalm of David. For this barbarian race is no less devoted to sacred things than it is to war." When one of the Crusader knights, Robert of Paris (Anna simply refers to him as *Latinus*, a Latin), insolently seated himself on the emperor's throne after taking the oath of allegiance to Alexios, she was appalled.

But her horror and fascination grew even stronger once the enormous Norman barbarian chieftain arrived at the court. Bohemond spurned the Lucullan feast Alexios had laid out for him, suspecting poison, owing to their past enmity, and then at first rejected the treasures and valuables Alexios offered before taking them. The Normans' history of aggressive animosity toward the Byzantines was hard to forget, and nobody trusted Bohemond, especially Alexios and Anna. "For by nature the man was a rogue and ready for any eventualities; in roguery and courage he was far superior to all the Latins who came through then, as he was inferior to them in forces and money."

However, Alexios perfectly understood Bohemond—after all, they had already met in battle, at Dyrrachium—and knew that the ambitious Norman, who lacked a kingdom of his own, most certainly had his eyes on Byzantium, or at least a part of it. He confided as much to Saint-Gilles (whom Anna refers to phonetically as "Isangeles"), thus sowing seeds of contention and doubt among the Crusaders.

> "After the Counts had all taken leave of the Emperor and reached Damalium by crossing the Propontis,[30] and the Emperor was relieved from the disturbance they caused, he often sent for Isangeles and explained to him more clearly what he suspected would happen to the Latins on their journey, and he also laid bare to him the suspicions he had of the Franks' intention. He often repeated these things to Isangeles and opened, so to say, the doors of his soul to him and, after stating everything clearly, he enjoined him to be ever on the watch against Bohemund's wickedness and if the latter tried to break his oath to check him and by all possible means frustrate his plans.

> "Isangeles replied to the Emperor, 'Bohemund has acquired perjury and treachery as a species of ancestral heritage, and it would be a miracle if he kept his oath. However, I will endeavour as far as in me lies always to carry out your orders.' And taking his leave of the Emperor, he went away to rejoin the whole Frankish army."

Thus was Urban's original ecumenical idea of a joint Frankish-Byzantine army marching on Jerusalem already null and void. Anna

---

30. The Sea of Marmara. She means the strait of the Bosphorus, which separates Constantinople/Istanbul from Anatolia/Asia Minor.

claims all too plausibly that Alexios "desired to march against the barbarians with the Franks, but their countless masses terrified him." Not
for nothing were the Byzantines known for their Greek cunning; Julius
and Augustus Caesar may have been their political forebears, but wily
Odysseus was their role model. Via a combination of bribery and duplicity, the Eastern Roman Empire already had managed to outlive the
Western Empire by six hundred years—no mean feat given the dangerous neighborhood in which it dwelled. Even if the troublesome Turks
and Fatimid Arabs were to suddenly disappear, Byzantium would still
have its hands full maintaining its territorial integrity against a host of
other enemies, including the Bulgars, Pechenegs, Alemanni, Cumans,[31]
and the Italian Normans—not to mention its own still-simmering
internal rivalries. At this point in its history, which historians have
likened to Rome in the third century, the Byzantines were fonder of literature, the law, and philosophy than they were the arts of war. Alexios
could ill afford to be away from Constantinople for any length of time;
meanwhile, the sooner the Franks and the Normans under Bohemond's
command departed for the eastern shore of the Bosphorus, the better.

For their part, the Crusader knights harbored a deep and abiding
suspicion of Alexios and his Greeks. Instead of accompanying the
armies, Alexios had sent along one of his most trusted generals named
Tatikios, a boyhood friend who was the son of a Turk captured by Alexios's father, the warrior John Comnenus. His job was to both guide the
Westerners and keep an eye on them. Tatikios stood out among the Crusaders for many reasons, one of which was that he wore a golden pros-
thetic nose in order to hide a disfigurement received during the fighting
that had brought Alexios to power a few years before. Tatikios was also
there to ensure that the Crusaders lived up to their oaths and dutifully
returned to Alexios any and all liberated Byzantine territories.

Considering the hardships the knights of the Princes' Crusade and

---

31. Another nomadic people of Turkic origin, also known as the Polovtsy by the Kievan Rus, who encountered them in battle. The "Polovtsian Dances" from the Russian
composer Alexander Borodin's opera *Prince Igor* are a rare surviving reference to their
existence. Several of the melodies found their way into the musical *Kismet,* including
"Stranger in Paradise."

their followers soon encountered, we can only marvel that so many endured and survived—and then, since territorial conquest was not the principal motive of the vast majority of Crusaders, simply returned home to Europe when the job was done. Their supply lines, such as they were, were always tenuous, dependent on the Byzantines during their journey through Asia Minor and, later, in the Levant, on the seafarers of the nautical Italian city-states, principally Genoa. Food for man, woman, child, and beast was always an issue. (Western mounts were larger than their Turkish counterparts, which meant they required much more food and water.) The lack of water crossing the dusty interior of Anatolia was brutal, and many died of thirst. Cannibalism, sometimes of the dead bodies of the Turks, was not unknown.

How did they do it? Looking for economic or political reasons does not divulge the real answer; important as those considerations might have been to some (principally the princes with no inheritances) they were secondary to religious zeal. More than anything, their faith in the Lord propelled them across continents and often was the only thing that sustained them in pitched battle with an enemy just as zealous in the service of his god as they were. The issue is often raised by the irreligious that, as adherents of the Roman faith, the biblical proscription against violence should have strangled the crusades in their cradle. But this is to misread both the nature and the history of Christianity. The idea of a "just war"—the *bellum iustum*—dates back at least to Augustine of Hippo. Mortal violence could be justified if the cause was just, the war was lawfully declared, and the war was fought with good and honorable intentions. The First Crusade, as preached by Pope Urban and bishops across Europe, qualified on all three counts. And while there were strictures about the proper conduct of a war (reflected still in the Geneva Conventions), in the heat of battle those were easily obscured by the *Friktion* of actual combat.

The first stop on the road to Jerusalem again was Nicaea, a Byzantine city only recently (1081) taken by the Turks under Kilij Arslan and incorporated into the Sultanate of Rum (Rome) as its capital. The recapture of Nicaea, so near to Constantinople, was important to Alexios, and, in this first encounter of Crusaders and Turks, his contribution was crucial. The city was formidably walled on all sides, with some two hundred towers; its only vulnerable spot was its western port on Lake Ascanius, which body of water was also controlled by the Turks. Having so easily defeated the largely amateur warriors of the Peoples' Crusade, Kilij Arslan had contemptuously moved his troops east to deal with the Danishmends, Muslim rivals in eastern Anatolia. Unconscious of the danger the genuine armies of Christendom posed to him, he had left his family and his treasury behind in Nicaea.

Arriving at Nicaea in the middle of May and encountering its formidable defenses, the first Crusaders on the scene, including Godfrey, Bohemond, and Tancred, promptly set about laying siege, something they were very good at, given their experiences with walled and castellated European cities. So they went to work building a siege engine and sending sappers to undermine the walls' foundations.

An opening skirmish outside the walls quickly convinced the Turkish defenders that they needed help, and so they got a message through to the sultan, who turned back to meet the Christians. He first encountered the forces of Saint-Gilles and Robert II of Flanders and was defeated after hard fighting. As further Crusaders arrived under the Norman Robert Curthose, joined by Stephen of Blois, Arslan decided to retreat, leaving the field strewn with the dead bodies of his warriors. In order to cast fear into the hearts of the defenders, the Christians beheaded the corpses and lobbed the heads over the besieged town's walls (a standard tactic, later used by both sides).

In the meantime, Alexios, following behind the Franks, had set up camp at Pelecanum on the Sea of Marmara and transported ships overland to Lake Ascanius, in order to attack from the rear. The Turks, surrounded, secretly engaged in negotiations with Alexios's general, Manuel Boutoumites, while Tatikios remained with the Latins outside the walls. The Turks surrendered to Boutoumites on June 19; the first thing the Crusaders knew of it was when they saw the imperial Byzantine flags flying from Nicaea's towers. And then they noticed the gates of the city remained closed . . . they had been euchred out of victory and its spoils.

This, of course, only amplified the Westerners' mistrust of Alexios and his Greeks. To assuage the Crusaders' anger at the lack of plunder, the emperor liberally spread around some wealth and then sent the Franks on their way, but not before words were exchanged between

Alexios and Tancred, and an undying enmity forged. The *Basileus* was in no mind to allow a bunch of barbarians to loot his property when he could simply pay them off. The proximate result of the victory at Nicaea was a boon for Alexios, who took advantage of the Crusaders' absence to now recapture much of the Asia Minor seacoast, and grab some important Turkish hostages. He also struck a deal with Kilij Arslan himself whereby Byzantine rule was reestablished in many places; Alexios made it clear that Rome would not be responsible for the behavior of the barbarian Franks as they went about the reconquest of now-Muslim territory and therefore the Anatolians would be better off back under Byzantine administration.

Arslan was happy to oblige. His experience with the Byzantines had taught him their limits; he could deal with them. But these Franks were a different story. Their march eastward indicated no signs of their going home any time soon. He had underestimated them once and would try not to make the same mistake again. Deprived of plunder, and the honor of liberating a city important in the catholicism of Christianity, the Franks and their allies were furious and now sought spoils of their own. They split their forces into two sections and set out toward Antioch, all the way across Anatolia and into Syria, far to the east: a crucial objective before any advance on Jerusalem could be made. The forward Norman guard under Bohemond, Tancred, and Robert Curthose, along with their minder Tatikios, was followed at some modest distance by Godfrey, Saint-Gilles, and the others.

Arslan's counterattack came on July 1, near the ruined town of Dorylaeum. It was the first test of the Crusaders' fighting ability against the unfamiliar tactics of an evenly matched foe. It was a battle that, but for Bohemond's daring tactical sense and the bravery of the Normans—not to mention the timely arrival of Godfrey's reinforcements—might have ended the First Crusade and the Western adventure in the near East before it had even properly begun.

As we've noted, it is possible to draw parallels between individual battles widely separated by history and geography. The unexpected (by the Franks) battle of Dorylaeum began as an ambush à la the Battle of Roncevaux in 778, turned for a while into a last stand that would echo forward as far as Custer at the Little Bighorn in 1876, and ended with a complete rout of the Turks reminiscent of Gaugamela. It gave a much-needed boost of confidence to the European knights, who for a time despaired of their lives, and once again proved the efficacy of discipline, a shield wall, and a fearless commander.

About a four-day march from Nicaea, their path east emerged from some hills and narrowed as it passed through a river valley. Kilij Arslan had struck a truce with his Muslim rival Danishmend himself, who rode to his assistance, reasoning that it was better to destroy the *Franj* (as the Muslims had begun calling the Europeans) on Arslan's turf instead of fighting them later in his own lands.

As they entered the valley, the Norman contingent spotted mounted Turkish warriors dogging and shadowing them from the hills, monitoring their path and taking note of their manpower, horses, and armaments. The weather was beastly hot, and the knights sweated profusely in their gear. These were not the knights of the later Middle Ages, armored from head to toe, but they were still formidably protected. Michaud describes how they were kitted out:

> The barons and knights wore a hauberk, or coat of mail, a sort of tunic, composed of small rings of iron or steel. Over the coat of arms of every squire floated a blue, red, green, or white scarf. Every warrior wore a casque, covered with silver for the princes, of steel for the knights and nobles, and of iron for the common men. The knights bore round or square bucklers, and long shields covered the foot-soldiers. The arms employed in fight by the Crusaders were the lance, the sword, a species of knife, a poniard, called *misericorde,* the club, the *masse d'armes,* with which a warrior could, at a single blow, strike an enemy to the earth; the sling, from which wove thrown stones and balls of lead; the bow, and the cross-bow, a murderous weapon, till that time unknown to the Orientals.

Man and mount thirsted. They made camp in a meadow near the wide plain west of the abandoned city, close by the river Thymbres and its marshlands. They had no inkling of what was in store. In his 1937 study *The Crusades: The World's Debate,* Hillaire Belloc, the Anglo-French Catholic intellectual, poet, and historian, observes:

Here, so early in the great adventure, was to come a test of life or death, and the Crusade came within an ace of extinction, a thousand miles short of its objective. The commander of the victorious Turks who had overrun Asia Minor and almost reached the gates of Constantinople, had, during the siege of Nicaea gathered every man he could to destroy the Western effort while yet it could be destroyed. Qilij Arslan, he the Seljuk, had in the presence of this peril made his peace with his rivals (Turkish also), and upon what was to follow depended the fate of Europe perhaps quite as much as upon any of the other battles fought between East and West.

The Western men, our people, had never yet met the light-armed, swift-riding Nomadic hordes from the steppes of Asia which had so recently all but destroyed Eastern Christendom. They had no experience of the Turkish tactic, which had destroyed the emperor's army those few years before at Manzikert. The Norman vanguard was taken completely by surprise, and outnumbered altogether by the swarms of mounted Turkish archers.

At dawn, Arslan's army attacked. It rained arrows. Women wailed and clerics prayed. Bohemond and his mounted knights charged, hoping to smash the Turks, but on their swifter, more mobile ponies the Muslim warriors easily evaded direct engagement yet maintained their hit-and-run tactics. And still the barrage of missiles continued.

Bohemond and his horsemen rode back into the besieged camp and dismounted, forming a shield of iron as they pushed back toward the river, where the marshes would hamper the Turkish horsemen. Although such a tactic is usually inadvisable, in this case it was the only possible solution. Suffering heavy losses, they would just have to stand and take it, as long as it lasted. The unknown author of the *Gesta Francorum*, who was traveling with the Normans, describes the scene:

On the third day the Turks made a fierce and sudden attack upon Bohemund and his comrades. These Turks began, all at once, to howl and gabble and shout, saying with loud voices in their own language some devilish word which I do not understand. The valiant Bohemund saw that there were innumerable Turks some distance off, howling and shouting like demons, so he ordered all the knights to dismount at once and to pitch camp quickly . . .

After we had set ourselves in order the Turks came upon us from all sides, skirmishing, throwing darts and javelins and shooting arrows from an astonishing range. Although we had no chance of withstanding them or of taking the weight of the charge of so many foes we went forward as one man. The women in our camp were a great help to us that day, for they brought up water for the fighting men to drink, and gallantly encouraged those who were fighting and defending them. The valiant Bohemund made haste to send a message to the others (the count of St Gilles and Duke Godfrey, Hugh the Great and the bishop of Le Puy, with all the rest of the Christian knights) telling them to hurry and come to the battlefield with all speed, and saying, "If any of you wants to fight today, let him come and play the man." . . . For our part, we passed a secret message along our line, praising God and saying, "Stand fast all together, trusting in Christ and in the victory of the Holy Cross. Today, please God, you will all gain much booty."

At one point, the Turks, led by their sultan, breached the defensive wall, crossed the river, and got into the center of the camp, where the women and children were. Even at this early stage of the war, everyone knew that a captured young woman would be subjected to the proverbial "fate worse than death"—that is, sexual slavery in the harems. Writes Michaud: "The Saracens massacred all who came within reach of their swords; sparing none but young and beautiful women, whom they destined for their seraglios. If we are to believe Albert of Aix, the daughters and the wives of the barons and knights preferred on this occasion slavery to death; for they were seen, in the midst of the tumult, decking themselves in their most beautiful vestments, and presenting themselves thus before the Saracens, seeking by the display of their charms to soften the hearts of a pitiless enemy." Wielding his deadly weapons to maximum effect and shouting the Crusader slogan *Deus lo vult!* (It is the will of the Lord!), Bohemond came to their rescue and sent the Turks scattering, and the women quickly fell back into line.[32]

After five hours, the reinforcements arrived. Some of the Normans swore that St. George, St. Demetrius (a fourth-century Christian martyr), and other spectral warriors were leading the charge. The Crusaders' battle line formed up now, into wings, with the Normans on the left and Godfrey and Robert of Flanders on the right, along with Saint-Gilles and Hugh of Vermandois, another important Crusader leader. Unseen by the Turks, forces under Bishop Adhemar managed to flank the main Turkish force and attack from the rear, sending them scattering in confusion as the combined Crusader forces mounted a frontal assault.

"They fled very fast to their camp, but they were not allowed to stay there long, so they continued their flight and we pursued them, killing them, for a whole day, and we took much booty, gold, silver, horses, asses, camels, oxen, sheep and many other things about which we do not know," according to the *Gesta Francorum*. Of course, it was all God's will: "If God had not been with us in this battle and sent us the other army quickly, none of us would have escaped, because the fighting went on from the third hour until the ninth, but Almighty God, who is gracious and merciful, delivered his knights from death and from falling into the hands of the enemy and sent us help speedily."

Miraculously the Crusaders had been spared; even more miraculously, they had won a smashing victory against a skilled and highly motivated, hitherto undefeated foe defending his turf. They counted their dead, among them Robert of Paris who had profaned the emperor's throne back in Constantinople; against the advice Alexios had personally given him, he broke under the sustained bombardment, rushed the enemy, and was cut to pieces. The Crusaders stripped the bodies of the Turks and wore their blood-stained clothes as they aped their mannerisms and mocked their corpses. "Though there was no destruction of the enemy force, Dorylaeum, as the sun sank somewhat lower in the bronze and dusty sky of that broiling afternoon, had proved

---

32. As this and other historical examples show, women will almost always go over to the enemy if they think their men have failed to protect them and their children.

to be a complete decision," writes Belloc. "The Seljuk Turks could attack no more: the long way to Syria was open, and, what was more, the West had proved, after so many generations, its superiority over the East. Loosely knit as these Crusading bands were, they had discovered sufficient energy in action to throw back the Seljuk menace to Christendom; they proved themselves capable of advance against Mohammedan armies in an ordeal to which the two religions had each summoned all the force at its disposal. The victory was won."

At Dorylaeum, the First Crusade had almost ended in the same bloody ignominy that had marked the Peoples' Crusade, which had given the Turks such a low opinion of the Franks. The crowned heads of Europe had very nearly been held up on pikes, their kinsmen slain, their women taken captive, all their possessions lost. Had the Normans been annihilated before the timely rescue by Godfrey and the others, it is perfectly plausible to suggest that the others might have turned back for home, their holy war stillborn. Certainly some of them would have—deserters were always a problem. Half their best leaders might have lain dead on the field of battle, their bodies stripped of their armor, carrion for the birds.

That they did not was largely thanks to the giant figure of Bohemond, whose commanding authority had held his panicky troops in good order under the ferocious barrage of the Turks. "In this extremity," writes the British military historian George Proctor in his *History of the Crusades* (1800), "the skillful and valorous conduct of Bohemond, never elsewhere so nobly contrasted with the baser qualities of his character, saved the whole crusading host from destruction."

Alexios had warned all the *Franj* about the Turkish way of war, which prized speed, ferocity, and surprise. The age of chivalry may have begun in Europe, a time in which gallantry was at least given lip service in the songs of the emerging minstrels, but in this strange and forbidding land of howling heathens there was no trace of it. Here, women were still possessions, to be bought and sold and used as their new masters saw fit. Christian boys were deflowered (the Turkish penchant for buggery was already notorious in Europe), sometimes castrated to become eunuchs in the harems or forcibly converted to Islam, and, by the fourteenth century, inducted into elite fighting units of Western slaves known as Janissaries. Still, the Turks had won the grudging respect of the Westerners. Writes Michaud:

> The intoxication of victory, however, did not prevent their doing justice to the bravery of the Turks, who, from that time, boasted of having a common origin with the Franks.[33] Contemporary historians, who praise the valour of the Turks, add, that they only wanted to be Christians to make them quite comparable to the Crusaders.

That was the solidarity of soldiers talking. For their part, the Turks discovered that the men of iron were every bit as fearsome as they appeared. Everything about them was larger than life, including their stature, their physical strength, the iron spine of their faith, and their steeds. They could slash a foe from head to toe, cut him in half as he rode by on horseback, or shatter his skull. Unprepared for this kind of warfare, the Turks counted on the fleetness of their horses to escape the mace. But in these early encounters, the Muslims were unable to field a proper allotment of six horses per mounted warrior to account for exhaustion, and when their ponies flagged or collapsed, the knights were able to catch up to them and pound them into dust.

"The quivers of the infidels were almost emptied," writes Major Proctor, then a professor at the Royal Military Academy at Sandhurst, "the length of the struggle had worn down their activity; and in the close combat they could no longer escape, their inferiority to the warriors of the West in bodily strength and martial equipment was signally displayed. The supple dexterity of the Asiatic was now feebly opposed to the ponderous strokes of the European arm; the curved scimitar and light javelin could neither parry nor return with effect the deadly thrust of the long pointed sword and gigantic lance; and in a direct charge, the weight and compactness of the Latin chivalry overpowered the loose order and desultory tactics of the Turkish hordes."

Dorylaeum for the Turks was what the Catalaunian Plains had been

---

33. They did indeed. By claiming they shared a common ancestor with the Franks, the Turks could partially rationalize their stunning defeat.

for the Huns: a sudden, bracing realization that they were not invincible after all. In confronting the Crusaders for the first time in open battle, the Turks had learned a new emotion: fear.

Belatedly—and this ultimately would take nearly a century—the Muslims also learned that no matter what their own doctrinal differences,[34] they would have to work together in order to repel the invaders. Had Kilij Arslan not been battling the Danishmends, he might have successfully defended his capital at Nicaea and thus throttled the *Franj* incursion in its cradle. The lesson that Darius III had learned at the hands of Alexander at the Granicus and Issus—both located in Anatolia—had evidently been forgotten or never learned in the first place: invaders from the West needed to be stopped as early as possible, before they had fully penetrated your territory and handed you a Gaugamela.

The next test of mettle came at Antioch. After their victory at Dorylaeum and the discomfiture of their enemies, the Crusaders expected to make quick progress through Asia Minor on their way to Syria. But Tatikios had other plans. His mission, after all, was a reclamation project, and so he led the Franks on a wandering path through Anatolia for maximum strategic territorial gain. Any Turks they encountered quickly fled, returning the land to Byzantine control and giving the Crusaders a morale boost but also a false overconfidence.

Along the way, both Tancred and Baldwin split off from the main body and headed south to the Armenian Cilician coast. The move made considerable strategic sense, since control of that stretch of coastline would protect the Crusaders and the sea lanes, but both men were ambitious and hungry for territory of their own. At Tarsus, St. Paul's birthplace, the two crusader forces even came to blows. Baldwin won out and handed control back to Alexios via Tatikios, while the headstrong Tancred hied off to rejoin his uncle in the march on Antioch.

Baldwin, meanwhile, remained in Cilicia, accepting an invitation from Thoros of Edessa, the Syrian city's Armenian-Byzantine ruler, to help him continue to fend off the Turks—a move that would soon

---

34. Islam, which lacks a central authority figure like a pope or the archbishop of Canterbury, split over questions of succession shortly after Muhammad's death in 632 A.D. The ensuing conflict between Shi'ite and Sunni remains to be resolved.

enough have considerable ramifications in the history of *Outremer*. There, he was welcome as a representative of the emperor Alexios and essentially handed the keys to the city. In short order, Thoros was killed in a not-coincidental popular uprising and the ambitious Baldwin acclaimed as the new lord of the city. Thus was born the first Crusader state, the County of Edessa (1098–1144).

After a harrowing passage over Mount Taurus, the main Crusader army finally made it to Syria, the rich and fertile former Roman province, and thus to Antioch, one of the principal cities of early Christianity, on October 21. Also known as Theopolis, the city of God, Antioch was the reputed site of the Apostle Peter's first ministry after a flight from Jerusalem, the place where his people first began calling themselves Christians. St. Paul had lived and worked there as well, from 47 to 55 A.D. Celebrated as "the eldest daughter of Sion," Antioch, the Queen of the East, had been a center of learning and disputation for centuries, and was second only to Jerusalem as the holiest site in Christendom. First taken by Arabs for Islam in 637, it was recaptured by the Byzantines in 969, then lost to the Seljuk Turks in 1084. Now the Crusaders were determined to capture it in the name of a Europeanized Christ, thus opening the way down the Levantine coast to their ultimate objective, Jerusalem.

It was not an easy journey. The vengeful Turks had preceded them, destroying crops and whole towns, poisoning wells, determined to make the Franks suffer. Horses died from lack of forage and water, forcing the mounted knights to either walk alongside their foot soldiers or ride on the backs of donkeys and oxen. Pregnant women gave premature birth, women with newborns and infants found that their milk had dried up and could not nourish their babies. Once again, they cried out to God to rescue them. Along the way, Raymond Saint-Gilles fell seriously ill, and his life was despaired of. And Godfrey, their moral leader and exemplar, was mauled by a bear while defending one of his soldiers from its predation. Although both leaders survived, each man had to be carried on a litter the rest of the way.

Like Constantinople, Antioch was a model of Roman-Byzantine fortification, engineered by the emperor Justinian in the sixth century. It was situated above the Orontes River and protected on its southeastern side by Mount Silpius, with the city's nearly inaccessible citadel—its keep of last resort—at the highest point. There were some four hundred defensive towers atop its massive walls; while the city had recently gone back and forth between Byzantine and Muslim occupation as a result of various treacheries, the walls had never been breached. Like all of the contested towns and cities in this part of the world at the time, it hosted a polyglot population of Christians and Muslims of various ethnic divides, including a sizable portion of Armenians, Greeks, and Jews, along with smaller Christian sects such as the Syriacs and the Melkites, whose ranks included early Jewish converts to Christianity. The city's Seljuk Turkish commander was Yaghi-Siyan, who controlled a garrison force of about six thousand men. Upon hearing of the approach of the Franks, he immediately requested assistance from other emirs in the area, including those in Mosul and Damascus.

Taking Antioch was vital to the success of the First Crusade. The city was situated directly north of Jerusalem and thus controlled the critical access points from the land. It was hemmed in by the bend of the river Orontes, which at one stretch ran very near the walls by the Bridge Gate on its way to the sea. It even maintained a seaport, St. Simeon, located some eight and a half miles to the west, control of which would be crucial for the Crusaders. Although the Crusaders had no formal command hierarchy, Bohemond, fresh off his heroics at Dorylaeum, had effectively taken principal command.

His challenge was formidable. Already the Crusaders' numbers had been seriously reduced via battlefield casualties, attrition, disease, and desertion. As they approached Antioch, they probably counted about forty thousand, including the noncombatants. They were entering the heart of enemy territory, where the Byzantine writ no longer held sway. And while their foes were disorganized and often at one another's throats, the Franks had learned that the Muslim warriors were not to be underestimated in either battlefield prowess, lust for triumph, or an unswerving belief that they were doing the Lord's work. True, there was no one dominant figure among the Turks and the Arabs as, a century later, there would be in the figure of the Kurdish Muslim general, Saladin, the personification of *jihad*. But neither was there among the Christian fighters. Add to that the princes' penchant for constant squabbling and jealousy and mutual suspicion that would have embarrassed the Greeks at Troy.

With Godfrey and Raymond partially *hors de combat,* it fell to Bohemond to plan the assault. Despite the relatively small garrison inside the gates, the Norman knew that reinforcements from other Muslim territories would soon enough be on their way. He had to somehow breach the impregnable walls before they arrived and could trap the Crusaders between the Orontes and the city walls. With nowhere to run and little room in which to maneuver in formation, they would certainly be slaughtered. They were in a tough spot, and it could only get worse from here.

In some ways, Bohemond's initial position was akin to Caesar's at Alesia during the Gallic Wars. He was approaching a strongly fortified hilltop city (far more formidable than Alesia). He lacked the numbers to overwhelm it and its still-potent fighting force. As with Caesar, he knew that a huge army of reinforcements was on its way; unlike Caesar, there was no way he could construct a second wall to keep the newcomers out while he battled the defenders within. His only chance was to capture the city before help could arrive. Once again, it looked like the First Crusade might end long before it sighted the walls of Jerusalem, still some three hundred miles away.

Thus the Battle of Antioch, a strategic masterpiece (although not recommended in its particulars except to those *in extremis*), begun in late October of 1097, was fought in several stages. Bohemond's genius was to square off at various bottlenecks and pressure points where he could project temporary numerical or tactical superiority over the Turks, who always outnumbered him in aggregate. The decision was made to try and starve the city into submission, despite the fact that he lacked the manpower to completely encircle it, and so stationed most of his forces at its weak spots, the gates. This, however, ensured almost continuous fighting, as the residents of Antioch and the crusader army both were facing a long winter of potential starvation unless they could be resupplied.

As the Crusaders settled into their encampments, inside the town all was quiet. With a false sense of security, the Christian forces spread out to enjoy the emoluments of the fertile countryside and the charms of the local women. But a tryst in the woods could end in sudden death whenever Turkish scouts would happen upon the lad and his inamorata and, after raping the woman, summarily beheaded the indiscreet lovers and tossed their heads back into the Christian camps. But when enough young noblemen were surprised *in flagrante* by roving bands of warriors and killed, Bohemond decided it was time to storm the walls, even though he had no siege implements to hand.

One advantage Bohemond did have was that his army was now a hardened, battle-tested group of warriors whose ability to get even this far had made them feel confident not only in their ability to handle the Turks and their legions of mounted archers, but also in God's manifest support for their cause. *Deus lo vult* was the watchword of the day. So far, the Almighty had bailed them out of every sticky situation, and as long as they kept the faith, there was no reason for Him to abandon them.

While Yaghi-Siyan had laid in provisions in anticipation of a siege, and the Crusaders had captured the city's port at St. Simeon to deny him aid from the sea, by Christmas the Crusaders had already stripped the countryside bare. On a foraging expedition, Bohemond and Robert of Flanders ran headlong into a ten-thousand-man relief force commanded by Duqaq of Damascus, who were routed and sent fleeing back to Damascus when the Crusaders charged them straight on (once again proving the superiority of the Europeans' heavy cavalry), but at a heavy cost in manpower; a war of attrition was one Bohemond could not win. Outside the city walls the Crusaders periodically had to fend off sorties from Yaghi-Siyan's men, one of which very nearly ended in disaster for the defenders when Saint-Gilles and his men not only turned the sally back at the Bridge Gate, hard by the Orontes, but very nearly got inside themselves.

Although they were now receiving supplies at the captured port from Genoese and Byzantine ships, the situation was nevertheless once again becoming dire. The Crusaders had exhausted the nearby fields and orchards, and famine was threatening. There was, of course, only one possible explanation. "We felt that misfortunes had befallen the Franks because of their sins and that for this reason they were not able to take the city for so long a time," wrote the contemporary chronicler

Fulcher of Chartres, a participant himself with the Norman contingent of Robert Curthose and Stephen of Blois. "Luxury and avarice and pride and plunder had indeed vitiated them. Then the Franks, having again consulted together, expelled the women from the army, the married as well as the unmarried, lest perhaps defiled by the sordidness of riotous living they should displease the Lord." Such proscriptions came and went, but throughout the crusade the men of the cloth remained very wary of the potent power of female sexuality. The cure was invariably days of chastity, fasting, and prayer.

We might pause here to observe that among the criticisms of *Gerusalemme liberata,* Tasso's great poem, were the interpolations of various love stories into the narrative. But a reading of the eyewitness chroniclers such as the author of the *Gesta,* Fulcher, and Raymond of Aguilers reveals countless allusions to matters sexual, most of which blame the women for tempting the warriors by their unbridled lust and wanton behavior, which is why in the poem several of the knightly encounters are with sorceresses and sultry, seductive witches.

Notes Michaud, "If contemporary accounts are to be credited, all the vices of the infamous Babylon prevailed among the liberators of Sion. Strange and unheard-of spectacle! Beneath the tents of the Crusaders famine and voluptuousness formed a hideous union; impure love, an unbounded passion for play, with all the excesses of debauch, were mingled with images of death. In their misfortunes, the greater part of the pilgrims seemed to disdain the consolations that might have been derived from piety and virtue."

The onset of the winter rains brought floods and disease. Tents floated away. Epidemics swept through the *laagers.* Man and beast died. Some soldiers headed north to Edessa, where Baldwin now held sway among the Armenians. Robert Curthose, the Norman, for a time went AWOL to Laodicea (Latakia), a port on the Syrian coast, until finally summoned to return to Antioch in the name of the faith and of the Lord Jesus. Peter the Hermit also slipped away, along with a valiant soldier known as William the Carpenter from the way he swung his axe in battle. They were both hauled back. No one could miss the irony that the man who had preached the crusade and celebrated the spiritual joys of fasting couldn't take the fast or the famine and refused to practice what he had so piously preached.

At this point, Tatikios also abandoned the Crusaders, telling them he was returning to Anatolia to get more supplies from Alexios, who was still engaged in mopping-up operations in Asia Minor. The defection of Tatikios only confirmed the notion of Greek treachery in the minds of the Franks, although Anna, in her account, says that Tatikios left at Bohemond's insistence, since the Norman wanted Antioch for himself and needed the spy out of the way. Then again, she would say that.

Things looked hopeless once more. Facing not only starvation but the relentless sapping of Turkish raiders, Bohemond experimented with psychological warfare of a particularly repellent nature. According to William of Tyre, a later chronicler who lived his entire life in the Kingdom of Jerusalem, Bohemond ordered that three Turkish prisoners caught spying be brought before him. A large fire was lit. Bohemond had them killed on the spot, then skewered with spits and roasted over the flames, proclaiming "all Turks or spies that shall henceforward be found in their camps, shall be, in this manner, forced to make meat with their own bodies." It's unclear whether the Christians actually ate these particular victims (although there are other accounts of cannibalism involving desperate Crusaders consuming Turkish corpses) but word of the object lesson soon spread far and wide, and the spying ceased.

In February 1098 news came that another relief force, this one under the command of Ridwan of Aleppo, was coming to lift the siege. Even though there was still no single leader of the crusading forces, it was now clear to everybody that Bohemond was the man most fit to formally lead the fight against the Muslims. He gladly accepted the offer, in part because, despite his pledge to Alexios back in Constantinople, he wanted Antioch for himself and had no intention of returning the city to the Greeks. He divided the Crusader forces between the foot soldiers, who were left behind to guard the camps against any sorties from within the walls, and bade the knights to follow him and Robert of Flanders.

Near the Lake of Antioch, north of the city, and with only about seven hundred mounted knights remaining, they secretly positioned five divisions of heavy cavalry near the lake, the Orontes, some marshes, and something called the Iron Bridge in order to ambush the oncoming Muslim force. "Gentlemen and unconquered knights, draw up your line of battle!" ordered Bohemond, and although hugely outnumbered by Ridwan's ten thousand warriors, they charged.

At first glance, this seems suicidal. No matter how brave the Normans and their allies were, to rush headlong into an engagement with such a superior force appears foolhardy. But Bohemond had taken the measure of his enemies. His position on a hill between the river and the lake, with the bridge across the Orontes nearby, was somewhat risky since a retreat would be difficult, but Bohemond counted on his knowledge of Turkish cavalry tactics and the importance they placed on encircling the enemy. The Christian position made that impossible. Further, he knew that the Turks were poor with both lance and sword, relying instead on their skill with the bow from a distance and their nimble horses to keep the Franks away. But Bohemond gave them no time to escape. At the Battle of the Iron Bridge, he had the fight he wanted, exactly where he wanted it, and on his terms—the hallmark of every great commander since Alexander.

Robert and his units headed straight for the emir of Aleppo's advance guard, colliding with them and pushing them back in retreat into the main forces, allowing the forces of chaos—*friction*—to take over. The Turks wanted nothing to do with the Crusaders' sword arms and lances, and at close range their bows were ineffective. Fierce hand-to-hand fighting on horseback ensued. But after the initial shock, the Turks began to rally and, as Ridwan's main forces moved to the front of the Western lines, even get the upper hand. Once again (according the *Gesta Francorum*), Bohemond stepped up, shouting:

"Charge at top speed, like a brave man, and fight valiantly for God and the Holy Sepulchre, for you know in truth that this is no war of the flesh, but of the spirit. So be very brave, as becomes a champion of Christ. Go in peace, and may the Lord be your defence!" So Bohemund, protected on all sides by the sign of the Cross, charged the Turkish forces, like a lion which has been starving for three or four days, which comes roaring out of its cave thirsting for the blood of cattle, and falls upon the flocks careless of its own safety, tearing the sheep as they flee hither and thither.

Another eyewitness chronicler, Raymond of Aguilers, the chaplain to Saint-Gilles, added this after-action detail in his *Historia Francorum qui ceperunt Iherusalem*: "With the battle and booty won, we carried the heads of the slain to camp and stuck them on posts as grim reminders of the plight of their Turkish allies and of future woes for the besieged. Now as we reflect upon it, we have concluded that this was God's command because the Turks had formerly disgraced us by fixing the point of the captured banner of the blessed Mary in the ground. Thus God disposed that the sight of lifeless heads of friends supported by pointed sticks would ban further taunts from the defenders of Antioch." About the same time, Yaghi-Siyan attempted an assault on the remaining Frankish infantry, but that too was repelled.

Further tests of arms lay ahead, including a Turkish attack on St. Simeon that imperiled both Bohemond and Raymond, who had ridden to its defense, leading to panicked rumors that they had been killed. With material brought from one of the relief fleets, the Crusaders began the construction of siege engines, and erected a fort outside the walls to block any exits from the city's Bridge Gate; Tancred also captured an abandoned monastery near St. George's Gate at the city's southern end and fortified it as "Tancred's Castle." Now the siege began to choke the life out of the Turkish garrison.

In April of 1098, an unexpected embassy arrived from Fatimid Egypt, proposing an alliance with the Europeans against their mutual enemy, the Turks, from whom the Egyptians were planning to seize Jerusalem. The terms were generous: if successful, the Egyptians promised to restore the Christian churches, protect pilgrims, and open the gates to everyone, with the proviso that they come unarmed and stay no more than a month. Since the capture and liberation of the Holy City was the objective of the entire enterprise, and the Crusaders had sworn a sacred oath to return Jerusalem to Christian control, the proposal was politely rejected. Still, the princes sent a small delegation of Christians

back to Cairo with the Muslims in order to explore possible cooperation.[35] After all, the enemy of my enemy often became my friend, at least
temporarily.

In May came ominous news: a third Muslim relief expedition was
underway, this one led by Kerbogha, the *atabeg* (governor) of Mosul. At
thirty-five thousand men, this would be the largest force sent against the
Christians to date, comprising Ridwan and Duqaq's armies as well as
troops from as far away as Persia. Instead of marching directly on Antioch, however, Kerbogha decided to detour via Edessa and try to wrest
that city from Baldwin. Kerbogha, however, could not take Edessa, and
after a few days gave up and began moving on Antioch. Time was of the
essence. Bohemond had to act.

In the end, the city was once again taken by treachery and greed.
For some time Bohemond had been cultivating a potential traitor, an
Armenian officer in Yaghi-Siyan's service named Farouz, who had op-
portunistically converted from Christianity to Islam for the purposes of
career advancement. Bohemond went to the other leaders with a proposition: if they would make him Prince of Antioch and abjure their oath
to Alexios, he would win the city. Now the dissension among the princes
exploded into the open. None of them had ever really trusted the ambitious Bohemond; for his part, the temperamental Norman was furious
that Baldwin had recently sent lavish gifts from Edessa to all the princes
except him. Raymond violently objected; they almost came to blows. Stephen of Blois—whom the Crusaders had just elected as the parliamentary
leader of their council, and who had been henpecked by his wife into
going on the crusade in the first place—deserted on June 2 and returned
to France, winning his place among history's greatest cowards.[36]

---

35. Unsurprising. Dating all the way back to the time of Alexander and the Battle of the
Granicus, opposing armies often had fellow countrymen, ethnics, or coreligionists fighting in the service of the other side.

36. His furious wife, Adela of Normandy, daughter of William the Conqueror, immediately
turned him right around and sent him back to fulfill his vows. Rejoining a secondary
crusade in 1101 (known as the Crusade of the Faint-Hearted for its number of deserters
having another go at salvation), he was captured at the Second Battle of Ramla by the
Fatimids and executed.

But their options were fast dwindling. Kerbogha and his huge army were coming. Bohemond got his deal, and that same night, just before dawn, he led a commando force into the city by climbing via a leather ladder one of the towers supervised by Farouz and opening a small service gate to let in his platoons. By morning, Bohemond's distinctive red banner was fluttering above the city, and Crusaders were rampaging through the town, shouting *Deus lo vult!* and killing everyone in sight. If you could not show a sign of the Cross or otherwise prove you were Christian, you died on the spot. Estimates (always unreliable) were that some six thousand people perished. "The pillage of Antioch had yielded them immense riches," wrote Michaud. "They abandoned themselves to the most extravagant excesses of intemperance and debauchery."

Yaghi-Siyan fled but was captured by some Armenian and Syrian Christians and beheaded. A small force of Turks under his son, Shams ad-Daulah, had managed to take refuge in the redoubtable citadel, where they held out against Bohemond's assaults. Still, the prize was won. But now their real troubles began.

Bohemond's position was at this point almost exactly analogous to Caesar's at Alesia in 52 B.C., sandwiched between two allied enemy forces: those in the citadel, which was almost impossible to take by storm and which in any case Shams had handed over to the atabeg, and the arriving massed army of Kerbogha outside the walls of Antioch. Bohemond therefore had to find a way to defeat the new Muslim army before they starved the Crusaders out of newly won Antioch and put them all to the sword. The hunter was now the hunted, trapped by his own victory.

At last it seemed the Turks had figured out what peril they were in from these barbarians from the west. The *Franj* were no effete pushovers like the Byzantines who, after Manzikert, could only buy their way out of trouble. Constantinople, they were sure, would someday be theirs, but before it was, they could lose Jerusalem.

Kerbogha, however, now made the fatal mistake of underestimating his opponent one more time. Someone brought him a fallen crusader's sword, all rusted, a useless spear, and a defective bow. "Are these the warlike and splendid weapons which the Christians have brought into Asia against us, and with these do they confidently expect to drive us beyond the furthest boundaries of Khorasan, and to blot out our names beyond the rivers of the Amazons? Are these the people who drove all our forefathers out of Rum and from the royal city of Antioch, which is the honoured capital of all Syria?" he inquired.

According to the *Gesta*, after boasting how he would drive the Christians all the way back to Apulia in Italy, Kerbogha was warned by his mother against taking the Crusaders too lightly; Bohemond and Tancred, the invincible warriors, were the special favorites of their god, she said, and from her study of astronomy and astrology, as well as predictions hidden in the Koran, the *Franj* were destined to win. "The Christians alone cannot fight with you, but their god fights for them every day."

"Be it so," replied the fatalistic Kerbogha, "yet will I not turn aside from battle with them." Although this story is surely fictitious (how would the author of the *Gesta* know?) it serves to reemphasize how strongly the favor of God was sought by both sides. The First Crusade had become a battle between warring divinities, Jesus and Allah.

Before the city was fully invested, but with Kerbogha's arrival imminent, a few more deserters had slipped away and joined the runaway Stephen of Blois in Tarsus in Cilicia. The sight of them fully convinced Stephen that Antioch was doomed—had probably already fallen—and so when by chance he encountered Alexios, fresh from his operations in western Anatolia and finally on his way to offer the Crusaders support at Antioch, he persuaded the Byzantine emperor that all had been lost. And so, incredibly but understandably, Alexios turned back, leaving the princes to their fate. It was not the worst possible outcome; if the Crusaders and the Turks managed to destroy one another, so much the better for him.

Upon hearing the news that Alexios had turned back, the Crusaders' fury at him reached fever pitch, an animosity that transcended generations until it culminated in the sack of Constantinople in 1204 by an army of Western knights during the Fourth Crusade. The news also increased their sense of despair so badly that for a time some of the Christian warriors refused to come out of their dwellings to answer the call of duty until the ruthless Bohemond set several city quarters on fire to drive them into the streets. An offer of surrender was sent to Kerbogha, who contemptuously rejected it. Kerbogha made two attempts to storm the city, on June 7 and 9, but was blocked each time, with losses on both sides. More soldiers deserted and made their way to the port of St. Simeon, but the Turks caught up with them, killed them all, and burned the ships they found in the harbor. Worse, the Turks who'd been holed up in the citadel sallied forth from time to time and attacked the Crusaders from the rear; in response—and in another echo of Alesia—the Christians built a wall around the keep to prevent further attacks. Thus the remainder of Yaghi-Siyan's garrison was now walled in the citadel, the Crusaders were walled inside Antioch, and a massive Turkish army awaited them outside.

Tancred bucked everybody up when he swore that as long as he had sixty men to fight beside him, he would never give up the quest to liberate the Holy City of Jerusalem. But the Crusaders would need yet another miracle—this one greater than Dorylaeum—to survive, much less emerge victorious.

Right on schedule, there were omens: natural phenomena, such as comets, earth tremors and even the aurora borealis, which the Crusaders had never seen. But it was the saints who came to their rescue: St. Andrew (one of the twelve Apostles), Jesus, and the Blessed Virgin made appearances to various holy men. The starving soldiers had visions. In one hallucination, Christ rejected the prayers of the licentious Crusaders and was willing to consign them to their doom until a timely intercession by Mother Mary saved the day. A Provençal named Peter Bartholomew had an even stronger, more specific revelation: St. Andrew had come to him in the night—in the aftershock of an earthquake—and told him that the Holy Lance—the spear that had pierced Christ's side at the Crucifixion—was buried under the floor of Antioch's Cathedral of St. Peter. While highly improbable, some in the Crusader leadership took this seriously; pieces of the True Cross had been floating around Europe since the time of Constantine's mom, and holy relics, including body parts of the saints, were much prized.[37] According to Raymond of Aguilers, Peter said:

---

37. Two of the most famous, the Veil of St. Veronica and the Shroud of Turin, did not go on public display until the fourteenth century, although there are earlier references to

I was alone abed in my hut without the reassurance of friends; it was dark, and as I have said the shocks continued at length, thereby adding to my anxiety. At this moment two men clad in brilliant garments appeared to me. The older one had red hair sprinkled with white, a broad and bushy white beard, black eyes and an agreeable countenance, and was of medium height; his younger companion was taller, and "fair in form beyond the sons of men."[38] [The older man] further commanded "Follow me and I shall reveal to you the lance of our Father, which you must give to the count because God set it aside for him at birth."

Peter recounted that he followed the apparitions into the church, where St. Andrew, the older man, dug in the ground and came up with the tip of the Lance. The saint then reburied the object and commanded Peter to announce his discovery to his master, Saint-Gilles, and to Bishop Adhemar. The story got increasingly convoluted, but here was Peter, six months after the fact, to report the vision. The next night, none other than Jesus the Christ appeared to a priest named Stephen of Valence and asked to know who the Crusader chieftain was.[39]

Stephen replied, "Lord, we have no unified command, but we trust Adhemar more than others." Then Christ commanded: "Tell the bishop that these people by their evil deeds have alienated me, and because of this he should command, 'Turn from sin and I shall return to you.' Later when they go to fight they shall say, 'Our enemies are gathered together and boast of their might; crush their might, O Lord! and rout them so that they shall know

---

the Veil well before that. The discovery of the True Cross, along with several of the Holy Nails, is attributed to Constantine's mother, St. Helena, who according to tradition found them as she was overseeing the construction of the Church of the Holy Sepulcher on a site previously occupied by a Roman temple and brought them back to Constantinople.

38. Peter later identified this figure as Jesus himself.

39. Like God the Father in the Garden of Eden in Genesis, who couldn't immediately locate Adam after the incident with the apple. It seems odd that Jesus wouldn't know who was in charge at Antioch.

thou, our God, alone battlest with us.' And add these instructions, 'My compassion shall be with you if you follow my commands for five days.'"

Even Mary got into the act: "While he spoke thus a woman, Mary, mother of Jesus Christ, whose countenance was haloed brilliantly, came near, looked towards the Lord and enquired, 'What are you telling this man?' And Christ answered Mary, 'I asked who were the people within Antioch.' The Lady declared, 'O my master! They are Christians who are so often in my prayers to you.'"

The author of the *Gesta Francorum* adds this piquant detail to Stephen's confabulation: "The Lord replied, 'I have given you great help, and I will help you hereafter. I granted you the city of Nicaea, and victory in all your battles, and I have led you hither and suffered with you in all the troubles which you have endured in the siege of Antioch. Behold, I gave you timely help and put you safe and sound into the city of Antioch, but you are satisfying your filthy lusts both with Christians and with loose pagan women, so that a great stench goes up to heaven.'" The New Testament god of the Crusaders, it seems, was just as preoccupied with fornication as his Old Testament counterpart.

Father Stephen was so confident in the veracity of his tale that he offered this challenge: "Gentlemen, if you do not believe this to be true, let me climb up this tower and throw myself down from it; if I am unhurt, believe that I speak the truth, but if I suffer any injury, then behead me or throw me into the fire."

Adhemar, the papal legate and fighting bishop, scoffed, but Raymond was taken in. The Turks in the citadel were increasingly on the offensive, threatening to break through the wall that was protecting the Crusaders. Famine was threatening, his forces were restive, desertions were increasing, and he was convinced not only that the situation was hopeless but also that the princes were scheming to flee to the port and leave the rest of the people to the tender mercies of the Turks. Raymond needed a game-changer. Accordingly, digging began immediately, but turned up nothing. Finally, Peter Bartholomew leaped into the hole in the floor of the church and began scrabbling at the earth with his bare hands.

We had been digging until evening when some gave up hope of unearthing the lance. In the meantime after the count had gone to guard the citadel, we persuaded fresh workers to replace the weary diggers and for a time they dug furiously. But the youthful Peter Bartholomew, seeing the exhaustion of our workers, stripped his outer garments and, clad only in a shirt and barefooted, dropped into the hole. He then begged us to pray to God to return his lance to the crusaders so as to bring strength and victory to his people. Finally, prompted by his gracious compassion, the Lord showed us his lance and I, Raymond [of Aguilers], author of this book, kissed the point of the lance as it barely protruded from the ground. I cannot relate the happiness and rejoicing which filled Antioch, but I can state that the lance was uncovered on the eighteenth day before the calends of July [14 June].

The Crusaders sent emissaries to Kerbogha, one of whom was the unsinkable Peter the Hermit, to inform him that Antioch by rights belonged to the Christians, but the leaders of the Franks would graciously allow the Turkish leader to withdraw peacefully with all his "goods, horses and mules, asses and camels, and to take with you all your sheep and oxen and other possessions whithersoever you may choose." On behalf of the Crusaders Peter also offered the Turks a choice of single combat, or a fight between small forces of equal number on both sides, winner take all.

Kerbogha sneered: "We neither want nor like your god and your Christendom, and we spit upon you and upon them. We have come here because we are scandalised to think that those leaders and commanders whom you name should lay claim to the land which we have conquered from an effeminate people. Do you want to know our answer? Then go back as fast as you can, and tell your leaders that if they will all become Turks, and renounce the god whom you worship on bended knee, and cast out your laws, we will give them this land and more besides, with cities and castles, so that none of you shall remain a foot-soldier, but you shall all be knights as we are: and tell them that we will count them always among our dearest friends. Otherwise, let them know that they shall all be slain or led in chains to Khorasan,[40] where they shall serve us and our children for all time, in everlasting captivity."

There was nothing left to do but fight. The Christians spent three days in fasting (probably not much of a sacrifice, given the conditions inside the city) and prayer. They took note of the day: the feast of Saints Peter and Paul, both patrons of Antioch. That was about as auspicious as things were going to get.

Now came Bohemond's *chef-d'oeuvre,* one not merely of bravery and tactics and keen understanding of his foe but of sheer bravado and effrontery. Kerbogha had enough forces to entirely surround the city, which was bad for the Crusaders but also good: the Turks couldn't be in full force everywhere at once, especially given the unfavorable conditions of the terrain, with its hills, rivers, lakes, and marshes. As at the Iron Bridge, Bohemond could pick his own battlefield and concentrate his forces on one or two spots, thus negating the atabeg's overwhelming numerical superiority. He didn't have to defeat the entire Muslim command—which in any case was operating under divided leadership, since its generals included the already once-defeated Ridwan and Duqaq—he just had to beat the forces outside whichever gate he chose from which to sally forth. The siege was going to—had to—come down to a single, decisive battle. *On s'engage partout, et puis l'on voit.* The Crusaders would attack the Turks head-on and see what happened.

Organizing his disparate forces into six lines of battle—headed by Hugh of Vermandois, who led a division of archers, Godfrey, Robert Curthose, Bishop Adhemar and Saint-Gilles, Tancred, and Bohemond himself—the sad-sack Christians, some of them mounted on asses and camels in the absence of horses, ran up the black flag signifying their decision to fight rather than surrender, opened the Bridge Gate, and trooped out. Thanks to the miraculous appearance of the Holy Lance, now held aloft by Bishop Adhemar as they marched into battle, their morale had soared; they were now the tip of God's holy spear against the infidels, and their priests blessed them with the Sign of the Cross from the battlements.

---

40. A remote province in what is today eastern Iran.

Incredibly, Kerbogha just sat there and watched the Crusaders deploy in an orderly fashion. The choice of the Bridge Gate over the Orontes as the sally point took the Turkish troops on the city side of the river out of the initial action. Had Kerbogha brought as many of his warriors as possible to bear on the chokepoint of the Bridge Gate, he might have made short work of the Christians and gained easy access back into the city. But, still contemptuous of the Europeans' fighting ability, he did nothing, reasoning that he could crush the entire Crusader army at one blow.[41] It was a decisive error.

Bohemond, from his earlier experiences with the Turks, knew that if their first attack with mounted archers failed, if the horsemen could be driven back and into the main body of the infantry, they would crack and run. They still were not accustomed to defeat, and had little inclination or training to learn how to regroup and rally. So although the Turks mounted a partial attack from troops stationed near several other city gates, and though some of the men at the Bridge Gate began fording the river in order to come up from behind the Christians, he held steady. His men fended off the attacks from the rear, while the main body formed a mobile iron shield wall as it approached the front lines of the Turks.

The Turks set grass fires to envelop the Crusaders in smoke and flames and thus impede their approach, but it had little effect. They engaged, and just as Bohemond had counted on, the advance line broke and—as at the Iron Bridge—fled in retreat backward, smack into Kerbogha's main army. At that moment, a trio of heavenly warriors in literally shining armor—the holy martyrs Saints George, Demetrius, and Theodore—came riding to their assistance. *Deus lo vult!* That only the Christians could see these apparitions didn't matter. The unwieldy Turkish coalition, much of it composed of raw recruits, shattered in panic at Bohemond's assault, with or without celestial assistance. Even Kerbogha ran: "He never dreamt of what despair and fanaticism are able to effect," notes Michaud. A few hours later, the holdout garrison

---

41. Michaud says that as Kerbogha watched the determined Crusaders take up their positions, he suddenly reconsidered Peter the Hermit's offer of a small, matched combat, but the Franks ignored him.

in the citadel surrendered. The Battle of Antioch, like the Battle of the Milvian Bridge, was over in a matter of hours. The date was June 28, 1098. Jerusalem beckoned.

The remainder of the First Crusade was, militarily, something of an anticlimax. Bohemond stayed behind in Antioch, establishing the Principality of Antioch as the second Crusader state. After six months of recuperation, the remainder of the princes (now minus Baldwin in Edessa and Bohemond in Antioch, as well as Bishop Adhemar, who had died in a typhus epidemic on August 1), moved on toward Jerusalem. Peter Bartholomew, still smarting from the disbelief evinced by many regarding his "Holy Lance" story, injudiciously and voluntarily underwent a trial by fire in April of 1099; he died two weeks later from his burns.[42]

The Crusaders arrived before the walls of Jerusalem on June 6, 1099—the same day that Tancred captured Bethlehem—and the next day set about besieging the city, aided logistically by the supply port at Jaffa, located near present-day Tel Aviv. The Fatimid Egyptian Arabs, who had indeed wrested the Holy City from the Seljuks while the Turks were bogged down with the Crusaders in Antioch, had expelled all the Christians from the city; the Jews who had not already fled during the intra-Muslim battles over the city were allowed to stay, and most of them did.

The outlying wells had been poisoned or filled in, and the nearest source of water was some six miles away; Saracen ambushes at watering holes were common. Nevertheless, the Franks managed to construct several siege engines, including two mobile towers. Before launching their main attack, Christian holy men called for the troops to march in a solemn processional around the city's walls, praying and dispensing alms while the Muslim and Jewish defenders jeered at them from the walls.

On the third day, a Friday, they stormed the city but were repulsed—some blamed Islamic witchcraft—but then one of the knights (the *Gesta*

---

42. The Provençals, Raymond of Saint-Gilles's men, insisted he had been crushed by the welcoming crowds after a successful passage through the flames. Raymond kept the tip of the Holy Lance for the rest of his days.

identifies him as Lethold of Tournai), "when that hour came when Our Lord Jesus Christ deigned to suffer for us upon the Cross," managed to get over one of the walls, causing the defenders to flee. The Crusaders entered the city, finally achieving their three-year objective—and the slaughter, led by Tancred and Godfrey, was tremendous:

> [O]ur men entered the city, chasing the Saracens and killing them up to Solomon's Temple,[43] where they took refuge and fought hard against our men for the whole day, so that all the temple was streaming with their blood. At last, when the pagans were defeated, our men took many prisoners, both men and women, in the temple. They killed whom they chose, and whom they chose they saved alive. (*Gesta Francorum*)
>
> With the fall of Jerusalem and its towers one could see marvellous works. Some of the pagans were mercifully beheaded, others pierced by arrows plunged from towers, and yet others, tortured for a long time, were burned to death in searing flames. Piles of heads, hands and feet lay in the houses and streets, and indeed there was a running to and fro of men and knights over the corpses. . . . In the Temple of Solomon and the portico crusaders rode in blood to the knees and bridles of their horses. . . . The deeds performed in the day-long battle were so marvellous that we doubt that history recorded any greater. (Raymond of Aguilers)

The surviving defenders were forced to drag the corpses outside the city walls, where they were piled into pyramids and set alight; "no one save God alone knows how many there were." Hardly anyone was spared, including the Jews who were viewed as allies of the Muslims.[44]

---

43. The Al-Aqsa Mosque.

44. David B. Green, writing in *Haaretz* on June 15, 2014: "The fate of the city's Jews at the time is also the subject of some historical controversy. There were Jews who sided with the Muslims in defending the city, and when Jerusalem fell, they supposedly retreated to their synagogue to wait to be slaughtered. Although some Muslim sources describe how the synagogue was burned down with the Jews inside, a contemporary letter found in the Cairo Geniza by historian S.D. Goitein, though it mentions the burning of the

The ghost of Bishop Adhemar appeared, offering religious counsel. The princes declared the Kingdom of Jerusalem and offered its throne to Raymond of Saint-Gilles, who turned it down. They then presented it to Godfrey, who accepted under the condition that he be called defender of the Holy Sepulcher rather than "king"; only Jesus could be king of the Holy Land. A third Crusader state was now in existence. The fourth and last, the County of Tripoli, would be proclaimed in 1102. Together, they would last until 1291, when Saladin retook Jerusalem.

The remaining Arabs retreated to Ascalon, on the Levantine coast south of Jerusalem, just north of the present-day Gaza Strip, there to regroup and await the arrival of a large Fatimid army from Egypt, some twenty thousand men strong. Carrying a relic of the True Cross, Godfrey left Jerusalem with the entire Crusader army, now reduced to about ten thousand men, and launched a dawn attack on the sleeping Fatimids encamped outside Ascalon, routing them in less than an hour,[45] and then spending the rest of the time slaughtering them en masse and looting the vizier Al-Afdal Shahanshah's tent of many valuables as he fled back to Egypt by ship. Foolishly, the Crusaders failed to occupy Ascalon itself, since the Muslims insisted they would surrender it only to Raymond, a condition Godfrey rejected. It was a strategic mistake they wouldn't rectify until 1153, when it was far too late.

As for Bohemond, the rest of his life proved less illustrious. In the year 1100 he marched out of Antioch with a small force of about three hundred knights to render assistance to a local Armenian chieftain against the Danishmends. At the Battle of Melitene, the Norman was ambushed, captured by the Turks and tossed into prison in the town of Neocaesarea (modern Niksar) in the old Hellenistic kingdom of Pontus,

---

'glorious sanctuary,' makes no reference to human victims of the fire. In fact, Goitein suggests that most of the Jewish population of Jerusalem had left the city during the course of the preceding century, as Seljuk and Fatimid Muslims fought for control. In any case, as opposed to the memorial chronicles written by Jewish communities of the Rhine to record the names of brethren who were massacred during the passage of Crusader armies through their towns, no similar documents have been found noting by name Jewish victims of the Crusader conquest of Jerusalem."

45. Connoisseurs of military history will note the resemblance to the Battle of San Jacinto in 1836, during the Texas revolution against Mexico.

incorporated into the Roman Empire c. 63 B.C. There he stewed for two years. The Danishmends offered him for ransom to Alexios, but the emperor was still seething over Bohemond's violation of his oath to return Antioch to Byzantine rule, and declined. Eventually, he was ransomed by Baldwin of Edessa and returned to his principality, where he found his nephew Tancred, now Prince of Galilee, ruling *pro tempore* in his stead.

Still hoping to enlarge his holdings, Bohemond, along with Tancred and Baldwin, was badly defeated by the Seljuks at the Battle of Harran in May 1104, in which Baldwin was captured and imprisoned for five years until finally ransomed. With his dreams of empire crumbling, Bohemond returned to Europe to recruit more troops. In 1106, while in France, he married Constance, the daughter of King Philip I, and they had two sons, the first of whom was named Bohemond II of Antioch. Still seething with hatred for Alexios—"not a Christian, but a mad heretic"—Bohemond attacked the Byzantines, once again at Dyrrachium in 1107–1108, but Alexios tied him up in a war of attrition and finally forced a negotiated settlement that reduced the mighty warrior to the status of Alexios's vassal. He died in 1111 in Bari in Italy without ever returning to Antioch, which was left once more in Tancred's hands.

In the end, his ambition exceeded his means, and it must have galled him to have had to take an oath of loyalty to Alexios. In a dangerous part of the world in which a man could use all the friends he could get, Bohemond had none. With grim satisfaction, Anna Comnena records the final defeat of her hated enemy, "the man of tyrannical mind who threatened to destroy the whole world." Nevertheless, with his defense at Dorylaeum and the capture of Antioch, Bohemond of Taranto takes his place in history as a master commander whose skill and iron will made possible the victory at Jerusalem and the creation of the Crusader States, and thus changed the history of both Christendom and the *dar al-Islam*, of both Europe and the Middle East. The unlovely Norman bequeathed us the Middle East that, in the main, we still have today.

Tasso, in Fairfax's classic translation, which preserves Tasso's original rhyming scheme and was first published in the year 1600, concludes his epic poem *La Gerusalemme liberata* thus:

> *Thus conquered Godfrey, and as yet the sun*
> *Dived not in silver waves his golden wain,*
> *But daylight served him to the fortress won*
> *With his victorious host to turn again,*
> *His bloody coat he put not off, but run*
> *To the high temple with his noble train,*
> *And there hung up his arms, and there he bows*
> *His knees, there prayed, and there performed his vows.*

Thus the First Crusade ended in complete military and religious triumph. It was an astonishing, bloody, impassioned, fanatical clash of arms, with an unseemly appetite for butchery that appalls us today but was perfectly acceptable by historical standards, which after all dated back centuries under the accepted practices of warfare. As with all historical events, it is a fool's errand to judge it by contemporary standards. But judge it we in the West now do. Whether others—less morally picky, less guilt-ridden, hungrier—share our fastidiousness remains to be seen. But, however ignored today, its lessons remain.

Eight

NAPOLEON AT AUSTERLITZ

Circumstances the most extraordinary have long kept me near the most extraordinary man that ever existed. Admiration made me follow him, without knowing him, and when I did know him, love alone would have fixed me for ever near his person. The world is full of his glory, his deeds, and his monuments; but no one knows the true shades of his character, his private qualities, or the natural disposition of his soul. This great void I undertake to fill up, and for such a task I possess advantages unexampled in history. I collected and recorded, day by day, all that I saw of Napoleon, all that I heard him say, during the period of eighteen months in which I was constantly about his person. In these conversations, which were full of confidence, and which seemed to pass, as it were, in another world, he could not fail to be portrayed by himself as if in a mirror, in every point of view, and under every aspect. Henceforth the world may freely study him: there can be no error in the materials.
—COUNT EMMANUEL-AUGUSTE-DIEUDONNÉ LAS CASES (1823)

WHAT REMAINS TO BE SAID ABOUT NAPOLEON BONAPARTE? DESPITE changing tastes, the Corsican-born Emperor of the French remains one of the most written-about men in Western history, alongside Jesus of Nazareth, Shakespeare, Abraham Lincoln, and Muhammad Ali, the boxer. Between the years 1799 and 1815 he was the Black Swan of Europe, which quaked before him, perhaps the least predictable cultural and political disruptor in European history. He was the epitome of the self-made man, a near-nobody (minor Tuscan nobility) from nowhere, Italian by heritage, French by accident, aspiring novelist, rising military officer during the French Revolution, First Consul of France and later Emperor, coronated with a facsimile of Charlemagne's crown, created for the occasion, that was proffered to him by Pope Pius VII at a ceremony inside Notre-Dame de Paris. He was a scourge of the aristocracy ennobled by himself, an education reformer, the architect of a concordat with the papacy, the discoverer of the Rosetta Stone (which unlocked the secrets of the Ancient Egyptian language and thus made the entire field of Egyptology possible), and the author of the Napoleonic Code, still in use in France and elsewhere today. And that in his spare time.

Above all, Napoleon was a battlefield general of genius, who at his peak in the first decade of the nineteenth century can only be compared to Alexander the Great in his command of kinetic land warfare and in his uncanny ability to know what his opponent was going to do before the enemy himself did. At his height between 1805, when he crushed a combined Austrian-Russian army during the Battle of the Three Emperors at Austerlitz, and the 1813 Battle of the Nations at Leipzig, which broke the spell of success, there was no contemporary who could rival him, and no one whom other generals feared more. Even the British army, which finally ended his career in 1815, had avoided a direct confrontation with the Little Corporal personally until the Duke of Wellington and a combined Anglo-Dutch-Prussian force stopped him at Waterloo, "the nearest run thing you ever saw in your life." No wonder Andrew Roberts, the contemporary British historian, entitled his magisterial biography of the man *Napoleon the Great*.

> The ideas that underpin our modern world—meritocracy, equality before the law, property rights, religious toleration, modern secular education, sound finances and so on—were championed, consolidated, codified and geographically extended by Napoleon. To them he added rational and efficient local administration, an end to rural banditry, the encouragement of science and the arts, the abolition of feudalism and the greatest codification of laws since the fall of the Roman Empire . . .

Napoleon's capacity for battlefield decision-making was astounding. . . . A general must ultimately be judged by the outcome of the battles, and of Napoleon's sixty battles and sieges he lost only Acre, Aspern-Essling, Leipzig, La Rothière, Lâon, Arcis and Waterloo. When asked who was the greatest captain of the age, the Duke of Wellington replied: "In this age, in past ages, in any age, Napoleon."

And yet Napoleon was even more than that. *Napoleone Buonaparte*, to give him his original Italian name, was the first Romantic, arriving on the world stage smack at the beginning of the turn of the century, the man who inspired not only political revolutionaries across Europe— and thus provided the impetus for the Continent-wide revolutions of 1848, which attacked institutional monarchies from Sicily, Italy, and France to Germany and Austria—but also poets, painters, composers, and musicians, who saw in him their abstract ideal of the Individual Agonistes, hero of his own story, unfazed by authority and unafraid to challenge it and bring it down. Even greater than his military legacy was the cultural and emotional effect he had on Europe long after the two decades of his ascendency and fall were over. Until the advent of World War I, Europe was what Napoleon had made it.

The turn of the eighteenth century into the nineteenth—in the arts, the turn from classicism to romanticism—was perfectly symbolized by his sudden emergence from the chaos that followed the end of the French Revolution, during which he fired on civilian insurgents in the streets of Paris in the name of the First Directory. As both a general and a member of the French Academy of Sciences, he had launched a major military campaign in Egypt and the Levant on behalf of the Republic, in which he crushed the Mamelukes at the Battle of the Pyramids but saw his fleet annihilated by Admiral Nelson at the Battle of the Nile; and who had seized power in a bloodless coup launched on the eighteenth day of the revolutionary calendar's month of Brumaire, November 9, 1799. His battles at Dresden and Leipzig and elsewhere in Germany helped spur the nascent German unification movement that would come to fruition under the Prussians and Otto von Bismarck in 1871. Parts of Italy, ruled by him as king between 1805 and 1814, eventually coalesced to become the unified Kingdom of Italy, also in 1871. Even in defeat, he had managed to wriggle from exile on Elba and return at the head of an army during the Hundred Days for one last grand gesture of defiance at Waterloo.

The Napoleonic Code he supervised, although much amended, remains the basis for the law in France, and has served as a model for other nations and provinces such as French Canada and much of Latin America. His invention of the corps system enabled him to split one large army into several practically self-contained units, moving in tandem with one another but at a distance, largely living off the land; in this way they could fight separate battles against smaller foes or quickly reassemble to fight as one large force. This was in large part because Napoleon, as he displayed in his tactical *tour de force* at Austerlitz, had mastered the art of maneuvering so as to make the enemy fight on his turf and on his terms, even when his forces were numerically inferior—an ability shared by all great generals. "For myself," he once said, "I have but one requirement, that of success." It wasn't until he lost the ability to win a battle even before it was fought, as he did at Borodino, Leipzig, and, finally, at Waterloo, that the hounds of Europe were finally able to run the wild hare to ground.[1]

Napoleon was all these things and more. In this chapter, however, I will be considering Napoleon not so much as a general or even a political leader but as an "artist of life"—an heroically successful *Lebenskünstler*, as the Germans say: the central character and doomed hero of his own self-written epic. An archetype, Napoleon achieved great triumphs and suffered stinging reverses, *volte-faces* that eventually brought him down. Fortune, who smiled on him until—as she does to nearly all men—she didn't, made him her fool for life; and eventually he found himself in the same position that has brought down so many great men—a tendency

---

1. Napoleon's epic losses all came when his opponent forced him to fight on unfavorable ground. The Russian general Mikhail Kutuzov had lured him to Borodino, on the way to Moscow, in 1812; the Sixth Coalition partners at the Battle of the Nations in 1813 had trapped him in Leipzig, a defeat leading to his first abdication; and at Waterloo in 1815 Wellington had interposed himself between the renascent Emperor and his objective of Brussels, forcing a disastrous frontal assault and the second abdication and permanent exile to St. Helena.

to go to the well once too often. And yet, the would-be novelist found his medium and scrawled it large, across the parchment of Old Europe.

In his *Mémoires d'Outre-Tombe* (*Memories from Beyond the Grave*, 1849–50), François-René de Chateaubriand, the influential French writer and philosopher considered to be the father of French Romanticism,[2] had this to say about Napoleon: "He had Italian blood; his nature was complex: great men, a very small family on earth, unfortunately find no one but themselves to imitate them. At once a model and a copy, a real person and an actor playing that person, Napoleon was his own mimic; he would not have believed himself a hero if he had not decked himself out in a hero's costume. This curious weakness imparted something false and equivocal to his astonishing reality."

Bonaparte was a poet in action, an immense genius in warfare, an indefatigable, able and intelligent mind where administration was concerned, a thorough and rational legislator . . .

I have read carefully what Bonaparte wrote, his first childish manuscripts, his novels, then his pamphlets . . . his private letters to Josephine, his five volumes of speeches, his orders and bulletins, and his unpublished dispatches ruined by the editing carried out by Monsieur de Talleyrand's office. I know a lot about it: I only recently discovered, in a vile autograph copy left on the Island of Elba, various thoughts which echo the nature of the great islander:

> "*My heart rejects familiar joys as it does commonplace sorrows.*"
> "*Not having given myself life, I will not deprive myself of it, as long as it demands something fine of me.*"
> "*My evil genius appeared and announced my end, which I met at Leipzig.*"

---

2. A distinction possibly shared with Étienne Pivert de Senancour, whose melancholic epistolary novel *Obermann* (1804) has a strong claim to being the first French Romantic novel. The pianist and composer Franz Liszt, much moved by it, gave us a musical interpretation of the author's alienation and love of nature in his piano piece, "Vallée d'Obermann," contained in the first volume of Liszt's *Années de pèlerinage* (1842).

"I have conjured the terrible spirit of novelty which tra-verses the world."

Something of the true Bonaparte is certainly captured there.

No one living in Napoleonic Europe during the first fifteen years of the nineteenth century, nor in the remaining decades until the outbreak of the First World War in 1914, was free from his influence. His life and works affected nearly every artist of note, no matter their fields or disciplines. He was depicted or caricatured (especially in England) in paintings and sculptures, in poetry and music, in drama and story, whether veiled or unveiled. His memory echoed throughout the twentieth century and into our own. Until the advent of the neo-Marxist assault on Western civilization via the destructive dogma of critical theory,[3] his place in the pantheon has seemed secure. Whether the brave new Orwellian world envisioned by another nineteenth-century disruptor, Karl Marx, would have room for the Alexanders, Caesars, and Napoleons of the past is highly unlikely—Stalin, of course, Marx would have loved—but the job of the interpretative historian is to analyze events in their correct context, not to predict the future.

Napoleon was not simply the actor but also the acted-upon: in 1808 he sought out Johann Wolfgang von Goethe—Europe's most celebrated intellectual, twenty years his senior—asking him to make the short journey from Weimar to Erfurt, where Napoleon had organized the Congress of Erfurt to cement a tenuous peace, if not an actual alliance, with young tsar Alexander of Russia. Like countless thousands of young men across Europe—some of whom committed suicide under the novel's emotional influence—Napoleon had been profoundly moved by *The Sorrows of Young Werther* (1774, revised 1787),[4] and was eager to display to the Germans his interest in their arts and letters. He was also keenly aware of Russia's cultural inferiority complex. He imported the stars of

---

3. See this author's *The Devil's Pleasure Palace* (2015) and *The Fiery Angel* (2018), both published by Encounter Books.

4. Later superbly and movingly set to music by the French composer Jules Massenet in 1892 as *Werther.*

the Comédie-Française, who staged sixteen plays, each one approved by the French emperor. The meeting got off to an odd start. As Goethe later recounted:

> I am called into the Emperor's study. . . . He is eating breakfast. On his right, at some distance from the table, is Talleyrand; on his left, Daru, with whom he discusses taxes. The Emperor signals to me to approach. I remain standing in front of him at a suitable distance. After looking at me for a moment, he says to me: "You are a man." I bow my head. He says: "How old are you?"
>
> "Sixty years."
>
> "You are well preserved. You have written some tragedies."
>
> He then brought the conversation to Werther, which he must have studied in detail. After several perfectly appropriate observations, he mentioned a specific part and said to me: "Why did you do that? It is not natural." And he spoke at length on this and with perfect accuracy.
>
> I listened with a calm face, and I replied, with a smile of satisfaction, that I didn't know whether anyone had ever made the same criticism, but that I found it perfectly justified, and that I agreed that one could find fault with this passage's lack of authenticity. "But," I added, "a poet can perhaps be excused for taking refuge in an artifice which is hard to spot, when he wants to produce certain effects that could not be created simply and naturally."
>
> The Emperor seemed to agree with me; he returned to drama and made some very sensible remarks, as a man who had observed the tragic stage with a great deal of attention, like a criminal judge, and who felt very deeply how far French theatre had strayed from nature and truth.
>
> He went on to talk about fatalistic plays, of which he disapproved. They belonged to the dark ages. "Why, today, do they keep giving us destiny?" he said. "Destiny is politics."

Goethe outlived Napoleon by eleven years. In 1828, seven years after the emperor's death, he offered this assessment of the man who had shaken Europe to its foundations:

Napoleon was the man! Always enlightened, always clear and decided, and endowed with sufficient energy to carry into effect whatever he considered advantageous and necessary. His life was the stride of a demi-god, from battle to battle, and from victory to victory. It might well be said of him, that he was found in a state of continual enlightenment. On this account, his destiny was more brilliant than any the world had seen before him, or perhaps will ever see after him.

There was also something of the whiff of the diabolical surrounding Napoleon, who struck fear and terror wherever he cast his basilisk gaze. No one, least of all his enemies, knew where or when he would strike, as the number of coalitions mounted against him—nine—indicates. He was the ultimate radical—another characteristic of the artist-as-hero— flouting convention in every direction, amorally unconcerned with the practical consequences, with the lives his actions cost, with the terrible physical destruction he left in his wake. In this, one might note, he adumbrated Marx, although the German's far greater damage was wrought by his philosophy, not his actions.

"There was in his indomitable dreams and ambitions something of the heroic that appealed to artists and poets and which came to epitomize the Romantic age," writes Alan Forrest in the introduction to his 2015 study of the battle, *Waterloo*. "If Waterloo was a defeat, it was a heroic defeat." And heroism, from the opening shots of the Napoleonic Wars to its death in Flanders's fields, was the highest ideal to which the Romantic hero could aspire.

Napoleon, the first Romantic hero, saw war—and thus saw his life—as theater, a *grand projet* dedicated to the furtherance of diplomacy *with* other means, the objective being total victory.[5] For him, war really was, in Clausewitz's phrase, *ein wahres politisches Instrument*. The connoisseur of the Comédie-Française brought a unique, stylish flair to the pursuit of bloodletting and mayhem. He could inspire his men with noble

---

5. In 1818, the poet John Keats said there were "two distinct tempers of mind in which we judge of things—the worldly, theatrical and pantomimical; and the unearthly, spiritual and ethereal." He judged Napoleon and Byron as belonging to the first group.

exhortations (one of his favorite tactics before a battle) and after action would reward them with medals and ribbons. As Roberts notes: "He convinced his followers they were taking part in an adventure, a pageant, an experiment and a story whose sheer splendour would draw the attention of posterity for centuries. He was able to impart to ordinary people the sense that their lives—and, if necessary, their deaths in battle—mattered in the context of great events. They too could make history."

In a dramatic callback to the legions of Julius Caesar, Napoleon made sure his well-drilled troops rallied 'round their eagle standards with the same fervor and protective ferocity as the legionaries of old. Although he had risen through the ranks from his days as an outsider, essentially a foreigner, at the military college of Brienne, and presented himself as a man of the people during the Revolution, he quickly developed a taste for luxury, his residences regally appointed in a manner that might make a Bourbon blush, his outfits fit for the highest royalty. "What a novel my life has been!" he exclaimed near the end of it, an outcast on the rock called St. Helena named, fittingly, after the emperor Constantine's mother.

Napoleon's family members, alas, were not up to his level of genius. The various relatives he placed on the thrones of Europe—notably his elder brother Joseph, to whom he entrusted kingdoms in Naples and later, disastrously, in Spain, and his younger brother, Jérôme, whom he made monarch of the short-lived Kingdom of Westphalia—lacked both his temperament and his genius, causing him not only a great deal of frustration but also, in the end, his own empire. Love-stricken by his first wife, the sexually adventurous, profligate widow Josephine de Beauharnais,[6] he bombarded her with love letters that were positively Wertherian in their ardency during their courtship; no wonder he was so passionate about Goethe's novel.

Later, as he learned of her various infidelities, he took a succession of

---

6. Born on the island of Martinique, a French possession, in 1763, making her six years older than Napoleon. Her first husband, Alexandre de Beauharnais, had been guillotined during the French Revolution, leaving her with two children. Her maiden name was Marie Josèphe Rose Tascher de La Pagerie. Before meeting Napoleon she went by the name of Rose, or Marie-Rose; it was he who dubbed her Josephine as a pet name. It stuck.

mistresses (Roberts puts the number at twenty-one), two of whom bore him sons, Charles Léon Denuelle de la Plaigne, who never amounted to much, and the accomplished Alexandre Florian Joseph, Count Colonna-Walewski, the son of Napoleon's beautiful Polish mistress, Countess Marie Walewska. Napoleon's only legitimate heir was Napoleon II—Napoléon François Joseph Charles Bonaparte—the issue of the emperor's second marriage to Marie Louise of Austria, contracted for diplomatic reasons in 1810. His marriage to Josephine was childless and was annulled on those grounds in order for Napoleon to marry the daughter of the Austrian emperor, Franz II, who was also the last Holy Roman emperor—a title that vanished into history in 1806 when Franz abdicated and dissolved the Empire rather than let it fall into the hands of a parvenu like Napoleon. Everything in the man's life resonated with the Muse of History.

Despite its bastardy, his first illegitimate child came as a great personal relief to Napoleon. Clearly, Josephine, the mother of two, was fertile. Clearly, the two of them enjoyed a robust sex life that may have exhausted even the Little Corporal: hence the phrase of unknown origin, "Not tonight, Josephine." And yet they had had no children.[7] Napoleon, the emperor, now assuredly potent, needed a dynastic son and heir. And so when he made the decision to offload Josephine (who was costing him a fortune), he had two diplomatic choices: Maria Louise (whose great-aunt was Marie Antoinette) or Tsar Alexander's youngest sister, the Grand Duchess Anna Pavlovna. His alliance with Alexander, formed after the catastrophic Austro-Russian defeat at Austerlitz in 1805 and the Russian disaster at Friedland in 1807 (sealed by the Peace of Tilsit), was fraying over the status of Poland. The Russians were dead set against that country's reestablishment, and a match with the duchess—all of fourteen years old at the time—would have gone a long way to papering things over, and ensuring that Poland stayed partitioned.

Napoleon, however, needed the flexibility that his client state, the Duchy of Warsaw, also known as Napoleonic Poland, gave him; he had multiple ethnicities to think of, including those of the restive Baltics.

---

7. The French emperor Napoleon III, who ruled France from 1852 to 1870, was Josephine's grandson, not Napoleon's.

He needed to keep the Russian bear on its back foot. He had already defeated both Russia and Austria on several occasions, but knew in his heart that soon enough he'd be back in conflict with one or both of them. And so the choice for Marie Louise was made—even though Napoleon knew that Russia would be the more formidable enemy, "I dread a march to St. Petersburg more than a march to Vienna." He was prophetic about that.

In any case, Napoleon's attitude toward women was characteristic of the Romantic age. The ardent swain in him adored them, the poet worshipped them, the general was irresistibly attracted to them, the emperor needed them in order to function as an alpha male.[8] But a deeply compartmentalized leader like Napoleon was not about to let a little thing like a love affair get in the way of the Great Game, mastery of the chessboard of Europe. "Women," he said, "should not be looked upon as equals of men. They are, in fact, only machines for making babies."

War, not women, was his real mistress. The battlefield was his art form, and his metaphor for life. Like all Romantic heroes, he saw life as a struggle, something to be conquered and mastered. The Hero raised his fist to the heavens, the way Beethoven was said to do as his last gesture during a violent thunderstorm at his death in March of 1827.[9] Napoleon was ferociously competitive, probably in ways even he didn't realize. And yet, from his point of view, war had been thrust upon him, not sought. Time and again, the great powers of Europe had ganged up on him, attacking revolutionary France as a cancer on the imperial system of the Continent (a relict of Rome, of course), mounting coalition after coalition against him, constantly imperiling *la belle France* and, as he saw it, forcing him, the offensive genius, to take the fight to them, peremptorily if need be. Which he did with gusto.

The iconography proclaims as much. Jacques-Louis David depicted him several times: atop the proverbial white horse (instead of the donkey

---

8. John F. Kennedy's famous remark that he needed a new woman every few days in order to prevent headaches comes to mind.

9. "The dying man suddenly raised his head, stretched out his own right arm majestically— like a general giving orders to an army. This was but for an instant; the arm sunk back; he fell back; Beethoven was dead," as one biographer described the scene.

he really rode) at the Saint-Bernard Pass in *The First Consul Crossing the Alps*; as the second coming of Caesar, his brow adorned by laurel leaves of gold; and at the moment of his coronation. Antoine-Jean Gros stationed him at the Arcole Bridge during his Italian campaign, flag in one hand, saber in another, leading a charge that never actually happened. One of the most famous images is by François Bouchot, immortalizing the fearless hero's bravado as he is expelled from the Conseil des Cinq-Cents at Saint-Cloud during the tensest moments of the Brumaire coup. At the far end of his career, Charles de Steuben portrayed *Napoleon's Return from Elba,* in which the leader is being rapturously hailed by the adoring soldiers who had been sent to intercept and arrest him.

But what of the other arts? Notwithstanding the terrible carnage unleashed by his relentless military campaigns against continental Europe and Russia, he was a hero to artists and intellectuals, painters and poets and composers, revolutionaries to nearly a man in both their private and public lives. Despite the relentless mockery of Napoleon by the London press, Lord Byron, an iconoclastic member of Britain's aristocracy, adored him. After abandoning England in 1816, he drove around Europe in a carriage modeled on the one Napoleon had abandoned at Waterloo. (Costing five hundred pounds, it broke down a lot.)

Liszt, the greatest celebrity in Europe during his heyday as a Byronic concert pianist in midcentury, found personal inspiration in the way Napoleon had flouted convention, forcing the world to take him on his terms, and not he on its. In 1839 Liszt, nearing his twenty-eighth birthday, sat for a formal portrait by the German-born French portraitist Henri Lehmann. The pose is a cross between the Napoleonic and the Byronic: Liszt is shown standing, in three-quarters view, arms folded confidently across his breast, the aquiline nose prominent (as was the young Napoleon's), a look of supreme confidence on his face, with a hint of superiority, expressing both his faith in his talent and his knowledge that he was one of the handsomest men alive. Like Napoleon and Byron, Liszt was iconographically instantly recognizable, and painters, like women, found him irresistible.

Napoleon's nearest contemporary, Beethoven, offers immediate insight. Beethoven, the Titan, never did anything by half measures. He was not Mozart, the obscene child-genius of Peter Shaffer's imagination in *Amadeus,* for whom everything came easily. Composition did not spring fully formed from Beethoven's brow, like Athena; rather, it was often the product of trial and error, writing and rewriting. The ferocity of his creative impulse is visible on the page, in the manuscripts; even the printed scores—instantly recognizable as Beethoven—simmer with it, and then explode.

In 1804 Beethoven, that indefatigable democrat, initially dedicated his Third Symphony, known today as the *Eroica,* to its inspiration—"Bonaparte"—although he violently scratched out the inscription after Napoleon declared himself emperor and replaced it with, "to the memory of a great man." As disruptive as its inspiration, the monumental symphony shattered the confines of the classical-era four-movement symphonic structure, remade the blueprints of the classical symphony's architecture, and was twice as long as any symphony before it (it can run almost an hour in some performances, although it shouldn't), with each of its four movements conceived on an epic scale.[10]

The *Eroica*'s first movement provides us with the best look at Napoleon as Beethoven saw him in 1804. It begins with two pounding, separate E-flat major chords, then introduces the main theme—which almost immediately goes sideways, slipping into fragments, harmonically sliding and slithering. But it is always driving forward, rhythmically ever forward (never was Beethoven's unflashy orchestration more suited to a work), building tension over syncopations, offbeats, chordal hammer blows, and supporting pedal points, all in three-quarter time.[11] At one point, during a quiet passage before the formal recapitulation of the main theme, a lone French horn makes a notoriously "wrong" entrance, jumping the gun but whetting our appetite for the climax, which finally bursts out in the full orchestra, a long-delayed, triumphant, and almost erotic apotheosis of the innocent virginal tune with

---

10. There is some internal evidence to suggest that the symphony might have been composed backwards, since the finale is based on a tune Beethoven had employed several times previously. The innocuous little tune's developmental possibilities obviously fascinated the composer, and it underlies each of the four movements.

11. Perhaps a nod to Mozart, whose 39th symphony—the first of the great last three symphonies—is also in E-flat major and whose first movement's main section is also in ¾ time.

which Beethoven began. For all that the *Eroica* has become a staple of the concert repertoire—its cornerstone, in fact—it remains a thrilling experience every time one hears it, the world begun again anew.

The second movement is a funeral march. Although the most heart-wrenching of Beethoven's funeral marches, and often viewed in hindsight as the composer's elegy to what might have been, no adumbration of the emperor's eventual fate should be read into this.[12] Funeral marches were a staple of nineteenth-century music (there's one in Beethoven's piano sonata in A-flat, Op. 26, written just a few years prior to the symphony), and composers continued to write them either as standalones or memorials throughout the century. Chopin famously interpolated one into his Op. 35 piano sonata in B-flat minor, and Liszt wrote several, including his virtuosic showpiece *Funérailles*. His son-in-law, Richard Wagner, wrote one of the most famous funeral marches in history for Siegfried after the character's death in *Götterdämmerung*, the last of the four "Ring" cycle music dramas; in Germany it continues to be performed at the deaths of great or important men, often musically introducing their deaths as the news comes over the radio.

The third movement is a playful scherzo; the word means "joke" in Italian but in the context of classical symphonic form it is a dance movement, growing out of the minuet, but with more energy; while the fourth is an extended set of variations on the theme the composer had used four years earlier in his ballet *The Creatures of Prometheus* and elsewhere. Here, he finally gets it right as the music flits through a kaleidoscope of colors and emotions, ending not in tragedy but in the triumph of the Individual over the forces of conformity and oppression. It is the perfect expression of the Napoleonic spirit in the run-up to Austerlitz.

It is coincidental but noteworthy (in the sense that history often rhymes) that in 1805, the year of the premiere of the *Eroica* in Vienna, both Napoleon and Beethoven were approaching the height of their powers. The symphony, first performed on April 7, would kick off Beethoven's so-called "middle period," during which his most popular works

---

12. Waterloo, after all, came twelve years after the *Eroica*.

were written; the Battle of Austerlitz, fought on December 2 that same year, announced the emergence of Napoleon's battlefield mastery.

But it was among writers that Napoleon found a special immortality—a kind of fame, one suspects, in which he would have taken great pride. Some feared him (and therefore ridiculed him); others looked up to him, admired him, saw in him the birth of modern man: self-actuated, beholden to no one but himself—the ideal of the individual taken to the extremes of narcissism and overconfidence in his own abilities and in the infallibility of his judgment. Indeed, catastrophic failure was the often—and oft-desired—end state of the Hero, for whom a noble death gave meaning to his life. But a rule of the game is that the Hero must dominate every scene, even those (or especially those) in which he does not appear. Said one of Napoleon's longtime courtiers who knew him well, "He was the only man in the world of whom it may be said without adulation, that the nearer you viewed him the greater he appeared."

The opening sentences of Leo Tolstoy's masterpiece, *War and Peace* (Война и миръ), invoke the fabulous beast lurking just offstage[13] in the voice of the St. Petersburg society hostess, Anna Pavlovna Scherer:

> Well, Prince, so Genoa and Lucca are now just family estates of the Buonapartes. But I warn you, if you don't tell me that this means war, if you still try to defend the infamies and horrors perpetrated by that Antichrist—I really believe he is Antichrist—I will have nothing more to do with you and you are no longer my friend, no longer my "faithful slave," as you call yourself! But how do you do? I see I have frightened you—sit down and tell me all the news. (Translation by Aylmer and Louise Maude)

Napoleon stalks the massive novel for hundreds of pages before we finally meet him in person at Austerlitz, saving the badly wounded Prince Andrey's life by getting him to a hospital tent. But what is of interest to us here is Tolstoy's focus on the French commander just before the battle. We see the Corsican chess master at work, maneuvering his

---

13. The opening title sequences of the BBC miniseries of the novel do the same thing: a shot of Napoleon from behind, looming over a potential battlefield.

troops so as to evoke a desired response from the Russians, who willingly oblige and thus march right into his trap:

Napoleon was positioned just ahead of his marshals, mounted on a little grey Arab horse, wearing the same blue overcoat he had worn through the Italian campaign. He was staring in silence at the hills which seemed to stride up out of the sea of mist, watching the Russian troops as they moved across them in the distance, and he was listening to the sound of gunfire in the valley. Not a muscle twitched on his face, which in those days was still rather thin; his eyes glinted as he stared at one spot. His predictions had come true. Part of the Russian army was going down towards the ponds and lakes in the valley; the other part was abandoning the heights of Pratzen, which he had planned to attack, since it was the crucial position . . .

Today was a day of celebration for him—the anniversary of his coronation. He had slept for a few hours before dawn and woken up feeling fresh, in good health and high spirits. Enjoying that happy frame of mind when nothing seems impossible and everything succeeds, he had mounted his horse and ridden out. He sat there now without moving, looking at the heights rising from the fog, and his cold face wore the odd look of well-earned but over-confident pleasure that you might see on the face of a lucky young man in love.

"That happy frame of mind when nothing seems impossible and everything succeeds." Later, as the Grande Armée marches on Moscow to administer a thrashing to the impertinent Tsar Alexander, the author views him quite differently. The mask of command, to use historian John Keegan's phrase, has changed. Far from being the ravening wolf of European imagination, Napoleon up close is short, chubby, vain, and sentimental. Here he is, on the eve of the fateful Battle of Borodino in 1812:

The Emperor Napoleon had not yet left his bedroom and was finishing his toilet. Slightly snorting and grunting, he presented now his back and now his plump hairy chest to the brush with which his valet was rubbing him down. Another valet, with his finger over the mouth of a bottle, was sprinkling Eau de Cologne on the Emperor's pampered body with an expression which seemed to say that he alone knew where and how much Eau de Cologne should be sprinkled. Napoleon's short hair was wet and matted on the forehead, but his face, though puffy and yellow, expressed physical satisfaction. "Go on, harder, go on!" he muttered to the valet who was rubbing him, slightly twitching and grunting. An aide-de-camp, who had entered the bedroom to report to the Emperor the number of prisoners taken in yesterday's action, was standing by the door after delivering his message, awaiting permission to withdraw. Napoleon, frowning, looked at him from under his brows.

"No prisoners!" said he, repeating the aide-de-camp's words. "They are forcing us to exterminate them. So much the worse for the Russian army. . . . Go on . . . harder, harder!" he muttered, hunching his back and presenting his fat shoulders.

As the battle is about to begin, Napoleon issues a proclamation to his troops, as he customarily did. Anniversaries were important to him, and he makes note of them in this historically accurate speech:

Soldiers! The battle you have been longing for is upon us. Victory depends on you. It is essential for us; it will give us all that we need: comfortable quarters and a speedy return home. Behave as you did at Austerlitz, Friedland, Vitebsk and Smolensk. May posterity long recall with pride your achievements this day! And may it be said of each one of you: he was there at the great battle before Moscow!

The emperor then issues a series of battle-plan orders, which the realities of the combat—the *Friktion*—precluded successful execution. "So it turns out that not one of the Emperor's instructions was carried out, and none of them ever could have been," writes Tolstoy. "But in the disposition it was stated that with the battle under way further instructions would be issued in response to enemy movements, so you might well imagine that all necessary arrangements were actually made by Napoleon in mid-battle. But this was not the case, and never could have been, because during the battle Napoleon was so far away that (as it later emerged) he could not have known how things were going, and not a single instruction issued by him during the battle could possibly have been carried out."

As the saying goes, history is written by the winners. Tolstoy's portrait of the emperor must be viewed in that light. By the time the greatest of Russian novelists was writing, Napoleon had passed into history, a bogeyman with which to frighten small children. The Hero had gone down to defeat. Borodino and the pointless capture of an abandoned Moscow led to the disastrous winter retreat and, little more than a year later, the calamitous Battle of Leipzig after which Napoleon was expelled from the German provinces and forced back to France, where in the face of a concerted allied assault, he abdicated and went into exile on Elba in April 1814. Returning to France early the following year, he was finally defeated by an allied army under the Duke of Wellington and Field Marshal von Blücher at Waterloo on June 18, 1815. He died on the island of St. Helena[14] in the South Atlantic on May 5, 1821.

While in exile, Napoleon produced a kind of four-volume autobiography, *Le Mémorial de Sainte-Hélène,* dictated to his private secretary Emmanuel-Auguste-Dieudonné Las Cases. By this time, he was not only defeated but ill, the stomach cancer that eventually killed him (as it had his father) gnawing away at his entrails.[15] Naturally, the novelist manqué cast himself as the hero of his own story, the way a proper artist

---

14. Discovered by Portuguese sailors in 1502.

15. Napoleon's cancer differed from his father's, as modern pathologists discovered in 2007. "This analysis suggests that, even if the emperor had been released or escaped from the island, his terminal condition would have prevented him from playing a further major role in the theater of European history," said Dr. Robert Genta, professor of pathology and internal medicine at University of Texas Southwestern and senior author of the study. "Even today, with the availability of sophisticated surgical techniques and chemotherapies, patients with gastric cancer as advanced as Napoleon's have a poor prognosis." The study also disposed of the notion that Napoleon had died from arsenic poisoning.

or amanuensis would, but even in exile his observations about things military still have much value:

> "The fate of a battle," observed the emperor, "is the result of a moment—of a thought: the hostile forces advance with various combinations, they attack each other and fight for a certain time; the critical moment arrives, a mental flash decides, and the least reserve accomplishes the object." He spoke of Lützen, Bautzen, &c.; and afterwards, alluding to Waterloo, he said, that had he followed up the idea of turning the enemy's right, he should easily have succeeded; he, however, preferred piercing the centre, and separating the two armies. But all was fatal in that engagement; it even assumed the appearance of absurdity: nevertheless, he ought to have gained the victory.[16]

Regarding overall generalship, and which qualities were the hallmarks of expert commanders, both of the past and the present, he had this to say:

> Turning to another subject, he said that the dangers incurred by the military commanders of antiquity were not to be compared with those which attend the generals of modern times. There is, he observed, no position in which a general may not now be reached by artillery; but anciently a general ran no risk, except when he himself charged, which Cæsar did only twice or thrice. "We rarely," said he, "find, combined together, all the qualities necessary to constitute a great general. The object most desirable is that a man's judgment should be in equilibrium with his personal courage; that raises him at once above the common level." This is what the emperor termed being well squared, both by the base and perpendicular. "If," continued he, "courage be a general's

---

16. This was delusional. Slamming his head against the brick wall of his opponent's center without first disrupting his flanks was something that Napoleon never did—it was the antithesis of Austerlitz—until Borodino and Waterloo: a sign of his declining powers, and fortune.

predominating quality, he will rashly embark in enterprises above his conceptions; and, on the other hand, he will not venture to carry his ideas into effect, if his character or courage be inferior to his judgment."

Something Napoleon prized in a general was something, of course, he possessed in spades: something he called "two o'clock in the morning courage." Like all geniuses, he could never figure out why others couldn't see or do things that he could. It was so obvious:

"I have very rarely met with the two o'clock in the morning courage. I mean, unprepared courage, that which is necessary on an unexpected occasion, and which, in spite of the most unforeseen events, leaves full freedom of judgment and decision." He did not hesitate to declare that he was himself eminently gifted with this *two o'clock in the morning courage*, and that, in this respect, he had met with but few persons who were at all equal to him. He remarked that an incorrect idea was generally formed of the strength of mind necessary to engage in one of those great battles on which depends the fate of an army or nation, or the possession of a throne. "Generals," added he, "are rarely found eager to give battle; they choose their positions; establish themselves; consider their combinations; but then commences their indecision: nothing is so difficult, and at the same time so important, as to know when to decide."

One must seize the moment, know exactly when to strike. But battlefields are among the largest possible canvases afforded any artist. Artists of extraordinary gifts in any field have a preternatural sense of their surroundings, a kind of second sight; they never have to think—there is no time—but only have to *do*. Their inner voice tells them exactly when that moment comes. "Success in war," said he, "depends so much on quicksightedness, and on seizing the right moment, that the battle of Austerlitz, which was so completely won, would have been lost if I had attacked six hours sooner."

Indeed, Napoleon had the soul of an artist: a penetrating insight into the natures of men. In every important respect except basic military skills, he was an autodidact. Always the outsider, even at his apogee, he was a keen observer of human beings and the nature of man—after all, he had to be. Alexander had taken the measure of Darius at Issus; a decade in the field against the Gauls had taught Caesar the essential nature of the Celts; Aetius knew his man Attila better than Attila knew himself. One evening in exile, the deposed emperor was reading the Comte Adrien de Sarrazin's collection of oriental tales, *Le Caravanserail* (1811), when he exclaimed:

> The moral of this story doubtless is that men never change. This is not true; they change both for better and worse. A thousand other maxims which authors attempt to establish are all equally false. . . . It is also said that when you know a man's character, you have a key to his whole conduct. This is a mistaken notion. A man may commit a bad action, though he be fundamentally good; he may be led into an act of wickedness, without being himself wicked.
>
> In truth, men have their virtues and their vices, their heroism and their perversity; men are neither generally good nor generally bad; but they possess and practice all that is good and bad in this world. This is the principle: natural disposition, education and accidental circumstances produce the applications. I have always been guided by this opinion, and I have generally found it correct. However, I was deceived in 1814, when I believed that France, at the sight of her dangers, would make common cause with me; but I was not deceived in 1815, on my return from Waterloo.

Yet neither exile nor death ended the world's fascination with him. Lord Byron—"mad, bad, and dangerous to know," as his lover Lady Caroline Lamb famously characterized him—kept a bust of Napoleon in his rooms while at Harrow, despite the fact that Britain was at war with the French. He sorrowed at Napoleon's reverses in Russia and at the Battle of the Nations in Leipzig in 1813. He thrilled at Bonaparte's escape from Elba two years later: "It is impossible not to be dazzled and overwhelmed by his character and career." He despaired when the emperor fell to earth again after the final defeat at Waterloo on June 18, 1815. Touring the battlefield in 1816 as it was already returning to nature, Byron interpolated his feelings into canto 3 of *Childe Harold*:

> *Stop!—for thy tread is on Empire's dust!*
> *An Earthquake's spoil is sepulchred below!*
> *Is the spot mark'd with no colossal bust?*
> *Nor column trophied for triumphal show?*
> *None; but the moral's truth tells simpler so,*
> *As the ground was before, thus let it be;—*
> *How that red rain hath made the harvest grow!*
> *And is this all the world has gained by thee,*
> *Thou first and last of fields! king-making Victory?*

For Byron, Napoleon was his alter ego, the aspirational man, the man who could make all Europe bow before him. In canto 11 in another of his masterpieces, *Don Juan* (1819–24), Byron wrote: "Even I— albeit I'm sure I did not know it,/ Nor sought of foolscap subjects to be king—/ Was reckon'd, a considerable time,/ The grand Napoleon of the realms of rhyme."

Byron's identification with Napoleon remained a constant throughout his short life—he died at Missolonghi in Greece in 1824 at the age of thirty-six, having forsaken his homeland in order to continue his meteoric roar through earthly existence—and even as he was creating his own archetype, the Byronic, Napoleon remained his beau ideal. He wrote five poems about him. Beginning with "Ode to Napoleon Buonaparte," the other poems are "Napoleon's Farewell," "From the French," "Ode on the Star of 'The Legion of Honour,'" and "Ode (From the French)." The first one, published in 1814, reads in part:

> *'Tis done—but yesterday a King!*
> *And armed with Kings to strive—*
> *And now thou art a nameless thing:*
> *So abject—yet alive!*
> *Is this the man of thousand thrones,*
> *Who strewed our earth with hostile bones,*

And can he thus survive?
Since he, miscalled the Morning Star,
Nor man nor fiend hath fallen so far.

But thou—from thy reluctant hand
The thunderbolt is wrung—
Too late thou leav'st the high command
To which thy weakness clung;
All Evil Spirit as thou art,
It is enough to grieve the heart
To see thine own unstrung;
To think that God's fair world hath been
The footstool of a thing so mean.

Fiona MacCarthy, in her richly detailed 2002 biography *Byron: Life and Legend*, notes another, concealed reference to Napoleon in Byron's 1815 poem, "The Destruction of Sennacherib":

And there lay the steed with his nostril all wide,
But through it there rolled not the breath of his pride;
And the foam of his gasping lay white on the turf,
And cold as the spray of the rock-beating surf.

And there lay the rider distorted and pale,
With the dew on his brow, and the rust on his mail:
And the tents were all silent, the banners alone,
The lances unlifted, the trumpet unblown.

She writes: "This vivid image of the unhorsed rider had contemporary connotations. Byron's poem was a jeremiad for the Emperor Napoleon, so recently and cruelly flung from his great charger."

At the very end of the century, in 1899, the German composer Richard Strauss premiered a new orchestral tone poem,[17] which he called *Ein*

---

17. A form invented and pioneered by Liszt in such works as *Tasso, Les préludes,* and even *A*

Heldenleben—"A Hero's Life." The proximate inspiration was Strauss's desire to follow in the footsteps of Beethoven's *Eroica Symphony* and write a work in E-flat major on a grand scale for large orchestra with an out-sized complement of horns and a similarly large brass section of trumpets, trombones, and tubas. In six sections, it depicts an unnamed Hero (although clearly Strauss himself, given the many quotations from his earlier works[18] embedded in the score), his critical adversaries, his beloved female companion (his wife, Pauline de Ahna), his martial exploits, his works of peace, and his "flight from the world and his completion." And while Strauss hastened to say, "I'm not made for battle," he did observe that he found himself to be "no less interesting than Napoleon."

Unintentional as it might have been, *Ein Heldenleben* presents us with the stirring spectacle of war as a form of dramatic art, which is surely the way Bonaparte saw it. The huge horn section is, as Strauss himself observed, "quite the thing to express heroism," and at the work's central climax, depicting victory on the battlefield, they dominate the soundscape, climbing up and over the rest of the orchestra, then descending in a descant of suspensions until, finally, one last leap into the sonic stratosphere to land on the tonic. No matter how many times one hears it, it's impossible not to be shaken by its majesty.

We may be grateful that we hear horns instead of cannons. Napoleon rose in his country's service as an artillery man, obsessed with finding exactly the right placement for his guns so as to inflict maximum damage on the enemy while keeping them at bay. It is correct to say that Napoleon essentially invented modern artillery placement, and he was known to get down on his hands and knees and scrabble about the guns, positioning them *just so*. Napoleon instinctively grasped both the necessity and the art of concentrated fire, which for a decade made the French army almost unbeatable. Combined with his command of topography, Napoleon made the offensive capabilities of his forces a

---

Faust Symphony, each of whose three movements is a musical portrait, of Faust, Gretchen, and Mephistopheles.

18. One of them being his earlier tone poem, *Don Juan*—based not on Byron but on a play derived from the work of the German poet Nikolaus Lenau. Still, the Byronic resonance is there.

terrifying thing to encounter on the battlefield; he was to artillery what Alexander was to cavalry charges: a stunning weapon against which his adversaries long struggled to mount a cohesive defense.

His aptitude for mathematics won him a coveted, scarce place at the École Royale Militaire and entry into the artillery corps; later he studied at the School of Artillery in Auxonne. He was thrilled; in his mind, the artillery corps was where the best generals came from. Advances in metallurgy had made the big guns lighter and thus more mobile, and the young Napoleon instantly understood how effective and lethal mobile artillery units could be. His favorites were the twelve-pounders. He called them his "pretty girls." He learned everything there was to know about guns, including gunpowder, gun carriages, and how to found the weapon itself.

What he never learned, however, was the proper use of naval power. For all his tactical military genius, Napoleon never grasped or mastered the importance of sea power—a fatal flaw in that he regarded Britain as his principal enemy, without whose defeat he could never achieve final victory.[19] Napoleon loathed the British—*une nation de marchands* (a nation of shopkeepers), he called them—a sentiment they returned in spades—and for a long time planned an invasion of England. The problem was that the Royal Navy stood athwart the English Channel and all the other sea lanes, shouting stop. In 1805 the French were already masters of the Continent, and well on their way to expanding their hegemony all the way to the Russian border, but the British held sway over the seas. The French navy was hampered by geography, with only one principal port at Brest, on the coast of Brittany, and the other far away at Toulon in the Mediterranean. Britain, being an island, had no such handicaps.

At the Battle of the Nile in 1798, Napoleon and revolutionary France had already experienced a disastrous defeat at the hands of Horatio Nelson, then a rear admiral and one of the ablest sea captains and warriors in naval history. At the outset of Napoleon's campaign in Egypt and the Levant, Nelson had been dispatched to pursue Napoleon and the

---

19. Odd, considering he was born on an island and the British lived on an island.

fleet and stop them, but Napoleon was able to evade them, capture the island of Malta, and land in Egypt. Nelson, however, caught up with the French fleet near Alexandria and pounded it to matchsticks, giving Britain control of the Mediterranean.

Napoleon, while preoccupied with his ongoing battles with the various European coalitions that kept mounting against him, needed a bold move as the Third Coalition, composed of Britain (Prime Minister William Pitt was the paymaster for the operation), the Holy Roman Empire of German states, the Russian Empire, the Kingdom of Naples, the Kingdom of Sicily, and Sweden; Austria joined later, but Prussia remained neutral. He hit upon amassing a huge army of 150,000 men, called the Armée d'Angleterre, at Boulogne, from which he would launch his invasion. The only problem was that the British were blockading his ports and harassing French shipping. But when a storm temporarily blew Nelson's fleet away from Toulon, the French admiral, Pierre-Charles Villeneuve, slipped through the Strait of Gibraltar and rendezvoused with an allied Spanish fleet at Cadiz and headed for the island of Martinique in the Caribbean. Nelson, of course, regrouped and followed, and so began a chase across the Atlantic and back as Villeneuve, with Nelson well behind him now, would attempt to break the blockade at Brest with the odds briefly in their favor and allow the invasion to go forward. "It is necessary for us to be masters of the sea for six hours only," said Napoleon.[20]

Instead of sailing to Boulogne, however, Villeneuve wound up back at Cadiz, driving Napoleon, who had no grasp of the finer points of naval maneuvering or indeed of seamanship, to distraction. "What a navy!" he exclaimed. "What an admiral! What useless sacrifices!" Meanwhile came the news that Austria was now mobilizing and that a joint Austrian-Russian attack on France itself was imminent. Unwilling to fight a two-front war, Napoleon postponed the invasion, moved his troops back into position to fight enemies along the Danube instead of

---

20. And even that would have been a bridge too far: "He never understood that a fleet which spent seven-eighths of its time in port simply could not gain the seamanship necessary to take on the Royal Navy at the height of its operational capacity," writes Andrew Roberts in *Napoleon the Great*.

the Thames, and made preparations to kill the Coalition in its tracks—
especially the perfidious Austrians. He sat and dictated his entire war
plan to a secretary, down to the last detail right up to the capture of
Vienna. Among his innovations was the establishment of the corps system, which he would shortly use to spectacular effect at Austerlitz. And
then he put it into motion.

On October 20, 1805, at the German city of Ulm, Napoleon trapped
the unfortunate[21] Austrian general Karl Mack, who had gotten too far
ahead of his Russian allies, led by General Mikhail Kutuzov, the fat,
old, one-eyed Russian commander who would later emerge as the hero
of Borodino. Unable to wriggle free, Mack surrendered his entire army:
infantry, cavalry, guns, ammunition, general staff, and all. The following
day, October 21, Nelson returned the favor by catching up with Villeneuve off Cape Trafalgar on the Spanish coast west of Gibraltar. Employing unorthodox tactics, the outnumbered Nelson—twenty-seven
ships of the line as opposed to Villeneuve's thirty-three—attacked the
French left flank, splitting the line, separating its vanguard and thus
evening the odds against the remainder. This was not without risk; the
British fleet was exposed to heavy fire as it sailed in and engaged at close
quarters. Nelson himself was shot by a French marine and died near the
close of battle, but his bold tactics had won the day. That was the end of
Napoleon's dream of a British invasion. He suppressed the news of the
defeat until 1814.

And so to Austerlitz, southeast of Brno in what is today the Czech
Republic. After Ulm, Kutuzov had retreated to Olmütz, where he was
joined by both the young tsar Alexander, keen for a fight, and the Austrian emperor Francis, bringing reinforcements with them. Napoleon
knew he had to move quickly. "Let us finish this war with a thunder-
clap!" he exclaimed.

The battle was fought on December 2, 1805, one year to the day from
Napoleon's coronation as Emperor of the French. The French had taken

---

21. A characterization employed by Tolstoy in *War and Peace*, when Mack bursts in upon
Kutuzov and exclaims, "'You see before you the unfortunate Mack,' he managed to say in
French, his voice breaking."

Vienna, in part by subterfuge, and the Austrians had fled to join up with the Russians. The Grand Armée had arrived on the plain near Austerlitz a few days before: this was where the Emperor wished to fight. His troops were tired, their supply lines were tenuous, and the last thing he wanted was to be counterattacked and possibly surrounded by the Coalition armies. The Little Corporal studied the seven-mile-wide terrain carefully, ordering some engineering changes in the scenery to give him every tactical advantage possible. Writes Roberts:

> He then rode over the ground, carefully noting its two large lakes and its exposed areas, and "stopping several times over its more elevated points," principally the plateau known as the Pratzen heights, before declaring to his staff: "Gentleman, examine this ground carefully. It's going to be a battlefield, and you will have a part to play upon it!"
>
> On that same reconnaissance, which took him in addition to the villages of Girzikowitz, Puntowitz, Kobelnitz, Sokolnitz, Tellnitz and Mönitz, Napoleon told his entourage: "If I wished to stop the enemy from passing, it is here that I should post myself; but I should only have an ordinary battle. If, on the other hand, I refuse my right, withdrawing it towards Brno, [even] if there were three hundred thousand of them, they would be caught *in flagrante delicto* and hopelessly lost." From the start, therefore, Napoleon was planning a battle of annihilation.

With the Coalition starting to converge, Napoleon activated his corps strategy and concentrated his forces, some fifty thousand infantry and fifteen thousand cavalry, with 282 guns. If his plan came off, he—like Bohemond at Antioch or, for that matter, Nelson at Trafalgar—would be able to outnumber his opponents at given, crucial pressure points, even though they had the overall advantage in manpower. At the end of November, Napoleon was acting like an ordinary soldier, mixing freely with his men, talking and joking with them, sleeping rough among them. He was satisfied. Like Alexander at Gaugamela, snoozing like a baby on the morning of the fight, he knew he had his opponents right where he wanted them. Even more: he could anticipate every move they would make once he had them in the snare, because his tactics combined with the topography would force them to. They would never know what hit them until it was too late.

The early morning hours of December 2 broke cold, but the battlefield was enveloped in a thick fog. This was all to the good. Thanks to poor intelligence, the allies still had no real notion of the size of his forces, and the dense mist made it impossible for them to see his battle array with any clarity. Napoleon stationed himself on what little high ground there was, from which he could survey almost the entire battlefield, which encompassed several villages where the battle would be first joined. For all the pomp of a battlefield array, modern combat had moved beyond the set-piece engagements of Alexander and Caesar. House-to-house fighting would become the norm, with a concomitant increase in civilian casualties and destruction of property. It couldn't be helped.

The key to his strategy was another deception: he would take the Pratzen Heights—the linchpin of his battle plan—and then hastily abandon them in full view of the enemy, thus dangling an irresistible poisoned pawn. With his right wing thus weakened, and with the allies on the heights where they could see his disposition, Napoleon was counting on them to take the bait and come swooping down on his exposed right flank at Telnitz and Sokolnitz, hoping then to envelop Napoleon's center from the rear. They were unaware that the French III Corps under the flamboyant Marshal Louis-Nicolas Davout was marching toward the field.

It was a fatal error. With the allied left having cleared the Pratzen Heights, Napoleon quickly counterattacked, sending Marshal Jean-de-Dieu Soult to regain the heights and splitting the allied line down the middle as his sacrificial lamb of a right flank fought fiercely and bravely, gradually falling back until Davout's army arrived. That was all the help the emperor needed as he brought the brunt of his force under Soult—who had suddenly appeared out of the mist, causing more consternation in the allied camp—to bear on the center of the allies' formations. Hampered by a split command structure and poor lines of communications, the Austrians and Russians were for a time frozen in place, confounded by the speed of Napoleon's assault. By noon, with the fog finally having lifted, Soult had conquered the heights and Davout had stabilized the French right.

To the north, however, fighting still raged between the forces of Marshal Joachim Murat[22] and Marshal Jean Lannes and those of the Russian general, Pyotr Bagration. A cavalry battle ensued, but the Russian force was bombarded by cannon fire from Napoleon's well-placed guns, forcing them back from the village of Bosenitz in the teeth of a ferocious charge by French heavy cavalry. In a last-ditch attempt to regain the Pratzen Heights, where Napoleon had now set his standard, the Russian Grand Duke Constantine threw in the final allied reserves. Although a French regiment lost its eagle during the Russian assault, Napoleon sent in his own Imperial Guard cavalry and thus broke the allied center for good. He then repositioned some of his artillery atop the heights.

Now it was time to mop up in the south, where Murat was still engaged in heavy fighting around Sokolnitz. French troops swooped down from what was now the allied rear and trapped the allied general Friedrich Wilhelm von Buxhöwden. The only way out was east, across some frozen ponds and lakes. The French guns opened up on them as they tried to cross the ice, sending some two hundred men to their deaths in the icy waters.

As Napoleon himself later said, the army he had at Austerlitz was the best he ever commanded. After Nelson's victory at Trafalgar he'd had to redirect his forces from Boulogne, where they were preparing for the invasion of Britain, to central Europe. From the hindsight of more than a decade, the idea appeared to some in both Paris and London ridiculous. But not to Napoleon. "Were the English very much afraid of my invasion?" he asked the Comte de Las Cases on St. Helena. "What was

---

22. Second only to Napoleon himself in glamor, the flamboyant Murat abandoned the Emperor after Leipzig. After re-defecting during the Hundred Days, he battled the Austrians hoping to save his throne as the King of Naples, but was defeated, captured, and executed by firing squad in 1815.

the general opinion at the time?" Came the honest reply: "In the saloons of Paris we laughed heartily at the idea of an invasion of England; and the English who were there at the time did so too."

> "Well!" replied the Emperor, "You might laugh in Paris, but Pitt did not laugh in London. He soon comprehended the extent of the danger, and therefore threw a coalition on my shoulders at the moment when I was raising my arm to strike. Never was the English oligarchy exposed to greater danger. I had taken measures to ensure the possibility of my landing. I had the best army in the world; I need only say it was the army of Austerlitz. In four days I should have been in London; I should have entered the English capital, not as a conqueror but as a liberator."

What comes next has not often been discussed by historians, and perhaps taken as the self-serving moonshine of a critically ill man, but it clearly links Napoleon with Alexander the Great in his quintessentially liberal notion of the brotherhood of peoples, even if it had to be accomplished by force of arms. Alexander had a vision of uniting Greeks and Persians; Napoleon was focused on the French and the English. It's worth reproducing his remarks, especially since it reinforces in an unexpected way the commonality of the great commanders—not just Alexander but in a sense William the Conqueror as well, the last successful invader of England:

> I should have been another William III[23]; but I would have acted with greater generosity and disinterestedness. The discipline of my army was perfect. My troops would have behaved in London just as they would in Paris. No sacrifices, not even contributions, would have been exacted from the English. We should have presented ourselves to them, not as conquerors but as brothers, who came to restore to them their rights and liberties. I would have

---

23. William of Orange, the victor in England's Glorious Revolution of 1688–1689.

assembled the citizens, and directed them to labour in the task of their regeneration; because the English had already preceded us in political legislation; I would have declared that our only wish was to be able to rejoice in the happiness and prosperity of the English people; and to these professions I would have strictly adhered. In the course of a few months, the two nations, which had been such determined enemies, would have thenceforward composed only one people, identified in principles, maxims and interests.

I should have departed from England, in order to effect from south to north, under republican colours (for I was then First Consul) the regeneration of Europe, which, at a later period, I was on the point of effecting from north to south under monarchical forms. Both systems were equally good, since both would have been attended with the same result, and would have been carried into execution with firmness, moderation, and good faith. How many ills that are now endured, and how many that are yet to be experienced, would not unhappy Europe have escaped! Never was a project so favourable to the interests of civilization conceived with more disinterested intentions, or so near being carried into execution. It is a remarkable fact that the obstacles which occasioned my failure were not the work of men, but all proceeded from the elements. In the south, the sea frustrated my plans; the burning of Moscow, the snow and the winter, completed my ruin in the north. Thus water, air, and fire, all nature and nature alone, was hostile to the universal regeneration which nature herself called for! . . . The problems of Providence are insoluble!

In his dazzling experimental work of historical fiction, *Napoleon Symphony: A Novel in Four Movements* (1974), Anthony Burgess sought to recreate the structure, architecture, and sequencing of Beethoven's *Eroica Symphony* while reimagining the emperor as a character in his own story. Here is the dying Napoleon, recounting the end of the Battle of Austerlitz to the doctors treating him during his last days on earth at St. Helena:

"Now that," the Emperor said, "was an example of initiative which I am disinclined to reprehend." For Bernadotte[24] had detached General Drouet's division to support the hard-pressed five squadrons of the Imperial Guard. "So now we order General Rapp to administer the final—Two squadrons of chasseurs and one of the fellow-countrymen of Roustam[25] here. How would you like to be out there, eh, Roustam, shouting *Allah chew their balls off* and so on?"

"Sire."

Oh, effective enough, very effective. Five hundred Russian grenadiers dead and two hundred officers of the crack and elite and nobly-born Chevaliers, personal escort of the Tsar or Czar, taken prisoner.

"Just after two o'clock, Sire."

"Well," smiled the Emperor, as Prince Repnine, Commander of the Holy Russian Imperial Chevalier Guard was presented to him, torn, dusty, cowed, but every inch a prince of the blood, "we gave you a run for your money, eh, my prince?" And then, brutally: "Some weeping and gnashing and so forth in St. Petersburg tonight or tomorrow, I should think. All these delectable aristocratic ladies bereft of aristocratic manly comfort. Very well, let our aristocratic guests be led away."

"Two-thirty, Sire."

"Very good. Final phase, I think, gentlemen."

The great supine body was cleansed of the infesting enemy. It was sluiced down, south of the belly of the Pratzen Heights,

---

24. Jean-Baptiste-Jules Bernadotte. He frustrated Napoleon with his passivity in battle, and was eventually sacked. In 1810 Sweden, hoping to ingratiate itself with Napoleon, offered Bernadotte the position of Crown Prince, a regency, and eventually the Swedish throne. He reigned from 1818 to 1844.

25. A reference to Roustam Raza, a Mameluke of Armenian or Georgian origin, who had been kidnaped at thirteen by Muslim raiders and sold into slavery in Cairo. He was presented to Napoleon in 1798 during the Egyptian campaign and returned with Bonaparte to France, where he acted as Napoleon's personal servant and bodyguard until 1814. The novel is dedicated to director Stanley Kubrick, who had directed the film adaptation of *A Clockwork Orange*.

to a region of frozen lakes and marshlands. The west was clear of enemy, and the column that retreated east towards Austerlitz was harried, battered, clawed, bitten, chewed, spat out. General Doktorov faced the north with frozen lakeland behind him. Every man for himself. Five thousand scattered, many over the iced waters.

"Bombard," ordered the Emperor. "All available cannon." He looked south to the white sheets, already cracking here and there under the weight of retreating gun-teams. Cannonballs stoned the ice, and the ice starred and shived and men went screaming into the black water, horses too, terrified and threshing, and the great useless guns.

"News from the north?"

"Enemy retreat under way, Sire. Just after three o'clock."

The Battle of the Three Emperors was over. The allies lost more than 6,000 men killed and another 11,000 wounded, while the French lost about 1,300 dead, and 7,000 wounded, with only 570 men captured. The French had taken some 11,000 prisoners. Alexander, Kutuzov, and their troops retreated home, while Emperor Francis was forced to sign the humiliating Treaty of Pressburg, paying a 40-million-franc indemnity to Napoleon and ceding territory along the Adriatic to his Kingdom of Italy.

The comparison with Gaugamela is apt, and it's impossible that a student of military history such as Napoleon didn't know that. A contained front, a poisoned pawn dangled on the right, the stretching out of the allied lines as they took the bait, enduring a hammering on his left that he was willing to take as long as his gambit on the right worked, the opening of a gap in the center that he knew must follow, and then the killer thrust. History repeats.

On the evening of the battle, the victorious emperor issued the following proclamation to the Grand Armée:

Soldiers of the Grande Armée: Even at this hour, before this great day shall pass away and be lost in the ocean of eternity, your emperor must address you, and say how satisfied he is with the conduct of all those who have had the good fortune to fight in this memorable battle. Soldiers! You are the finest warriors in the world. The recollection of this day, and of your deeds, will be eternal! Thousands of ages hereafter, as long as the events of the universe continue to be related, will it be told that a Russian army of 76,000 men, hired by the gold of England, was annihilated by you on the plains of Olmütz.

When news of the disaster at Austerlitz reached Pitt, he is supposed to have exclaimed: "Roll up that map of Europe. It will not be wanted these ten years." He died a month later. Napoleon would rule Europe for the better part of the next decade. He rests today in his sarcophagus in an open crypt at Les Invalides in Paris, still the center of attention.

Nine

PERSHING AT ST.-MIHIEL, NIMITZ AT MIDWAY, PATTON AT THE BULGE

Battle is the most significant competition in which a man can indulge. It brings out all that is best and it removes all that is base. You are not all going to die. Only two percent of you right here today would be killed in a major battle. Every man is scared in his first action. If he says he's not, he's a goddamn liar. But the real hero is the man who fights even though he's scared. Some men will get over their fright in a minute under fire, some take an hour, and for some it takes days. But the real man never lets his fear of death overpower his honor, his sense of duty to his country, and his innate manhood.

We'll win this war, but we'll win it only by fighting and showing the Germans that we've got more guts than they have or ever will have. We're not just going to shoot the bastards, we're going to rip out their living goddamned guts and use them to grease the treads of our tanks. We're going to murder those lousy Hun cocksuckers by the bushel-fucking-basket.

—GEORGE S. PATTON, JR., MAY 31, 1944

UNTIL THE ADVENT OF THE AMERICAN CIVIL WAR, THE CONCEPT OF desk-jockey generals—"rear-echelon motherfuckers" or REMFs, in contemporary parlance—was pretty much unknown. From Alexander to Napoleon, generals had fought on the same fields of battle as their men—indeed, they led them into battle. John Keegan's formation—in front always? Sometimes? Never?—was universally applicable. But with the arrival of mechanized warfare, trains, planes, and automobiles, not to mention tanks, battlefields grew ever larger. Theaters of war became more widely spaced, encompassing whole countries, then continents. Even with improvements in communication it became impossible for one man, or even a small general staff, to manage the tactical, strategic, logistical, and other demands of modernizing warfare. Soon enough, war became too important to be left to the generals, and so arose the civilian leaders who were also the political leaders in their respective countries. For them the answer to Keegan's question about the proper placement of the commander has been: are you kidding? American generals now "lead" from offices in Tampa while losing war after war and never wondering why or suffering any career consequences.

How much has warfare been changed by the push-buttoned, air-conditioned generals? Hard to say, but the fact that America has not won a war since World War II might provide some indication. As warfare has become more remote, so has it become less effective. Americans once thrilled to the exploits of warriors like Grant, Custer, and Patton. Today, they have been replaced by overweight, beribboned, plush-bottomed widebodies of both sexes proudly displaying chests full of fruit salad, preening about "metrics" and prattling about "inclusivity" and sexuality when the only thing they should be discussing is total victory.

Imagine, then, the contempt a man like George Patton would feel for them today. America's greatest fighting general since Grant, Patton—as is readily gleaned from the excerpt above from his famous speech to the Sixth Armored Division shortly before D-Day—had no patience with, and little respect for, desk jockeys: men without chests who fought wars in the map room rather than in the field. His bluster and outspokenness and sometimes even borderline insubordination delayed his career advancement and, even in theater, got him relieved of command, much to the astonishment of the German General Staff, which couldn't fathom why Dwight Eisenhower would yank his best commander just for slapping a soldier whom he viewed as a shirker and a coward.

And yet Patton, more than any other American military figure of the twentieth century, frames the rise and fall of the country's military might. Expert horseman and marksman, a champion with the sword, personally wealthy yet coming from a long line of soldiers stretching back to the Revolution, utterly fearless in the face of fire, sure of his battlefield instincts, which tactically rivaled those of Alexander and Napoleon, Patton exemplified all that was best about an America that no longer exists. From his early service in the punitive Villa Expedition, during which he personally shot and killed several men, through his pioneering exploitation of a new mechanism of war, the armored tank, to his tactical masterpiece at the relief of Bastogne during the Battle of the Bulge, Patton distinguished himself in the annals of American military history in a way that no one has since.

In the annals of potent military leadership the United States mustered from America's entry into the First World War to the formal surrender of Imperial Japan on the deck of the battleship *Missouri* in September 1945, which concluded World War II, it is Patton's warfighting ability and clear-eyed tactical and strategic sense that helped win both global conflicts. There was nothing coy about him, and he very rarely resorted to subterfuge; he simply did what other generals fervently believed could not be done, and in that lay his element of surprise. He was an embodiment of Nietzsche's Will to Power, a human battering ram who liked nothing better than going toe to toe with the enemy, and destroying him.

Despite his reelection-year promises in 1916 to keep the U.S. out of the European conflict, President Woodrow Wilson acted as quickly as possible after declaring war on Germany in the spring of 1917—in large part owing to Germany's renewed policy of unrestricted submarine warfare—to get troops onto the battlefields of France and Flanders. There was only one problem: America barely had a functioning Army, led by a tiny officer class. Grant's armies had been disbanded as quickly as possible at the end of the American Civil War, and a career in the military of an isolationist nation was not seen as particularly desirable to young men on the make and in a hurry. Luckily for the U.S., Patton and a few of his coevals—men who would later play a leading role in winning the Second World War in both the European and Pacific theaters—were an exception.

But at this time they were still junior officers. To command the American Expeditionary Forces (AEF), Wilson turned to the veteran

General John J. Pershing, the leader of the punitive American incursion into Mexico a few years earlier in the wake of Pancho Villa's raid on Columbus, New Mexico, in March 1916.[1] "Black Jack," as he was known, was one of those men who hadn't originally sought a military career— West Point was free and a better option than any of the universities in Missouri at the time—but who discovered his true métier in the command of other men. He was a descendant of German immigrants (the name Pershing was originally Pfoersching) who had graduated from the Academy in 1886, and immediately marked for success. He saw action against the Apaches in the American Southwest, then served with the Sixth Cavalry up and down the frontier as it closed. In 1890 he took part in the last battles of the Indian Wars against the Sioux from his base at Fort Meade in South Dakota. In 1895 he was given command of the Tenth Cavalry Regiment, a contingent of black "Buffalo Soldiers"[2]; it was there that he acquired his nickname.[3]

Pershing won a Silver Star in Cuba during the Spanish-American War, where he was the Tenth's regimental quartermaster, a role that Grant had fulfilled for the Fourth Infantry during the Mexican War half a century earlier. Nerveless, Pershing saw action throughout the war, from Cuba to the Philippines, including America's holdover conflict against the Filipino *insurrectos* inherited from Spain. He later served as an observer in the Russo-Japanese War of 1905, which saw Russian Baltic-based battleships sail halfway around the world only to be annihilated at the Battle of Tsushima, and which announced to the world Japan's entry into the sweepstakes of potent militarism.

After bouncing around the ranks via a series of brevet promotions, he was appointed a brigadier general by his biggest fan, President Theodore Roosevelt, and married Helen Frances Warren, the daughter of a prominent senator from Wyoming, with whom he had four children.

---

1. New Mexico had entered the Union just four years earlier, in January 1912, followed a few weeks later by Arizona, thus completing the continental United States.

2. A name given to black soldiers by the Indians, since their thick curly hair reminded the Sioux of buffalo hide.

3. Originally "Nigger Jack," later ameliorated to "Black Jack." Throughout his life, Pershing wore it as a badge of honor.

Tragically, Frances and their three daughters were killed in a house fire at the Presidio of San Francisco, then an important West Coast army base, while Pershing was away planning their move to Fort Bliss in El Paso; only his son, aged five, survived.

In 1917, Pershing took command of the AEF that would soon enough be on its way to France. Here is where the former quartermaster's talent for war shone. Essentially, he created an American Army where there had been none, trained it, supplied it, transported it in June of 1917, and led it during its first action as a standalone unit in the critical Battle of St.-Mihiel in September of 1918. Two months later the war was over; the American troops had been the decisive addition with which to break the nearly four-year stalemate on the Western Front. By the end of the war, Pershing had risen to the rank of General of the Army, skipping the three stars of lieutenant general and thus becoming the first four-star general since Philip Sheridan, Grant's cavalry commander, in 1888.[4]

One of Pershing's hand-picked lieutenants was George S. Patton. The two men had first met during the Villa campaign and had become social; indeed, Pershing was even engaged to his flamboyant young protégé's sister, Anne Wilson "Nita" Patton, in 1917–1918, but the relationship foundered when he was sent to France. He didn't remarry until 1946 (he died in 1948), to a woman thirty-five years his junior named Micheline Resco, a Romanian-born French artist he met when she painted his portrait and who had been his mistress for many years. Patton, however, would serve under Pershing with spectacular distinction during World War I as a brevet colonel in charge of a tank brigade, leading a charge—from the front, of course—that helped win the Battle of St.-Mihiel on the Meuse River in northeastern France, blunting a major German salient and turning the tide of the war for good.

The Battle of St.-Mihiel took place not terribly far from where the

---

4. "Little Phil," the son of Irish immigrants from County Cavan, was an outspoken advocate of total war. It was he who had burned the Shenandoah Valley in Virginia late in the war to deny its fruits to the starving Confederates, and who relentlessly pursued Robert E. Lee during the endgame that resulted in Appomattox. It was also Sheridan who famously, or notoriously, said, "The only good Indians I ever saw were dead."

Battle of the Catalaunian Plains had been fought almost fifteen hundred years earlier—and where another great battle would be fought again in 1944–1945, near Bastogne. Stretching just a little, we can also include the Battle of Tours in this relatively small geographic region. Although unsung today, St.-Mihiel is one of the turning points in modern American military history. With the surrender of the Russians at Brest-Litovsk in March 1918, the Germans were hastily redirecting soldiers from the Eastern Front to the west, hoping that the additional manpower would finally allow them to crack the trench warfare stalemate. The Americans were much needed by the exhausted allies to fill in holes in the lines and prevent such an eventuality, but St.-Mihiel marked the first time the American soldiers in France had fought as an American army, and not seconded off to various British and French units. It was also the first time that the designations D-Day and H-Hour were employed by the U.S. military.

In 2020, the distinguished American poet Elizabeth T. Gray, Jr., published her poem *Salient,* her response to months spent walking the battlefield and communing with the souls of the men who had fought and died there just a century before. It's an extraordinary work, impressionistic and analytical, observational yet engaged. More effectively than a mere narrative of the terrain over which armies had clashed time and time again, it paints a picture of what those men experienced as seen through modern eyes:

CAMOUFLAGE: TRENCHES

The way a new trench
is best concealed by making it look like
an abandoned one and an abandoned one
is best concealed by making it look like
a meadow, or a digression, say,
one that has cast off its lines
and is moving slowly away from us
downriver, and is just now—see?—passing
under a bridge, making its way to the coast,
and as it drifts through the small trading towns

no one who sees it thinks to ask why
it was held or who had been there.[5]

The proud Pershing had been dead set against having his men employed piecemeal; he was the one who had raised them, farm boys with no prior service experience, plus the dregs of the cities, urban thugs who knew how to fight with their fists, teeth, broken bottles, and paving stones.[6] They were his men, goddammit, and they were *Americans*. So when a window of opportunity opened for the AEF to strike out on its own in September 1918, Pershing snapped it up. He would show the exhausted Europeans how to deal with Jerry and get this war over with.

Pershing's staff and subordinate officers included just about everybody who would go on to supervise, fight, and win the Second World War: George C. Marshall, the quintessential staff officer; Harry Truman, an artillery officer, later vice president and president of the United States; Billy Mitchell, head of the First Army Air Service; Eddie Rickenbacker (whose parents were German-speaking Swiss immigrants), the nation's first flying ace; Brigadier General Douglas MacArthur, like Patton an Army brat[7] of Scots heritage as well as another massive egotist fearless under enemy fire; aviator Hap Arnold; Chester Nimitz, who served aboard a refueling vessel in the North Atlantic and later became

---

5. New Directions Books, used with permission. Writes the author: "This work began by juxtaposing two obsessions of mine that took root in the late 1960s: (1) the Battle of Passchendaele, fought by the British Army in Belgian Flanders in late 1917, and (2) the chöd ritual, the core 'severance' practice of a lineage founded by Machik Lapdrön, the great twelfth-century female Tibetan Buddhist saint. I have no complete explanation as to why these two subjects have remained of abiding interest to me . . ."

6. Including the notorious Lower East Side gangster Monk Eastman, who volunteered to fight at the age of forty-two. When doctors examined him during his physical and saw the number of scars and bullet wounds tattooed there, they asked him if he had ever been to war: "I been in a lotta little wars around New York," he replied. He fought with the 106th Infantry Regiment of the Twenty-Seventh Division (O'Ryan's Roughnecks) and emerged from the war to public acclaim as a decorated hero, returned to crime, and in 1920 was shot to death in front of Tammany Hall. He was buried with full military honors.

7. His father was Arthur MacArthur, Jr., who had served the Union in the Civil War and also saw action in the Indian Wars, the Spanish-American War, and in the Philippines, where he served as military governor in 1900–1901.

an aide to the commander of the Atlantic Fleet's submarine service; and Patton himself. Dwight Eisenhower, then a second lieutenant eager to see action, served stateside at Camp Colt in Pennsylvania; later he would become Supreme Allied Commander in Europe and the thirty-fourth president of the United States.

In March of 1918, the desperate Germans mounted Operation Michael, their last major offensive of the war, in an attempt to smash through the Allied lines. St.-Mihiel was a small town that hitherto had not been considered of strategic importance, but with the Allied advances on the Western Front early in the war, it had found itself behind enemy lines at the tip of a salient, a bulge as it were, thrust into French territory and obstructing communications between Verdun and Nancy. Salients—as the Germans were to learn again in less than thirty years—are tricky things. On the one hand, they represent a degree of success on the part of the attacker, whose goal in warfare since Alexander has been to break the enemy's front line, get in his rear, and then either wheel and destroy him or sprint toward a further objective: a capital city, for example. On the other hand, a salient is by definition surrounded on three sides by the opposition, leaving the offensive forces open to flanking fire from each direction. So its success or failure relies on perfect execution combined with speed and overwhelming force—and the ability to hang onto it.

Six months later, *les Boches* were still holding on. Pershing saw that the Germans had left themselves vulnerable. They were no longer on the offensive, for one thing. Indeed, they were busily trying to vacate St.-Mihiel, an important railway depot, and pull back to the more significant railhead at Metz, which would give them access to—or prevent the Allies from accessing—the Briey Iron Basin and the coal fields of the Saar. In fact, Metz initially was to have been the secondary but more important goal of the St.-Mihiel attack until Marshal Ferdinand Foch, the Allied supreme commander, informed Pershing that the new Allied battle plan would require the Americans to move north in time to join the final "grand offensive," which would take place in the Meuse-Argonne region. They would have two weeks to take St.-Mihiel.

The German salient had stalled. The dice had been thrown in an attempt to split the lines, cutting the French off from the American Expeditionary Force under the overall command of Sir Douglas Haig and forcing them to fall back in order to protect Paris. Now, with the growing realization that the war was lost, the best the Germans could hope for was an armistice and a border settlement that included the disputed provinces of Alsace and Lorraine (Elsaß-Lothringen), which had changed hands throughout the centuries of French-German rivalry, most recently going to Germany as spoils of the Franco-Prussian War. And that itself was a reaction to the Napoleonic conquest and occupation of the region by the French a century before. Some grievances never die, and indeed seem immune to the kind of "negotiated settlement" so beloved of modern-day Metternichs.

The action at St.-Mihiel saw the full complement of American theory and might, waged with infantry, tanks (cavalry), and air power, then in its infancy. Pershing, who occupies the strange nether land of American military action and philosophy that obtained between 1865 and 1917, could not completely foresee how thoroughly the First World War would change the battlefield calculus for every war going forward. But he immediately grasped that the static trench warfare (a remnant of Grant's siege of Petersburg that had effectively ended the Civil War) which had chewed up so many lives unnecessarily and caused so much destruction to property, had to stop, and that new ways of offense would have to be created in order to solve the problem.

The U.S. had been highly reluctant to become involved in Europe in what was essentially an interbred family squabble between the Hanoverian Queen Victoria's grandchildren. King George V and Tsar Nicholas II were first cousins, as were Nicholas and Kaiser Wilhelm II, while Wilhelm and George were third cousins; physically they were three peas in a pod. Although born in London, Her Britannic Majesty was German on both sides of her family, and she spoke German with her husband, Prince Albert of Saxe-Coburg and Gotha (whose English was weak), with whom she had nine children—all of whom spoke German fluently—and who was also her first cousin, as well as her third cousin once removed. They were born just months apart and shared the same midwife as infants.

So German was the British royal family in 1917 that in the interests of patriotism King George V changed their name from the house of

Saxe-Coburg and Gotha to "Windsor," denominating themselves after the castle rather than the other way round, as is commonly supposed. His action was precipitated by the arrival in the skies above London of the German heavy bombers of the Gotha G.IV class (earlier raids were largely carried out by airships) and the forced abdication of Tsar Nicholas in March of 1917. Both Germans and monarchs had lost favor with the people of Europe, a development of which the British royals were keenly aware—and which was driven home by Nicholas's murder by the Bolsheviks, along with that of his entire family, in July 1918. Nothing could be less democratic than fighting for a trio of inbred royals in the name of saving the world for democracy, but there it was.

America had another major reason for not wanting to join in a war against Germany: the largest ethnic group, especially in the Midwest, was (and still is) of German descent. But Wilson, who regularly flouted the Constitution, a document he held in low regard, waged a fierce propaganda war against German-Americans.[8] Prohibition, which became law in 1920 during Wilson's last year in office,[9] was in part aimed at them and their well-known fondness for brewing and drinking beer. The result was a sad litany of overt prejudice, changed names, shuttered businesses, and general public opprobrium. German-American periodicals were shuttered, books banned and destroyed, music forbidden to be performed, German-language classes outlawed. Anti-German propaganda posters were everywhere, depicting the Hun as a rampaging ape wearing a spiked helmet, holding the prostrate body of virginal Belgium in one arm, a club (marked "*Kultur*")[10] in his right hand. "Destroy This Mad Brute," it read, "Enlist." The most familiar image from that period is undoubtedly the iconic picture of Uncle Sam, dressed in red, white, and blue and wearing a top hat, pointing directly at the viewer and announcing: "I want YOU for U.S. Army."

---

8. The irony being that German-Americans were instrumental in winning both world wars for the U.S., Pershing, Eisenhower, and Nimitz prominent among them.

9. At which point he was seriously incapacitated by the stroke largely kept from the public.

10. As opposed to Anglo-French *civilisation*—a major philosophical distinction in the late nineteenth and twentieth centuries. Very broadly speaking, the difference is between a societal overlay ("civilization") and its essence ("*Kultur*").

In short, the atmosphere was decidedly hostile. No one was exempt from the aura of suspicion and fear. Consider the case of the German-born conductor Karl Muck, a Swiss national, who was imprisoned at Fort Oglethorpe in Georgia for a year and a half and then deported to Copenhagen, for allegedly refusing to conduct the "Star-Spangled Banner" (it was not yet the national anthem; that didn't happen until 1931) at a concert with the Boston Symphony in Providence, Rhode Island, in the fall of 1917. Some orchestras had begun doing so after America's entry into the war earlier that year, but it was far from customary, much less mandatory. Muck, a fine conductor who at this point in his career considered himself an American, had even offered his resignation once America declared for the Allies. Still, the music director of one of America's greatest orchestras was hounded by the editor of the *Providence Journal,* one John Rathom, whose motto was "raise hell and sell newspapers" and who had first planted the suggestion that Muck was an untrustworthy sinister foreigner a few days before the concert. Such was the tenor of the times that Muck—a known friend of Kaiser Willie!—wound up in a Georgia prisoner-of-war camp, along with many other Germans. He eventually found his way back to Germany, where he continued his career under the National Socialist regime, and died in Stuttgart in 1940 at the age of eighty.

Such demonization of the Triple Alliance[11] and its descendants in America, however, was routine. President Wilson denounced "hyphenated Americans." The American ambassador to Germany from 1913 to 1917, James Watson Gerard, declared, "Every citizen must declare himself American—or traitor!" Tempers soared at the sinking by the Germans of the British ocean liner RMS *Lusitania* off the southern coast of Ireland near Kinsale on May 7, 1915, which killed 128 of the 139 American citizens on board. The publication of the notorious "Zimmermann telegram"—a January 1917 missive from the German foreign secretary to his minister in Mexico—inflamed the crisis with its revelation that Germany was about to recommence unrestricted submarine warfare in the Atlantic, and the proposition that should America enter the war,

---

11. Germany, Austria-Hungary, and Italy.

Germany could form an alliance with Japan and Mexico against the United States. The idea that a hostile nation might exist on the southern border spurred the U.S. to action, and war was declared on April 6, 1917.

Once in the war, however, Americans had responded with headlong commitment. Practically from scratch, an entire army was conjured out of thin air. The right man, Pershing—of German descent—was given the task. Young German-Americans were keen to join the fight, to display their patriotism and assist the war effort with their language skills. Although Wilson had campaigned for reelection in 1916 on the slogan, "He kept us out of war," the American public forgave the deception and rallied to his side. Aside from the Indian Wars, Americans had not been involved in a major conflict since the Civil War, now safely in the past, its veterans aging, infirm, or deceased. Memories were fading: upon election in 1912, the Virginia-born Wilson had become the first southerner to be elected to the highest office since James K. Polk in 1848, and his reelection in 1916 made him the first Democrat elected to a second term since Andrew Jackson in 1832.

And so on September 12, 1917—the day before his fifty-seventh birthday—Black Jack Pershing and fourteen divisions of the American Expeditionary Forces, about half a million men in all, found themselves at St.-Mihiel. Pershing knew that everything was riding on this battle, and under very difficult conditions. First, he had to win, or face the relegation of his army back to support and reinforcement duty. Second, he had little time to do it, since he had to join the Meuse-Argonne offensive in a matter of days. Third, the Germans under Lieutenant General Georg Fuchs had been dug in there for a long time, and even though their units were exhausted from four years of fighting, were under strength, and had started to pull back and thus couldn't muster a counterattack—the order to evacuate and pull back behind the Hindenburg Line had been issued on September 8—resistance would still be fierce. There were entrenchments, barbed wire, and machine-gun nests everywhere. Further, the enemy had been alerted by a report in a Swiss newspaper regarding the timing of the opening Allied artillery barrage. There was still plenty of fight left in the frontline German soldiers. They were as ready as they could be.

So were the Americans, although still largely untested and unbloodied. There was plenty to do, including acquiring homing pigeons from the Signal Corps, prepping arms, studying plans. Still, there was the inevitable ennui that always precedes any fight. As the saying at the time went, "War is long periods of boredom punctuated by moments of sheer terror." One of the Americans with ants in his pants, of course, was George Patton, who had organized the AEF's tank squadrons and eagerly awaited the news of what his troops' role would be.

Prior to arriving in France, Patton had served on various bases, in 1911 landing the quartermaster's post[12] at Fort Myer, just across the Potomac from Washington, which was chockablock with peacetime brass. He owed that transfer to George C. Marshall, a rising staff officer with whom he would soon serve in France. As a wealthy American aristocrat—he brought his own horses with him—Patton mingled easily with other men of his social class, including Henry L. Stimson, the secretary of war under President William Howard Taft at the time.[13] Stimson took Patton on as his military aide and introduced him to everybody who was anybody in the capital.

A native of San Gabriel, California, near Los Angeles, Patton (b. 1885) came by his military career naturally: an early relation, Hugh Mercer, was a brigadier general in the Continental Army during the American Revolution, killed at the Battle of Princeton in 1777, while his paternal grandfather, George Smith Patton, had commanded the Twenty-Second Virginia Infantry under Jubal Early in the Civil War and was killed during the Third Battle of Winchester in 1864; his great uncle Waller T. Patton was killed at Gettysburg during Pickett's Charge, fighting for the South. He could be gracious, with a refined sense of *noblesse oblige*;

---

12. Another quartermaster, like Grant and Pershing, he understood the art and science of feeding, housing, and transporting large numbers of men—living proof of the adage that "amateurs talk tactics, professionals talk logistics." This knowledge would pay off spectacularly at the Battle of the Bulge during World War II.

13. A nonpartisan Republican, Stimson would serve as Herbert Hoover's secretary of state and again as secretary of war for presidents Franklin Roosevelt and Harry Truman. He died in 1950.

he could also swear a blue streak, even in polite society. It was hard for normal people to know what to make of, or what to do with, him. His real métier was for war, and it was his and his country's great fortune that the Great War and the Big One were the making of the one and the salvation of the other.

As a student at the Virginia Military Academy he struggled with reading and writing owing to undiagnosed dyslexia, but excelled at military drill. After being appointed to the U.S. Military Academy at West Point, he flunked first-year mathematics and had to repeat it. Nonetheless, in 1909 he graduated 46th in his class of 103 cadets. An artist with the sword, he was selected to go to the 1912 Olympics in Stockholm to compete in the modern pentathlon: fencing, swimming, equestrian jumping, cross-country running, and pistol marksmanship. While in France preparing for the Olympics, he had studied at the École de cavalerie at Saumur, just west of Tours—a part of Europe he would come to know very well in both world wars.

In resurrecting the Olympics, Baron Pierre de Coubertin said he wanted to recreate the Greek warrior ideal under the conditions a Napoleonic officer might have faced: "He must ride an unfamiliar horse, fight enemies with pistol and sword, swim, and run to return to his own soldiers." That, of course, was right up Patton's alley. He idealized his famous military predecessors—Alexander, Hannibal, Scipio, Caesar, Bonaparte—and in fact believed he was the umpteenth incarnation of the Soldier throughout history: the eternal recurrence of the military hero. He even wrote a poem about it:

So as through a glass and darkly
The age long strife I see
Where I fought in many guises
Many names—but always me.

In Sweden he placed fifth overall; the first four finishers were Swedes. He might have placed higher, or even won, but for his performance in the pistol event. Everybody knew he was a crack shot, a record-setter in his handling of a sidearm. During the Villa expedition he had personally gunned down three of the Mexican leader's aides with his trademark Colt .45 single-action revolver, roaring up to their Rancho San Miguelito hideout in a convoy of 1916 Dodge motorcars of riflemen and engaging in an old-fashioned western shootout. In the pentathlon, however, he was charged with one complete miss on the silhouette target. Patton insisted he hadn't missed, but that his shot went through the same hole as an earlier one, but the judges disallowed. He was probably right.

Still he defeated the French world champion in fencing and was named the sword-fighting champion of the Army. Inspired by the way the French used their swords as stabbing rather than slashing weapons, he invented something called the "Patton saber," a kind of modern reincarnation of the ancient Roman *gladius,* whose purpose had been to pierce an opponent's entrails, not chop his arm off. By World War I, however, Patton's military career seemed to be going nowhere. He chafed at his lack of progress in the peacetime army, which promoted young officers very slowly, if at all. While waiting for his summons to war, however, he had latched onto the tank as the modern incarnation of the Persian cataphracts or the heavy cavalry of Napoleon's armies and had become the foremost proponent of its use in battle—despite the fact that the tank itself was relatively new and had never been tried in combat prior to the war.

His chance finally arrived at St.-Mihiel, three weeks before the battle was to commence: Patton would employ his 144-tank brigade—French-made Renault FTs, their two-man crews filled by Americans—in a direct assault on the salient while other forces would attempt to encircle the Germans from the rear. This meant the enemy would be right in his kill zone, a prospect that pleased him immensely. Not for him was an Austerlitz-style chess match, with gambits and poisoned pawns; instead, he would head right at them. The tanks were primitive affairs, with fifty horsepower engines and a top speed of four and a half miles per hour. They were armed with either a 37 millimeter cannon or a 9 millimeter machine gun, fired by the commander, who sat above the driver, who could not see out. Directions were given by the primitive expedient of kicking the driver in the back and shoulders. But they were still formidable and, as yet, still largely untested as an offensive weapon.

Ten days before the battle, the orders changed, again to Patton's dismay. Now he would only be supporting the Forty-Second Division, which had never worked with tanks, and on entirely different ground from the one he had, in imitation of Napoleon, earlier traversed in preparation. He quickly surveyed the area, which was promptly drenched by rain.

Donald A. Carter, a historian at the Center for Military History of the United States Army in Washington, describes what the Americans were facing:

> The Germans had the advantage of occupying the highest ground in most of the area along the salient front, on which they had constructed strong defensive positions supplemented by vast stretches of barbed wire. Although the Germans had defended the salient against French attacks since late 1914, they had few illusions regarding the security of the position. Its wedge shape made it highly vulnerable to a pincer attack. Allied successes in the north also indicated that the static nature of positional warfare no longer defined tactical realities on the Western Front. Moreover, the Germans needed to conserve manpower in the light of their losses earlier in the year, requiring them to shorten the line wherever possible.
>
> As early as June 1918, the high command began work on a planned troop withdrawal from the salient, code-named *Loki*.[14] So long as the sector remained quiet, they would hold their current positions, but as soon as they detected a major Allied assault in the offing, the defenders would withdraw to the shorter, more defensible Michel position across the base of the salient to make their stand.

The fledgling air force had three primary missions: to bomb enemy positions, to conduct aerial reconnaissance, including shooting down observation balloons, and to prevent any German planes from doing the same thing to the Americans. Billy Mitchell, the commander, knew

---

14. The Norse god of trickery.

the Americans would need at least two days' worth of air superiority, if not actual supremacy, to give the attacking forces their best chance for success. To help, both French and British bombers had overflown the attack zone in the days preceding.

D-day was set for September 12, and H-hour was 0500, after the four hours of artillery bombardment. The opening artillery barrage duly came at 1 A.M. The soaking rain had already turned the battlefield to mush. The tanks instantly got bogged down. Patton pushed forward anyway. He never demanded more from his men than he was ready to give himself, and he knew this was his big chance to show what an armored column could do. He walked ahead of the tanks into the village of Essey, then German-held. In the front? Always.

During the fighting, Douglas MacArthur's Eighty-Fourth Infantry Brigade was getting hit hard by machine-gun fire and the heavy mortars called *Minenwerfer*. Patton's tanks were having trouble negotiating the field, not only muddied by now but pockmarked by shell craters, which made it hard for them to keep up with the advancing infantry they were supposed to be supporting. Worse, they were running out of fuel.[15] Meanwhile, in the air, the inexperienced American pilots, largely unfamiliar with their British-made DH-4 biplane bombers now outfitted with the new four-hundred-horsepower American-made "Liberty" motors, were having to learn on the fly. The weather was making photographic reconnaissance impossible.[16]

Patton left his command headquarters on foot and met up with MacArthur. The two of them stood there in the middle of the carnage, coolly discussing the way forward while bullets and shells whizzed around them. "Each one [of us] wanted to leave but each hated to say so, so we let it [the barrage] come over us," recalled Patton in a letter to his wife,

---

15. According to author Winston Groom in *The Generals* (2015), Patton "learned a valuable lesson about tank battle tactics: a reliable fuel supply must be far more abundant and closer behind the fighting tanks."

16. Thus did the Americans get their first tastes of aerial combat. Among them was one of the earliest aces, Second Lieutenant Frank Luke, Jr., who scored his first kill, a piloted balloon, on the opening day of the battle, and collected a total of eighteen scalps in ten sorties over eight days of combat before he was shot down and killed on September 29.

Beatrice. Patton had finally met an ego as big as his own. If a shot was going to get you there was nothing you could do about it, so why worry?

There was nothing to do but forge ahead. As his troops entered the nearby village of Pannes, Patton rode atop one of his tanks until the German machine-gun fire grew so intense he had to take cover. Soon the overall attack had made such rapid progress that IV Corps had already achieved most of its first-day objectives and began to move ahead on the next. The two sides of the German salient, attacked from both sides, had been pincered; caught in the bulge, the Germans began to fall back, under fire from supporting French troops.

German resistance stiffed on September 13 as they approached the "Michel Line," their ultimate fallback, unleashing devastating coordinate artillery and machine-gun fire at the approaching Americans. Pershing's troops kept coming. On the fourteenth, with the Germans pushed back and out of a severely pounded St.-Mihiel and environs, the Americans consolidated their positions as the weather cleared. By the sixteenth, the salient was gone. Pershing was tempted to push on to Metz but his staff advised against it: the defenses there were formidable, and while the First Army had been bloodied, the men were tired. Further, Pershing had to honor his word to Foch that the AEF would now move north to the Meuse-Argonne, where in fact they arrived on the twenty-second. The Americans had won their first victory, in heavy hand-to-hand fighting, close fire, and death from the skies[17]—and they had won. With the Germans in retreat, the end of the war was now in sight.

Despite the Americans' limited action during World War I, the nature of the country was radically changing from what it had been at the turn of the century. War does many things to nations, elevates or destroys them, but no country is ever unaffected by it. And no matter how fervent the wish at war's end to revert to some sort of prelapsarian state of innocence, it never happens. How you gonna you keep 'em down on

---

17. Off the effectiveness of the air campaign, Mitchell was promoted to brigadier general after the battle.

the farm after they've seen Paree?[18] Virgin boys from Tennessee and Iowa got their first tastes of exotic French sexual practices in the many bordellos that sprang up near the fields of honor (prostitutes, as we have seen, are always a significant portion of camp followers), and brought home some naughty French postcards to prove it. The eruption of flapper hedonism that marked the Roaring Twenties[19] was in large part grounded in the doughboys' experiences Over There.

At the same time, the returning soldiers found the civilians they left behind profoundly uninterested in their exploits and experiences. The crowds that had cheered them off from the New York piers were absent at their return. They found their jobs gone and, often, their girls too, who after all couldn't be expected to wait forever while they were overseas playing soldier boy. Further, violent criminal gangs had appeared in the streets of New York and elsewhere, reacting to the instant Prohibition-inspired black market in bootleg beer and bathtub gin. Organized mostly along ethnic lines and often run by the Democrats of Tammany Hall,[20] they were composed of the dispossessed and the unwanted: brawling Irish rabble from the Lower East Side and, later, Hell's Kitchen; Italian hoods, quick with the stilettos; canny Jews who not only kept track of the money but (until the assassination of Dutch Schultz in 1935) boasted some of the toughest gunmen and ice pick artists of early gangland. Their world was memorialized in Herbert

---

18. One of the big hits of 1919, first sung by Sophie Tucker.

19. Also the name of a 1939 movie starring James Cagney and Humphrey Bogart, who had both served in the Navy during the war. They played two of three doughboys who meet in the trenches and then return home to an America they hardly recognize—and which doesn't care to recognize them. Bogart becomes a violent criminal, Cagney a taxi-driver-turned-bootlegger and nightclub owner. The third man (Jeffrey Lynn) becomes a lawyer. Things end badly for both Bogart (the heavy) and the luckless Cagney. "He used to be a big shot," goes the film's famous last line.

20. One of whose founders was the treacherous Aaron Burr, Jefferson's vice president, who killed Alexander Hamilton, a Founding Father, in a duel in 1804. Three years later, out of office, he was tried for, and acquitted of, treason for seditious conspiracy. Although arrested on President Jefferson's order and almost certainly guilty of planning a rebellion in the western territories, Burr skated on the technicality that his plan of breaking off American territory and founding his own country had not actually been put into action.

Asbury's 1928 book, *The Gangs of New York,* later made into a 2002 motion picture directed by Martin Scorsese.

While America partied, however, the rest of the world was roiling with political discontent. Defeated Germany, pummeled by the Treaty of Versailles, had begun to plot revenge in the person of a German corporal named Adolf Hitler, gassed at the front and awarded both the Iron Cross second class in 1914 and the Iron Cross first class in 1918 for bravery under fire. In 1920 Hitler commandeered a fringe party, the German Workers Party, changing its name to the *Nationalsozialistische Deutsche Arbeiterpartei* (National Socialist German Workers Party), or NSDAP. In 1923 he and General Erich Ludendorff, one of the top German commanders during the war, failed in a coup attempt to overthrow the Bavarian state government.

Hitler was sent to Landsberg prison, where he dictated much of his memoir, *Mein Kampf* (My Struggle, or My Battle), first published in 1925 and again in 1927. He was released in 1924, having spent 264 days in jail. By the end of January 1933, he was chancellor of the Weimar Republic. By March, he was its dictator. On September 1, 1939, he launched the Second World War with an attack on Poland from the west, aided by his communist ally,[21] the Union of Soviet Socialist Republics, which on September 17 steamrolled the helpless country from the east. Both Britain and France, bound to defend Poland by treaty, declared war on Germany on September 3.

Meanwhile, on the grave of tsarist Russia, the new Union of Soviet Socialist Republics had been proclaimed in 1922, uniting by concordat Russia, the Ukraine, Byelorussia (today's Belarus), and the short-lived Transcaucasian Federation of Georgia, Armenia, and Azerbaijan. It was led by Lenin until his death in 1924, when he was succeeded by a Georgian, who had briefly studied the priesthood in the Russian Orthodox Church, named Ioseb Dzhugashvili, changed later to Iosif Vissarionovich Stalin—the man of steel.

In the wake of the Bolshevik Revolution, the new USSR had successfully fended off military interference by both the Europeans and the

---

21. By virtue of the Molotov-Ribbentrop nonaggression pact of August 23, 1939, which lasted until June 22, 1941, when National Socialist Germany invaded the USSR.

Americans, who in 1918–1919 under Wilson's orders had landed five thousand troops of the AEF around the Arctic Circle port of Arkhangelsk ("the Polar Bear expedition," they called themselves) to assist the British in an attempt to overthrow the Bolshevik government. At the same time, the eight thousand men of the AEF Siberia, deployed at the Pacific port of Vladivostok in the Russian Far East, were there to prevent the Japanese from seizing the region.

As well they might have. The Rising Sun of the Empire of Japan was making its presence felt. After the Japanese sent the Russian Baltic Fleet to the bottom at the Battle of Tsushima over two days in May of 1905, the world suddenly realized that the Japanese had become a formidable naval power. Now it was busily enhancing the prowess of its modern national army, which had in part been formed and trained by first the French and then, after their loss in the Franco-Prussian War of 1870, by the victorious Germans. Cresting on a rising tide of militarism that combined the warrior code of *bushido* with fanatical emperor worship, the Japanese nursed their grudges against their archenemies China and Korea, as well as the West after a century of humiliation, and bided their time.

Like England, Japan had a problem with both geography and natural resources. Just as the Industrial Revolution never could have come about were England to have relied purely on what it could produce, but instead required a vast overseas trading network to provide the raw materials Britain lacked, so did Japan. The Japanese islands were mountainous in their interior, which meant that the population mostly lived on the littorals. This forced them to turn to the sea for sustenance and trade. The problem was that—thanks to pesky Jesuit missionaries[22] and unscrupulous traders—Japan had been closed for two centuries to all but a few foreigners in the Nagasaki trading quarter until in 1853 the American commodore Matthew Perry forced it with gunboats (the *kurofune raikō*, the "arrival of the black ships") to open up to the outside world.

---

22. Beginning with the Spaniard St. Francis Xavier, one of the founders of the Jesuit order, in 1549. He proselytized in Japan, India, and Borneo and had arrived off the coast of China when he died in 1552 at the age of forty-six. For many years, Irish Catholic boys named "Francis" often were given "Xavier" as their middle names.

The country had been making up for lost time ever since. The failure of the Satsuma Rebellion of 1877[23] spelled the end of the old tribal loyalties, and the restored Japanese Meiji monarchial government had begun forging a new, pan-Japanese identity that included a nationwide revival of the indigenous Shinto religion to displace foreign Buddhism, as well as the legalization of Christianity on the theory that Western countries would now adopt a softening attitude toward Japan.

In the wake of Perry's ultimatum and the Treaty of Kanagawa the next year, which formally opened Japan to trade and diplomatic relations with other countries, Japan was almost immediately rocked by transformational changes. The feudal Tokugawa shogunate,[24] which had ruled the country since 1603, collapsed in 1867, spelling the end of the warlords and their rigidly maintained four-tier culture that distinguished traditional Japanese society: *samurai,* farmers, merchants, and artisans, with essentially no mobility between and among them. Everyone knew his place: the class into which you were born was the class in which you died. This caste system ensured a continuing supply of food and marketable products (silk, paper, porcelain, *sake*) while funneling commerce with Portuguese and Dutch traders through the island of Dejima ("exit island") a man-made atoll off the shores of Nagasaki constructed by digging a canal across a small peninsula and then connecting it to the southern island of Kyushu with a bridge controlled by the shogunate.

The opening of Japan had exactly the results the shogunate had feared. Now succeeded by the imperial Meiji dynasty as its leader, Japan quickly embraced industrialization and modernization, adopting Western standards in many things, including military. Leaderless samurai were called *ronin*; under the rules of *bushido* they were supposed to kill themselves upon the loss or the disgrace of their master, but many instead chose the life of a wandering paladin or mercenary. They were shunned by polite society, which regarded them as little better than bandits. Meiji Japan had no further need for their skills or services, abolishing them

---

23. Semifictionalized in the 2003 film *The Last Samurai*, starring Tom Cruise.

24. The word *shôgun* means "great general."

as a warrior class upon taking power. It was a terrible blow to the caste that had repelled a Mongol invasion from China in 1274 and again in 1281—in large part thanks to ferocious thunderstorms and typhoons that destroyed the Mongols' attempts at amphibious landings, winds that became known as the *kami-no-Kaze,* or "winds from the gods." In short, "divine winds."[25] But a modern nation had no need for a hereditary warrior class when it could organize a professional army of trained officers and conscripts to fill out the ranks.

The samurai were therefore seething with resentment when in 1873 one of their representatives in the Meiji government, the nobleman and samurai Saigō Takamori, proposed that he travel to Korea and once there become so obnoxious and insulting that the Koreans would have to kill him, thus providing Japan with a reason to mount an invasion led by the dispossessed warriors that would both advance Japanese foreign policy against one of their principal enemies and provide the *ronin* with a proper samurai death. When it was rejected, Takamori returned to his home prefecture in Kagoshima (Satsuma), on the southern tip of Kyushu, and plotted rebellion. He established a number of private military academies (*Shi-gakkō*) to educate and train warriors, including an artillery school, although in the end the number of artillery pieces used in his uprising against Mutsuhito, the Emperor Meiji, was small.

Alarmed at Saigō's provocative activities, the central government in 1876 sent a police detachment to investigate. The Kagoshima government, functionally independent from Tokyo, captured and tortured the cops into admitting they were actually assassins. Early the following year Tokyo sent a gunboat to raid the arsenals. The students fought back. Takamori signed on to lead a popular revolt, and with a small force of about twenty thousand men he began to march northward. There were a series of pitched battles, mostly reverses for the rebels culminating in the Battle of Shiroyama on September 24, 1877, in which the retreating rebels, now down to about five hundred men, encountered thirty thousand soldiers of the Imperial Army, dug in and well-fortified, and augmented by firepower from five warships.

---

25. The name *(kamikaze)* they would later give to their aerial suicide attacks against the U.S. Navy in 1944 and 1945 during the Pacific War.

Surrender was demanded and rejected. The army opened up a total front assault on the rebel position, but its young conscripts, unused to samurai swordsmanship, were at first repelled. Still, there was no way the samurai could hold out against such massed might. Saigō was killed by a bullet that struck his femoral artery; as he died, his adjutant, Beppu Shinsuke, severed his head to give him a proper samurai's demise. Then, out of ammunition, Beppu charged the enemy and was shot to pieces. The few remaining samurai drew their katana swords and charged as well. All died. The rebellion was over, and unquestioned modernity was now the order of the day.

And so Japan began nearly a century of expansion and preparation for its new role in the world order. Although Japan had been smarting from its treatment by the West for decades, at the same time, however, it needed and even desired what the West had to offer. A kind of inferiority complex had developed at the upper levels of society. The Japanese knew the *gaijin* considered them lowly Orientals and had little to no respect for or appreciation of Japan's long history, its complex and beautiful culture, its arts, its masculine code of honor, and its alluring women. It was all beneath them. At the same time, though, the Japanese began to mistake the trappings of Western civilization for the civilization itself, and thought that by adopting Western clothing, manners, faiths, and certain Western forms of art (especially classical music) they could begin to comprehend what made these strange, big-nosed, hairy foreigners so potent.[26] They looked to Europe first, to France and Germany for inspiration; when their gaze turned east, across the Pacific toward the United States, however, they saw only a looming threat.

The Hawaiian Islands lie between Japan and the West Coast. They were a relatively new American possession. A constitutional monarchy until 1893, Hawaii had long hosted American whaling ships and New

---

26. This belief only intensified after the Japanese defeat in World War II, which was taken as proof that Western ways were superior to those of the Japanese. Japanese affection for things Western doubled and redoubled: when Sony and Philips were developing the compact disc in the early eighties, one of the Japanese conditions for backing the new technology was that a CD had to be able to accommodate in its entirety Beethoven's *Ninth Symphony,* which had become Japan's unofficial New Year's Eve anthem.

England missionaries and had gradually become the linchpin of the American presence in the Pacific. Although located some twenty-five hundred miles southwest of California, Hawaii's quasi-Westernized culture had become remarkably sophisticated for such a remote chain of islands, boasting two of the oldest private schools in the nation west of the Rocky Mountains: Punahou (1841), for the white aristocracy, and St. Louis (1846), a Catholic boys' school, mostly for natives. The royal family was overthrown by a consortium of pineapple and sugar cane planters, assisted by U.S. Marines, and, after some controversy, the islands were annexed as a U.S. territory on July 7, 1898, with new president William McKinley setting his signature on the deal. Hawaii entered the Union along with Alaska in 1959.

On December 7, 1941, residents and military personnel at Pearl Harbor on the principal Hawaiian island of Oahu woke up to the sounds of Japanese bombs and guns. It was a colossal failure of intelligence combined with American naiveté that would be unmatched until the events of September 11, 2001. In a surprise attack masterminded by the Harvard-educated Japanese Marshal Admiral Isoroku Yamamoto, much of the American Pacific Fleet, including its eight prized battleships, was caught in the harbor and largely destroyed, including the *Arizona* and *Oklahoma*,[27] while the *Nevada* was badly damaged as she tried to escape Battleship Row and beached at Hospital Point. The *Arizona* and *Oklahoma* were lost for good; the other six, including the *Nevada*, the *Maryland*, the *California* (sunk), the *Pennsylvania*, the *Tennessee*, and the *West Virginia* (sunk), were either lightly damaged or salvaged and refloated. All six saw later action, island-hopping in the Pacific. A former battleship, the *Utah*, which had been converted into a target ship for American practice, was also sunk during the attack.

Many other vessels were damaged as well, including three cruisers, three destroyers, and a number of other ships, and significant damage was done to airfields, aircraft, fuel dumps, and personnel. One hundred and eighty-eight aircraft were destroyed and another one hundred and fifty-seven damaged. Two thousand three hundred and thirty-five

---

27. While a total loss, *Oklahoma* was raised, stripped, her parts sold off for scrap. Her hulk sank in a storm in 1947 while being towed to San Francisco.

service members were killed, along with sixty-eight civilians. The Japanese lost twenty-nine planes and five minisubs; their total killed in action was one hundred and twenty-nine.

The attack was not wholly unexpected. Storm clouds had been gathering for some time. At the time of the Pearl Harbor attack, the Americans had only recently moved the Pacific Fleet headquarters from San Diego to Hawaii the year before, as a warning to Japan and a bulwark against its growing bellicosity. In the weeks leading up to the attack, a Japanese delegation was holding peace talks with American officials in Washington, ostensibly to try to defuse the tensions over oil[28] and Japanese Far Eastern hegemony. The hapless commanding naval officer, Admiral Husband E. Kimmel, along with his army counterpart, Lieutenant General Walter C. Short, had both been warned that war might soon be on its way; indeed, on November 27 Kimmel received a message from Washington that "negotiations have ceased," while Short was told that "hostile action is possible at any moment." That, however, did not necessarily mean that Pearl was going to be the target, and so Kimmel had husbanded his ships in the harbor, from which they could be deployed quickly in any direction. It was a textbook response, but one that played right into Japanese hands, and wholly inadequate to the developing, kinetic situation.

By chance, at the time of the Japanese ambush, several ships were not in harbor at Pearl, and this accident of history is what ultimately determined the course of the Pacific War. These happened to be the three American aircraft carriers in the Pacific: the *Lexington,* the *Saratoga,* and the *Enterprise.* The other four—*Ranger, Yorktown, Hornet,* and *Wasp*—were stationed on the East Coast, to deal principally with marauding German submarines.

The day of the assault, *Enterprise* was returning from a run to Wake Island, which lies some 2,300 miles west of Honolulu, and to which she

---

28. After Japan occupied French Indochina in 1941, America had countered by freezing Japanese assets in the U.S., thus making it difficult for Japan to buy oil on the world market. Their only recourse was to simply take it from British Malaya and the Dutch East Indies, which would have been an intolerable provocation for the Americans. Thus the attack on Pearl Harbor, meant to cripple any possible American response before proceeding.

had ferried twelve Wildcat fighters for use by the Marines stationed there. *Enterprise* was only about 215 miles from Oahu when the Japanese struck. She had sent aloft eighteen Dauntless dive bombers to return to Pearl ahead of the carrier: they ran smack into the Japanese air attack. Seven of them were shot down, the rest went on a hunt for the Japanese ships that had transported the Zeros and other aircraft. They couldn't find them, so they returned to the carrier while its fighter jets were launched for Hawaii to take part in the defense of Pearl. In the confusion, some of them were shot down by friendly fire.

The *Lexington* had been on her way to the small atoll of Midway, northwest of Hawaii, but when news of the attack reached her, she turned around and, after a futile search for the Japanese fleet, made for port. Meanwhile, *Saratoga* was in San Diego finishing up a retrofit. She left for Hawaii on December 8, arriving December 15. Ironically, Yamamoto knew the carriers were not at Pearl, but the chance to kill the mighty battleships, ducks in the Row, could not be missed. Even as savvy a commander as he had not yet realized that the future lay with carriers, not with the dinosaur dreadnoughts.

Why the focus on the battleships? The hulking armored floating battle stations with the big guns had evolved from the Russo-Japanese clash at Tsushima into the mightiest predators of the high seas: the top-of-the-line ships of the line. During World War I, the British had watched in horror as, at the Battle of Jutland (May 30–June 1, 1916), battleships both British and German pounded one another, the Germans trying to crack the British blockade of their North Sea ports by luring the Grand Fleet into favorable German waters, where they could fight it out for control of the North Sea and perhaps even break their own fleet out into the North Atlantic by rounding Scotland. It was not to be. The naval chess match, during which both sides had to seek out the other, and which featured enormous broadsides by battleships firing directly at one another—Nelson would have felt right at home—ended in a stalemate, which amounted to a British victory. The German High Seas Fleet never saw the high seas.

At Jutland, the British lost three battle cruisers (similar to battleships but smaller, lighter, and faster), three cruisers, and eight destroyers, while the Germans lost one battleship, one battle cruiser, four light cruisers, and five torpedo boats. It was the biggest battle in naval history to that time. Watching the action, and seeing the HMS *Indefatigable* and the *Queen Mary* explode and sink when their magazines were struck by German shells, British admiral David Beatty exclaimed, "There seems to be something wrong with our bloody ships today." Few present thought much about the presence of HMS *Engadine,* a seaplane tender, one of whose aircraft flew a reconnaissance mission off her decks during the battle. But she, not the battleships, would turn out to be the future of naval warfare.

At Pearl, Admiral Kimmel was quickly relieved of command. His replacement was a quiet, German-speaking, classical-music-loving former member of the submarine service, Chester W. Nimitz. Nimitz, fifty-six, had been born and raised in Fredericksburg, Texas, in the hill country west of Austin. Fredericksburg had been founded by German immigrants in 1846, part of a huge nineteenth-century wave from the Rhineland and elsewhere that left its mark on places like New Braunfels and even San Antonio.[29] It was named for Prince Friedrich Wilhelm Ludwig of Prussia—a contemporary of Clausewitz—and had maintained its semi-insular German-speaking ways for almost a century.

Nimitz, born in 1885, had grown up with German as his first language—something he dropped during the furious anti-German sentiment of the First World War. His father, Chester B. Nimitz,[30] had died six months before he was born, but his mother had married his uncle, William Nimitz, five years later. If it seems strange that a boy born in a landlocked part of Texas should want to go to sea, his paternal grandfather, Charles H. Nimitz, had been a merchant sailor back in Germany and often regaled the boy with sea yarns; in America, Charles became a Texas Ranger, and wound up fighting for the South during the Civil War. He gave this advice to his grandson: "Learn all you can, then do your best, and don't worry—especially about things over which you have no control."

---

29. To this day, one sees "Tante Emma Laden" (Aunt Emma's Shops, aka "corner stores") all over this part of Texas.

30. The name is derived from the Slavic word for "foreigner" or "German." In Russian, for example, the word is Немецкий (*Nemetsky*). The root meaning is "the people who can't speak any language."

Like Patton, Nimitz's forebears had fought for the Confederacy, whose patriotic warrior culture had far outlasted the demise of the CSA. Nimitz's first wish was for West Point, but there were no places available; instead he got an appointment to the U.S. Naval Academy at Annapolis, from which he graduated in 1905. His career nearly ended in 1908 in the Philippines when as an ensign he grounded the *Decatur* in a shallow harbor. He was duly court-martialed but because of his hitherto sterling service record was only given a letter of reprimand, and later became a submariner. He saw action during World War I, serving aboard the oil tender *Maumee,* servicing for the first time in naval history a fleet of American destroyers while they were underway.

He rose through the ranks, losing part of a finger in the process while trying to fix a diesel engine, serving in various positions until as Rear Admiral Nimitz he was appointed to the Bureau of Navigation in Washington, a desk job, which is where he was at the time of Pearl Harbor. He was already a favorite of Franklin Roosevelt, who had once served as Assistant Secretary of the Navy under President Wilson. "Tell Nimitz to get the hell out to Pearl and stay there till the war is won," FDR barked at Frank Knox, his secretary of the navy, shortly after the attack. Nimitz did, and stayed to the end, present at the Japanese surrender on the decks of the battleship *Missouri*[31] on September 2, 1945.

He knew the job was going to be tough, maybe impossible. Aside from the carriers, the shattered Pacific Fleet had few remaining assets. And while he had been appointed Commander in Chief, Pacific (CinCPac), he was going to have to report to the imperious, hard-driving Admiral Ernest J. King, who had fully earned his reputation of being extremely difficult to work with. As Commander in Chief of the worldwide Navy as well as Chief of Naval Operations in Washington—he enjoyed his unwieldy acronym, COMINCH-CNO—King would be overseeing, and second-guessing from halfway around the world, every move Nimitz would make.

In Hawaii, Nimitz got a brevet promotion to four-star admiral, which came with the command. In his change-of-command address aboard

---

31. Now a museum ship, stationed at Pearl Harbor.

the submarine *Grayling*, he took note of his unlucky predecessor Admiral Kimmel, now reduced to the two stars of a rear admiral once more. "We have taken a tremendous wallop," he said, "but I have no doubt of the ultimate outcome." Asked by a reporter what he proposed to do now, Nimitz replied, "All we can do is bide our time and take advantage of any opportunity that might come along." He knew how bad things were; brave words, false hopes, and fiery speeches were not for him. In the teeth of such a disaster, there was nothing for it but hunker down, take stock, appoint the right subordinates, rally the troops by example, shut up, and get back to the battlefield and see what happened.

Things looked pretty bleak. Pearl Harbor was an enormous blow to the American psyche, the worst since the Lincoln assassination in 1865 and Custer's Last Stand in 1876. It quickly became a byword for treachery, and anti-Japanese sentiment instantly surpassed the anti-German hatred of World War I. Starting in February of 1942, however unfairly, Japanese Americans were rounded up as potential enemy agents and saboteurs and sent to internment camps across the West but as far east as Arkansas under President Roosevelt's Executive Order 9066, upheld by the Supreme Court by a six-to-three decision in *Korematsu v. U.S.* in 1944.[32]

But all was not lost. The sparing of the carriers had proven to be a stroke of pure luck, and it was quickly put to good use. In April 1942, an army lieutenant colonel, James Doolittle, organized a raid on Tokyo and other sites in the Japanese home islands, launching sixteen B-25B Mitchell bombers from the deck of the carrier USS *Hornet*, now deployed in the Pacific. Although the raids didn't cause much damage—and the unescorted bomber crews had to ditch their planes over occupied China—the shock to the Japanese was considerable. Just four months after Pearl Harbor, the Americans, who were practically counted out of the war, had embarrassed the Imperial armed forces and demonstrated they could even threaten Emperor Hirohito where he slept. Meanwhile, the raid

---

32. Partially redressed in 1983 when Fred Korematsu's conviction for refusing to relocate was vacated; the Roberts Court abandoned its support of the decision in 2018 as part of its decision in *Trump v. Hawaii*, which upheld the president's travel ban from certain Muslim countries.

was a huge morale boost to the American population, especially those on the West Coast who feared another Japanese strike, this one on the homeland.

At this point Yamamoto understood his error in not taking out the American carriers. He would have to correct that. And so planning began for what turned out to be the pivotal Battle of Midway.

By this point in the war, the Japanese had already conquered much of the Far East and Southeast Asia. Three days after Pearl Harbor they sank the British battleship *Prince of Wales* and the battlecruiser *Repulse* off the coast of Malaya, a British colony. Two months later, they shocked the British even more by capturing their major military base at Singapore via the simple expedient of attacking the island from the landward side down the Malayan Peninsula—something the British had considered impossible given the thick jungles—instead of from the Singapore Strait. The result was one of the worst humiliations the British Army ever suffered. Churchill—who had ordered the garrison commander Sir Arthur Percival to defend the island to the last man—called it the worst disaster in British military history.[33] Some eighty thousand British, Indian, and Australian troops were taken into captivity, among them Percival himself.

The American ground troops weren't faring much better. The Japanese invasion of the American territory of the Philippines had begun ten hours after Pearl Harbor; combat in the archipelago lasted January to April 1942. Under orders from Washington, General MacArthur abandoned his troops for refuge in Australia, leaving behind some seventy-six thousand American and Filipino defenders at Bataan, whence they were forced into the infamous Bataan Death March on which many of the POWs died under the barbaric lash of their captors. All told, in the first few months of the Pacific War—MacArthur's theater—the Japanese blitzkrieg had taken the Philippines, Malaya, Singapore, Guam, Wake Island, New Britain, the Dutch East Indies, and the Gilbert Islands.

---

33. Churchill knew something about military disasters, given that he had been the architect of the Gallipoli fiasco in February 1915. Churchill fancied himself a master strategist but continued his blunders throughout World War II, particularly in his "soft underbelly" gambit that resulted in the Allied misadventure at Anzio in early 1944.

The swaggering, braggadocious, well-connected MacArthur, he of the aviator sunglasses, scarf, and corncob pipe, is surely among the most overestimated commanders in American military history, serviceable in many areas but, aside from the Inchon Landing in Korea in 1950, brilliant in none. In the direct aftermath of Pearl Harbor, he kept his planes snuggled wingtip to wingtip on the tarmac, where they were quickly destroyed by the Japanese; during the Philippines disaster he acquired the nickname "Dugout Doug" for his lack of presence to the troops. Running the Korean War from the safety of Japan, after the successful Inchon Landing he ordered the Marines and some Army units to push toward the Yalu River; the Battle of the Chosin Reservoir, in which the bravery of the First Marine Division saved him from total disgrace, was the result. His defenders point to his successful rule of postwar Japan as supreme commander for the Allied Powers, but he was rightly sacked by President Truman in April 1951 during the Korean War for insubordination. Writing of MacArthur's 1964 autobiography, *Reminiscences,* General James M. Gavin, who served with Patton, noted, "There is about it a self-righteousness and an air of infallibility that become a bit irksome." And yet he was awarded seven Silver Stars, the Distinguished Service Cross, and the Medal of Honor, among other honors.

In early May 1942 came the Battle of the Coral Sea, and the future of naval combat suddenly presented itself. Fought entirely in the air, it was the first naval battle in history in which the opposing fleets never engaged, or even sighted each other. In an attempt to capture the strategic town of Port Moresby in New Guinea, elements of the Japanese Combined Fleet (*Rengō Kantai*) under Admiral Shigeyoshi Inoue, which included three carriers, were to provide air cover for the ground forces. What the Japanese didn't know was that the American codebreakers in Honolulu had partially broken the Japanese naval codes, and so a combined American-Australian fleet was dispatched to intercept them. What they also didn't realize was that the carrier *Yorktown* had been redeployed to San Diego in late December 1941 and was now safely in the South Pacific along with the *Lexington*.

At the same time, Admiral Yamamoto was planning a killing strike on the American base at tiny Midway Island. Its destruction would open the way for another attack on Hawaii, this one intended to drive the Americans all the way back to California. His plan, however, was still unknown to the Americans. From his headquarters on Oahu, Nimitz placed Admiral Jack Fletcher in command of the Allied naval forces at the Coral Sea with orders to report only to him, even though the area was nominally MacArthur's. The last thing Nimitz needed was a prima donna like MacArthur (now sheltering in Australia) mucking about.

The two American carriers surprised the Japanese during their invasion of the island of Tulagi, near Guadalcanal in the Solomons, which was to precede the seizure of Port Moresby, known as Operation Mo. Planes from the carriers shot down a number of Japanese aircraft and sank a destroyer, but Tulagi was taken on May 4, 1942. Now alert to the presence of American carriers in the area, the Japanese carriers were tasked with finding and destroying them. On May 6 the two fleets came very near each other without detecting the other's presence, but the carriers' aircraft engaged in the skies over the Coral Sea off the northeast coast of Australia on May 8. The Japanese sank the *Lexington,* the destroyer *Sims,* and the oiler *Neosho* (scuttled after she offloaded her crew), and damaged the *Yorktown,* which limped back to Hawaii. The Japanese only lost one small carrier, the *Shōhō,* but suffered significant damage to a fleet carrier, the *Shōkaku.* It was thus a tactical victory for Japan, although it came with a heavy price: Port Moresby, the centerpiece of their strategy to cut off Australia, remained in Allied hands.

Like the Doolittle Raid, the Battle of the Coral Sea gave another lift to American spirits. True, the U.S. Navy hadn't yet won an encounter with its Imperial Navy counterparts, but the fact that America's still-green fighters, torpedo bombers, and dive bombers had gone toe to toe with the far more experienced and expert Japanese pilots was encouraging. And there was a grim satisfaction in knowing that for every Japanese pilot they killed his replacement would be someone far less experienced and dangerous—and the Japanese didn't have the superior manpower the Americans did. Nor did they have the industrial capacity to replace the aircraft as rapidly as the Americans could.

For their part, the Japanese high command was confident in its plan to take Midway, even without the *Shōkaku.* Yamamoto's plan involved a feint toward the vulnerable Aleutian Islands of Alaska, lightly manned when manned at all. His reasoning, very Japanese, was that the Americans would be unable to sustain the loss of face that would come with the loss of U.S. territory. They would move to defend the Aleutians rather than sacrifice them. At the same time, his huge fleet would gradually converge on Midway, where it would annihilate the American garrison there, and then launch a killer strike on the Hawaiian Islands. With Hawaii in Japanese hands, the Imperial Navy would have the freedom of the seas, and MacArthur would be isolated and quarantined in the Antipodes until such time that Japan felt like adding Australia to its list of conquests. With Singapore fallen, the British certainly had no means to stop them.

On May 10, 1942, Lieutenant Commander Edwin T. Layton came into Nimitz's office with news. Layton had been Kimmel's intelligence officer, and as such he oversaw the basement-dwelling codebreakers—Station HYPO—who had already deciphered parts of the Imperial Navy's dispatches. Layton was the perfect man for the job: he had been sent by the Navy to Tokyo to learn Japanese, and spoke the language fluently; he had also spent time in China. He itched to be given command of a destroyer, but Nimitz had kept him on because he judged that Layton could be very useful. "You can kill more Japs here than you could ever kill in command of a destroyer flotilla," Nimitz told him. "You are to see the war, their operations, their aims, from the Japanese viewpoint and keep me advised about what you are thinking about, what you are doing, and what purpose, what strategy, motivates your operations." In other words, Nimitz wanted Layton to *be* Yamamoto.

Layton's eyes and ears on Japanese signal intelligence ran through the eccentric Lieutenant Commander Joseph Rochefort. A native of Dayton, Ohio, Rochefort had joined the Navy in 1918, while still in high school, lying about his age to get in. His skill at crossword puzzles and bridge brought him to the attention of the cryptographers. As it happened, Rochefort had met Layton en route to Tokyo to also study the Japanese language. Now, just two days after the Coral Sea, Layton reported to Nimitz that the Japanese appeared to be massing a huge force of up to four aircraft carriers, two battleships, and many other ships. The target was Midway. Nimitz had three weeks to deal with it.

This ran counter to everything the analysts in Washington were saying. They too had detected activity, but in their view the target could just as easily be Australia, New Caledonia, or Fiji—or any or all of the above. This posed a big problem for Nimitz. The damaged *Yorktown* had arrived in port, and his instinct had been to send her to the Puget Sound Naval Shipyard in Bremerton, Washington, for retrofit and repair. But now he would need her for the defense of Midway; he put her in drydock at Pearl with orders that she be ready to sail in three days— impossible, but so what?

He would also need his best fighting admiral, the combative William "Bull" Halsey, but Halsey, who had been commanding the *Enterprise* in the South Pacific, came down with a debilitating case of shingles and was ordered to hospital for treatment. He would not be available for Midway.[34] In his place, Nimitz selected Admiral Raymond A. Spruance, as calm an officer under fire as could be imagined. It proved to be an excellent choice as Spruance took command of Task Force 16, which included the *Hornet* and the *Enterprise,* while Jack Fletcher was given Task Force 17, which included the *Yorktown.*

In order to be sure that Midway was indeed the target, the Americans needed better proof, and so laid a trap. For weeks they had been puzzling over the designation "AF" that kept turning up in the Japanese signals. Rochefort and Layton were sure that designation referred to Midway, but Nimitz needed more than guesswork. Accordingly, on May 19, they had the station at Midway broadcast a message *en clair* that their saltwater evaporators had broken down. Sure enough, two days later the Japanese reported that "AF" was running low on drinking water. Midway it was. It had to be.

And so the chess pieces were now in motion for one of the greatest ambushes in military history, one that the intended victims themselves

---

34. "Hit hard, hit fast, hit often," was Halsey's motto. The day after Pearl Harbor, contemplating the wreckage, he swore: "Before we're through with them, the Japanese language will be spoken only in hell." During his months-long convalescence, he told an audience of cheering midshipmen at the Naval Academy, "Missing the Battle of Midway has been the greatest disappointment of my career, but I am going back to the Pacific where I intend personally to have a crack at those yellow-bellied sons of bitches and their carriers." He was the Patton of the Navy. Americans don't talk, or fight, like that anymore.

rushed right into. The Navy may have been running short of flattops, especially with the loss of the *Lexington* at the Coral Sea, but the beauty of Midway with its airstrips was that it was essentially a stationary carrier all by itself. It would be the irresistible poison pawn proffered to the Japanese. What they wouldn't know was that hiding behind Midway to the northeast would be Nimitz's strike forces, preparing to give Yamamoto the nastiest surprise of his life.

The Japanese armada boasted four of their top-of-the-line fleet carriers: the *Akagi*, the *Kaga*, the *Sōryū*, and the *Hiryū*, all of which had participated in the attack on Pearl Harbor a few months earlier. They also brought along two battleships (one of them, the *Yamato*, Yamamoto's flagship), two heavy cruisers, one light cruiser, twelve destroyers, thirteen submarines, and two hundred and forty-eight aircraft. In addition to his one hundred and twenty-seven planes on Midway itself, Nimitz had the *Enterprise*, the *Hornet*, and the *Yorktown*, fresh from its seventy-two-hour turnaround. (She wasn't quite her old self: there had not been time to repair the damage to her power plant, so her top speed was limited. But the old girl was game.) He also fielded seven heavy cruisers, one light cruiser, fifteen destroyers, sixteen subs, and two hundred and thirty-three carrier-based airplanes.

Nimitz's air forces consisted primarily of fighters, torpedo bombers, and dive bombers. The fighters' principal task was to keep Japanese bombers away from the American carriers and to escort their own bombers through enemy defenses. The torpedo bombers' mission was to come in low and slow, dropping torpedoes aimed at hitting their targets below the water line. The dive bombers, the cowboys of the skies, came in high and then dove straight down toward the decks of the opposing carrier, dropping their payloads at the last minute and then pulling up for dear life. It was not a job for the squeamish since the pilots experienced tremendous G forces both diving and climbing and in the teeth of shipboard antiaircraft fire.

Like so many crucial battles, Midway was—to paraphrase Wellington at Waterloo—a "damned near-run thing." The American torpedo bombers were clobbered by the Japanese fighters and, to make matters worse, the torpedoes often turned out to be duds even when on target.

The American Devastator torpedo bombers took a beating, their Mark 13 torpedoes all too often futile, leaving them sitting ducks for the Japanese antiaircraft gunners and supporting fighters.

Both sides made critical errors. Flying over the open ocean and observing radio silence as much as possible, it was often hard for the naval aircraft to find the enemy. With no sophisticated electronics, they had to rely on human spotters, and even when ships were sighted from the air, it was hard to tell whether they were the main forces or ancillary vessels. Sometimes they just followed hunches. During the search for the main Japanese fleet, Lieutenant Commander Wade McClusky—running low on fuel—spotted the destroyer *Arashi* and guessed she was tailing the main fleet. His hunch proved correct and he led his air group from the *Enterprise* in a dive-bombing raid. Together with his top pilot, Lieutenant Richard Best, they destroyed the *Kaga* and *Akagi*, while dive bombers from the *Yorktown* took out the *Sōryū*.

The *Akagi*'s fate had been sealed early in the engagement. During the initial attack on Midway Island itself early in the morning of June 4, the Japanese inflicted heavy damage on the American planes but failed to take out the runways or the defensive installations. Despite Yamamoto's order to keep his reserve strike force for later, Admiral Chūichi Nagumo (Yamamoto's old-school chief deputy) ordered another attack. He may have been spooked by a near-miss on his command ship, the *Akagi*, when a crippled B-26 torpedo bomber buzzed its flight deck before crashing at Midway.

Just then, word arrived that the American fleet was emerging from behind Midway, and so Nagumo countermanded his own order. The munitions crews were in the middle of switching from bombs to torpedoes when the Americans struck. Caught with his pants down, Nagumo was forced to abandon ship when American dive bombers scored direct hits on the *Akagi,* causing the exposed munitions to explode, and sank the *Kaga* and *Sōryū* as well. Near the end of the battle, *Hiryū* joined the other three carriers at the bottom, scuttled after being hit by dive bombers from the *Yorktown* and the *Enterprise.*

It was a stunning, unimaginable defeat for the Japanese. In one stroke, the Americans had wreaked a terrible revenge for Pearl Harbor on the guts of the Imperial Japanese Navy, sinking all four of the carriers with which Yamamoto had so confidently sailed into battle. Japan's worst nightmare had just come true. Senior Japanese commanders, among them Yamamoto, had known that Japan's only hope was to knock the U.S. out of the Pacific quickly, before the nation's greater industrial might and larger population kicked in.[35] Japan couldn't afford to go toe to toe with the U.S. Japan couldn't replace the pilots or the planes as fast as the U.S. could, and the advantages of combat experience tilted toward the Americans with every Japanese pilot shot down in flames.

As the smoke cleared on June 7, the Japanese had lost not only their carriers but more than three thousand men, one cruiser, and hundreds of aircraft. The U.S. casualties were put at 362 men, one destroyer, 144 aircraft—and Admiral Fletcher's heroic *Yorktown*, which had been crippled by bombers from the last of the Japanese carriers, the *Hiryū*. Her last act was performed by one of her scout aircraft, which spotted the *Hiryū* and called in the killer strike from bombers from the *Enterprise* and orphaned planes from the sinking *Yorktown* herself. Admiral Fletcher abandoned ship and ceded operational control to Spruance for the remainder of the fight. The badly listing *Yorktown* was taken in tow, but while being tugged it was hit by a salvo of torpedoes from a Japanese submarine, which also sank the destroyer USS *Hammann*, which had been providing the *Yorktown* auxiliary power. Early in the morning of June 7, the *Yorktown* rolled over on her port side, then turned upside down and sank, stern first, into the Pacific.

Just six months after Pearl Harbor, the tide of war had dramatically shifted. The run-up to Midway marked the high-water mark of Japanese offensive capabilities in the Pacific; from then on they would be defending a consistently shrinking perimeter. The worst of the fighting still lay ahead, borne in large part by the U.S. Marine Corps, who executed the brutal "island-hopping" strategy that eventually led to the Battle of Okinawa on April 1, 1945—the last redoubt of the Japanese and the stepping stone to the island of Kyushu and thus Japan itself.

The fanatical Japanese, however, showed no willingness to surrender.

---

35. Their position was thus militarily analogous to that of the Confederates during the American Civil War.

American estimates of potential casualties were astronomical: the war would last another year and a half, and fatalities (based on Peleliu,[36] Okinawa, and other pitched battles) could rise as high as eight hundred thousand out of a total of some two to four million casualties. With President Roosevelt having died on April 12, 1945—Hitler killed himself eighteen days later—and Germany out of the war, President Harry Truman decided the price was too high. America's secret weapon, the atomic bomb, was dropped on Hiroshima on August 6 and upon Nagasaki on August 9. Even then, some elements of the Japanese military wanted to fight on, mounting an abortive coup known as the Kyūjō incident against the Emperor Hirohito on the night of August 14–15. It failed, and Japan surrendered the next day.

The surrender was formally accepted at 9:04 A.M., on September 2, 1945, on the quarterdeck of the battleship USS *Missouri,* anchored in Tokyo Bay. Receiving the surrender from the Japanese foreign minister Mamoru Shigemitsu and General Yoshijiro Umezu were MacArthur, a glory hound to the end, Bull Halsey, and Chester W. Nimitz. They were later joined on deck by the unhappy Sir Arthur Percival, emaciated but still standing after his long captivity at Hsian in Japanese-occupied Manchuria, and the American general Jonathan Wainwright, who was left holding the bag in the Philippines, and who also had endured the hell of Hsian for three years; both had been rescued by an American OSS operation just a few weeks before. Despite its decisive role in amphibious and ground combat throughout the Pacific War, there was no representative from the Marine Corps, which made Nimitz privately furious and is yet another blot on MacArthur's escutcheon.

But MacArthur, failing upward, had already been named by Truman

---

36. Another of MacArthur's bright ideas, part of his self-justification campaign to fulfil his vow to unnecessarily retake the Philippines near the end of the war, and conducted over Nimitz's objections with FDR's approval in September–November 1944. Advertised as a walkover, the attempt to capture a Japanese air strip on the small coral island proved to be an extremely costly battle for the Marine Corps' First Marine Regiment, which took more than sixteen hundred casualties in the first two hundred hours of the fight. In the end, it accomplished nothing except to fan MacArthur's ego. But MacArthur needed his "I shall return" moment; hence the photo op of him wading ashore at Leyte on January 9, 1945.

to oversee the occupation of Japan, and the flamboyant General of the Army was not about to let the moment pass. Two American flags were flying on the *Missouri* that day. One was the flag that had been flying over the Capitol on December 7, 1941; the other was the flag of the USS *Powhattan*, Commodore Perry's flagship when it sailed into Tokyo Bay in 1854. It was Dugout Doug MacArthur's day, and he wanted everybody to know it.

After the war, Nimitz returned to Washington, succeeding Admiral King as Chief of Naval Operations, with the unenviable task of downsizing what had risen from the ashes of Pearl Harbor to become the most powerful navy in the world—in great part thanks to him. He wrote an affidavit in support of Admiral Karl Dönitz (who had briefly succeeded Hitler as the leader of Germany in the closing days of the war in Europe) during the German's Nuremberg trial in 1946. Nimitz testified that he himself had employed unrestricted submarine warfare in the Pacific; partially as a result, Dönitz escaped the hangman's noose and spent ten years in prison. Nimitz, the former submariner, also championed then-Captain Hyman Rickover's proposal for the *Nautilus,* the first nuclear-powered submarine in the fleet. Although inactive after his retirement in 1947, he retained his rank of fleet admiral for life.

He died on February 20, 1966, in his quarters at the naval base on Yerba Buena Island in San Francisco Bay, just short of his eighty-first birthday. The boy from the Texas hill country—the hero of the war in the Pacific—died surrounded by the open water upon which he had lived his life. Nimitz is buried in San Bruno alongside Admiral Spruance, and two other friends from the Navy.

On the far side of the world, George Patton was still awaiting his moment. Despite his heroics in World War I, until the outbreak of the Second World War he had spent most of his time on the shelf. Even after the war, it was just as hard for junior officers to move up as it had been before, no matter their combat record. The nation's longstanding aversion to maintaining a large standing army saw to that.

During the Meuse-Argonne offensive that won the First World War for the Allies in 1918, Patton had been seriously wounded one morning while leading a small platoon and a tank into the German lines near

Cheppy in an attempt to silence a German machine-gun nest. They walked right into a trap, however, and enemy fire strafed them from all sides. Typically, brevet Colonel Patton, then thirty-two years old, was carrying his ceremonial walking stick, waving it over his head to encourage the men to follow him, when it happened. Accompanied by his orderly, Private First Class Joseph Angelo, he kept moving forward as his men were killed around him. Finally, a bullet struck him as well, and down he went. He had visions of his dead ancestors, military men like himself who had fallen in battle, and thought to himself, "It's time for another Patton to die." He was wrong about that.

The bullet went through his left thigh and exited from a buttock, near his rectum, punching a good-sized hole through his behind. Under fire, Angelo rolled Patton into a shallow shell hole, cut away his trousers, and dressed the wound as best he could with his field kit. Only half conscious, Patton refused to be rescued until the remainder of his troops had destroyed the emplacements. For this he was later awarded the Distinguished Service Cross.

Patton returned to an America just happy its brief experience of war was over. The country was reentering its traditional isolationism—George Washington's Farewell Address, with its admonition against "the insidious wiles of foreign influence," was still heeded—and had little work or love for the doughboys. Stationed at Fort Meade, Maryland, Major Patton[37] developed his theories of tank warfare, elevating the tank from its wartime role supporting the infantry into a fighting force in its own right—in other words, into a more Alexandrine offensive unit to break through enemy lines and allow the infantry to catch up later, a mechanized cavalry. In 1927 he was in Washington serving with the Office of the Chief of Cavalry and was developing his plans, but they died stillborn when Congress yanked the funding. In 1931, still going nowhere, he did a stint at the Army War College, then located in the District of Columbia. But he was itching to fight.

In mid-1932, the ghosts of World War I came back to haunt both him and Douglas MacArthur, now the Army's chief of staff, and cemented

---

37. With the war over he had lost his brevet rank and reverted to captain but was immediately promoted to major.

their lifelong animosity. MacArthur's superb social- and rank-climbing skills annoyed Patton, little realizing that it was his own uncontrollable mouth and pungent vocabulary that was holding him back; he was, after all, even more of an aristocrat than MacArthur. It was clear to Patton that MacArthur already had his eye on the White House and was polishing his résumé as best he could in the peacetime army, a skill that eluded Patton.

For some time, some ten thousand veterans—enlisted men and conscripts—of the Great War had been gathering on the mudflats of Anacostia in the capital to protest their economic plight. The war had set their careers back, and then along had come the Depression to really put them in the hole. They thought their country owed them something for their blood, sweat, and toil in France. True, in 1924 Congress had passed the so-called "Bonus Act," guaranteeing them a pension based on a formula, and which would in sum amount to between $500 and $625— payable in 1945. The "Bonus Army," as it quickly became known, wanted and needed the money now.

Among them was Joe Angelo, who had saved Patton's life during the war. "I could go right over to this cavalry camp across the river and get all of the money I want or need from Colonel Patton," he testified before a congressional committee. "But that ain't right. . . . He owes me nothing. All I ask is a chance to work or a chance to get my money on my certificate." But the best Congress could do was authorize the vets to borrow against their certificate, just enough money for them to travel home. Somehow that failed to satisfy the nearly destitute men.

On July 28, Herbert Hoover's attorney general, William D. Mitchell, ordered the vets to be dispersed. District of Columbia police moved in on them. Fights broke out. Rocks flew. The cops fired at the protestors, killing two of them. Now the president himself got into the act, directing MacArthur to clear the area by military means, including columns of infantry and six tanks. Patton, as his subordinate, led six hundred men of the Third Cavalry against the marchers, a job he found profoundly distasteful. MacArthur's infantry and tanks arrived. Things escalated. Somebody set the makeshift encampment—called "Hooverville"— ablaze. Tear gas filled the air. That was the end of the Bonus Army. Patton and his family visited Angelo at Walter Reed Hospital. Recalled Patton's daughter Ruth Ellen: "He was a sad little man, all eyes, and we wondered how he could have dragged Georgie into the shell hole and saved him."

That was the low point, although Patton didn't know it yet. In 1934 he was promoted to lieutenant colonel and shipped off to Hawaii to work in intelligence, where he pondered the likelihood of a war involving the Japanese, who had invaded Manchuria in 1931 and were preparing for a second Sino-Japanese War. He wondered about the necessity of interning Japanese-Americans should war break out and wrote a paper called "Surprise" forecasting a Japanese sneak attack on Hawaii. Among his points: "The vital necessity to Japan of a short war and of the possession at its termination of land areas for bargaining purposes may impel her to take drastic measures. It is the duty of the military forces to prepare against the worst possible eventualities."

Patton made full colonel in 1938, and after a stint in Texas as commander of the Fifth Cavalry, he was made a brigadier general (one star) in October of 1939. Once again he was stationed at Fort Myer, where he renewed his relationship with George Marshall, the new Army chief of staff. The calm and steady Marshall never got a field command of his own, mostly because dating from his time as Pershing's aide-de-camp in France he was indispensable to the proper administration of a modern American army. (After the war, Marshall became the U.S. special envoy to China, secretary of state, and secretary of defense in the Truman administration. He was the eponymous force behind the Marshall Plan, which aided in the reconstruction of Europe.) But Marshall knew talent when he saw it, and despite Patton's manifest personal eccentricities and shortcomings, he became one of his strongest advocates.

When war broke out in the Pacific, Patton was ready. He trained armored units stateside for a while, during which period he rose to major general (two stars): maneuvering tank units around the South to demonstrate how speedily it could be done, and "capturing" the city of Shreveport, Louisiana, during war game exercises in June 1941. He cultivated a dramatic, theatrical personal image to inspire his troops: after all, that's what Caesar had done (and MacArthur was doing). In addition to a riding crop or swagger stick, he carried an ivory-gripped, silver-plated single-action Colt .45 revolver on his right hip, and a matching Smith & Wesson Model 27 .357 Magnum on his left. Like Alexander, he got his men to believe they were part of something far greater than themselves, and he never asked them to do anything he wouldn't do himself.

The legend began in earnest in North Africa, when Patton and his men came ashore at Casablanca as part of Operation Torch and liberated Morocco from Vichy French forces. Awarding him the Order of Ouissam Alaouite, the sultan of Morocco observed: "*Les Lions dans leurs tanières tremblent en le voyant approcher*" (In their dens, the lions tremble at his approach). After the disastrous Battle of the Kasserine Pass in February 1943, in which inexperienced American and British armored units were routed by Erwin Rommel's Afrika Korps, Patton was promoted to lieutenant general (three stars) and replaced the wholly inadequate Lloyd Fredendall. He quickly installed discipline and dignity, and brought in Major General Omar Bradley as his deputy. Together, they would command the Seventh Army across Sicily, culminating in the capture of Palermo and Messina in July 1943.

In a piece for *The Atlantic* in February 1965, James M. Gavin—the dashing young paratrooper general adored by his men for jumping into combat with them—recalled Patton during this period:

General Patton had given us a send-off talk about a week earlier, when we were still in North Africa. His talks on such occasions were usually quite good, earthy, and I was impressed. One thing that he said always stuck with me, for it was contrary to what I had believed up to that moment, but after being in combat only a short while, I knew he was right. Speaking to all of us late one afternoon as we assembled in the North African sunset, he said, "Now, I want you to remember that no son of a bitch ever won a war by dying for his country. He won it by making the other poor dumb son of a bitch die for his country."

Then Patton's career was derailed again, and by his own intemperate actions. First was the Biscari Massacre of Italian and German prisoners of war by troops under Patton's command when the American soldiers obeyed his admonition to take no prisoners if opponents continued to resist within two hundred yards of their position. No charges were brought against Patton. It was a judgment call, *Friktion*.

Alas, this was followed by the infamous slapping incident, in which Patton berated and struck a soldier under his command hospitalized from "battle fatigue," a condition someone like Patton refused to admit existed. How could anyone be tired of battle? Eisenhower reprimanded him and ordered him to apologize to the soldier, the doctors and nurses at Nicosia, and publicly to all the soldiers in his command. Ike hushed the matter up, but it leaked out to the press, which then set about excoriating Patton; their former favorite was now their favorite whipping boy. In the ensuing uproar, Eisenhower—perhaps with a thought ahead to his own presidential ambitions—put Patton on ice for almost a year.

And so it was that Bradley, not Patton, was given command of Operation Overlord, the Normandy invasion. Temperamentally, the Missouri-born Bradley was much more in sync with the Kansas-raised Ike than with a flamboyant Angeleno like Patton. In England, Patton stewed, finally given command of the new Third Army during the first six months or so of 1944. To the German high command (Oberkommando der Wehrmacht, or OKW) it was inconceivable that the Americans would sideline their most potent fighting general in any plans to invade the Continent via France, especially over something as trivial as the incident in Italy; Ike and Bradley made use of this by making Patton the leader of a "phantom army," disinformationally tasked with invading France at the Pas de Calais. With the Germans' attention thus misdirected, the Allies would land at Normandy.

It was there, on May 31, 1944, that he made the (here unexpurgated) invocation that has come to exemplify the man. Addressing the men of the Sixth Armored Division, he said:

> An army is a team. It lives, eats, sleeps, and fights as a team. This individual hero stuff is bullshit. The bilious bastards who write that stuff for the *Saturday Evening Post* don't know any more about real battle than they do about fucking. . . . Why, by God, I actually pity these poor bastards we're going up against.
>
> Each man must think not only of himself, but think of his buddy fighting alongside him. We don't want yellow cowards in the army. They should be killed off like flies. If not, they will

go back home after the war, goddamn cowards, and breed more cowards. The brave men will breed more brave men. Kill off the goddamn cowards and we'll have a nation of brave men.

Sure, we all want to go home. We want to get this war over with. But you can't win a war lying down. The quickest way to get it over with is to get the bastards who started it. We want to get the hell over there and clean the goddamn thing up, and then get at those purple-pissing Japs. The quicker they are whipped, the quicker we go home. The shortest way home is through Berlin and Tokyo. So keep moving. And when we get to Berlin, I am personally going to shoot that paper-hanging son-of-a-bitch Hitler . . .

Some of you men are wondering whether or not you'll chicken out under fire. Don't worry about it. I can assure you that you'll all do your duty. War is a bloody business, a killing business. The Nazis are the enemy. Wade into them, spill their blood or they will spill yours. Shoot them in the guts. Rip open their belly. When shells are hitting all around you and you wipe the dirt from your face and you realize that it's not dirt, it's the blood and guts of what was once your best friend, you'll know what to do.

I don't want any messages saying "I'm holding my position." We're not holding a goddamned thing. We're advancing constantly and we're not interested in holding anything except the enemy's balls. We're going to hold him by his balls and we're going to kick him in the ass; twist his balls and kick the living shit out of him all the time. Our plan of operation is to advance and keep on advancing. We're going to go through the enemy like shit through a tinhorn.

My men don't surrender. I don't want to hear of any soldier under my command being captured unless he is hit. Even if you are hit, you can still fight. That's not just bullshit either. I want men like the lieutenant in Libya who, with a Luger against his chest, swept aside the gun with his hand, jerked his helmet off with the other and busted the hell out of the Boche with the helmet. Then he picked up the gun and he killed another German.

All this time the man had a bullet through his lung. That's a man for you!

Then there's one thing you men will be able to say when this war is over and you get back home. Thirty years from now when you're sitting by your fireside with your grandson on your knee and he asks, "What did you do in the great World War Two?" You won't have to cough and say, "Well, your granddaddy shoveled shit in Louisiana." No sir, you can look him straight in the eye and say "Son, your granddaddy rode with the great Third Army and a son-of-a-goddamned-bitch named George Patton!"

All right, you sons of bitches. You know how I feel. I'll be proud to lead you wonderful guys in battle anytime, anywhere. That's all.

This is how men talk to each other, or used to. There was nothing "offensive" about it; no one was made to feel "uncomfortable"; the only people who should have felt "threatened" were the Germans. Today, because total victory is no longer a primary military objective, such a speech would get any male officer cashiered for creating a hostile working environment.

Patton finally got his wish to get back into the field on August 1, 1944, when the Third Army joined the fighting as part of Bradley's Twelfth Army Group. Immediately, the Third struck at the enemy in every direction. At Supreme Headquarters Allied Expeditionary Force (SHAEF), Eisenhower and the other top brass had to wear several hats: warfighters, diplomats, politicians. Patton had only one: the helmet with three stars on it.

The Germans had invented the concept of *Blitzkreig* in the early days of World War II. Now Patton was going to show them how to do it properly. Everything he had learned in the field, from his days facing down the Villistas in Mexico through his development of tank and armored column tactics in the First World War, and even the book learning and practical experience he had acquired in the run-up to the war, now came into play. Like Caesar at the Rubicon, Patton had met his moment, and at age fifty-nine he was ready for it.

L'audace, l'audace. Patton had made the expression his motto, which dated back at least to the French revolution if not actually to Frederick the Great of Prussia, but it might as well have been Hitler's, too. From his own rise to power and seizure of the Weimar Republic in 1933 and the remilitarization of the Rhineland in 1936, through the bloodless annexation of Czechoslovakia in 1938, to the Molotov-Ribbentrop Pact of 1939 and the subsequent *Blitzkrieg* against Poland a week later, his lightning victory over France in 1940, Hitler consistently wrong-footed his opponents. Like Napoleon, he kept the other European heads of state constantly guessing, rationalizing his intentions while wondering where he would strike next. And then, with his catastrophic surprise attack on the Soviet Union in 1941 and his crushing defeat at Stalingrad in 1943, his luck had run out.

Now the wheel of our story comes full circle. Throughout the remainder of 1944, Patton and the Third Army chewed up the Wehrmacht and spit it out, hell-bent for Berlin. Just as Patton had wanted to beat Field Marshal Montgomery to Messina in Sicily, now he wanted to beat the Soviets to the Reich *Hauptstadt*. Patton had little use for the Russians, whom he regarded as semi-civilized "Asiatics," sadistic drunks who were fighting a butcher's war against the Germans on the Eastern Front. The Russians under Kutuzov in the Napoleonic Wars may have disproven the theory that a country collapsed once its capital was taken, but Germany was different. Berlin *was* National Socialist Germany, its command and control.[38] Allied bombers could blow the other German cities to smithereens but until the Führer was buried in his bunker in the heart of Berlin, the war would not be over.

By this point, even Hitler had come to realize his war was, in the main, lost. The GROFAZ—*größter Feldherr aller Zeiten*[39]—had failed. Operation Barbarossa, his dramatic double-cross of his erstwhile socialist partner Stalin, had failed in its objectives, which were to capture Moscow, Leningrad (St. Petersburg), and Stalingrad (formerly Tsaritsyn), an important manufacturing city on the Volga River in southwest

---

38. Although Munich—*Hauptstadt der Bewegung* (capital of the Movement)—was its heart.

39. "Greatest Supreme Commander of all time," as he was now being mockingly called by some of his generals, although never to his face.

Russia. True, the Wehrmacht had gobbled up a vast amount of territory, but vast amounts of territory were something the Soviet Union had in abundance. As they had done versus Napoleon, the Russians simply fell back, moving their government and, in 1941, much of their manufacturing capability to the east. Marshal Georgy Zhukov knew his Napoleonic history better than Hitler did, ceding turf for time until the Soviets could fully mobilize their population and crank up their manufacturing might. And then, in Operation Bagration,[40] they began to roll the Wehrmacht back.

At this point, time was no longer on Hitler's side in the East, and his only option now lay in knocking the Western Allies back on their heels and, he hoped, to the bargaining table to free up his troops in France and elsewhere for use against the rampaging Russians. The spot he chose was very near the St.-Mihiel salient of the First World War, except this time it would be a new "bulge," an offensive thrust into the Allies' still-forming lines, instead of a defense of territory that was being abandoned anyway. In its massed force, it was also a replica of the tactics used on the same turf in 1940, during Germany's lightning conquest of France. In retrospect, the plan had little to no chance of success, but it was the slender reed the German High Command (some of whose confreres had tried to assassinate Hitler a few months earlier, in July 1944, at his forward command post, the *Wolfsschanze*, in Prussia) had to hang on to if Germany wanted to salvage anything from the war.

And so, on December 16, 1944, twenty-five German mechanized divisions smashed into the thinly held Allied lines of the Ardennes between Belgium and Luxembourg. The German strategic objective was to take the Allies by surprise, split the British from the Americans, and punch their way through to Antwerp—a critical deep-water port that could handle the Allies' supply-line needs and which had only become operational on November 28—in order to close it to Western shipping, and also to annihilate any Allied forces encountered along the way. Moving significant tank forces through the dense woods of the

---

40. Named after General Pyotr Bagration, who served during the Napoleonic Wars, including at Austerlitz and Borodino.

Ardennes would not be something the Allies would expect,[41] and in fact it was expertly done. The surprise was complete.

Still, the prospects for success were not good. Allied air superiority—at this point, effectively air supremacy against the collapsing Luftwaffe—meant that German ground movements were severely restricted and had to take place under cloud cover or darkness. German tanks were critically short of fuel—at the start of the offensive, they only had enough for six days—thus putting many of their immediate objectives out of reach unless they could capture and loot allied supply depots along the way.

That meant feigning to be Americans in order to approach the depots before the Allied garrisons could destroy the fuel dumps, so the Germans recruited commandos who could speak fluent English and even pass for American (because some of them in fact had been born in the U.S.). In command was the daring, duel-scarred Otto Skorzeny of the Waffen-SS (the man who had rescued Mussolini in 1943 from Italian partisans). Operation Greif met with only limited success, and many of the commandos were executed under the laws of war regarding spies, but it put a scare into the Americans and forced a dramatic tightening of security. No one was exempted, even General Bradley, who at one point had to answer questions about American football and the pinup girl Betty Grable—nice gams!—before passing a sentry point.

For both sides, the weather was terrible, foggy, snowy and cold, the skies overcast—something that actually aided the Germans since it kept Allied reconnaissance planes on the ground. Ancient warriors had always taken the winters off, but modern armies could not afford such a luxury. With the front still in flux, the American First Army had few operational objectives other than to wait; there were only six undermanned divisions in the area. Another Allied weakness had been the sheer speed of their advance across a very broad front, which meant it would be difficult—if not, under certain weather conditions, impossible—to rapidly unite the various command elements should the need arise.

In a sense, the overall Allied position was similar to that of the Turks at Antioch in 1098, with the Germans starring as the Crusader forces

---

41. Just as the British hadn't expected the Japanese to come down through the jungles of Malaya to conquer Singapore.

inside the city. With its twenty-nine divisions, of which twelve were armored, the Wehrmacht had to break through against an overall superior force, one with the wind at its back, and so their only hope was to concentrate everything at the tip of the spear, direct it at the weakest link, and hope for the best. *On s'engage et puis . . . l'on voit.*

Bastogne, which was being held by the Twenty-Eighth Infantry Division, proved to be the sticking point. The Belgian town lay at the convergence of seven of the principal routes through the Ardennes, and thus was vital for the Germans' mobility; the German battle plan called for the capture of Bastogne by the second day. One thing the Germans had going for them was that their Panzer tanks were far superior to the American Shermans, which couldn't compare with them in either firepower or armor. Further, the American Twenty-Eighth was composed largely of weary veterans getting a breather and new recruits freshly arrived from the States.

But the defenders weathered the initial attack long enough for reinforcements from the 101st Airborne under its acting commander Brigadier General Anthony McAuliffe, and remnants of the Tenth Armored Division, to arrive on the nineteenth. Nonetheless, in short order the Americans found themselves encircled by General Heinrich Freiherr von Lüttwitz and his XLVII Panzer Corps. Lüttwitz then sent the following communication to McAuliffe:

> To the U.S.A. Commander of the encircled town of Bastogne.
>
> The fortune of war is changing. This time the U.S.A. forces in and near Bastogne have been encircled by strong German armored units. More German armored units have crossed the river Ourthe near Ortheuville, have taken Marche and reached St. Hubert by passing through Hompre-Sibret-Tillet. Libramont is in German hands.
>
> There is only one possibility to save the encircled U.S.A. troops from total annihilation: that is the honorable surrender of the encircled town. In order to think it over a term of two hours will be granted beginning with the presentation of this note.
>
> If this proposal should be rejected one German Artillery Corps and six heavy A. A. Battalions are ready to annihilate the

U.S.A. troops in and near Bastogne. The order for firing will be given immediately after this two hours term.

All the serious civilian losses caused by this artillery fire would not correspond with the well-known American humanity.

The German Commander.

To which McAuliffe replied,

To the German Commander,
NUTS!
The American Commander.

When Lüttwitz asked Colonel Joseph Harper, the American officer who had delivered the reply, what "Nuts" meant, Harper informed him: "In plain English, it means go to hell."[42]

Now Patton painted his masterpiece. His three divisions had been heading east, into the Saarland, some 260 kilometers from Bastogne. The beastly weather had been hampering him as well, and he had outrun his supply lines. On December 8 he rang up the Catholic chaplain, Father James Hugh O'Neill, and asked him to write a prayer to the Almighty for the weather to break. "Sir, it's going to take a pretty thick rug for that kind of praying." Replied Patton: "I don't care if it takes a flying carpet." When the man pointed out that chaplains didn't usually pray for good weather in order to kill fellow human beings, Patton responded, "Are you trying to teach me theology or are you the chaplain of the Third Army? I want a prayer." He got it:

Almighty and most merciful Father, we humbly beseech Thee, of Thy Great goodness, to restrain these immoderate rains with which we have had to contend. Grant us fair weather for Battle. Graciously harken to us as soldiers who call upon Thee that, armed with Thy power, we may advance from victory to victory,

---

42. Legend has it that the actual reply was saltier.

and crush the opposition and wickedness of our enemies, and establish Thy justice among men and nations. Amen.

The weather broke. Patton got the divine a Bronze Star. "God damn!" he exclaimed. "Look at that weather! That was some potent praying."

On the night of the sixteenth, Patton got the word that the Germans were attacking across the Ardennes. He had suspected something like this; intelligence had suggested the Wehrmacht was massing men and materiel. At once, he ordered his staff to start planning for what would be an unprecedented logistical feat: wheeling an army already in motion and traveling fast, through a ninety-degree turn, and arriving ready to fight without missing a beat. Privately, he blamed Bradley and Ike for having lost forward motion along the front, something that had left Bastogne a sitting duck. And, since he had been there, he immediately recalled Ludendorff's failed Operation Michael from 1918 and felt confident that the new thrust would similarly fail. At this point in the war, the scholar-warrior knew every move the Germans were going to make.

Summoned the next day to an emergency conference at Verdun with Eisenhower and other top brass, Patton was told that the six divisions under his command were needed to counterattack the Germans as quickly as possible. How long would it take? "I can be there on December 22nd with three divisions," Patton told the room, with the calm confidence of (in Mark Twain's famous formulation) "a Christian holding four aces." He wasn't bragging; hadn't the Lord just come through for him? When Ike wondered whether three divisions would be enough, Patton told him the extra speed and mobility would be well worth not spending the time to assemble the extra three divisions, which in any case existed largely on paper.

As the meeting broke up, Eisenhower—who as Allied supreme commander had just received his fifth star—pulled Patton aside and remarked, "Every time I get a new star I get attacked." As it happened, Ike had gotten his fourth star—with the rank of full General—just before the Kasserine Pass, which had sent the Americans reeling from their encounter with Rommel. Now with five stars he was General of the Army, a rank shared after the Civil War by only Ulysses S. Grant, William T. Sherman, and Philip Sheridan, and during World War II by Marshall, MacArthur, Hap Arnold (all within a few days of each other in December 1944), and, later, Omar Bradley in 1950.[43] Patton responded, "Yes, and every time you get attacked, I pull you out!" Now he would do it one last time.

No one but Patton could have pulled this off. When he had taken command of the Third Army in England, it was filled with green recruits; now it was a lethal fighting force that would follow him to hell and back. His background in armored vehicles meant he had witnessed the development of tank warfare firsthand and had partly written the manual himself. His time spent as a quartermaster, combined with his experience in the First World War, had given him an instinctive grasp of how to train, feed, motivate, supply, and move an army. Most important, his kinetic sense of the battlefield—his ability to predict what the enemy was about to do and foil him before he could react—had made him the best fighting general in the U.S. Army. The Third Army had become for Patton what the army of Austerlitz had been for Napoleon: the pure expression of his will.

Patton arrived in Bastogne on the twenty-sixth, breaking the German siege and relieving "the Battered Bastards of Bastogne." By the end of January he had pushed the Germans all the way back to where they had started, and then shoved them farther east, back over the Rhine on March 22. To show his contempt for the Germans he took a leak in the mighty river as he crossed it. He thrashed his way through Germany, from the Rhine to the Elbe, capturing 32,763 square miles of territory, while losing two thousand men killed to the Germans' twenty thousand. On April 14, 1945, he got his fourth star; Patton may have been a pain in the ass, the reasoning went, but he was *our* pain in the ass.

Because Eisenhower and the other allies had decided to give the Soviets the honor of capturing Berlin, he was brought up short, much to his frustration. But from August 1, 1944, the day the Third Army went operational, to the end of the War in Europe on May 8, 1945,

43. At the same time, the Navy was creating a similar rank, fleet admiral, for William D. Leahy, Ernest King, Nimitz, and Bull Halsey.

the Third Army was in continuous combat for 281 straight days, killing some 47,500 of the enemy from Normandy to Pilsen in Czechoslovakia. Patton couldn't have been happier. George Patton combined Alexander's fearlessness with Caesar's tenacity and Napoleon's celerity. To say he was the best tactical general America ever produced is an understatement.

But having played a leading role in the Allied victory in the heart of central Europe, his fortunes changed as the god of war, Mars, decided his usefulness was at an end. In postwar Europe there was no room for Patton; he wished openly for a command in the Pacific, but it was not to be. That was Doug MacArthur's territory and MacArthur outranked him. Marshall came up with a lame excuse, and finally Henry L. Stimson, the secretary of war, officially scotched the idea.

Patton went on a speaking tour of the U.S., getting a hero's welcome everywhere, including in his hometown of Los Angeles, where he spoke before a crowd of one hundred thousand people in the L.A. Coliseum. He returned to Germany as part of the Occupation, but his brief stint as military governor of Bavaria came a cropper over the issue of denazification and his general hostility toward the Soviets. Never a philo-Semite, he began to equate Jews with Communists and was openly hostile toward the Jewish reporters in the American press, who returned the sentiments. "So far as the Jews are concerned, they do not want to be placed in comfortable buildings," he injudiciously wrote in an October 4, 1945, letter to a former aide, Lieutenant Colonel Charles Codman. "They actually prefer to live as many to a room as possible. They have no conception of sanitation, hygiene or decency and are, as you know, the same subhuman types that we saw in the internment camps."

The press responded by gleefully reporting some remarks he made about Germans who had joined the National Socialist Party. Asked at a press conference whether SS soldiers would be treated differently than ordinary Wehrmacht soldiers, he was quoted as saying, "Hell no, SS means no more in Germany than being a Democrat in America—that is not to be quoted." But of course it was. Wrote *Time* magazine:

General George S. Patton Jr. had kept mum for quite a while. It was unlike him. Last week, in Bavaria, where he is U.S. military governor, he broke the irksome silence, brandished his riding crop and informed the press: "Well, I'll tell you. This Nazi thing. It's just like a Democratic-Republican election fight." The fact that General Dwight D. Eisenhower had just instituted an investigation of Bavaria's Nazified German bureaucracy did not seem to cut much ice with Georgie Patton. In his opinion, too much fuss was being made about denazification. Said Patton: "I'm not trying to be King of Bavaria. . . . To get things going, we've got to compromise with the devil a little bit."

Ike promptly relieved him, kicking him sideways into a paper-shuffler desk job as "commander" of the Fifteenth Army in Bad Nauheim, a rump outfit charged with compiling a history of the war in Europe. His long-rumored affair (disputed by some of this biographers, although both Patton's wife and daughter both believed it to be true) with his beautiful niece-by-marriage, Jean Gordon, which had begun in Hawaii in 1936 and continued during her service as a Red Cross nurse in Europe, finally came to an end.[44] After VJ day, he openly fretted that Clio, the muse of history, had no further use for him. "Yet another war has come to an end, and with it my usefulness to the world," he confided to his diary.

On December 9, on his way to a hunting party, Patton's staff car collided at low speed with an army truck. It was a minor accident: the other occupants of the car, including his chief of staff, Major General Hobart Gay, were uninjured, but Patton—in the days before seat belts—banged his head on the glass partition separating the driver from the passenger compartment. He complained of difficulty breathing and loss of bodily sensation. Rushed to a military hospital in Heidelberg, doctors discovered he had suffered a compression fracture and dislocation of his third and fourth cerebral vertebrae. In plain English, his neck was broken and he was paralyzed from the head down. When a chaplain arrived, Patton barked, "Well, let him get started. I guess I need it."

---

44. After the failure of another affair she had been having with a married American officer, Jean returned to America, where she learned of Patton's death on December 21. She killed herself in a friend's apartment in Manhattan by asphyxiation by gas stove, surrounded by pictures of the general.

His wife, Beatrice, was flown in from America and camped out in the hospital to be constantly near him. She read to him daily, from military histories of Greece and Rome. "I should have done better," he told her. He never realized he'd already matched them on the battlefield, the only comparisons that mattered. Only a few others were allowed to see him.

Doctors did their best, but it was no use. To relieve the pressure on his spine they put him in traction with a torture device called "Crutchfield hooks," fishhooks lodged painfully beneath his cheekbones, attached to his skull. They didn't help. When Patton asked one of the docs what chance he had ever to ride a horse again, the answer was "none." At age sixty, Patton decided that if life had no further use for him, he had no further use for it. Among his last words were, "This is a hell of a way to die."

Despite his condition, Washington—not wanting him to die in Germany, enemy territory—ordered him to be returned to the States, but it was too late. His rage to fight, to *conquer*, had subsided. It was time to die. Encased in a plaster cast and thus completely immobile, he developed pulmonary edema and congestive heart failure and passed into history in his sleep on December 21, 1945, just a year after his greatest triumph at Bastogne. His daughter, Ruth Ellen, offered this valedictory: "For him I think it is seemly that he rode out on the storm, and escaped the dullness of old age, while he was at the height of his fame."

In *The Generals,* Winston Groom writes that the morning Patton died in Europe, both his daughters reported that he had communicated with them. Just after midnight in Washington, Bee got a phone call from a distant voice that asked, "Little Bee, are you all right?" after which the line went dead. Ruth Ellen said that she suddenly awoke to see her father "lying across a bench in the bay window of her bedroom, in his uniform, with his head propped up on his arm. He gave 'his very own smile,' she said, and then he was gone." The next morning, not having heard the official announcement of Patton's death, the two sisters spoke. "I guess he's dead, then," said Ruth Ellen. "Poor Ma," replied Bee.

Three days later, on Christmas Eve, he was buried with full military honors in the Luxembourg American Cemetery in Luxembourg City, in honor of his wish to be interred with the men of the Third Army.[45] His marker is a simple white cross, with his name, rank, and serial number. He rests there still.

---

45. Eight years later, in 1953, Beatrice died from an aneurism while riding her horse at her estate in Massachusetts. She was cremated and is buried with her husband in Luxembourg.

AFTERWORD

The Battle of 9/11

No one would have believed in the last years of the nineteenth century that this world was being watched keenly and closely by intelligences greater than man's and yet as mortal as his own; that as men busied themselves about their various concerns they were scrutinised and studied, perhaps almost as narrowly as a man with a microscope might scrutinise the transient creatures that swarm and multiply in a drop of water. With infinite complacency men went to and fro over this globe about their little affairs, serene in their assurance of their empire over matter. It is possible that the infusoria under the microscope do the same.

Yet across the gulf of space, minds that are to our minds as ours are to those of the beasts that perish, intellects vast and cool and unsympathetic, regarded this earth with envious eyes, and slowly and surely drew their plans against us.

THUS DOES THE FABIAN SOCIALIST H. G. WELLS BEGIN HIS 1898 META-phor for international conflict, *The War of the Worlds.* Just two decades later, the civilizational confidence of Victorian and Edwardian England, Wilhelmine Germany, and Imperial Russia lay face down in the mud of Flanders, killed in trenches, gassed blind, slaughtered by machine guns, left to die suspended from barbed wire in a barren moonscape called No-Man's Land. Fortuna is a fickle mistress. Even the strongest empires fall.

George Patton and his coevals were the last American flag officers to win a major war, and Harry Truman the last president to preside over an unequivocal victory. Since Patton's death, the U.S. has participated in the inconclusive Korean War, as part of a United Nations coalition; the failed invasion of Cuba at the Bay of Pigs in 1961; the disastrous Vietnam War, a classic example of a war without an objective; a small, pushover engagement in Grenada in 1983, with no strategic purpose; the Gulf War of 1990–1991 to expel Iraq from Kuwait, a war in which the country had no national or compelling interests; a pointless and bloody failed intervention in Somalia highlighted by the Battle of Mogadishu in 1993, which saw the bodies of American soldiers dragged through the streets; a pointless intervention in a religious conflict in Kosovo in 1998–1999 under the fig leaf of the North Atlantic Treaty Organization, a military alliance whose mission was accomplished in 1945; the civil wars in Bosnia from 1992–1995 that resulted from the collapse of communist Yugoslavia, again without any national interests at stake; and the Afghanistan War from 2001 to 2021, which, after an initial, punitive success following the attacks of 9/11, became a spectacular military and diplomatic failure ending in an ignominious retreat that is without precedent in American history. That long and futile conflict includes the briefly successful Iraq War, which settled the unfinished business of the Bush family left over from the first Gulf War, but left intact the imaginary Sykes-Picot country of Iraq as a wholly owned subsidiary of Iran; and the purposeless bombing of Libya under the Obama administration in 2011, which resulted in the death of Muammar Gaddafi and rendered that country leaderless and rudderless but was celebrated by then-secretary of state Hillary Clinton in her maladroit evocation of Caesar: "We came, we saw, he died." A less Caesar-like figure than the wife of a former president and a defeated candidate for the presidency in 2016, a woman of no particular distinction, and animated almost exclusively by bitterness and resentment, can hardly be imagined.

It's an impressive litany of futility, made even more noteworthy by whom the U.S. did *not* fight in what has come to be called the Forever Wars: Iran, the architect of the hostage crisis of 1979–1981 that brought down the Jimmy Carter administration; Saudi Arabia, which helpfully contributed fifteen of the nineteen hijackers on 9/11 and birthed al-Qaeda's ringleader, Osama bin Laden; and the People's Republic of China, which attacked the U.S. in Korea and, after the end of the Cold

War with the Union of Soviet Socialist Republics in 1991, supplanted the Russians as the principal enemy of Western, and especially American, civilization. As of this writing, none has yet been decisively confronted.

One notes that in all the conflicts cited above, none conforms to the Clausewitzian dictum that "war is an act of force, *and there is no logical limit to the application of that force.*" In each case, these wars of choice were fought along the invented limiting principle (found nowhere in the ancient world) that wars (a) should be defensive, fought in response to some provocation, and (b) any response should be "proportionate" to the initial injury. In other words, the goal has always been a return to the status quo ante—a recipe for an unstable stasis that must eventually fly apart.

Call it diplomacy with no other means. Among other things, an irrational fear of *Friktion* on the part of the politicians and fruit-salad generals and scrambled-eggs admirals is why there has not been an un-equivocal victory among them. As well, American public opinion, goaded by the corporate media, has become obsessed with the chimera of an "exit strategy" even before a war is fought, much less won. A war fought not to win is by definition unwinnable—and these are precisely the wars the U.S. has welcomed since 1945, since they keep the Pentagon's war machine humming, and the only cost is in the lives of the cannon-fodder volunteers, few of whom come from the self-appointed "elite" classes of sitcom-writing Harvard graduates and Yale Law attorneys.

Consider, for example, the fetishistic emphasis on "stability" that became evident at the end of the Cold War, when George H. W. Bush—a former director of the Central Intelligence Agency—took the reins from Ronald Reagan at the conclusion of the latter's second term. With the "cowboy" Reagan gone, the striped-pants set breathed a profound sigh of relief. "He's a safe pair of hands," said one ("conservative") British cabinet official of my acquaintance at the time. Translation: there would be no more of this "Evil Empire" nonsense.

For the truth was that neither the Soviet nor the American intelligence community welcomed the end of the Cold War; indeed, both resisted it to the end. The KGB and the CIA had reached a comfortable *modus vivendi,* in which the rules were clear to everybody. No cowboys needed apply: the unspoken dictum was that neither side would

actively undermine the other, because neither wanted fundamental regime change. Back-alley battles in Berlin and elsewhere were conducted
between low-level operatives, any or all of whom could easily be sacrificed or hung out to dry or left out in the cold as circumstances permitted.[1] The real work was done in expensive restaurants in Washington,
New York, London, and Paris. The cozy arrangement that had obtained
from the creation of the agency—Ivy League, hard-drinking, Protestant—
in 1947 and the KGB—earnest, fumbling, sweaty—in 1954 (a year after
Stalin's death) to the fall of the Berlin Wall in 1989 had been ideal, and
now it was gone.

One might also observe that no military figure of stature emerged
from these wars. These two things are not unrelated. Wars that are
fought with the single objective of total victory are led by men who
embody that philosophy. Had Caesar been defeated in Gaul, that would
have been the end of him. Had "Unconditional Surrender" Grant failed
in the endgame against Lee, he likely would have been relieved of command, and the war-weary Union might have rushed to the bargaining
table (which is all the South wanted) at the prospect of years more of
fighting. Without Patton's logistical miracle at the relief of Bastogne, the
Germans might have punched through and taken Antwerp, and the end
of the war would have looked vastly different.

A reading of history reveals another flaw in postwar America. Alexander fought to extend Greek culture (to which he was originally a
semi-outsider) across the known and unknown world. Caesar fought
for himself, to be sure, but always in the name of the Senate and People
of Rome; he died at a meeting of the Senate. Constantine the Great
fought to restore the length and breadth of the entire Roman Empire—
an empire in which even the Greeks of the east called themselves
"Romans"—as well as to establish Christianity as its new, unifying
faith. Aetius fought a rear-guard action to preserve the *idea* of Rome

---

1. The best fictional depiction of this chess match is to be found not in the baroque novels
of John le Carré, literarily brilliant as they are, but in the *Game, Set and Match* trilogy by
British thriller writer Len Deighton, especially *Berlin Game* (1983). Deighton perfectly
captures the tension and the tedium and heartbreaking betrayal of the midlevel op's existence.

against—literally—the Huns, even after the effete Romans had abandoned it as (to use the voguish term) "unsustainable." Bohemond and the Crusaders fought to reclaim the holiest sites in Christendom. Napoleon (another outsider)[2] fought for France. Pershing fought for the emerging idea of "America." Patton and Nimitz—from vastly different economic and ethnic backgrounds—fought for America herself.

Like the late Romans, though, the "idea" of America today has as little meaning as "Rome" did in the ruins of 476 A.D. We are told repeatedly that America is a "notional" nation, which is to say not a country by European standards—one of consanguinity, however imperfect—but one founded on an idea. While this is a pleasing fiction to some, even a cursory reading of *The Federalist Papers* shows this to be a falsehood. None of the Founders thought the nation-state they were creating was anything but a product of the British Enlightenment, the economic child of Adam Smith (whose *Wealth of Nations* was published the same year as the Revolution), the religious child of Anglicanism (with an admixture of Deists, such as Jefferson). One's allegiance was not to a piece of parchment called the Declaration of Independence or the Constitution but to the United States of America. And for two centuries, this proved to be true. The opening line of Mario Puzo and Francis Ford Coppola's script for *The Godfather* sums up the zeitgeist perfectly: "I believe in America." Everybody did. Ask yourself whether this is still true today.

The lone American victory in post–World War II warfighting came not in a hot war but in a cold one. President John F. Kennedy rightly responded to Soviet provocation when the Berlin Wall started to go up in August of 1961. In October of that year, tanks were briefly met with tanks at Checkpoint Charlie. A long standoff then ensued, occupying much of the next thirty years. But it was not until Ronald Reagan took office in 1981 and succinctly articulated the objective—"We win, they lose"—that the will was in place to finish it. Although Reagan had left office by the time the Soviet Union imploded—it was left to Bush senior

---

2. Alexander wasn't Greek, Constantine was born in what is today Serbia; Aetius was born in modern Bulgaria, Bohemond of Taranto was a Norman born in Italy, and Napoleon wasn't French. For that matter, Hitler wasn't German, Stalin wasn't Russian, and Churchill was half American.

to ineptly handle the aftermath—there was never any doubt that the victory belonged to the Gipper, the last effective American commander in chief.

Indeed, we can date the decline of the United States as an international power to the first Bush presidency, and that decline's emphatic punctuation with the presidency of his son, George W. Bush. "Poppy," as the elder was called, essentially ceded control of the events that followed the end of the Soviet Union and the liberation of Eastern Europe—the cornerstone of American foreign policy for nearly half a century—to other players: to Boris Yeltsin in Russia, Helmut Kohl in Germany, Vaclav Havel in Czechoslovakia, and, critically, to the Hungarian-born George (Schwartz) Soros, who invested a great deal of money in the rebuilding of the East Bloc and was widely hailed at the time as a moneyed capitalist savior from the wreckage of communism.

America under Bush I, however, did almost nothing. The U.S. could have bought Russia and the rest of the Warsaw Pact for ten cents on the dollar, maybe less; instead, it left the field to KGB *ronin* like Vladimir Putin, various thugs and gangsters, and canny opportunists like Soros. By this point, however, America had become "notional," and the fall of embarrassing plastic-shoed, stinky economic Communism was of little interest to the emerging Washington supra-national, anti-"jingoistic" *nomenklatura*.

And then came the Battle of 9/11.

The hijacked-airplane attacks on the symbols of American capitalism and military might were conducted by nineteen spies and saboteurs, mostly young men in their twenties—fifteen of them from Saudi Arabia, the other four from the UAE, Egypt, and Lebanon, all semifictional Muslim political entities formed in part from conquered lands but all part of the *ummah*. In spite of decades of Islamic assaults on U.S. targets both at home and abroad, in most cases the fifth columnists had been admitted to the U.S. in an excess of naiveté masquerading as goodwill with an admixture of guilt, and in an ongoing perversion of Christianity called "political correctness"; several of the attackers were even admitted to American flight schools, despite manifest misgivings about both their skills and their intentions. Especially when they evinced little interest in learning how to land their aircraft.

Osama bin Laden, from an Arab family directly adjacent to the much-proliferated Saudi "royal" family, had studied his enemy for a long time, dating back to the days of American involvement with the *mujahidin* in Afghanistan in the 1970s and throughout the 1980s. They were fighting in opposition to a Marxist, Soviet-aligned Afghan government that had seized power in a 1978 coup, and began receiving military aid from the U.S. The movement attracted fighters from all over the Muslim world, among whom was bin Laden, who established al-Qaeda— "the Base"—while in country. After the Soviet withdrawal in 1989, bin Laden took his movement international, issuing a worldwide declaration of a state of war between Islam and the West in February of 1998 and blowing up two American embassies in Africa six months later just to illustrate his intentions.

On February 26, 1993, al-Qaeda operatives detonated a bomb— thirteen hundred pounds of urea nitrate from fertilizer, hydrogen gas cylinders, and cyanide packed into a stolen Ryder rental van—in the public parking garage underneath the World Trade Center in Manhattan. Their intention was to so destabilize the North Tower that it would topple and take out the South Tower along with it. Six people were killed and more than a thousand injured, mostly from smoke inhalation, which rose high into the upper floors. They failed, however, to bring down the towers, and then the usual dance of "bringing them to justice" began as American authorities, led by the FBI, saw the bombing as mere terrorism and sent the feds and New York City cops chasing after the cell, instead of treating the event as the act of war it so clearly was.

Al-Qaeda learned from its failure—not so much about the physics of destroying the towers as the lack of will on the part of the United States to do anything about it. From the time of his inauguration to what was supposed to have been Reagan's third term, George H. W. Bush spoke of a "kinder, gentler" nation—the most bald-faced preemptive declaration of weakness in American history. He followed that up by bungling the end of the Cold War—he and his chief of staff, James A. Baker III, seemed almost to regret that it had happened—allowing canny opportunists to step into the central-European power void and snatch away the American victory. The first attack on the Trade Center came early in Bill Clinton's first term, and met with a typically feckless response from the president involving some tough talk but little action; after all, Monica Lewinsky beckoned. Throughout his two terms, Clinton was always more concerned about the domestic political resonance of any of his pre-poll-tested options than he was about the nation.[3]

And so it was left to George W. Bush, who was reading a book to grade-school children in Sarasota, Florida, when the planes struck, to handle 9/11. From the start, his instincts were bad. "Today we have had a nat'l tragedy," he wrote in some notes before his first meeting with the press as the event was still unfolding. "Airplanes have crashed into the World Trade Center in an apparent terrorist attack." This was at the time, and remains even more so in hindsight, precisely the wrong response. Future historians are likely to mark the destruction of the Twin Towers in lower Manhattan, the wreckage of an airliner in a Pennsylvania field—brought down by the hijacked passengers, who chose death before dishonor—and the simultaneous damage and loss of life sustained by the Pentagon in suburban Virginia by Muslim *mujahidin* directed by bin Laden, as the end of the American Century.

The immediate death toll was 2,927 innocents, with many dying later from toxic inhalation of the destruction, but the attack's effects went far beyond a casualty list. It will be seen as the turning point that marked the end of American military and cultural hegemony and heralded the financial and moral collapse of the U.S. as a global power: an unanswered act of war, proclaimed in the name of Islam and celebrated by Muslims around the world, some of them in the U.S.

And yet the object of the attack, the United States of America, categorically refused to see it that way. "These acts of violence against innocents violate the fundamental tenets of the Islamic faith. And it's important for my fellow Americans to understand that," Bush said during a visit to the Islamic Center of Washington, D.C., taking the side of the enemy less than a week after the atrocity. "The face of terror is not the true faith of Islam; that's not what Islam is all about. Islam

---

3. Clinton's mentor in Hot Springs, Ark., his home town, was the Irish-American gangster Owney Madden, who had left New York City immediately after the assassination of Dutch Schultz (Arthur Fliegenheimer) in 1935 and resettled in Hot Springs, where he died in 1965. I recounted his story in my 2003 novel, *And All the Saints*.

is peace." Bohemond, his mace still bloody from Antioch, would have laughed in his face.

Bush dutifully responded with something more than the random missile strikes of his predecessor, launching an attack on Taliban-controlled Afghanistan, which had given safe harbor to the fugitive bin Laden and from whose territory the plot had originated, and quickly toppling that fundamentalist government (itself a poisonous byprod-uct of American meddling in the Soviet-Afghanistan war). But rather than hold the governments of the countries from which the hijackers and their leaders had come responsible, he opted instead to announce a fruitless "global war on terror" that eventually led to the belated, irrel-evant, but strategically disastrous toppling of his father's old nemesis, Saddam Hussein, in Iraq in 2003.

Neither basket-case Afghanistan or strongman-state Iraq, however, had anything to do with the actual attacks by a stateless paramilitary united only by its religion—in Islamic theology, all observant Muslims are members of a worldwide *ummah,* which supersedes transient na-tional identifiers—and conducted against economic, military, and po-litical targets in New York City and Washington, D.C. But instead of immediately directing the nation's ire at Saudi Arabia—the chances that some of the familially interconnected "royals" in that desert sheik-dom were unaware of the plot and did not offer financial assistance are zero—Bush and his vice president, Dick Cheney, let their close allies and business partners off the hook. They immediately provided police protection for the Saudis beginning the day of the attacks because the the Saudis "feared harm," and began preparations to spirit them away even before the airports had officially reopened. On September 13, the Bushies flew some 160 members of the bin Laden extended clan—many of them attending high schools and colleges in the U.S.—and other Saudi nationals out of the country. Ask yourself what Achilles or Alex-ander would have done with them.

In fact, almost everything the administration did in its panicked re-action to September 11 was wrong. It instantly declared—to the hosan-nas of the media and the utter disbelief of the public—that the religion of Islam had nothing to do with the attacks, and that the word "Islam" meant "peace" rather than "submission." Harmoniously, King Fahd of

Saudi Arabia called on America to "protect the innocents" while Prince Bandar had the chutzpah to quote one of the students saying that until that moment "he never really appreciated why the Japanese wanted a memorial or an apology for their treatment in World War II. I understand now that when you are innocent, in the face of emotion, nothing, not even common sense, can help argue your case." Incomprehensibly, with many of the dead not even identified yet, the Saudis were considered the real victims as they returned to their plush lives in Riyadh, London, Paris, and elsewhere, miniskirts and Victoria's Secret underwear under their women's burkas and hatred in their hearts.

Instead, Bush and Cheney punished the American people. Civil liberties were shredded in the name of "safety." A vast new unaccountable bureaucracy was set up, spearheaded by the Orwellian Department of Homeland Security. The Director of Central Intelligence was demoted and bigfooted by a Director of National Intelligence. The transparently unconstitutional Patriot Act—an overreaction to a monumental intelligence failure that had allowed 9/11 to happen—was rammed through a compliant Congress and remains at this writing on the books; it allows warrantless cyber-snooping, "sneak and peak" searches of the private information of American citizens; as well as the blatantly illegal FISA law that allows the intelligence agencies to spy on Americans, and which has been the primary cause of the transformation of the Republic into a fiefdom of the intelligence community, the Surveillance State, leading to all kinds of real and imagined mischief that have done great harm to the nation-as-founded. Because of nineteen Muslims, every American has lost his or her right to privacy and freedom of assembly and expression. Patton would have thought this an obscene bargain.

Most insultingly, the Transportation Security Administration—another excrescence of the Bush administration—promptly deemed all three hundred-plus million American citizens as potential criminals, in open defiance of the Fourth Amendment's proscription of unreasonable searches and seizures, and forced them to shuffle shoeless and beltless (like the plotters against Hitler in Nazi judge Roland Freisler's courtroom) through endless queues at airports and to suffer the indignity of having their luggage searched without warrant and themselves subjected to bodily invasion as well. And all because the Bush administration refused to name the enemy, then engage him, then punish and destroy him. What would Caesar have done in the face of such provocation?

Much legalistic pettifogging was expended on the fact that al-Qaeda was a "non-state actor," and hence there was no legitimate entity for the Americans against which to strike back, other than an amorphous "terror." Never mind the fact that the plot was hatched by a Saudi national and carried out in large part by Saudi nationals, which in any other time and place would be considered a prima facie *casus belli*. The overrepresentation of lawyers in every facet of American life has never been such a danger to the Republic, and while it may seem "humane" to have every battlefield action subject to second-guessing and, occasionally, a court martial or even civilian criminal charges, it defeats the very purpose for which a standing military stands. Besides REMF, the dirtiest word in a soldier's vocabulary is JAG.[4]

Eventually, bin Laden was hunted down and killed on May 2, 2011, in Abbottabad, Pakistan, just north of the Pakistani capital of Islamabad, where by sheer coincidence he was hiding out a stone's throw from the Pakistan Military Academy, the West Point of the only nuclear-armed Muslim nation. A "non-state actor" indeed. Unsurprisingly, his death occasioned handwringing in some quarters about whether he should have been taken alive to "face justice." The fact that he got an approximation of the justice that was coming to him was lost on his apologists.

Even in death bin Laden, a savvy commander, had taken the measure of his enemies. He understood there was no longer an American flag to rally round—much of academe and the media had long since decided that the United States was an illegitimate country, invalidated by African slavery and a legacy of "colonialism" and hence unworthy of respect or allegiance. He sensed that since Vietnam the fighting spirit had gone out of the Americans, that total victory was now considered excessive and even rude, and that the pusillanimous George W. Bush

---

4. "Judge Advocate General," commissioned officers who are nonfighting lawyers, effectively hired to represent the enemy against the men they serve with. They are regarded with the same loathing that cops have for Internal Affairs, little more than spies and snitches.

was a far cry from the American president who, the day after Pearl Harbor, had angrily declared:

No matter how long it may take us to overcome this premeditated invasion, the American people in their righteous might will win through to absolute victory. I believe that I interpret the will of the Congress and of the people when I assert that we will not only defend ourselves to the uttermost but will make it very certain that this form of treachery shall never again endanger us.

With confidence in our armed forces—with the unbounding determination of our people—we will gain the inevitable triumph—so help us God.

Then Franklin Roosevelt unleashed Admiral Nimitz on the Japanese, breaking the back of their navy at Midway, rolling them up via the island-hopping campaign in the Pacific, and even assassinating Admiral Yamamoto—the architect of Pearl Harbor—by shooting down his airplane in April 1943 in the skies over Bougainville Island near Papua, New Guinea; the mission was unapologetically called "Operation Vengeance."

There it was, the now-vanished America: the Clausewitzian Roosevelt had said publicly there would be *no limit to the application of force*; that this act of perfidy would be kept firmly in mind as the nation took its revenge; that "absolute victory" was the objective; that such a "form of treachery" would never again endanger the U.S.; that "hostilities exist" (refreshingly direct); that the situation was "grave"; and that "so help us God" the American triumph would be inevitable. And he declared war—the last time an American president would so. In August of 1945, Harry Truman fulfilled the deceased FDR's promise and dropped the atomic bomb on Hiroshima and Nagasaki. Here ended the lesson. But when Bush dubbed his response to 9/11 as "Operation Infinite Justice," and described the mission as a "crusade," the usual suspects immediately decried its bellicosity and implicit lack of respect for Islam, and so it was withdrawn in favor of "Operation Enduring Freedom"—another sign that the war was lost from the start.

For his part, Osama bin Laden intended the 2001 attacks to be the opening salvo in the continuation of the religious, political, and cultural war between Islam and Christianity that had begun with the early conquests of Muhammad and was punctuated more than a millennium ago with the sack of Constantinople in 1453. He seethed with resentment about the *Reconquista* of Iberia by the European Christians. He believed fervently in the Manichean notion—a tenet of his faith—that the world is divided between the *Dar al-Islam* and the *Dar al-Harb*, the World of War in which Islam and its disciples are locked in mortal combat with Christian and Jewish enemies until their final, Allah-bestowed, and thus inevitable triumph.

On 9/11 bin Laden took advantage of the manifest weaknesses of late twentieth-century America in order to shoot a gullible nation in the back: the desire to be liked rather than respected or feared; a politically correct hesitation in judging other cultures, even when they are openly, proudly, inimical; and the decline of its own Christian faith. A war over something as silly as religion was inconceivable to the *illuminati* of the West—but not to him.

We know from history what other, more secure and confident, cultures would have done. The imperial Romans would have gone full *delenda est* on Saudi Arabia, razed its cities, destroyed the Kaaba, leveled the mosques, occupied the oil fields, seized its wealth, executed its leaders, and sold the populace into slavery; they knew an existential struggle when they were in one. Constantine would not have stopped until Greco-Roman writ applied without resistance across his realm. Bohemond would immediately have known the holy warriors for what they were: dedicated, merciless enemies in a religious war in which there could be only one victor, and helpfully converted their mosques back into churches as he put them to the sword. Napoleon would have as handily defeated them as he did the Egyptian mamelukes—former slaves who had risen to power over the centuries—and added their territory to his empire, sending scholars and scientists to preserve and protect the ruins and artifacts and where possible restore the preexisting nations and faiths that had been overwhelmed by the Islamic conquest, especially in Persia, a once-great nation that has not been the same since the Arab conquest in 654 A.D.

Americans, however, have never had a taste for empire. True, the U.S.

successfully rehabilitated Germany and Japan as allies, in large part by Americanizing them via its pervasive popular, even vulgar, culture. But that was only possible after both nations had been convincingly beaten. As for Russia, the Cold War foe, it is still feeling the effects of its loss of manpower during the Great Patriotic War, the collapse of its moral structure under atheistic Communism, its reliance on abortion as birth control, its corresponding declining birth rate, and a host of other ills brought on by its self-imposed, prolonged absence from Western civilization during most of the last century. Once an enemy, Russia is now simply an adversary, and not a particularly potent one at that.

The *Dar al-Harb,* however, is still out there, itching for a fight. For more than half a century, it has provided provocation after provocation, from the 1983 bombing of the Marine barracks in Beirut up to and including the declaration of hostilities that accompanied 9/11. "Why do they hate us?" we ask, helplessly, when the real question is why we do not hate them back. But that would be rude, and "not who we are."

Meanwhile, across the Pacific and despite their unequaled record of military ineptitude, the Chinese are eyeballing the U.S. Most likely their aggression will continue to be more Sun Tzu than Clausewitz: "Supreme excellence consists in breaking the enemy's resistance without fighting." The Chinese way of war is waged with money—our own, as it happens. Still they haven't won a war against a Western power since they lost the Battle of Talas in 751, when a Tang dynasty army was defeated by Ziyad ibn Salih; otherwise, the only people they seem able to defeat is themselves, as their record of calamitous civil wars illustrates.

The end of the draft, which coincided with the American defeat in Vietnam, means the U.S. now has a standing professional army employed latterly as a laboratory for social change rather than as a lethal fighting force. The purpose of war may still be killing people and blowing things up, but that no longer seems the foremost concern among the generals and admirals. The armed services have lost their dominant position as the most trusted of American institutions, and all their branches now struggle with recruiting, owing in large part to their fixation on social fads driven by a tiny minority and pushed hard by the media. To quote Sun Tzu again: "One may know how to conquer without being able to do it." It's not alarmist to suggest that under current management at least, the American military, rageless and thus impotent, may well know everything about fighting except how to actually do it, not to mention why.

To paraphrase Fannie Hurst, or Leon Trotsky, or whomever actually said it: we may not be interested in war anymore, but war will always be interested in us. The United States is too rich, too populous, too influential to focus solely on domestic matters, which at least since the sixties has largely amounted to a series of futile variations on the theme, "the poor will always be with us," with the potent addition of an obsession with race. But international affairs are the arena of war—*policy with other means*—and every dominant culture since Athens is closely watched for the first signs of weakness by those who would replace it. Much to the delight of its enemies, a nation that refuses to defend its territorial integrity, its culture, its language, and its legitimacy is on an express train to the ash heap of history.

Let us therefore conclude our *tour d'horizon* of epic and epochal battles, and the circumstances that incubated them, with a return to Clausewitz and *On War*. Despite the modern distaste for combat and disdain for its historical functions, the Prussian's precepts remain as timely and true as ever, especially this one: "In war, the result is never final." How can it be? It is the oldest of human group activities. No matter the outcome, the crisis continues, the strife goes on. Any solutions, even total victory, are only transitory; as Immanuel Kant famously observed, "The state of peace among men living side by side is not the natural state; the natural state is one of war." Perhaps in that sense, and in the long run, it's true that war "never solves anything." But in the long run, as John Maynard Keynes quipped, "we're all dead." Each generation is therefore concerned with the here and now; the cycle always begins anew. The last line of *Hamlet* belongs to Fortinbras: "Go, bid the soldiers shoot."

It is, then, not a question of *if* war comes again, but *when*. The Kellogg-Briand Pact of 1928 outlawed war, but war is itself an outlaw and so has chosen to ignore it. Thus it is the duty of all but the suicidal to be prepared when history calls. As Clausewitz says, "Everything in war is very simple, but the simplest thing is difficult." Even the best and most confident generals must keep in mind the quasi-Napoleonic dictum, *On s'engage partout, et puis l'on voit.*

There's the human condition in a nutshell. Be prepared in mind, will, soul, and body, then start the battle and see what happens. It's the best we can do. In the end, it's all we can do.

ACKNOWLEDGMENTS

WRITERS MAY BE SOLITARY AND UNSOCIABLE CREATURES, BUT FEW are hermits. From the outside, the process might appear to consist of reading and researching combined at some point with typing, but going on inside the writer's head is a riot of competing facts, narratives, thoughts, propositions, and dramatic structures, all struggling to be aligned, tested, and combined in an overall story. A writer is doing his most important work when he seems to be doing nothing at all.

It's no accident that the first historians were first and foremost storytellers, bards, poets, shanachies, and not academicians—all trying to make sense of their cultural pasts and passing along what they learned and deduced to instruct future generations. From the works of Homer and Herodotus through Livy and Tacitus to the biblical evangelists to the medieval scribes who rode with the Crusaders to Gibbon and Paul Johnson, and down to the present day, a good history should read like a good biography or novel: not merely a collection of facts—that is the job of journalists—but rather a ripping yarn, with a point, and a purpose. A mere recitation of gleaned facts won't do, except as a referential doorstop or paperweight.

My thanks, therefore, goes to them and also to the editors past and present at St. Martin's Press who acquired and published *Last Stands* and encouraged and effected the publication of the current volume: Adam Bellow, Pronoy Sarkar, and Michael Flamini. The best editing is not correction but suggestion; not rewriting but navigating the rocky shoals of a writer's ego by explaining which chapters need work and then insisting on it, calling out needless repetition of fact or sentiment (almost inevitable in any first draft), and backing their authors to the hilt once the manuscript has been accepted. I certainly have been blessed in this regard.

Thanks also to my agent at Don Congdon Associates, Cristina Concepcion, who's read just about everything ever published and always steers me straight; and the late Don Congdon, who brought me into a stable that has included Ray Bradbury, William Manchester, Jack Finney, Tom Berger, Evan Connell, William Shirer, Richard Schickel, and many others. Fast company indeed, and one that I strive to be worthy of with each new book.

Thanks also to my friend, the late Caleb Carr—novelist and military historian—whose endorsement of *Last Stands* contributed greatly to that book's commercial success, and to Victor Davis Hanson for unselfishly encouraging me to work his side of the street.

Writers are generally born, not made, but like all human beings, they are greatly dependent upon their upbringings and their families—mothers and fathers, siblings, wives and husbands, their own children and grandchildren. First, for their relatives' understanding that the writer's Hobbesian path is uncertain, subject to the whims of fate: solitary, sometimes nasty, troublingly brutish, for long stretches poor, and all too often short. And second for the emotional, physical, financial, and moral support they provide, even as the writer skirts the boundary between aspiration and accomplishment while waiting for Fortune to smile upon him.

To that end, then, let me thank my parents, who indulged my obsession with reading and writing from a very early age; and my four siblings, including my three younger sisters, Victoria Batease, Pamela Bard, and Martha Campbell, women of accomplishment and all now helping take care of our 98-year-old father in Florida, a Marine officer to the end. And my younger brother Stephen, a retired Naval officer and accomplished pianist, who provides me with historical and musical expertise whenever called upon.

I thank also my two daughters Alexandra and Clare (now deceased), who had to grow up in Germany with an often-absent journalist father and, later in New England, with the thing in the attic pounding away at one book after another or commuting to Los Angeles while working in the picture business. Thanks also to Alexandra's husband, my son-in-law Conall Doorley, the father of my three Dublin-born grandchildren, Ada Clare, Sorcha Kathryn and, newly arrived just as the final manuscript of this book went to the publisher, Oscar Oisín Doorley.

And last but far from least, to my wife Kathleen, without whom none of this would have been possible, and to whom everything is owed.

INDEX

ABOUT THE AUTHOR

The author of *Last Stands* and seventeen other novels and nonfiction books, **Michael Walsh** was the classical music critic and a foreign correspondent for *Time* from 1981 to 1997. He received the 2004 American Book Award for his gangster novel, *And All the Saints*. His books *The Devil's Pleasure Palace* and *The Fiery Angel* examine the enemies, heroes, triumphs, and struggles of Western civilization from the ancient past to the present. He divides his time between Connecticut and Ireland.